AF411601

OF
HAPPINESS

OF HAPPINESS

An Essay

VOLTERRA

Andover Books

Chapel Hill

ISBN 0-9660806-0-2
Library of Congress Number 98-070640
Printed and published in the United States of America

First Edition

Contents

In writing this book on the subject of happiness, one difficulty I faced was the discovery of a style capable of expressing truths.

Clever and involved prose strikes me as a medium by means of which a man may say very little and rant much. Prose cannot be too simple in structure, vocabulary, and, therefore, tone. I will go further and say that a man should do everything in his power to write in as simple a manner as the language allows, even to the point of banality. Now, only a writer who actually has something to say will have the courage to publish his thoughts in the very simplest language possible, and not feel compelled to puff them up with an involved or clever style. On the other hand, he who has nothing to say naturally cannot afford this banality, for then his lack of ideas will be obvious to all. Difficult, involved prose or cleverly witty or erudite prose therefore is always only a product of necessity, and the resource of those who lack ideas.

For the description of ideas, Montesquieu's extremely simple and flexible style has always appeared to me greatly preferable to Proust's or Foucault's, or for that matter Kant's or Freud's, however odd this may seem, for unlike theirs it does not allow for chicanery to creep in at every quarter under the old guise of arcane truths and yet allows for the expression of even the most difficult or delicate thought.

A book on the subject of happiness puts its reader under the unhappy obligation of examining his own heart at every moment to find there confirmations, or the lack of them, for what he is reading. In this regard, if this be not an unreasonable request, I ask the reader to do himself the favor of not permitting vanity to cloud his reasoning in forming a judgment of what he reads.

He can do no greater disfavor to the author than to completely, or even to greatly, agree with him; for every careful reader of the essay itself will very soon note that if its central thesis is in fact the truth, two results *necessarily* follow: *universally*, there *must* be great exception taken to its chief ideas, and secondly and more interestingly, for more precisely conclusive, in *every* reader the illusion that the author has, at the very *least*, an overweening touch of the arrogant about him. The one person who would not have suffered this revelatory illusion is no longer alive; as for the rest....

BOOK ONE

’Tis in ourselves that we are thus or thus.

Othello

Chapter I

Of Happiness

Pleasure is that sensation which one would prolong or have prolonged, if possible. Pain is that sensation which one would stop or have stopped, if possible. Happiness is that sensation to which one would sacrifice all others, if necessary; it is what one would feel rather than feel anything else, and, being so delicate and opinionated a matter, it is what many find difficult to pinpoint, even as regards themselves.

Beauty, the sensation produced by the promise of pleasure or happiness. It is then necessarily a product purely of the imagination and not, properly speaking, a quality contained in the object considered beautiful.

Beauty is instantly felt as beauty, i.e. a man wishes the sensation to continue.

You may instantly feel the beauty of a flower, a car, or a woman, but have to make an effort to feel the beauty of a Leonardo painting or *Ulysses*. But another man with more imagination, which he has taken time and care to exercise, will enjoy the works of Leonardo or Joyce as instantly and naturally as he would a flower, etc.

A man with less force of imagination may find the Grand Canyon or a Mozart opera as immediately pleasing as would a more sensitive one, but the intensity of the pleasure felt is correspondingly less.

The more lively a man's heart, the more well stocked his mind becomes in time with ideas that produce pleasure. Such a man, being predisposed to find as many things as possible that please his senses, and ideas that please his heart, is *sensitive to beauty*.

Even the greatest sensations of beauty inspired by the most pleasing object are fleeting. At best, no effect of beauty lasts more than a few days. It is not then possible for the same object to produce the original sensations, unless years have passed in its absence and you suddenly come across it again. It must strike your imagination as possessing the charm of novelty.

With age, weariness, suspicions, and disillusionments, a man becomes less susceptible to the sensations of beauty.

The true sensation of beauty, that delicate glow of pleasure, is sometimes but faintly linked in the mind with the object that inspired it. One goes about in a daze of pleasure, thinking about the object now and then, but the pleasure permeates every thought and every other sensation.

Civilizations themselves and their by-products, religion, science, engineering, philosophy, the arts, the social passions and manners as well as all the forms of love are all equally only the overall practical consequences of the general desire for happiness.

Beauty may be discovered not only in tangible objects, but also in their retrospective images set forth in any of the arts. The *mediums* themselves of the arts, by becoming objects of perception in and of themselves, can inspire the sensation of beauty, though faintly in comparison to natural objects.

Man is not free *not* to pursue every pleasure he perceives or imagines unless fear prevents him.

The true historian, that very rare type of man, ought to study the past in order to discover the changing ideas of happiness. The Elizabethan or the Roman would have found repugnant the progress that many today are so proud of. The early Roman would have considered the love of wealth beneath him, and a society dedicated to the idea of wealth a relic of barbarism. Today, he is the barbarian.

What is beautiful to one is as likely as not the object of ridicule or scorn to the other. Neither is right but for himself, and neither can persuade the other against his will. Politics: the field of contest in which each such party attempts to advance his (more usually than her) interests against those of others, and makes use of perceived similarities and differences of opinions and interests to persuade others to grant him more power to do all that he wishes. Those who believe in freedom of thought (and thus democracy) will not happily bear with those who deny this means of organizing societies to produce the greatest happiness for the greatest number. They cannot afford to.

Happiness can be classed and described only according to the type of imagination used.

Happiness can proceed from two sources, and so may be most generally divided into two distinct classes.

1) The happiness from vanity. This class includes nearly all that goes by the name of beauty, happiness, advancement, philosophy, art, friendship, love, etc. I group all these under the same heading because what happens in the heart so far as the sensation of pleasure is concerned in each is the same.

The pleasure that one finds in owning an elegant or expensive car is the same in nature that another finds in following religious rules, in producing metaphysical opinions, in gossiping, in attaining fame or a high office, in reading *King Lear*, or in knowing that a beautiful woman or her heart is his. The difference is in the degree of imagination required, and in the object and manner of its employment.

The sadist's vanity is only gratified when he hurts the object of his love. Sadism is the consequence when a man is weak and cowardly by nature, and only by hurting others is he able to attain a feeling of security.

A poet may write a great poem about the woman he loves, and shower upon her the most generous attentions, but it is possible that he only loves out of vanity.[1]

In describing politics, the classifier of varieties of vanity has to consider the nature of the object desired, and how much toleration of opposed interests is genially borne, how much borne with pain, and how much not borne at all.

2) The happiness of passion. By passion I mean passionate love. Passion exists beyond the limit of beauty, although in its initial stage its victim's pleasures are those of beauty and vanity. Although the effect of beauty is instantaneous in passion as well, it accumulates through the course of passion and is not balanced by vanity.

There is, properly speaking, no such thing as beauty in passion. That certain thing X which the passionate lover feels his beloved possesses, and which delights him when he thinks of her, has unfortunately no name. It can only be called "beauty" by default, since it is for the lover a veritable fact, not merely a promise of happiness.[2]

---

[1]Catullus, Petrarch, Spenser, Shelley, Pushkin, etc.

[2]"Apologies to all women for making general statements that seem to exclude them. It would be best to state at the very beginning here that in many cases the ideas stated apply equally to women.

"To say 'men and women,' or 'he or she' every time would make for unnecessary awkwardness, and to vary from men to women arbitrarily would be ridiculous. Out of a desire to be impartial, I considered referring to women consistently, but this is irregular

The object of passionate love is transformed and perfected in and by the imagination to a degree altogether unheard of and unknown to those whose only passion is vanity. The transfiguration is so deep and thorough that the lover cannot help feeling deep in his heart that he is not seeing the beloved in a clear and impartial light, yet he is utterly unable to see her as otherwise than absolutely perfect.

Vanity-beauty cannot survive intact the contradiction natural to passion. Where the slightest doubt about the worth of the object arises in all cases where the pleasure derives from vanity-beauty, the result is either unhappiness, or the object of doubtful beauty is discarded in the hope or expectation of finding one more likely to give pleasure.

Passionate love, since there is nothing of vanity left in the heart when it has been born, weakens the will to act; the lover cannot will an effective act in the presence of the beloved, or cannot act upon his will, or both. It is no longer the simple matter of trying to secure the object of love.

Whereas in the pleasures of vanity, *perfection* is the end of idealization, after which there arises the wish to come into possession of the perfected object which promises so much happiness to its possessor, in passion the perfection of the beloved is the starting-point for the heart. The transports of passion that give those who feel them sublime happiness would in all probability be painful to those who only know the happiness of vanity, if they could at all feel them.[1]

My aim here is only to describe dispassionately the secret motions of the heart, and I have no aim beyond that of a logical study of the mechanics of happiness. There are no doubt many other methods than mine. I do not make a great claim for the methodology of this essay, but I see no reason to think that it interferes with the truth of the observations made.

---

enough to falsify the meaning; and nothing is more affected than the 'person' commonly used today by prim and proper journalists whose sole motive in doing so is to flatter themselves and the petty vanity of some women.

"Whenever only the one or the other sex is being spoken of, this fact is made clear."

Louis Rollefort, the author of this essay, wrote these words on the margins of his manuscript. I have placed them here at what seems to me to be the first convenient place.

I am not at all sure that Rollefort wanted to publish his obscure notes to the world, *pace* the lines quoted above, and some others like them. In fact, there are some indications that he only wrote them to keep himself from blowing his brains out out of despair. These pages were left in my hands by one of his friends, who did not tell me what had brought this strange man to such a pass.

[1]They fortunately cannot.

Chapter II

Of Vanity

The simple wish to have power over objects and men is imaginatively the least demanding form of vanity-beauty, although otherwise identical in nature with more poetical ones.

Such pleasures as provincialism, regionalism, nationalism, racism, etc. require slightly greater efforts of the imagination, although considerations of security and survival are never absent.

Devotion to ideas of groups, nations, races, is not only a matter of social order, which is simply the specific overall result,[1] on the level of society, of the pleasures they offer to the heart and mind. The sole reason for this type of devotion, as well as for much of philosophy and religion,[2] is man's *need* to adopt as good an opinion of himself and of his consequence as he can: in other words, vanity. As soon as survival is not at stake, vanity comes in, and if it remains ungratified, unhappiness results. But if survival is at stake, considerations of vanity are usually ignored, though there are sometimes Catos in the world, too.

For the vast majority of men and women, religion ostensibly offers the greatest consolation to their vanity, by, at the least, making them a part of a grand scheme. Not many take the doctrines too seriously, at least as far as their practical affairs are concerned, but religion offers a final pillar against which their vanity may rest. There are sadists and masochists among believers of religions, too, the latter quickly swinging from joy to misery and back again as vanity is gratified or dealt a blow by some scruple of thought.[3]

Fear plays a large part in stimulating the pleasures of vanity, the more so in cases of petty vanity where the imagination does not play a great part. Where the pleasures of vanity are concerned, there is an inverse relation between the degree of fear of losing whatever supports vanity and the degree of imagination required to sustain it, with neither ever

---

[1]Accidentally brought about or deliberately contrived by some in whose interest such order lies.

[2]The truth or falsehood of religions and philosophies is not under discussion here, but only the mechanics of their operation upon the soul.

[3]Augustine, Jonathan Edwards.

disappearing entirely.[1] Owning a fine car will give some pleasure to its delighted owner, but the fear of not having one, and of being known not to have one, contributes much to the pleasure. "How unhappy I would be if I could not afford a car," a man thinks, "and how happy am I that I can."

Fear is the effect of imagining yourself in a worse situation than the present one, or than the one you wish to be in in the future. But this is not the imagination of pleasures; even when the fear is that of losing an object of worth, the pleasures whose loss is feared are not clearly known. It is the fate of those who cannot rise above petty vanity to be constantly beset with fear unless nature has given them a sanguine and cheerful temperament that checks the imagination when it wanders into gloomy areas of thought.

Religion operates through rewards (tangible heaven or the idea, pleasing to a man's vanity, of being part of a cosmic plan) and threats of punishments (divine or social). Other varieties of vanity, such as nationalism or racism, similarly survive on vanity and the fear of pain or death.

Demanding souls convert religion, which appeals to the majority only when simple and awesome, into poetry or abstruse and vague philosophy, sometimes to the point of departing from accepted religious opinions altogether.

Philosophers, being cold and vain by nature, are not susceptible to the more tender passions even when they are otherwise informed by the most generous sentiments. They cannot include in their philosophies sensations they have not felt. Taking aside the many hypocrites and fools, even those few with an excellent understanding of politics and society and of the motives that rule the heart (the subject of all true philosophy) have described both the tender and the artistic passions erroneously or incompletely.

Those of more than commonplace imagination, whose sensations are more lively, i.e., artists, delight in the fancies of their mind, and nothing stops them from raising everyday matters or objects to the status of objects of celestial beauty by the use of their imagination, beauty being nothing but any pleasing impression made upon the imagination. The sensation of beauty improves in purity and quantity (i.e., in relative

---

[1]Napoleon's pleasures in 1810 consisted of greater elements of petty vanity than his pleasures in 1796.

quantity of pleasure felt), from the simple feeling of commonplace utility
and petty vanity to a pleasure without these last two; and from acts in
the course of which the heart is dominated by fear, affectation, and
avarice to art and love. This fact can obviously only be known when you
can feel more than one type of pleasure.

In love is found the greatest purity and quantity of this sensation—
but precisely because of this fact, not all are susceptible to love above the
level of vanity and physical passion. Shakespeare observed of those in
love,

> The lunatic, the lover, and the poet,
> Are of imagination all compact.

Vanity love produces, for some, the greatest, most lively sensations of
beauty that life offers. Even physical pleasures are less *common* than
those of petty vanity. Its pleasures are less intense than those of physical
love. A woman is looked at in the same light as is a fine house, a
respectable lawn, smart clothes, etc., if even that high.

In warm temperaments, vanity love can be tender and generous.[1]

In *all* cases of vanity and beauty, the following occurs:

1) Desire for pleasure and happiness exists in all men and women.

2) An object is found that gives pleasure when seen, heard, smelt,
touched, tasted, or thought about. Or it may be an idea which has a
tangible symbol that represents it to the mind, such as, for example, the
idea of flying, or of helping those in distress.[2]

3) He thinks, "X gives me pleasure to see, touch, think of, etc. How
much pleasure I will feel if I could thoroughly enjoy X." At this point,
this object X (person, thing, or idea) is felt to have beauty to the degree
of the pleasure it promises. As much is ascribed to this object as possible,
and the richer the imagination, the more worthy of admiration and
possession X comes to seem.

4) He thinks, "It must always be in my power to enjoy the pleasures that
I know X can give me." The greater the promised happiness, the
stronger the desire to secure it, and the more that alternate pleasures are
willingly sacrificed to this end.

---

[1]Mozart and Jane Austen.

[2]Helvétius, Hobbes, Locke and others have shown that all ideas arise from sensory
perceptions, and from the pleasure or pain caused by these perceptions. The instincts are
comprehended under the law of pleasure and pain.

If this end is difficult and the hold the object has on the imagination weak, the process stops. Some other object must be found; unhappiness results otherwise. If the pleasure promised is strongly enough impressed upon the heart, difficulty in securing it only intensifies hope, although it is attended with grief and fear. At this point, the thought, "My happiness will always be incomplete, I can never be happy, if X never becomes mine," takes hold of the heart.

5) When and if the man can say, "X is mine," the happiness that he knows depends upon how much imagination is still involved in construing the object as beautiful, as capable of giving him happiness. With possession, the *need to imagine* the beauty and worth of the object declines precipitously, and thus the commonly perceived fact that there is usually more pleasure in the acts of pursuing and hoping than in that of possessing. But the fear of thinking oneself, or being thought of, a fool also comes in at this point.

The quicker a man obtains power of possession over the object[1] once it has inspired great desire or hope, the greater will be the immediate pleasure of possession, ceteris paribus. In such cases, he feels fully the sensations both of beauty and vanity. If there is a delay of more than a few days between the birth of desire or hope and possession, the pleasure is chiefly that of vanity; and as the interval increases, there will be more of the last, so long as the pursuit does not begin to bore him.

A man derives his happiness from the knowledge, "X is mine." For this happiness to last, the worth of the object must always be present to the mind, or at least the fear of losing it must give a worth to it. The image of its worth may dim in time as the man becomes bored with the object; and he then seeks something else, and only when fear of losing it overrides boredom will he be moved to make further efforts to prolong or re-secure the possession of the object.

With sensitive or artistic souls, because of their ready and active imagination, the worth of the object is more likely to remain imprinted on their thoughts. They continue to be subject to the charm they had dreamed of earlier, and although this charm of an object decreases when it is theirs, this disappointment is sometimes more than made up for by the new charm of secure possession: the sensations of beauty are united with the pleasures of vanity. But in such people there also is often the balancing love of novelty.[2]

---

[1]Here as always, by object is meant object as object as well as object as sensible symbol of a pleasing idea.

[2]Rousseau, Shelley, Tolstoy, Delacroix, etc.

Regardless of the particular shades of the pleasures of vanity that make for happiness, the five stages described above of vanity-beauty remain the same. The object that calls up pictures of happiness may be a tangible object, or it may be an idea formed by the comparison of objects. One thinks: "This limousine belongs to me," "The best house in town is mine," "the most beautiful woman in town is mine," "the arrogant and proud woman is mine," "the handsome man is mine," "that rich man is mine," "I have a husband/wife," "I am a pious man/woman," "I am a great politician/scientist/engineer/economist/artist/beauty, etc.," "I am a successful businessman/townsman/organizer/lover, etc.," "I am a good citizen/patriot /friend/advisor /father/mother /daughter/son/ revolutionary /conservative/feminist, etc."

Nature has made man so that all happiness save that of passionate love arises from the gratification of vanity that follows the pleasures of the senses.

Physical love and sports are felt to be pleasing even without the aid of vanity. The pleasures of great application of mind or body such as are felt in solving mathematical, scientific, or engineering problems, in conducting affairs of state or business, in mountain-climbing, playing polo, managing a household, etc., are the results of exertion. But both of these types of pleasures are (at best) temporary and tiresome if vanity is not gratified in the process.

When you are incapable of or unsuccessful at any one of the steps of vanity-beauty, the process stops, resulting in unhappiness. All unhappiness save that of passionate love has this failure as its cause. You tell yourself, "I do not deserve this unhappiness."[1]

----

[1]Here I may as well make clear that by such quoted thoughts are meant what goes on in the heart only. Johnson wrote in one of the *Rambler* numbers:

> And surely, if we are conscious that we have not contributed to our own sufferings, if punishment fall upon innocence, or disappointment happens to industry and prudence, patience, whether more necessary or not, is much easier, since our pain is then without aggravation, and we have not the bitterness of remorse to add to the asperity of misfortune.

This is good as far as a smooth and sonorously solemn style and the *effect* of having logically studied the matter go. But it would be ridiculous to be confused by the use of words, or by what people tell themselves they feel. There will be no end to his errors in matters of the heart if a man cannot detach himself from all feelings but that of a respect for facts.

When someone feels, "I was foolish and made a blunder. I deserve this consequence," or "I committed a moral error and therefore deserve the worst fate," he is unhappy because

The greatest happiness for those who cannot rise above vanity is to feel, "I have all the consequence I could wish for. I have everything I could desire." The intensity of this happiness depends entirely upon the number of ideas of pleasure[1] that led to a man to this thought.

The number of such ideas only increases beyond the minimal with the increase in the number of *clear and exact* ideas of the shades of pleasures of other men—and women—you have.[2] Every man and woman has his or her own shade of vanity, each of different degrees of intensity, each deriving from different objects, ideas, and rhetorical phrasings of those ideas.[3]

---

his wishes met with failure, and he has only to blame himself for this; but the unhappiness of one who feels, "I was foolish and made a little blunder, but the consequences are unfairly painful," or "I did nothing that should bring upon me this great a misfortune," is much greater because vanity is more unsatisfied here. He blames himself, but the pains of guilt, remorse, or self-contempt are proportional to the degree to which he feels that they are undeserved.

[1]This number being proportional to the number of entirely different types of objects whose possession gives him *intense* pleasure. An automobile, a house, a sauna bath, a private jet, a very presentable and ambitious wife, etc., make up only *one* type of object. To have the heart so deeply stirred by a majestic valley that you lose yourself in reveries of happiness would make up another type of object. The subject of those reveries may make up a third. The beloved, if different from the subject just mentioned, makes up a fourth. And so on.

[2]I.e., the number of others whose happiness you can feel as they do themselves, exactly and with utter conviction that there is no other.

[3]Cervantes, for example, or Betty Grable knew a very great number; Napoleon, Verdi, and Baudelaire knew fewer; Freud knew even fewer than Schopenhauer. But since few men, though they may admit others to be wittier, more talented in some specific matter that to them is not the most important for their own vanity, or stronger, admit anyone to be wiser than themselves, as Hobbes pointed out, and since a man is under necessity to admire in others only his own ideas, as Helvétius pointed out, with few exceptions, everyone thinks his knowledge of what pleasures there are to be the maximum, and thinks others' to be great also only when they are seen to match his own. So, Freud admired Sophocles, Shakespeare, and Dostoevski, because by chance they and their great fame helped him support his own vanity, deriving from love of fame, as Foucault did Nietzsche, and thus do their admirers Freud and Foucault, etc. In a very rare case, such as that of Shakespeare, the popular opinion may match facts, but in his case only because even a fool can tell that Shakespeare produced a great number of very different characters. This kind of man or woman will find only something called a pedant's "illusion vs. reality" theme (with its mild pleasures of benign vagueness and ignorance) in Cervantes and think it a "complex" or simple matter according to his or her own vanity, and nothing at all in Betty Grable— whom the *Harvard Lampoon* once selected as the Worst Actress of the Year; she wrote to the editors and cheerfully agreed. Will what I am about to say be believed? Though Cervantes and Betty Grable seem to me among the greatest geniuses of the world, I agree with them very little. Opinions like this one will, I admit, make this work seem very trivial to a serious-minded man or woman or a hypocritical one. Such a reader is requested to not

The pleasure of self-esteem is empty without the esteem of those who are esteemed, and their esteem is always necessary in order for a vain man or woman to feel his or her happiness to be complete.

The happiness of contented vanity of each man has no definite relation to the varying intensities of sensations that can be known by other hearts.

Too strong a passion is, in fact, generally regarded with dread and suspicion, and felt to be perilous in oneself unless inspired by the instinct for self-preservation, and in others unless its object would protect one in times of danger.[1]

Only that much intensity of even common passions is admitted by a man as beneficial, desirable, or, indeed, tolerable as he himself has known. Anything exceeding that in others is looked upon as unintelligible and perilous.

Happiness is a relative matter. The man who has been held in solitary confinement for a year will be overwhelmed at the opportunity of exchanging a few words with a friendly janitor. But this is merely the cessation of pain felt as pleasure. So long as the imagination is not stimulated to imagine delights there can be but little positive pleasure. If that man is allowed to converse with a faithful mistress for a few hours, or given some news regarding his fellow insurgents, he will feel joy according to his nature and interests. How much pleasure is felt upon obtaining what has been desired depends greatly upon how much pleasure was expected generally at the moment it was obtained.

No one tolerates another's idea of beauty unless he believes it to derive *in the end* from the same source as his own, i.e., unless he feels that the other agrees with him in matters he regards to be of consequence—the differences are seen as being of a nature where mutual compromises would leave both men content. The greater his intelligence and imagination, the more passionate his nature, the more deeply beyond the surface will he look for agreements in opinions, but if none

---

bother himself or herself any further with it. Should many come to say that they have read this essay all the way through and disliked or despised it, I shall be forced to regard my powers of inspiring deep interest and then gratifying it to be much greater than I had ever dared to suppose, for what but overwhelming interest can possibly motivate such readers to read any further?

[1]The reason why physical love has been sharply discouraged in some ages and nations, and religious fanaticism in others, but the *idea* of patriotism has never been publicly discouraged except by traitors who sense victory.

is discovered, he develops an aversion for the other man. This comparison of opinions and interests is so much a matter of opinion as opposed to logic, and thus open to idiosyncrasies of misjudgment, that it is no wonder that friendship is an idiosyncratic and, seemingly, an arbitrary affair.

The unvarying sameness of any (even the most beautiful) object makes it boring, unless fear of losing it revivifies the image of its worth. The rapidity with which boredom sets in depends upon the sensibility of the man,[1] and upon how deeply the object affected him. The inevitable birth of boredom is one of two reasons for the love of novelty. The other reason is the existence in some of a type of vanity which seeks its chief pleasure in constantly turning from one object to another. This type of vanity commonly does not outlast youth. It arises from suspicion of boredom.

You must turn to artists to find the men and women who have had the gift to express the happiness of contented vanity, or the unhappiness of discontented vanity.[2]

The ideas of beauty a man associates with a woman are made up of the perceived physical charms plus the moral qualities she is thought to possess. The aggregate equals her beauty. The word *beauty*, though, is generally used only when the happiness promised is of a more than commonplace nature.

Love, the sensation felt towards the object that inspires this sensation of beauty, is born when some accident or circumstance that gives rise to hope makes a man dwell on the beauty of a woman. He seeks to make the object of his love his. A sensitive man has the additional wish to be able to express fully to the beloved his feelings, which he can do only if she returns his love to some degree. He fears that far from returning his love she will not even understand him. He thinks, "I would be happy if she loved me."

---

[1] A man with a lively sensibility finds innumerable perfections in a lovable object, but he is also moved to boredom more easily than dull men are.

[2] E.g., see Nabokov's and Chateaubriand's autobiographies for examples of gratified vanity, and the confessions of Augustine, Rousseau, Tolstoy, Edwards' *Personal Narrative*, as well as the novels of Dostoevski and Proust and the works of Schopenhauer and Pascal, for vanity disguised as misery. In the cases of Flaubert and Kafka (excepting *The Castle*), the bitter humor and the cold icing of style are affectations that do not quite manage to hide the unhappiness of the writers. Has Chateaubriand's autobiography anything more to say than Franklin's? Each relates anecdotes in what he hopes is an amusing manner, and each expresses in the language he thinks most effective his pleasures and aversions. Where lies the difference, save for the different shades of vanity?

The greater the effect of beauty, and the more precipitously increasing its hold on a man's imagination, the greater is the vanity love inspired, and hence the greater the wish to reach the stage of intimacy.

Once this goal is attained, the thought, "She is beautiful, she is morally perfect; I wish she loved me," is replaced by, "This adorable creature is mine." He counts the perfections of the beloved, and every detail that excites his admiration and love makes him happier by the knowledge that she is his. The more perfect he thinks his beloved the greater is his happiness.

The quality and degree of the happiness of vanity depend entirely upon the imagination of a man.

The relative power of two mental faculties separates us from other animals.[1] One is our imagination's power of seeing what we already know in new lights. This power leads to the birth of new pleasures and pains, and, therefore, of new knowledge, which is acquired to ensure future gratification of the new desires and to dispel the new aversions.[2] If there be any in the world who are not susceptible to boredom, they will, I imagine, be the very dull witted men, but who would envy them their dreary contentment?

The other faculty consists of our powers of memory by means of which we can retain many of the imagination's products for later use.

What are considered *thoughts* and *ideas* (as opposed to feelings and sensations) are feelings or sensations resulting from the comparison, not of things, but of *words*.

Language itself, the product of imagination and memory, allows us to compact a whole range of sensations in a symbol, thus allowing us to juggle with symbols only—as is the case in mathematics, which is but a type of language and can be used for sustaining fantasies as well as common words. Thought itself is but a type of feeling. Its directions and subject matter are controlled by the law of pleasure and pain. The seeming unpredictability of what springs into the mind at a given moment is due to the fact that our will generally has little control over the powers of memory and imagination, or over our pleasures and pains.

The power of the imagination indicates merely the degree to which objects have an effect on the soul of a man. It depends upon his inner makeup and upon the degree of his experience. The greater and wider

---

[1] Our erect posture and our thumbs are the obvious physical advantages.

[2] Sciences, engineering, the arts, manners, institutions, etc. are born in this manner.

his experience, the more well stocked his mind will be with different ideas of beauty. By the inner makeup I mean the degree to which that energy in the mind and heart is habitually exercised which leads him to compare pleasures and pains in order to arrive at the maximum of the former and the minimum of the latter.[1]

The greater the habitual exercise of the imagination, the larger is the number of ideas that are brought to bear upon the objects that give pleasure (thoughts of objects that induce pain are avoided to the degree that prudence deems safe), and the greater is the harmony imagined between these. Compare Hugh Lattimer[2] to Calvin or Milton.

It follows that the greater the imagination, the more an object that inspires pain or pleasure is likely to become a *symbol*. As such, its worth begins to be exaggerated by the imagination.

The man of greater imagination knows fully the pleasures of another of less imagination, so long as their pleasures derive from the same objects and ideas, but not vice versa. In all likelihood, the latter will think himself the more intelligent and imaginative. There is no way to prove one's superiority to another against his conviction.

Those with great powers of imagination need not, and usually do not, have better knowledge of facts than others not so gifted or fortunate as regards experience, but they have more facts about the heart at hand.

There is, in the vast majority of cases, more vanity, as well as a greater susceptibility to beauty, where there are greater powers of imagination: this is where vanity grades into pride, its highest reach.

In terms of quantitative units of pleasure possible, if I may be allowed the use of such terms for the sake of clarity, love comes first, with art and love of power closely following.[3] All other forms of pursuing happiness either require less imagination altogether, or waste it where there is no motivation to look for ever new perfections and proofs of happiness. But a great scientist or philosopher may have much more

---

[1]Ideas of beauty increase when you learn to admire what those whom you respect or fear admire; and when you try to discover in an object that has proved pleasing already, or in anything associated with it, new beauties to admire. These newly perceived qualities belonging to an object already admired lead the imagination to recognize them for the first time as beautiful.

[2]An English Protestant reformer and martyr of the 16th century.

[3]The maximum degrees to which the soul can be affected by different pleasures vary. Men, individually taken, though, have often not the power to derive much pleasure from this or that object which rouses the imagination to a fierce tempest in others.

imagination (and use it as well) than is called into play in Mr. X and Miss Z by love or a work of great art. In all probability, the scientist's or the philosopher's imagination will be thrown into greater agitation by some natural mystery or a question of national consequence than by art or love. Many cannot rise to the knowledge of any lively pleasure.

All such passions as envy, anger, indignation, hope, joy, fear, zeal, valor, cowardice, desire to please, hatred, most of the shades of love, etc., are aspects of vanity, and make up the various possible responses to circumstances. Sometimes they are the responses to the threat of death or great peril, to problems of survival rather than vanity.

The passions of sympathy, empathy, or pity always run parallel to the degree to which an active imagination is present, for none of these can be felt but when you imagine yourself to be the victim. You can only be made unhappy by your own misfortunes, or by imagining those of others to be happening to you.[1] In civilized societies, these generous passions are taught to the young in order to produce in them a lifelong conscience about the suffering of others, but the pity and empathy that have been thus taught produce in themselves little pain, and are of use only to society and its established manners in general.

The virtuous man and the vile criminal both are made happy or unhappy by vanity, the difference lying only in the power to imagine themselves in the shoes of another. Among both classes is found the whole range of degrees of courage in the face of grave dangers.[2]

---

[1]For this reason, excessive pity (the sort where there is a nervous reaction) for the suffering of others is often a sign of moral or physical cowardice, occurring more commonly among women. So is excessive empathy, perhaps more common among men.

When the sufferer is someone you love, you immediately share her pain as if it were your own, to which is added, in cases of deep love, an additional (and worse) dose of pain because pride cannot step in to forestall self-pity.

[2]To go on at length about vanity and how it operates in different circumstances, and in relation to different objects would have been so tedious that I would probably have given up after a few pages from boredom. The pattern is always the same, but the notable and necessary features of each different combination of the degree of desire, the circumstance, and the nature of the object or objects of desire will naturally be different. The dispassionate study of this subject (true philosophy, that is) may have existed in a primitive form here and there in history, but it was Hobbes in the seventeenth century who established the first principles of philosophy by combining logic, the study of the passions as motions of the soul, and ethics. He was followed by his politically more liberal imitator, Locke, who, being the soul of pedantry, was idolized in the eighteenth century. Subsequent English philosophers of note were either poets (the famous Berkeley, for example), charlatans (such as Hume), or men of talent, though also of limited range of imagination and therefore knowledge (such as Mandeville, Bentham, Spencer, and Malthus). The hard

Before proceeding further, I want to state that I have no wish or intention to demean or vilify. I have emptied myself of all personal feelings in order to describe facts. I do not praise or censure. I merely observe.

Chapter III

Of Art

Art is the product of the desire to please by other means than direct flattery or advancement of those interests that require the cooperation of others. Many actions and manners have an artistic side, but few have nothing but it. It is the products of this last group that are most properly called the works of artists. A work of art has no purpose but to give pleasure to the soul through the senses, and does not generally inspire any action or wish but the desire to prolong the sensation. The work made with didactic aims in mind relating to society, manners, or opinions yet is made to please those who enjoy[1] discovering the particular sentiments it expresses because they agree with them.

Art only exists as such in the minds and hearts of an audience. One audience can reject the application of the description *art* to what another proclaims to be the acme of art.

An artist always seeks to express in his work whatever seem to him the most beautiful things or ideas imaginable, those which hold the

---

and exact method of Hobbes was taken up in France by Condillac, Helvétius, Condorcet, Tracy, and Cabanis. I refer the reader to their works, especially to that of Helvétius, whose *De l'esprit* is the finest work of cold philosophy I know, followed by Helvétius' *De l'homme,* Hobbes' *Leviathan* (the first twelve chapters, and a few other ideas here and there), and Cabanis' *Rapports du physique et du moral de l'homme.*

These great men, even the sublime Helvétius, were largely incapable of the more lively passions, and their accounts of these are spare and wanting in full truth. I have, therefore, largely confined my essay to a study of those sensations they ignore. This essay could not have been possible without many contributions by others, not only by writers, philosophers, artists, statesmen, scientists, etc., but also by those whom the author observed in order to understand the passions of the heart.

In the remainder of this essay I am only interested in the stronger passions that operate upon the heart, in great actions of the *soul.*

[1]Much as I tried, I could not locate in any dictionary a drier and less romantic word than "enjoy" with which to express in a word the idea, "To derive pleasure from."

greatest possibilities of producing happiness. The work of art created is a picture, a symbolic suggestion of what is held by the artist as beautiful, and it is the artist's hope that this picture will inspire in others the reveries that he associates with his favored objects of beauty.

At their respective bests, except for love, all other human actions are inferior to the making or enjoying of art, insofar as the degree of pleasure is concerned. Much of philosophy, from Plato (and before him) onwards through Aristotle, Epicurus, Aquinas, Spinoza, Descartes, Leibniz, Hume, Berkeley, Kant, Hegel, Schopenhauer, Kierkegaard, James, Freud, Wittgenstein, etc., consists chiefly of poetry with odds and ends of facts thrown in for good measure.[1]

Religion, as it loses its primitive qualities (as it does among followers of genius), tends towards the arts: I refer not only to such great artists as Dante, Michelangelo, and Bach, but also to religious mystics and visionaries. Are not the writings of some lesser mystics identical to what is today called symbolist poetry and symbolist literature: all reflecting the search for Novalis' "blue flower"?

Art may consist of very complicated effects, such as those of Tolstoy's *Anna Karenina*, or of relatively simple ones, as of Balzac's *Illusions perdues*. A reader may, though, very well ignore in his deriving pleasure from it, or be ignorant of, how the work was intended to be enjoyed by its maker(s). He will enjoy *Anna Karenina* in a simple direct way, and find all sorts of complicated and clever effects and artistic manipulations in *Illusions perdues*. The pleasures of the artist and the pleasures of specific audiences need never coincide.

Art may be divided into seven classes according to how the heart is affected. These are the seven manners by which an artist can attempt to make an impression upon the souls of others. Or they may be considered seven manners in which an audience can derive pleasure from works of art. To clarify matters, I give examples of artists who produced works in these classes, but an audience will always derive pleasure from these works in the only way it can.

---

[1]Or alternately, Confucius, Mencius, Lao-tzu, Buddha, Shankara, Ramanuja, Avicenna, al-Ghazali, Averroës, etc. It will be noted that the author seldom refers to names that are not illustrious. Is this a fault? He would not be taken to mean that by philosophers he means only these great names, and by artists only those he names later. But their very fame makes of them excellent illustrations of what the author means, as the reader is more likely to have heard of them than of obscure and uncelebrated names.

Their lasting fame also indicates that they supply enough literary material for later men of widely removed ages and nations to put to use in furthering their own interests.

There are many who enjoy only what has pleased others they esteem, or for the pleasure of being able to say that they, too, can find pleasure in it. Others enjoy or esteem only those works which conform to their pet ideas.

Perhaps the following categories will seem arbitrary, and a clever reader may come up with different ones. Such rhetorical scruples do not affect the following truths concerning how the heart is affected by works of art.

1) When the clever manipulation of the constituent elements of the medium, be they words, images, ideas, paint, lines, sounds, gestures, demeanors, etc., is such that it gives pleasure by the surprising arrangements and patterns produced. This is the harmonic aspect of art, and the works of art which give pleasure *chiefly* (though naturally not exclusively) in this manner may be called works of harmonic art.

Among the artists who have produced harmonic masterpieces are Horace, Giotto, Chaucer, Rabelais, Fra Angelico, Ariosto, Titian, Rubens, Marvell, Pascal, La Fontaine, Bach, Swift, Pope, Sterne, Haydn, Chateaubriand, Coleridge, Pushkin, Keats, Gogol, Flaubert, Manet, Tolstoy, Chekhov, Delacroix, Degas, Gauguin, Rimbaud, Machado, Matisse, Joyce, Kafka, Khodasevich, Nabokov, Jean Renoir, Hawks, Keaton, Cary Grant, Groucho Marx, and Mr. Ashok Kumar.

He who derives from the very clever, varied, and complicated effects of manipulation of the resources (the stock material of the medium) and of the conventions the artist must use more pleasure than he does from anything else in art will tend to produce or enjoy a work of art harmonically; this man will discover, whenever possible, harmonic qualities in all works he or she enjoys, and not only in those which were composed with the intention of displaying them.

Nabokov, who described harmonic art more completely than anyone else, echoing Coleridge and Flaubert, put it in this way: an artist begins with the materials of this world, takes them apart in his mind, and recomposes them in a new and harmonic manner in his works.[1] The philosophic justification, which is in fact a poetic excuse, is similar to Kant's vague reveries about beauty in the *Critique of Judgment*: the harmonic pattern is taken to reflect the larger pattern of some "superhuman reality", of which one can get hints (which are regarded as

---

[1] I paraphrase. The idea itself is old, its expression most precise and complete in Nabokov.

hardly falling short of the status of proofs) through harmony. Rationally considered, this notion is very silly, but it reflects the passion which the harmonic artist considers the most pleasing.

The pleasures of harmony are the pleasures of regarding yourself to be enormously clever, and, as the harmonic manipulations become very complicated and clever, regarding yourself to be the maker of destinies.[1] They are purely the pleasures of vanity. The artist feels clever as he composes his work, and the audience feels very clever in following the cleverness. At the highest levels of harmonic complexities, religious sentiments also come in. The simpler pleasure is similar to the pleasure one gets from watching difficult feats of acrobatics, gymnastics, figure skating, sports, etc.. The idea of the difficulty overcome, and the elegance with which it was overcome, inspire the joys of vanity through empathy with the artist.[2]

Harmonists have this advantage, that as long as the medium survives (the language, the canvas, etc.) their works can continue to give pleasure to those who are susceptible to the pleasures of harmony. Harmonic art is then as little susceptible to changes of fashions as art can be. It is only when the medium itself is no longer understood or extant that a harmonic artist is relatively neglected: the fate of Chaucer's poetry for centuries.

The vanity of all great artists is usually also great, but it is often hidden behind a show of great generosity of spirit. I doubt that more than a few knew true passion; they did not have the simplicity for it.

For some strange reason I cannot fathom, unless it be either insincerity, or a desire not to appear common and ridiculous, the pleasures of harmony are often called by those who feel them "disinterested" pleasures. What they mean, I think, is that the source of pleasure is not any particular object, or the thought of an object, which is true to a degree, because their vanity is more a matter of pure self-

---

[1]For this reason, only men produce works of harmonic art, though women can derive some pleasure from them. See chapters XXXVII and LII. One exception, the only one I know, that maker of those curious joke-poems often masquerading as metaphysical (i.e., pedantic) riddles, Emily Dickinson.

[2]Nabokov knew as much. See the sections on Mascodagama in one of his three best novels, *Ada*. *Pale Fire* is a slow-motion demonstration of harmonics in action, and a making explicit of the philosophic-poetic backdrop of harmonic art. Nabokov spent his entire life collecting and ordering all of the ideas regarding the pleasures of harmonic art. For this reason it is surprising that his three masterpieces, all harmonic in design, turned somehow into works of ideal art, a phenomenon I find only in Nabokov.

esteem deriving from knowledge of their powers in matters of art. Considering the degree of difficulty that the greatest harmonic artists gaily put before themselves as a challenge, and the elegance with which they solve these self-devised problems, what would it be but ill-nature that would ridicule them for deceiving themselves with regard to the disinterestedness of their pleasures?

Style originally had the function of raising the dignity of what was being described. As men come to stand in increasing awe of the advancements of science and technology, and to worship the ideas of liberty and equality, a difficult or sonorous style begins to be regarded with suspicion. Simpler styles have come into fashion as a consequence, but their function is the same, only the specific methods have changed.[1] That is to say, style changes only according to the tastes of the public.

On the other hand, style has been given a greater emphasis than ever by artists in the last two centuries; e.g., by Shelley, Keats, Pushkin, Manet, Matisse, Flaubert, Cézanne, Joyce, Chateaubriand, Baudelaire, Rimbaud, Dickens, Yeats, Mallarmé, Stevens, Melville, Stravinsky, Schoenberg, Ozu, Gauguin, Nabokov, Proust, James, etc.

2) The idealists, those who have each their own idea of what is beautiful, and express it and enjoy it as best and as fully as they can. By far the great majority of artists and audiences belong to this class.

The difference between great artists and minor ones is always only a matter of opinion. All that may be said about greatness in art is that great artists are those who search for and find their own unique idea of what is most beautiful, and minor artists are those who reflect the fashions of their time, and cannot rise above these. The popular success of an artist depends upon how closely his ideas coincide with those of his public; but a great artist can surpass the ideas which his public is capable of, and yet be popular because his ideas tend generally in the same direction as his public's.[2]

Among ideal artists some famous names are Homer, Virgil, Kalidasa, Tu Fu, Dante, van Eyck, Rumi, Masaccio, Ghirlandaio, Hafiz, Michelangelo, Titian, Veronese, Tintoretto, Caravaggio, Guido Reni,

---

[1]Consider modern best-sellers, films (both those that are popular, and those with greater pretensions), MTV, the "modern music scene," etc.

[2]I.e., his public feels that they are being given what they want. They usually want flattering portraits. Since many today flatter themselves by claiming to have a low opinion of themselves and their passions, "anti-heroes" and "anti-heroines" are produced to flatter this group. Men and women also want what is already fashionable in a more flashy guise.

Lope, Cervantes, Tasso, Rembrandt, Corneille, Molière, Handel, Vivaldi, Fielding, Goethe, Cimarosa, Canova, Beethoven, Hölderlin, Burns, Kleist, Balzac, Schubert, Shelley, Verdi, Tchaikovsky, Wagner, Offenbach, Delacroix, Baudelaire, Dickens, Ghalib, Tolstoy, Dostoevski, Melville, Twain, Picasso, Yeats, Proust, Stravinsky, Blok, Rilke, Jean Renoir, Vigo, Hawks, Lernet-Holenia, Faulkner, Nabokov, Ozu, Mr. Kurosawa, Grable, Astaire, Saigal, Meena Shorey, etc.

Since the pleasure that a work of art produces can never surpass the capacity of the man who derives pleasure from the work, it depends on his previous knowledge of pleasures, although in time he may discover new beauties from repeated acquaintance with a work that has greatly pleased him. All the genius of Madhubala or Mozart is of no avail if the audience has little knowledge of the finer and stronger feelings.

The pleasures of ideal art are then those which a man already knows, and which are inspired by the impression the work of art makes on his senses.

There are many who are absolutely indifferent to any form of art; their only pleasure is the advancement of their worldly interests.

Some learn to enjoy works of art through rules or prescriptions. The only way their heart can be affected by works of art is if in them they can discover what those whom they respect have taught them to esteem.[1]

By describing what a man thinks of as beautiful, the artist can produce the sensation of beauty in that man, but it is necessary that he not know exactly how the artist has described it.

The first time you hear a piece of music, read a poem or story, or see a film or painting, etc., you can enjoy it fully, so long as you are not distracted by other thoughts. But as you hear, read, or see the same work again, it is memory that you are calling upon to help you enjoy it, and the effect is less beautiful than it was originally. It may happen that during the inital experience you did not understand the work. It is the first time you understand the work (to the maximum degree you are likely to) that you derive from it the greatest effect of beauty it can give.

When memory comes in to stimulate pleasure, what we have is the pleasure of vanity. The man now thinks, "This work is pleasing because it has such and such a beauty." But now that beauty itself cannot be felt, since it was merely the promise of a happiness now attained and known.

---

[1]The type almost universal today.

If, however, you have not gone back to the work for so long a period that you have forgotten it, you will derive from it as much pleasure as you did the first time. But a work that is loved will be fondly remembered in detail, and will be less beautiful as it is more loved. The pattern of the general course of vanity-beauty is the same here as in other objects of pleasure.

New works also gratify the love of novelty that already known works cannot, and so there is always a demand for new works. But new works do not only represent a reworked appeal to exactly the same ideals and ideas, since both artists and fashions keep changing. A slight change from current fashions that meets with public favor is then imitated and exaggerated in the future, and in time many such small changes lead to changes in fashions. Where there has been a great political change, the change in artistic fashions is commonly as sudden.

Harmonic artists are also ideal to the degree that they must represent some ideals in their works. The difference is that the ideals take second place to the cleverness of the artist.[1]

Proust was a clever writer, but Flaubert, who was less clever, obtained his chief effects solely through the cleverness of his art. He was pleased to call it *purity of style*. Proust's cleverness was always at the service of his ideas and opinions about what constitutes pleasure. These are paramount even when they praise the cleverness of artists. If you think as he did you will derive pleasure from reading his works, otherwise you will not unless your vanity drives you to enjoy generally esteemed works, a very common phenomenon. The mental effort required by the greater harmonic artists results in their ideal side's being felt more vividly by the audience up to it.

There are often harmonic qualities in works of ideal art,[2] but these do not predominate over the expression of ideas and images.

Every artist and most men are capable of producing or deriving pleasure from some work or the other of ideal art, but the taste for harmonic effects is rarer. *Anna Karenina* and *La règle du jeu* are among

---

[1]Except in the unique case of Ghalib, whose *ideal* was harmonic in the nature of its sensations. He was an ideal artist purely, but his personal pleasures of composing poetry, his greatest pleasure, lay in the originality and clever orderliness of his use of poetic devices and conceits. But it is not the manipulations themselves that gave pleasure, as in the case of Joyce or Nabokov, but the *idea* of manipulation; even in the case of Nabokov, it was the *possibilities* of manipulations that gave pleasure in an ideal form, not the idea.

[2]In Ozu or Milton, for example.

the greatest harmonic masterpieces, but Tolstoy and Renoir also produced in *War and Peace* and *The Golden Coach* great works of ideal art. Harmonic works are usually enjoyed in an ideal manner by audiences.

A man can discover whatever he desires in a work and derive pleasure from his discovery, although the work may be thought by most not to describe what he sees in it. You cannot change another's opinions against his will.

3) Dramatic art, which expresses with exact truth the sensations felt by a man or woman in the midst of active encounters with other men and women. The only examples of dramatic art I know are some of the works of Shakespeare, Guercino, Mozart, Madhubala, and Clark Gable. There is an overlay of ideal pleasures on top of the dramatic ones in these works.

4) The melodic genius of *Hamlet, Don Giovanni,* and Madhubala's performance as Bela in *Kal Hamara Hai* ("Tomorrow is Ours").[1]

Shakespeare, Mozart, and Madhubala were in their lesser works dramatic artists, but in these three works they have produced works that are different from the rest of their oeuvres.

Ideal works have the effect of beauty when what the works seem to him to express and what a man considers beautiful coincide for the first time. In the only three works I know that belong to the melodic class, the effect of beauty is produced merely by the effect of the medium on the senses of the audience. This is a difficult, if not an impossible phenomenon to explain clearly, for why should it take place in only these cases?[2]

---

[1]From this point in this chapter, the works named display increasingly deep knowledge of the human heart. These works provide a gauge by which can be measured the sum experience and knowledge of ideas of pleasures of a man by the degree and nature of his pleasure, if any.

Madhubala plays two roles in *Tomorrow is Ours*. The one where the effect is melodic is that of Bela. The role of Madhu is played seemingly in normal dramatic manner, but in such a way that it contributes to the melodic art of Bela; it is therefore a *necessary* part of Madhubala's achievement. (The difference is the same as that between the lines of Hamlet and those of the other characters.) The film needs to be edited so that all the non-Madhubala sections are cut out, and this can easily be done on video copies.

Bela is not even the central character of the film.

[2]You may ask, Why write about this class only by mentioning a play, an opera, and a film? A little knowledge of beauty is possessed by everyone, and it is drawn upon when deriving pleasure from new situations in life, and from new works of art that are felt to express that beauty when first encountered. The melodic effect is thus a part of the ideal

That Shakespeare and Mozart had great verbal and musical powers respectively is universally granted by all men who take an interest in the matter, and who are not led to their opinion merely by the desire to praise someone else in their place[1]—and the case is exactly the same with Madhubala, except that almost no one as yet has recognized her great genius. But this fact regarding their powers in itself tells us nothing.

The melodic effect is difficult to describe. I quote the attempts Keats made in some of his famous letters, although his description is not precise:

> "Several things dovetailed in my mind, & at once it struck me, what quality went to form a Man of Achievement especially in Literature & which Shakespeare possessed so enormously—I mean *Negative Capability*, that is when a man is capable of being in uncertainties, Mysteries, doubts, without any irritable reaching after fact and reason—Coleridge, for instance, would let go by a fine isolated verisimilitude caught from the Penetralium of mystery, from being incapable of remaining content with half knowledge. This pursued through Volumes would perhaps take us no further than this, that with a great poet the sense of Beauty overcomes every other consideration, or rather obliterates all consideration."

In another letter, he wrote,

> "As to the poetical Character itself, (I mean that sort of which, if I am any thing, I am a Member; that sort distinguished from the wordsworthian or egotistical sublime; which is a thing per se and stands alone) it is not itself—it has no self—it is every thing and nothing—It has no character—it enjoys light and shade; it lives in gusto, be it foul or fair, high or low, rich or

---

effect—but the power to remain in the realm of beauty, and not fall into vanity even with continued acquaintance with the same object is *very* rare, and if Shakespeare, Mozart, and Madhubala rose to that height when producing their melodic masterpieces, this is as much to say that at this level of art, the artist has *almost* no match among the rest of mankind. This last fact leaves a describer of the mechanics of how art affects the soul no choice but to limit himself to describing the nature of the works, and the effects consequent to that nature.

[1]E.g., Voltaire and a host of other Frenchmen on Shakespeare; Gould on Mozart.

poor, mean or elevated—It has as much delight in conceiving an Iago as an Imogen. What shocks the virtuous philosopher, delights the camelion Poet. It does no harm from its relish of the dark side of things any more than from its taste for the bright one; because they both end in speculation."

Keats seems to have taken some of Hazlitt's ideas and used them to make the distinction between harmonic art—his own, which he confuses with the dramatic (i.e., non-melodic) art of Shakespeare—and ideal art, which for him was always in danger of declining into a "wordsworthian or egotistical sublime," thereby sacrificing harmonic emphases. His application of his ideas to Shakespeare confuses the subject because Shakespeare was not a harmonist, although his verse has a rapid and brilliant quality that a harmonist naturally will take to be harmonic verse. Keats' description of what a great poet is is an example of the poetic-philosophic justifications of harmonic art that its practitioners sometimes invent if they have an inclination for pedantry.

I am not sure how useful are Keats' ideas here. Perhaps I ought to delete them, since in these two letters he is only praising harmonic art. I finally include them because if Madhubala, Shakespeare, and Mozart did not possess harmonic genius as well as other qualities, they could not have been the artists they were. To have understood beauty as they did, they must have felt a greater number of things to be beautiful than almost all men or women do. They must also have been able to distinguish clearly between the various shades of pleasures they had felt, and to classify them accurately.

Hamlet, *Don Giovanni*, and *Tomorrow is Ours*, are works entirely different in kind from *King Lear*, *Le Nozze di Figaro*, and *Mr. and Mrs. 55*, which are works of dramatic art.

The effect of melodic art is limited to the inspiration of the sensation of beauty, and it is possible because beauty, being a *promise* of happiness, is a uniform sensation, whose various shades of color do not differ very much. In this respect, the pleasure of beauty is entirely different from the pleasures of vanity whose shades of color are widely different, and make up as innumerable a number of different shades of pleasures as there are numbers of combination of temperaments, situations, and elements of fortune (i.e., chance). The subject matter of the three works cannot be too important for the *effect* they produce. Yet the melodic masterpieces were perhaps the most personal works of these artists.[1]

The effect of pure beauty that melodic art inspires often is felt no more than one or two times in the course of the performance or reading of the work, and then only for a few seconds.[2] Then there are those times when its sway over you lasts all evening.

Melodic genius is, I conclude from the fact that only Madhubala, Shakespeae, Mozart have expressed it, a natural result of dramatic genius of a certain kind.

5) The reveries inspired by pictures of happiness, which make up the sensation of beauty, are by nature transitory. Sooner or later, only vanity remains.

Love produces in those who are at all susceptible to this disease of the imagination the greatest sensations of beauty nature has allowed mankind. That this is true is a physiological fact, not only a

---

[1]In *Hamlet*, the chief theme of a man of genius surrounded by commonplace run of men and women incapable of understanding his generous sentiments and passionate love of moral purity reflects the situation of Shakespeare himself, and of all geniuses. Hamlet is a man who is disappointed and distressed by the truths he sees, and by the time he overcomes this oversensitivity, it is too late to prevent the tragic end. How *practical* are his responses to his growing convictions is another matter. But then we would not have the great play.

In *Tomorrow is Ours*, Bela is a woman who has left the ordinary walks of life in order to gain wealth, power, and fame through her beauty. She sacrifices everything else a sensitive woman would want to protect, her modesty and pride, her reputation, and her chances for a sincere, happy love, for the power and wealth which her beauty wins her, because ambition draws her more agreeable pictures of happiness than virtue and love. The parallel with Madhubala's own life is clear, and love comes, but, as in Hamlet's case, the happy and settled frame of mind is come upon too late to prevent the tragic end.

The case of Mozart was only apparently different. His weakness for the pretty charms of women and the pleasure of winning their favors form the chief theme of *Don Giovanni*, but the somber tone of the work, which finally overrides its considerable wit, expresses Mozart's discontentment with the undiscriminating nature of these desires. Love for him was a very serious matter, but he was at the same time susceptible to the charms of many pretty women.

[2]In the past few months, I have known the sensation twice, curiously enough, in each of the three works: during the trio between Don Giovanni, Masetto, and Zerlina just before they join the party in the first act; when the Stone-Guest breaks into and silences Don Giovanni assertions during the last few minutes of his life; during the scene when a stooge of the rich businessman offers Bela the diamond necklace; when she discovers that Bharat does not love her; when Hamlet tells Horatio that he is the best of men; and when Hamlet suddenly reveals himself and jumps into the grave of Ophelia.

These are merely *personal reactions*, and worth nothing more.

Sept. 1, 1991

psychological one. Stendhal called the peculiar form of idealization that occurs in love *crystallization*, and I see no need to invent or substitute another word for it. Crystallization is the strongest, most powerful of idealizations, in which all known ideas of happiness come into play.

The lover thinks, "How much pleasure I shall feel if I could see, touch, hold her hands, kiss her, etc." All the senses participate in the pleasures of love, but sight is the most important, because it is the source of the majority of our ideas.[1] The artist who wishes to produce the phenomenon of crystallization in men must then appeal above all to the eyes, and only thereafter can he hope to inspire ideas of moral beauty.

For an artist who wishes to inspire in his audience sensations similar to those that occur during the first crystallization when the heart is delighting in rendering the beloved increasingly perfect, the chief problem is that every man has his own opinion of what is beautiful. A modest reserve in manners might attract one and bore another. The solution, if one exists, can only lie in expressing every idea of great beauty possible (i.e. in discovering and expressing the common factors, if any, underlying the idea of a lovable woman), since each man can then see the reflection of his own ideas of perfect beauty.

The art of Raphael and Ophuls resembles that of *Hamlet*, *Don Giovanni*, and *Tomorrow is Ours* in that only that much beauty will be felt by any individual which he or she knows from experience, but where Shakespeare, Mozart, and Madhubala allow you to feel the beauty of any object or situation that you take pleasure in, Raphael and Ophuls restricted themselves to beauty in love. Raphael's and Ophuls' greatest masterpieces were produced with the sole intention of inspiring the greatest transports that are to be found in the heart at the most advanced stage possible of first crystallization.[2]

As the first crystallization proceeds, the object of love is finally so magnified in the imagination that she seems to contain within herself the sum of all available happiness; the lover correspondingly underestimates his own worth. This is roughly the effect of the portraits that Raphael and Ophuls made. For this sensation to arise in a man, *all possible* ideas of vanity-beauty that can arise in the soul must be known by him, as Raphael and Ophuls knew them.

---

[1] Addison, among others.

[2] This fact cannot be proved to someone who has never loved deeply. You cannot *prove* the existence of colors to a man blind from birth.

This painter and this filmmaker were able to express the very illogical *logic of crystallization.*

The degree of pleasure they can inspire in a man depends entirely on his experience of love; it may vary from boredom, through rococo pleasures to the highest peaks of moral beauty.

The far-away and fairy-tale effect of their settings and techniques is important because the object of beauty must remain finally inaccessible; otherwise only vanity will be left to give its paltry pleasures.

Nietzsche and Miss Bina Rai are related to Ophuls and Raphael in that they are artists of maximum vanity. More exactly, they produced one or more characters through whom they express varying degrees of vanity (and their bases), up to the maximum possible pride.

6) The art of Correggio and Jean Arthur, who expressed the one side of first crystallization that Ophuls and Raphael had to ignore.[1]

I separate Correggio, Jean Arthur, Nietzsche, Miss Bina Rai, Raphael, and Ophuls from ideal artists because they are scientific artists of maximums. Their aim was to express the maximum possible degree of that nuance of vanity or beauty which gave them most pleasure.

7) Stendhal, Audrey Hepburn, and Nargis, the artists of passion, the exact describers of the movements of the soul during the course of passion.

Passion has nothing to do with beauty, or rather is born when love survives the limits of beauty and vanity. Those who would describe exactly the nuances of feelings felt in passion must describe the exact truth about every nuance, how it arises, what it thrives on, how it dies, etc., and not content themselves with vagueness, which pleases or displeases according to the tastes of a man.

The effect sought is neither the feeling of beauty nor vanity, since neither exists in passion. The works of the three artists of this class may be enjoyed ideally by those who have never known passion; I have not read or heard anything regarding any one of the artists of this class that was not an ideal response to their works rather than a true description of what they do, and why.

Passion for truth, and truth in the depiction of the passions and states of happiness, these are the two chief qualities of the works of Nargis, Hepburn, and Stendhal, and found in no one else to my knowledge.

---

[1]Leonardo, Annibale Caracci, Emily Brontë, Kate Chopin, and Miss S- also belong to this class. They expressed fewer ideas than Correggio and Jean Arthur, and these are such as were known to the two but which they overcame and surpassed in the pursuit of ever deeper happiness.

Cimarosa's *Il Matrimonio Segreto* and Meena Shorey's *Ek Thi Larki* ("A Girl There Was") also belong marginally to this class for in these they expressed the phenomenon of the birth of passion—the motion of the soul as it rises above vanity-beauty happiness to the happiness of passion.[1]

Chapter IV

Of Laughter

Nobody has improved upon Hobbes' description of the cause of laughter. I quote from his *Leviathan*,

"*Joy* arising from imagination of a man's own power
and ability is that exultation of the mind which is called

---

[1]Some of the names mentioned in this chapter may not be known to all readers. Saigal and Mr. Ashok Kumar were Indian actors, and Meena Shorey, Madhubala, Miss Bina Rai, and Nargis, Indian actresses. All of these great women gave their best performances between 1947 and 1967, easily making those two decades in India one of the greatest periods in world art, equaling Renaissance Italy, perhaps even surpassing it.

The twentieth century has lost all sense of passion and beauty, so it is no wonder that the great masterpieces have remained unrecognized. Indian cinema of the period was condemned by Indians who pretended to intelligence and taste*; they had imbibed their ideas of beauty from moribund artists and journalists of those nations that had forgotten the stronger pleasures. Add to the masterpieces produced then in India the films of Hepburn, Ophuls, Jean Arthur, Betty Grable, and Clark Gable, and you have the greatest age of art the world has known in the midst of as violent a century as any, which had neither the time nor the sensitivity to recognize what was taking place. The decline since then, in the West and in the East, has been precipitous.

The great passions of this century of great political and social changes are *collective* vanity, the vanity of groups, and the undisguised love of wealth, and I wonder if the sensibility for art has not altogether vanished, except for pockets of resistance here and there in the world. Sourness, gloom, and love of gain have been the order of the day for the last ninety odd years (a legacy of the nineteenth century), or there is love of cloying prettiness. It is possible in the twentieth century to feel a little pride in being able to despair over the "absurdity of the universe and of history"; conversely, unhappy self-pity is still fashionable, though less so since 1980. The reader will note that I do not name many living men and women in this chapter. It is not my intention to flatter dead or living artists or philosophers, but if the reader has any favorite names he may add them in his copy of this book—probably to the list of ideal artists, the idealists.

* These same pious folk were scandalized when, in 1980, Nargis publicly called that solace to Indian mediocrity, Satyajit Ray, a "peddler of India's poverty," a man who made films calculated to please the Western journalists and pedants who hand out awards. But then, how could Indian journalists and pedants have understood a *psychologist?*

GLORYING, which, if grounded upon the experience of his own former actions, is the same with *confidence*, but if grounded on the flattery of others, or only supposed by himself for delight in the consequences of it, is called VAINGLORY, which name is properly given because a well-grounded *confidence* begets attempt, wheras the supposing of power does not and is therefore rightly called *vain*....

"*Sudden glory* is the passion which makes those *grimaces* called LAUGHTER, and is caused either by some sudden act of their own that pleases them or by the apprehension of some deformed thing in another, by comparison whereof they suddenly applaud themselves. And it is incident most to them that are conscious of the fewest abilities in themselves, who are forced to keep themselves in their own favor by observing the imperfections of other men. And therefore much laughter at the defects of others is a sign of pusillanimity. For of great minds, one of the proper works is to help and free others from scorn and compare themselves only with the most able."

I have no quarrel with the conclusion this great philosopher draws from his definition of laughter, but is it not better to have laughter and carefree gaiety than sour solemnity[1] The power to laugh deeply shows a certain energy of the mind, of which when there is general lack in a society, there is, in consequence, much affectation of power, rank, wealth, and the like.

Extremes of riches and poverty usually lead to gloominess of temper as considerations of wealth and social standing hold sway over the hearts of those afflicted with either fate. Even in the cases of those societies, getting ever rarer today, where an established and secure aristocracy exists, as it did in seventeenth-century France, or eighteenth-century Austria, or in Japan and India until the nineteenth century, wealth and position seldom lead to gaiety of temper. The rich are so caught up in the affectations of their station and oppressed by the fear of being shown up by others that they seldom can laugh but at the expense of some rival.

---

[1]Hobbes was attacking thoughtless inanity, not wit, for he was one of the sharpest wits at the court of Charles II.

Passion has been out of fashion around the world for a long time; it probably never was in fashion except sporadically here and there through the centuries. But if we cannot have passion, must we have no gaiety either? The temper which looks for a good laugh as a relief from the general pursuits of life is far removed from insouciance, and the former is usually the best that is met with. A heart empty of ideas of pleasure can only derive joy from the meanest and most dilute of pleasures.

An analogy will explain this idea; and the analogy I have chosen should delight even those whose chief passion is love of wealth. Pleasure is like the interest one expects to earn from an investment: the returns depend upon the amount of money already invested, and the wisdom of choice of investment. The less you initially have to invest, the less real profit you will make. You may turn $500 into $2000 in less than a year, but if you had invested $5000 in the same stocks, ceteris paribus you would have made a profit of $15,000; as for repeating your success, it should be remembered that fortune is a whimsical goddess.

Even if you have an initial fund of several million dollars, were you to simply put it in a bank, you would really be losing money. You pay hard cash for security. For more profit from your money, for a greater percentage interest, so to speak, you must invest it in risky ventures. You can turn ten million into a hundred million, perhaps, but you can also lose everything you have. You cannot expect to earn a large interest return from your investments unless you have put *all* of them in high yield, high risk gambles. The richest profit-maker is above all the most knowledgeable, prudent, and reckless gambler.

True passion comes about only as a result of protracted grief that does not have as its cause injured vanity.

A lover who has long suffered the disfavor of his beloved, whose passion has been met by indifference or aversion, who has had as many or more moments of despair as of hope, who has met with imagined or true setbacks, who has had moments when he *dare not hope* although he cannot live without hope, this lover alone may be said to know passion. His happiness, should he gain her love, would be out of all bounds, and of a nature utterly incomprehensible and unknown to all the more complacent members of society, who probably would laugh at his situation if he let them discover it. What would surprise them is that this happiness he so long coveted and has at last gained has no element of what is called *joy* in it; not only is it not the joy of success generally, it is not even the joy they associate with amorous successes. How mysterious must be the unhappiness of such a madman to others who have known only the grief of vanity.

Chapter V

In art as in life, laughter is the effect of what Hobbes called sudden glory. It can only be inspired, therefore, in a narrative context, no matter how sketchy, although perhaps it is possible for some to laugh at little, sudden, and unexpected changes of tempo or melody in a symphony or concerto; this they do by substituting in the place of the abstract notes some vague image of sudden glory that they habitually rely upon to rouse themselves.

One way to bring about laughter is by producing a sudden feeling of superiority in the audience. Harmonic artists are best at doing this. The stylistic high jinks of Nabokov, Matisse, Gogol, Rubens, Haydn, Flaubert, Joyce, or Chaucer can often make you laugh by a turn of phrase, a patch of color, a little spurt of a violin's counterpointing dash, without recalling the exact narrative context.

It is also possible to laugh at some sudden great show of emotion in a drama, film, or novel; the sudden inflow of knowledge of superiority that one feels when one identifies with a character can make one laugh in the middle of a most tense and dramatic scene. A clever writer or filmmaker will often make his hero laugh as well at these moments.

Comedy usually relies chiefly on making the audience feel superior to the characters. In Petronius, Swift, Aristophanes, etc., you see this principle carried out without reservations. The effect is harsh, and usually the works are general satires or simple farces.

When Sterne[1] produced his Uncle Toby, Walter Shandy, Yorick, and Tristram Shandy, he set an example of how to use comedy to lead to the inspiration of gentle sentiments, an example imitated by Gogol, Flaubert, Dickens, Chekhov, Proust, Joyce, Kafka, Nabokov, Renoir, Hawks, Ozu, Keaton, Chaplin, etc.

These artists produce comedy by making one laugh at their characters; when vanity is thereby gratified a little, a man is less liable to

---

[1]On the heels of Farquhar's *The Beauxs' Stratagem*. Cervantes and Molière were the first ones, but their genius could not be imitated, whereas Farquhar's and Sterne's could be.

be suspicious, and more likely to feel inspired with fine and generous sentiments for the character responsible for the pleasure. As much amicable feelings as he is capable of generally exist in a man who sincerely seeks pleasure through art, and the pleasure of laughter can increase them. He is then less likely to ridicule the grief of a character, or envy his or her happiness.

The chill of Northern temperaments is in no way more dislikable than when one sees it represented to the public at large in art. Think of Ibsen, Strindberg, Garbo, both Mr. Ingmar and Ingrid Bergman, etc., and what you have is not the melancholic but the phlegmatic temperament[1]; and nothing is worse than when this type gets a notion in his or her head to be whimsical or comical.[2]

Solemnity has crept into the works of the French and the British;[3] there was always very little wit among American artists, excepting many in films, where America has had such great comic artists as Arthur, Grable, Gable, Astaire, Keaton, Hawks, Wayne, and Mr. Don Adams. But what humor is there in Emerson, Poe, Thoreau, Hemingway, Ellison, Stevens, Eliot, West, Welles, O'Neill, Williams, Pollock, etc., and many living writers, painters, and filmmakers, which is not spoiled by sourness or puerility of ideas (i.e., by considerations of petty vanity)?

Melville was at his worst when he imitated Dickens in *Moby Dick*, and Hawthorne's comic effects were equally strained. Ford did hardly better, though he had the advantage of talented comic actors like Wayne and Fonda. It is difficult to imagine Melville, Hawthorne, or Ford breaking into deep laughter.

There is nothing in Whitman but verbose petty vanity of a coarse grain, but he at least has great representative worth.

Lest the reader think these statements are motivated by alien taste, I repeat again that my interest is solely in men's expression of ideas. And in this regard there are, in my opinion, a few American books not entirely spoiled by sourness, pedantry, and puerility of ideas: *Huckleberry Finn, The Awakening, The Sound and the Fury, Ada*. Twain's description of American humor—the telling of a series of ridiculous anecdotes by a narrator who does not understand what he is doing—holds true for some great American artists. Keaton, Hawks, Mr. Don Adams, and John Wayne, each in his own way, produce comic effects in this manner.

---

[1]See Cabanis.

[2]*Smiles of a Summer Night, Indiscreet, Peer Gynt.*

[3]I except British television.

Filmmaking, a cooperative effort, has its drawbacks. Hawks recalls having been exasperated with Miss Katharine Hepburn during the filming of *Bringing Up Baby*. He wanted her to play the role of Susan Randall seriously, so that the film would be amusing, but Miss Hepburn, who habitually overacted in all her films, persisted in *trying to be comical*.[1]

How can you expect a gloomy individual, suspicious of laughter, envying and hating those who laugh at the drop of a hat, to esteem comedy? It should not be a matter of mystery that the greatest artists that this country has ever produced are for the most part dismissed as minor league popular artists not to be compared to the revered gloomy names. For my part, I think it best that Jean Arthur, Astaire, Hawks, *et al.*, are not put by the custodians of taste[2] among the greatest American artists. One is spared the comments of pedants, critics, men and women of letters, and suchlike.[3]

Comic effect is common in painting, e.g., Titian, Rubens, Bosch, Rembrandt, Vermeer, Delacroix, Manet, Matisse, Picasso, Klee, Miró, Tintoretto, Hogarth, Goya, Brueghel, etc., all have comic effects.

A comic effect can still produce laughter when encountered again for the same reason that a harmonic effect does not vanish in repeated encounters with a work of art. The shift of focus is still felt to be so great that you let yourself believe that you are surprised. A man wishes to think himself happy, and the less real happiness he feels, so long as he is not miserable, the more he deludes himself; at least this is true of the sanguine temperament.

---

[1]See the very amusing interview book, *Hawks on Hawks*. Though the interviews were conducted by a then young critic who proceeded to make a complete fool of himself in the introduction, Hawks' wit, pride, and charm in conversation make you forget that fact. Hawks was finally able to get Miss Hepburn to give the least unnaturally exaggerated performance of her career.

[2]By both those who express the opinions that have the greatest sway, and by those who want to supplant those opinions with new ones. In this regard, I should state that I wish to change no one's opinions, for, in my opinion, new pleasures cannot be taught. (I am imagining the obvious jest, and answering it in advance.)

[3]The author evidently hopes that, with any luck, on account of sentiments like these they will not ever be tempted to enroll him into the distinguished lists of men and women of letters to which they themselves belong. This gives me a poor opinion of his judgment, for he assumes the existence of pride where there is only complacency—THE EDITOR

Chapter VI

The tender passions are most effectively inspired by comedy, for the reasons I have given. But there are other, simpler methods, those of Shakespeare, Madhubala, and Mozart. They simply changed the dramatic sensation they were expressing as the circumstances of their characters changed a little.

Van Eyck and Fred Astaire belong in a special class by themselves among comic artists. Theirs is not the comedy that inspires violent laughter, or even unrestrained amusement. Rather, it is an expression of a special type of contented vanity, about which I need only say that the reader will best understand it by seeing *Shall We Dance*, *The Gay Divorcée*, or some of the famous paintings of van Eyck.[1] Their laughter is a product of that type of idealized vanity love in which extreme tenderness goes hand in hand with easy and good-humored self-importance. Fielding and Betty Grable, whose souls knew deeper thoughts, had more serious tenderness and less complacency.[2]

True and unaffected insouciance is uncommon. At this moment, I can think only of Cervantes, Molière, Cimarosa, Meena Shorey, and Mr. Hugh Laurie as having expressed it.

On account of their education, chiefly, but sometimes also due to their constitution, there are many who cannot bring themselves to give the title of great artists to those who do not express the passions attendant on fear, especially fear of powers surpassing human ones. These same claim a veneration for some of the Greeks; for Dante and Milton; for Michelangelo, Titian, El Greco, and Rembrandt; for Bach and Beethoven; for Racine, Goethe, Blake, Wordsworth, Baudelaire, Melville, Tolstoy, Dostoevski, Yeats, Proust, Kafka, Conrad, Mann, Musil, Faulkner, Kazantzakis, Camus, Hitchcock, Welles, Mr. Bergman, etc.

They even admire Shakespeare and Mozart for identical reasons.

I may as well warn such readers that they will not understand this chapter, nor perhaps much of this treatise; to those who are astonished by what they are reading, and find the contents of this essay scarcely credible, I can only reply by asking, "Who is to say who is right and who color-blind?"

---

[1]As well as the not-so-renowned, such as for example, the *Virgin and Child with Saints and Donor*, at the Frick Collection in New York.

[2]*Tom Jones, Coney Island.*

So long as we continue to have logical and scientific opinions, which, in spite of all the idiocies that abound today, is still how I would finally describe today's developed world, the art of grand and sublime fears will not be produced; the Sweden that Mr. Bergman grew up in was not what Germany is today, but neither was it the Germany of Goethe's age.

The examples of Kazantzakis, Eliot, Klimt, Mizoguchi, Dreyer, Bresson, Mr. Pynchon, and Mr. Bergman illustrate that such an art has become impossible in the twentieth century. Our knowledge makes us less susceptible to the primitive power that animates art dependent upon fear, the source of wonder when overcome to a safe degree; the comforts we have gained have been at the expense of the primitive power. Perhaps Faulkner in his minor works failed least of any writer of this century, but even his attempt, like Blake's, to pretend to himself that he shared the temperament of the writers of that collection of poems called the Old Testament failed, not out of lack of special genius, which, for example, Blake and those writers lacked, but because, in spite of himself, he saw too many things too clearly—you cannot task the poets who made the Old Testament or Blake with clarity of sight.

Most of those who profess admiration for the tragedies of Shakespeare or the frescoes of Michelangelo borrow what idea of terror they have from the great massacres of our century (when they are not expressing what they think they ought to feel, often deluding themselves in this, too), but that is a matter of simple fear of extinction and disgust, not of terror raised to even the melodramatic, let alone the sublime, which has as its source the lack of dispassionate curiosity and knowledge regarding causes. No one has even attempted to depict the Holocaust or Stalin's and Mao's purges in order to extract the sublime from them, and for good reason. They are seen too clearly even by the most confused men and women. The wars of this century have not produced the heroic art of an *Iliad*[1] or a *War and Peace*; Picasso's *Guernica* seems anemic and precious in comparison to Rubens' or Goya's paintings; and Mr. Pynchon's novel *Gravity's Rainbow*, whose sales have been helped along by academic interests and some fans of rock music, and Mr. Kubrick's films are even more cheerfully puerile[2] than Picasso's paintings or Mr.

---

[1]When I wrote this, I had forgotten Mr. Ludlum's *The Bourne Identity*, the *Iliad* of our century, as well as some of his other fine novels.

[2]I describe the tone here, which is different from Mr. Mailer's *The Naked and the Dead*'s, *The Executioner's Song*'s, and *Ancient Evenings*' gloomily puerile one.

[36]

Grass' prettily harmonic *The Tin Drum*. Our artists today generally cannot rise above sour comedy to the melodramatic, and neither can their audiences.[1] All of this in spite of the fact that there has been a much more eager attempt to produce such effects in our century than ever before, from affectation and vanity: artists want applause, and gloom, sourness, and anger are equated by critics and audiences today with depth of thought and feeling. This equation is a sign of to what degree petty vanity, or more precisely wounded petty vanity, has evolved in this odd century.

Comedy, arising as it does from humbler forms of vanity, we are still susceptible to.

Chapter VII

Of Style and Manners

Style is a matter of manners, which are practical outcomes, specific to each group or people, of the desire among men to live together in peace, mutual contentment, and collective vanity. Style consists of the pattern of affectations and poses adopted to impress others. It is born of the fear of ridicule.

The proud woman who disdains the friendly addresses of all save a chosen few imitates the manners of other proud women. The polished and obsequious, or verbose and domineering, manners of a good salesman or saleswoman are matters of style; as are the genial and relaxed manners of the hosts and the guests at an evening cocktail party.

To act according to custom and conventions, to fly deliberately and with calculated effect in the face of them, or to habitually act according to your nature, these are the choices. *Natural* manners are so rare because the ideas and passions of most men and women are almost entirely determined by the society they live in, by their form of government, etc., so that the individual characteristics are lost among the general

---

[1]Dostoevski and Van Gogh were the last ones who did not fail completely, but their half-successes show that perhaps the idea of the sublime was dying by the late nineteenth century. They did not succeed any more than did Faulkner, but neither did they possess his clarity of sight.

prevailing ones, and do not differ among themselves as much as the general ones agree. An idiosyncratic Syrian who has lived his entire life in his native land is felt to be less different from his fellow countrymen than is an Irani visitor, etc.

Being natural, what is called "letting it all hang out," has become a matter of pride in the United States and the nations it has most influenced. This affectation, born in the 1960's, was adopted by young men and women who did not see that the idea "to let it all hang out" imposed very rigid rules on their manners, many of which those young today continue to observe religiously. Only in matters relating to physical love was there any true advance, but since it is a very powerful passion, the affectation of the 1960's has had a general influence on the manners of the citizens of half the nations of the world.

A jot of cold naturalness in the actions and words inspired by physical passion becomes forcefully evident as a part of the general manners of an age and nation only in the declining periods of advanced and militarily dominating societies.[1] These ages of decadence are perhaps the only instances when a type emerges that is indifferent to the *opinions of others*: Some fringes of the aristocracies during the first century of the Roman empire; the reign of Louis XV; the period between the two World Wars among the rich of Britain and France, etc. The reason why this type only develops then is simple. Only advanced and dominant societies will produce a *refined* passion for superiority to the common run of men, and it is only when such societies have lost their vigor and relative love of public virtue and good that this passion can be freed from the restraining idea of social duties.

The distinguishing fact about the sixties was that the decadent and natural manner was by and large adopted only by the youth of all classes; it was the expression of youthful animal spirits, and, though the product of an unprecedentedly wealthy society, it did not seriously affect the productive part of that society. But precisely because America was still a healthy and strong society, the new ideas quickly became accepted, especially when the youth became the new crop of leaders.[2]

Style plays a decisive role in the popularity of works of art, philosophy, political persuasion, in that of a celebrity or would-be

---

[1]Or among savages.

[2]Such propitious circumstances not obtaining, the way of the English Restoration wits died with them.

celebrity (e.g., a politician, a comedian, a pundit) who presents himself to the public, etc.

The function of style in manners and in works of art, as well as of form generally, is to present a matter or act in the most favorable light possible, to dispose others in its favor. In the ancient world, the upper classes, who wrote, commissioned, and judged the works, wanted the stories of gods and heroes to inspire respect among the masses. In more recent times, aristocratic manners and fashions developed from the same motive.

The other function of style and form is to aid the faculty of memory. An agreeable form makes a lively impression upon the imagination, and is more easily recalled than an indifferent one.[1] And when a favorable impression upon a possible lover, financial contact, an audience, etc. is desired, one wants any admiration that was felt to be remembered.

When a nation has existed with the same monarchical and aristocratic government and institutions for several hundred years, refinement may be expected to set in, especially among those of the upper classes, who begin to despise the manners of their ancestors even as they proclaim their pride in being descended from them. During these periods, great refinement or elevation of style is demanded of artists. If there are any then who can win the admiration and patronage of the makers of taste (be they courtiers, ladies of the court, princes, popes, pedants, etc.), their styles exercise a dictatorial prestige for later generations.[2] The powers of critics, as well as of women, have become less absolute in the West since the end of the age of monarchies.

To inspire the masses with ideas of the great superiority of those of noble birth was one of the chief motives for the affectations of manners, customs, dress, and art—the other was self-flattery, and among artists, flattery of those in power. A form such as pastoral poetry developed its style in order to let the rich dream of a different manner of life, be it ever so mean, in such a manner that they could delight in the charms of novelty without impairing their dignity. All aristocratic and royal

---

[1]In the poems of pre-literate societies, rhyme, alliteration, assonance, regular meters, etc. were mnemonic as well as ornamental devices.

[2]The prestige and influence that the styles of Virgil, Cicero, Petrarch, Raphael, Poussin, Racine, Dryden, and Beethoven exercised for up to several centuries each—the style of Cicero became fashionable again among pedants after Petrarch. The Ottomans under Suleiman, the Indians under Akbar, Jehangir, and Shah Jehan, the Japanese under the Ashikaga shogunate, the Chinese under the Mings.

affectations, when refined over time, have one aim and therefore one type of manifestation: to distinguish one group from the rest of men, and to do so most generally by censuring all natural actions and words, and praising their very opposite—thus the table manners, the manner of greeting and conversing, of dressing, of all those with aristocratic affectations, with all their differences, have a similar manifestation. Everything natural is thought gross and indecent.[1]

As the masses got educated and became the greater public, and the source of bread and butter for most artists, the fashionable modes of styles (not to mention the subject matters) of painting, writing, and composing had to change accordingly. As social hierarchies by birth become as little of a tyranny as they are ever likely to, the envy of the lower classes for the diversions and fashions of the upper decreases.[2]

The shrill insistence on the consequences of style by the prouder artists of the last two centuries is the result of skepticism about the ideas and opinions trumpeted as the acme of nobility in earlier centuries. Style was the last resort of the intelligent few who wished to be able to believe in the worth of something in centuries when anarchical thought seemed the only consequence of honesty; vanity always creates dissatisfaction in over-lively minds.

I should mention the philosophic style in literature and philosophy, a cut and dry style popular since the age of Hobbes, Newton, and Locke, which is often used to mask ignorance and win the esteem of the gullible. It decorates the books of some of the most famous philosophers,[3] and works of art as well: the essay portions of *War and Peace*, *The Idiot*, or *À la recherche du temps perdu*—although Proust, like Montaigne, seems to have wanted it both ways, to be known as a cold examiner of passions and manners, and to have a cleverly rich (as opposed to Montaigne's cleverly witty) style.

It is generally a cold temperament that responds with what little passion it can to flourishes of style. This insipid pleasure is utterly unknown among passionate souls. It is the more affected version of the

---

[1]See Montesquieu on education in a monarchy.

[2]Also, critics become more powerful of their own, and so a whole class of works of art is born which panders to their tastes, though their opinions have less general and absolute an authority because the public has neither time nor motive to consult them.

[3]They gives themselves away by emphatic qualities, though, that, when examined closely, are a little ridiculous: Spinoza, Hume, Kant, Russell, Wittgenstein, Freud, etc. Descartes perhaps began this tradition.

identical pleasure felt by a man or woman who sincerely falls to admiring an ornate wall-paper pattern, or a group of flowers, furniture, an automobile or yacht, a neatly laid out garden, an ancient vase, etc. Love of prettiness rules out the pursuit of deeper pleasures.

Chapter VIII

Of Harmonic Art

I have already touched upon harmony; now I describe it at greater length.

Since the pleasures of harmony arise from the cleverness of the work, they will be proportionate to the degree of cleverness. No artist can be entirely free of ideal pleasures. Even those who delight in harmony often prefer a work less harmonic than another, because they prefer the ideal pleasures it expresses.

The pleasure of vanity is not incompatible with tenderness.

With the least complicated works of harmonic artists, you are shown either little else but the simplest cleverness, or you must have felt and enjoyed what the artist is depicting (which generally does not amount to much) as best as you can: Horace, Petronius, Ovid, Chaucer, Fra Angelico, Ariosto, Rabelais, La Fontaine, Sterne, Haydn, Chateaubriand, Keats, Gogol, Flaubert, Manet, Rimbaud, Degas, Gauguin, Joyce, Kafka, Cary Grant, Groucho Marx, etc.

The effects of Rubens, Giotto, Pushkin (*Eugene Onegin*), Hawks (*The Big Sleep* and *Rio Bravo*), Nabokov (*Transparent Things*)[1], Mr. Robbe-Grillet (*Topologie d'une cité fantôme*), Ozu (*Late Spring*),[2] Mr. Ashok Kumar, Messrs. Grant and Naylor (*Red Dwarf*) are more complicated. A greater effort of the imagination is required to understand *all* of their harmonic pleasures.

---

[1]*Lolita, Ada,* and *Look at the Harlequins!* are works of ideal art; *Pale Fire* is on the lower level of harmony, that of Joyce, Pope, etc.

[2]Ozu is an ideal artist, not a harmonic one as I mistakenly thought him until I saw this film for the first time yesterday (July 4, 1993) in at least two years, but I leave what I wrote more than two years ago here as a proof of how easy it is to be misled in the most obvious cases.

The most complicated harmonic effects occur in some of the works of Titian, Bach, Tolstoy (*Anna Karenina*), Renoir (*La règle du jeu*) and Mr. Robbe-Grillet (*Projet pour une révolution à New York*). The surface cleverness as cleverness is less apparent here: Compare the ornate stylistic concentration of Rubens to Titian's,[1] of Nabokov to Tolstoy's, of Mr. Robbe-Grillet of *Topologie* to Mr. Robbe-Grillet of *Projet*, etc. Their cleverness is mainly to be seen in the *general organization* of ideas and designs of the harmonic masterpieces, within the context of which there is a very high rate of harmonic effects at all points of the works. The effects of other harmonic artists are relatively more local in orientation.

Titian and Tolstoy, even Mr. Robbe-Grillet, are praised for the simplicity of their styles. The confusion is due to general blindness to harmony. No one to my knowledge has called the style of *La règle du jeu*, or that of the *Mass in b-Minor, simple*.

✳✳✳✳✳✳✳✳✳✳✳✳✳✳✳✳✳✳✳✳✳✳✳✳✳✳✳✳✳✳✳✳

I have thought over the distinctions drawn above and discussed them with Desmoulins; I had some doubts regarding Rubens, Nabokov, Hawks (*The Big Sleep*), Mr. Robbe-Grillet (*Topologie*), and Messrs. Grant and Naylor. He confirmed my doubts and suggested that they belong in a separate class higher in degree of harmony than Giotto's and lower than Titian's.

Pushkin changes his tone as well as the object and style of lyric or satiric parody every few stanzas or less in *Eugene Onegin*, and balances this harmonic side with his ideal one gracefully. But he does not express a pleasure in very complicated abstract movements of designs and forms as such. Neither does Giotto, Hawks, or Ashok Kumar.

The very involved nature of the art of Rubens, etc. is chiefly responsible for the condescension with which they are often regarded.[2] Unlike Giotto, Pushkin, Bach, or Tolstoy, they offer few ideal pleasures. For them the gossamer web was everything.

In Titian, Bach, Tolstoy, and Renoir, the effect is of a painting or piece of music, etc., that seems to express the most important ideas

---

[1]Giotto's only *seems* less so, but only if you see his paintings ideally and not harmonically as he intended them to be seen.

[2]E.g., the work of Nabokov that is the most fashionable today, *Pale Fire*, is as trivially pedantic (and therefore as entirely suited to our age) a novel as *Ulysses* or *Madame Bovary*, and more so than *Tristram Shandy* or the *Satyricon*; but the livelier pleasures of his last two novels remain unknown, and for this reason they are held in much lower esteem.

about moral truths and errors in apparently the most serious, even solemn manner.[1] There is less of *apparent* self-praising in their works than in those of Rubens, Nabokov, etc.

At this most complicated stage of harmonic art, it is most difficult to make out the harmonic nature of the effects because the most generally esteemed ideal works seem to express similar moral sentiments; but the idea of *play* (i.e., of the artist's consequence) is the chief one for harmonists; it is the chief pleasure. How difficult it is to understand this idea of consequence appears clearly from the generally ideal enjoyment of *La règle du jeu, et al.*

The initial ideal effect is the inspiration of melancholy in Bach; of vigorous self-complacency and physical tenderness alternating with a bilious and surly temper in Titian, and with bitter disenchantment in Tolstoy; of sourness alternating with bitter laughter in Renoir; and of fear and concupiscence[2] in the Robbe-Grillet of *Projet*. Perception of the harmonic manipulations provokes a species of vanity-pleasure that a man thinks more noble and worthy of esteem than others by virtue of the resistance of melancholic or bitter sensations it must overcome.[3]

Chapter IX

Of Ideal Art

Proust occupies among ideal artists the same position Nabokov does among harmonists: not the greatest artist, but the chief describer or philosopher of the nature and mechanics of ideal art (both its production and enjoyment).[4]

---

[1]Renoir produced one harmonic masterpiece, Tolstoy several, Titian many, and Mr. Robbe-Grillet, like Bach, has produced only harmonic works.

[2]The nature of these sensations has prevented Mr. Robbe-Grillet's novel from attaining an equal degree of fame. Though universal passions, they are not the most admired ones for they do not gratify vanity to the degree that Renoir's or Tolstoy's ideal passions do; and the fame of ideal works on this harmonic level depends upon the ideal side, the only one generally visible.

[3]Comedy and conspicuous artificiality prevent the initial pain from arising in the cases of *Transparent Things* and *Red Dwarf*.

[4]Along with Renoir in *The Golden Coach*, who expresses the same ideas with much greater clarity and less affectation.

Proust wrote much on art; the following is one of the least affected passages. The narrator is describing the pleasures he felt as a boy when reading in the family garden at Combray.

"And did not my thoughts also form just such another enclave, in the depths of which I felt that I could remain buried, and so observe what happened outside?... On the sort of screen dappled with different conditions which, while I was reading, my consciousness would simultaneously unfold, and which ranged from the most deeply hidden aspirations in myself to the most external view of the horizon that I would have, at the center of the garden, before my eyes, what came first and was of the innermost part of myself, the handle ceaselessly in motion that governed the rest, was my belief in the philosophic richness, in the beauty of the book I was reading, and my desire to appropriate them for myself, whatever the book was....

"After this central belief which, during my reading, would execute incessant motions from within outwards, towards the discovery of truth, came the emotions that the action in which I was taking part gave me, for these afternoons were more crammed with dramatic events than often occur in a whole life. These were the events occurring in the book I was reading. It is true that the people they affected were not "real people", as Françoise would have said. But all of the sentiments that make us feel the joy or the misfortune of a real person are not produced in us but by the intermediary of an image of this joy or misfortune; the ingenuity of the first novelist lay in his understanding that in the apparatus of the emotions, the image being the sole essential element, the simplification which consisted purely and simply of the suppression of real people would be a decisive improvement. A real being, profoundly as we may sympathize with him, for the great part is perceptible through our senses, that is to say, remains opaque to us, presents a dead weight that our sensibility cannot lift. If he is struck by misfortune, it is but in one small part of the total notion we have of him that we can be moved by him; indeed it is but in one small part of the total notion he has of himself that he can be moved himself. The novelist's fortunate discovery was to have the idea of replacing these parts impenetrable to the soul with an equal quantity of immaterial parts, that is to say, those things that our soul can assimilate. What matters then that the actions, the emotions of these beings of a new kind appear to us as truths, since we have made them ours, since it is in us that they produce themselves, that they are holding court, while we feverishly turn the pages of the book, the quickening of our breaths and the intensity of the gaze? And once the novelist has brought us into this state, where, as in all purely inner states, every emotion is magnified ten-fold, where his book comes to disturb us in the shape of a dream, but a dream clearer than those that we have in sleep, and whose memory lasts longer, why then, here he sets loose within us for an hour all the happiness and miseries possible, of which in life we can come to know only some in years, and the most intense of which would never be revealed to us because the slowness with which they develop prevents their perception....

"Already less intimate a part of myself than this life of personages, would come in turn, more or less projected before my eyes, the landscape in which the action was unfolding, and which exerted a much greater influence on my thought than the other, the one I had before my eyes when I raised them from my book. It was thus that for two summers, in the heat of our Combray garden, I had had, on account of the book I was then reading, a deep longing for a hilly and fluviatil land, [etc.]... And as was the dream of a woman who will love me that was always present in my thought, that dream in those summers was impregnated with the fresh coolness of running water; and whoever the woman was whom I would evoke, bunches of violet and reddish flowers would immediately spring up on each side of her like complementary colors."

Proust cleverly put this exactly accurate description of the motion of the soul in the sway of ideal art at the beginning of his novel and concluded with the fine sounding and elegantly phrased, but purely fanciful theory of art (a ridiculously exaggerated version of the one above, if considered dispassionately) that is set forth in *Le temps retrouvé* to forestall criticism by anticipation. Proust's great flaw of logic here (a typical one for him) lies in the narrator's first explaining that real people have a weighty solidity that prevents imaginative perception, and that the feelings inspired by art are idealized (i.e. exaggerated) as they are in dreams, and then claiming in the same paragraph that the feelings inspired by art are of the same kind as those of lived life. Ideal art sensations are not lived-life sensations. The claim that life-feelings unknown in one's experience can be known through art is an equally fatal flaw.

Proust was not deeply affected by women, he preferred the other sex. He had too strong a sense for physical beauty to feel any save the most pettily self-admiring of passions.[1] Nonetheless, there is no reason to throw aside the idea that the passion of love lies behind the greatest works of ideal art for the simple reason that it produces the greatest sensation of beauty that the heart can know. The greater a work of art is, the closer its effect is to love. But love has at least a thousand nuances.

In enjoying ideal art, a man puts in as much as his own pleasures into what he is presented with as he can persuade himself the work contains, which may be more or less, or completely different in nature from what the artist had in mind.

When Hölderlin, Twain, or Cervantes (I deliberately choose unrelated masters) describes a setting (or an idea or a passion), or Mr. Kurosawa or Mr. Antonioni shows it, or when Leonardo, Rembrandt, or Claude paints a landscape background or a face, or when Beethoven, Offenbach, or Verdi draws forth a descriptive strain, the pleasure that is inspired depends upon how much happiness one has known in such a setting (in the case of music and literature, the setting or idea which springs into the imagination), derived from that idea or passion, or else one imagines how much pleasure one may have in the best of circumstances.[2] In this latter case of ignorance and lack of experience, *vagueness* of ideas is the keynote.

One man will imagine himself standing by the shore, a king admired and envied.

Another will imagine the ship is about to take him and a beautiful woman or his beloved to a distant land.

Yet another will compare the sea and ship to what he saw in his local port the last time he was there, etc.

There will be another whose vanity will lead him to enjoy only the *cosmic* or *religious* aspect of the sea. Not always unrelated in their pleasures are those whose knowledge of the heart is so little that if they enjoy the painted scene at all, it is for the brush-technique or the school

---

[1] All human pleasures are necessarily self-pleasing, but there are different degrees of idealization of the object of love. Proust could crystallize very little.

[2] Ideal art is possible because of a certain type of power that words, sounds, colors, images, etc. have over the imagination. Bacon called these, when used to lead men to illusory thoughts, "Idols of the Marketplace." He observed that ideas and words can and do become facts for people; not only false philosophy but ideal art becomes possible because of this phenomenon.

to which the painting belongs, or because "Everyone knows that Cézanne is a great painter," etc.

The first effect of a work of art that has produced any strong effect on a person is beauty, and it decreases in time. Only pleasures of memory then remain.

The advantage the ideal artist has over nature is that he can concentrate his forces to please as much as nature has given him power to. Everything that does not please immediately may be excluded, or may be included to heighten the pleasing images by contrast. Excepting simple lyricism, all art relies on contrast. The best description of the most pleasing idea bores the most well-disposed man if sustained without variety for too long.[1]

To derive any intense pleasure at all from a work of art, a man more often than not allows himself as a preparation the luxury of a conciliatory humor even as he would put himself in an amiable humor were he preparing to meet a woman he suspects he may fall in love with. Unless some prejudice guides him in a particular case, he wants to be as pleased by a work as possible. Only something unpardonably ugly or ridiculous will be wholly rejected. It is not an uncommon event to find a man pleased by a fictional character he would have hated in life, as there is nothing to fear from him or her.[2]

Since tastes and fashions change, a work of ideal art which is praised by everyone in one period is forgotten or ridiculed thirty years later. It is only when it has the power to divert or impress several types of people that it lasts for more than a few years. Often the vanity of nations comes in, and a poor artist is dragged through the centuries and doled out to all

---

[1]Although the patience of readers, viewers, etc., is often incredible. A little less than two hundred years ago, all of Europe became agog over the interminable descriptions of Walter Scott and his imitators, as all the world has by the much more tedious special effects of Mr. Kurosawa (I refer to his inferior films such as *The Seven Samurai*, *Throne of Blood*, *Ran*, *Rashomon*, not to his masterpieces), Mr. Coppolla, Mr. Lucas, Mr. Spielberg, and their many imitators.

[2]Do not many protective fathers of young girls profess to love *Don Giovanni*, the opera as well as its cheerfully profane and obscene hero? In puritan societies, a Don Giovanni on stage would not be tolerated to seduce and abandon women with complete freedom in the view of all the public, even if he were ultimately punished. There are undoubtedly many today who are delighted more by the intelligent evil of Iago than by the noble simplicity of Othello. I bring in Mozart and Shakespeare because they are almost universally and mistakenly understood in an exclusively ideal manner.

the schoolchildren as someone who brightens the glory of their nation, which he does.[1]

The ones who arouse fear in their audience are respected most.[2] I do not mean those who paint horror stories, which frighten only children and uneducated men and women. Men like Sophocles, Homer, Dante, Giotto, Michelangelo, Leonardo, Titian, Shakespeare, Cervantes, Milton, Racine, Rembrandt, Goethe, Bach, Mozart, Beethoven, Wordsworth, Melville, Tolstoy, Dostoevski, Kafka, Proust, Hitchcock, Mr. Bergman, etc., are esteemed largely because for many people only what has to do with death, social injustices, or moral pains merits the title of great art, and the general esteem of nations.[3]

For example, the case of Chaucer, who used to be dismissed with empty words of praise as a great poet, but not as much of a glory to the English as Shakespeare or Milton. Today, after Joyce, Proust, and Nabokov have made popular the idea of artist as mischievous gamesman, Chaucer has come to seem to not have been a very frivolous artist after all, but rather one who wrote about serious moral subjects, but in a gay and mischievous manner; he is granted greater solemn esteem.

He who shows the worst miseries of mankind, and is able to console his audience with some sort of a "spiritual" hope, however distant and bare his artistic rhetoric claims this hope to be,[4] guarantees himself lasting popularity if he is not unfortunate.[5] The bilious temperament in this regard is decidedly an advantage.

---

[1]Dante, Racine, Shakespeare, Michelangelo, Rembrandt, Goethe, Tolstoy, Van Gogh, etc.

[2]Helvétius explains why.
Since fear and the pains of wounded petty vanity are common to all, their descriptions are universally understood; so that when they are expressed together with the flattering idea of the struggling nobility of man, in an eloquent, illogical, vague, and emphatic manner, the work wins general esteem.

[3]Try, as an amusing experiment, to convince a *soi disant* man or woman of discriminating taste that Fielding and Betty Grable are much greater artists than Tolstoy, Dostoevski, Rembrandt, Leonardo, Van Gogh, or Bach, great men though these others were. Modestly, in the manner of a scientist, I predict that if my theory is correct you will be laughed at and despised.

[4]E..g., Beckett, who got this pattern down to a slick formula: "I can't go on, I'll go on": the central idea and the last words of one of his most famous novels.

[5]I do not ignore women here. The favorites of feminists are promoted for two reasons: first, the promoters must make their reputations by appearing to be novel; and second, to console themselves, either with the idea of cruel persecution heroically countered, or by identifying with the sorrows of female characters or lyric personae.

You will commonly have seen philosophers, eccentrics, bohemians, journalists, academics, comedians, etc. who apparently are more than commonly intelligent, but who yet have little knowledge of the heart. Self-knowledge is the beginning of all true knowledge, and they lack it from laziness and the fear of wounding their vanity.

When more than usual liveliness of thoughts and feelings and love of pleasure exist without the courage for self-knowledge, the powers of the mind are employed in finding every connection imaginable between things and ideas that is capable of giving him or her pleasure. They seem to be facts. In this manner, the ideal artist is born. His or her pleasures are just more lively than those of others.

The different arts do not affect us in the same manner.

Music is the most passionate, and literature (even poetry) the most logical.

Painting and the cinema fall in between. Dance, sculpture, architecture, pottery, jewelry, etc. are increasingly cold arts which call forth a man's admiration by the display of craftsmanship and the overcoming of apparent technical difficulties; his soul is not affected by descriptions of passions.[1]

Music affects our souls by making the attainment of perfect happiness seem not as impossible as it usually does.[2] For this reason, it brings vividly to mind thoughts of love. No other art can equal music in this effect perhaps, but it need not be great music that transports the listener to heaven. Who is to say that a composer has discovered new beauties, when the response is always a matter of feelings?

Only if some artist manages to express the greatest pleasures of love in another medium can he hope to give greater pleasure than the most ordinary composer often can.

---

[1]The proof of this lies in the effects of Michelangelo's great statues. We are awed into admiration of his Moses, David, and Mary, but the human form by itself and isolated from all detailed contexts cannot describe precise nuances of any of the passions. Architecture, chinaworks, etc., appeal only to the taste for prettiness, and have, at best, the beauty of spacious, heroic simplicity. Gothic architecture is, if the truth be told, as drearily pretty as the music of Berlioz. It is admired by those who like to exaggerate their mild sensations of pleasures to themselves since the baroque excesses visible to even the most dull imagination give them seemingly good justifications for claiming they are feeling transports of exalted joy.

[2]The types of music most popular today prove that our youths have a meager number of pleasing ideas.

The dramatic effect is the reproduction in an audience of those sensations which come into play in our active interactions (social, personal, and intimate) with others.

Those other pleasing sensations that arise in solitary reveries about your own fate, pleasures, future, past, acquaintances, etc., form the class of ideal sensations that most artists seek to inspire. These include what you feel when you look at a beautiful view, a stretch of woods or a lake, etc. The thoughts and feeling regarding friends, lovers, enemies, neighbors, etc. are those which you would feel if they were to remain images whom you will never meet in real life.[1] All non-dramatic ideal art is a phenomenon of solitude.[2]

Harmonic artists are of the poetic (i.e, non-dramatic) type, and so are most ideal artists.

I have never succeeded in explaining the distinction I make here to those who respond only to poetic effects, even in the works of dramatic geniuses.[3] The dramatic passions (or at least a good number of them) are known by all, but they cannot distinguish them from those other sensations that arise in moments of quiet from thoughts of the people they do not know and places they do.

---

[1]Why so many fall in love with actors, actresses, singers, etc., and why so many of those who are fortunate enough to meet their idol and make him or her fall in love in return fall out of love in the long run. Miss P. Pr-, some of the wives of Cary Grant, etc.

[2]The pleasures of *War and Peace* are of the poetic class, for all the seeming dramatic quality of the work. *Moby Dick*, for example, is *obviously* a non-dramatic work. Rossini and Verdi are no less poetic than Wagner. They are merely lighter on their toes. Tintoretto, whom Stendhal was as usual the first and perhaps only one to understand clearly, surpasses all other painters in portraying dynamic activity, in using all the possibile resources at his command to bring out in heightened tone the interrelating situation, character, and passion of the *moment described*. But the heightening means that the sensations inspired are yet only ideal ones. The only painter of dramatic genius, so far as I know, was Guercino.

[3]John Stuart Mill has something to say on the subject of the solitary nature of ideal art, but could anyone be less of a poet or artist than this dull Englishman? His ideas are to a degree accurate because he himself was a very prosaic man. He had just sufficient sensitivity to poetry to feel a little pleasure from it. But it was his dull side that made it possible for him to see clearly the nature of the effect that poetry had on him. And so he sounds less exaggerated and affected than Proust, who says largely the same thing.

<h1 style="text-align:center">Chapter X</h1>

Dante and Proust produced very different effects by relying upon what happens when the imagination wearies from a sustained effort in one direction. Plato and Schopenhauer (who were poets also, but dry ones) express sentiments very similar to those of Dante and Proust, respectively, but the pleasures the former express remain rhetorical ones, and inferior in intensity, in the number of constituent ideas to the pleasures, of Dante and Proust.

Dante and Plato lived in ages of superstitious faith, transitional ages that had inherited (and had come at the end of) a long-standing tradition rife with the most extravagant speculations based on nothing more than fancies unsupported by interest in observation and facts.

Proust and Schopenhauer lived in ages of skepticism, and they had to adopt a pseudo-logical style, but at the expense of the power of passionate faith. For this reason, they seem enervated and decadent compared to the austere sublimity of Plato and Dante.

Michelangelo and Beethoven are identical in all respects, save that of medium, to Dante.

Each strips away whatever does not reflect sublimity of ideas. The respective arts of Dante and Michelangelo consist of eliminating all prettiness, softness, and gentleness. Only those effects are used that are characterized by great violence, magnitude, or speed. The style in each case is blunt, simple, and plain. The effect arises from the ideas of terror, not from affectedly elevated language or affectedly contrived chiaroscuro.[1]

Rembrandt and Wagner belong with Proust.

---

[1]Since music is all style, all embroidery, it would be ridiculous to talk of a simple style: that could mean little besides saying that the piece is cheaply pretty. Beethoven's third and fifth symphonies are equivalent to Dante's *Inferno* and Michelangelo's *Last Judgment*. However, they have more moments of tenderness, but these are needed in music if effects of terror and grandeur are not to becoming cloyingly repetitive. Dante has descriptions as well as comic and dramatic conversations and actions to give breathing spaces to his effects of terror, and many of Michelangelo's figures on the wall respond with energy but with a show of neither great pleasure nor pain to Christ. Beethoven's sixth, seventh, and eighth symphonies parallel the *Purgatorio* and the frescoes of the prophets and sibyls on the Sistine ceiling surrounding the central portion depicting the biblical myth of creation.

Think of these six artists and you have a fairly complete picture of the relationship of genius to the medium in which it is seen, as well as to the age, country, and society. Centuries separate Dante and Michelangelo, whereas Schopenhauer and Beethoven were near contemporaries.[1]

Plato, Dante, and Michelangelo lived when strong faith was common in their societies, Beethoven when its decline was still being bitterly felt, and art was being exalted in the place of religion.[2] He felt free to express his ideas of terror and grandeur because they were heroic in nature and could be considered to be an expression of the age. Unlike Dante or Michelangelo, but like Plato, he did not have to use a specific popular mythology.

With Rembrandt, Schopenhauer, Wagner, and Proust, you are in the world of the bourgeoisie, the world of the soft, modern middle classes of highly developed and specialized societies (in spite of all surface appearances to the contrary).

What would Schopenhauer or Beethoven have become and done had they been Italians living in Naples or Genoa? How much does a particular type of society influence genius? Dante's poem is Italian through and through, and nothing could be more German than the choral ending of the Ninth. Every man and woman is to a very great degree formed by the social and political institutions and manner of his people, which, in turn, depend to a large extent upon climate, geography, historical accidents, etc. On the other hand, how are the special qualities of Jean Arthur or Cervantes to be explained?

There is one thing, genius, and then there are social as well as artistic circumstances. The latter can prevent genius, but they cannot produce it.[3]

But why isolate Plato, Dante, Michelangelo, and Beethoven on the one hand, and Rembrandt, Schopenhauer, Wagner, and Proust on the other, from other ideal artists? Why not Leonardo, Masaccio, Twain, Yeats, Gluck, or Verdi? These artists would have you believe in the beauties that they present *as they are described.*

---

[1]Not to mention the fact that Michelangelo was forced against his will to work upon what turned out to be his greatest masterpiece, the Sistine chapel frescoes. The *Last Judgment* was a later addition to the chapel. He was the greatest sculptor the world has known, but it is for the Sistine Chapel that he will always be famous. Like Beethoven, he did not conceive of his masterpiece *in toto* from the beginning.

[2]Rousseau.

[3]No one distrusts and hates the word *genius* more than the man who knows himself to be lacking it. Great genius is nothing but a more than ordinary mental energy that manifests itself in any number of manners.

A Leonardo portrait brings to mind (when ideally seen) melancholic thoughts because that is how Leonardo seems to have felt about the woman and the desolate setting.

But what you have in Michelangelo and Proust is, first, one type of effects. The final effect of pleasure is of another type altogether, and arises automatically when the mind tires of dwelling on the first.

The sensation that Plato, Dante, Michelangelo, and Beethoven thought the most pleasing is the love for a being or power in comparison to which all human affairs are morally inconsequential, and which has made man inconsequential in comparison to itself.

Since these men were clever, they brought in every idea of terror and power and used every rhetorical device they could to express this sensation.

The other four artists valued above all a feeling of reposed self-complacency. The distorted, dream-like images produced by Rembrandt's chiaroscuro, the desire of withdrawal from the Will to Life in Schopenhauer, the soporifics of Wagner's music (as Nietzsche accurately described it), the idea of sleep and dreaming that encases Proust's novel, and which lies behind his reveries regarding character, personality, time, memory, and art,[1] these are the various rhetorical postures that give a mild pleasure in themselves. Their object in praising the charms of exaggerated dream-like vagueness was to awaken that mild vanity of being in awe of what one can convince himself he feels.[2]

---

[1]Through the "metaphysical" theory of metaphor, which he applies indiscriminately to all subjects, wherein neither of the compared objects is important, a sort of vague metaphysical truth lying in the connection discovered by the great artist. Proust claims he was capable of feeling pleasure only when the objects that inspired pleasure seemed to him to be remote, inaccessible, and incapable of being possessed. He was apparently incapable of possessing an object and esteeming its worth at the same time, and foolishly thought everyone else incapable as well.

[2]In the difference between them and the greatest harmonic artists one can see the difference made by how one explains and glorifies (i.e., by the rhetoric thought fit for adequately expressing) an emotion felt. Therein only lie the differences between Rembrandt and Titian and Rubens; between Proust and Tolstoy, Nabokov, and Mr. Robbe-Grillet; between Wagner and Bach; between Schopenhauer and Kant. It is not to be wondered at that Tolstoy should have written *Anna Karenina* after coming under the influence of Schopenhauer. In *War and Peace*, in spite of and in contrast to the weakly argued and pedantically mechanistic theory of history that is put forward, the chief quality praised is that of the mild but unabashedly acknowledged egotism (Natasha tells Marya that the depressing limitation of Sonia is her lack of egotism) which finds its nesting place in a bourgeois (in the mental sense) marriage. A different brand of egotism may be found in the three films celebrating art and love that Renoir made in the 1950's which is repressed in *La*

They describe ravishment of the senses and the imagination too painstakingly to have truly felt it; the *aesthetic ravishment*, if I may be allowed the use of this absurdly exaggerated phrase in order to describe the claim from inside, is pure affectation.

The art of these men was based on a particular sort of action and reaction of the heart: thus there being so many artists who worked in identical ways.[1] Theirs were two specific paths to happiness.

The peculiar focus which Rembrandt, Wagner, and Proust wish their audiences to assume is a state of mind from which, when they are released (because of either weariness or fatigue), there arises a pleasing sensation. The forced attitude led them to regard everything in the works in a falsely exaggerated way, to feel that they are being led into the secrets of the most intense raptures. Afterwards, there arises the pleasing sense of vanity at being able to feel so much and so deeply.[2] Proust wrote once to the Princesse Bibesco, "A sensation, no matter how disinterested it may be, a perfume, or an insight, if it is present, is still too much in my power to make me happy."

This pleasure is very similar to the effect of harmonic art, the difference being that the harmonic artist achieves the effect by emphatic manipulations of the medium and conventions while Rembrandt *et al.*, through the expression of a vague and very exaggerated state of reverie, encourage the audiences themselves to persuade themselves to be equally sensitive.

Looking over Rembrandt's oeuvre, the viewer is persuaded to admire the man for being a deeply sensitive and heroic genius. Now, this is the universally observed reaction. The biblical, mythical, historical, and the landscape paintings and the portraits are the works of the master, and he himself we see in the famous self-portraits as a deep, tragic, witty, and mysterious soul.

---

règle du jeu, where the cleverness of achieved harmony gives zest to an apparently melancholic mood.

[1] I except Plato and Schopenhauer from the following description. They please in the manner of normal ideal artists, i.e., directly. But even this is a half-truth. The final effect is missing because it is a purely emotional one. They rest content with rhetoric as pleasure.

[2] It is this latter effect that Schopenhauer could not manage. His genius was for rhetoric, and what was needed was genius for fiction and sentiments, which Rembrandt, Wagner, and Proust possessed. Rhetoric by itself cannot fill the imagination to the degree required for the second stage to arise because the number of ideas expressible through it is limited.

Wagner claimed that it was in his operas in which the beauties of all the arts are combined. For Wagner, and for the true Wagnerians, all musical compositions excepting his own elephantine productions were rudimentary and primitive affairs. There never had been anything like Wagner's Bayreuth following.

In Proust, the reader is directly asked to admire the special genius of Proust (or Marcel) who has at long last found the key to true art, a key which had formerly been dimly espied, perhaps, but never truly possessed.

The pleasures of their works can only be known fully by those who can identify completely with them to the extent of placing themselves in the shoes of their idols. Since this transformation is practically impossible, the response, when there is a positive response, is commonly half-way: the vanity consequent upon release from the state of exaggeration is felt to be one's own contribution only. But there are also the pleasures of kinship with genius.

Much greater, much more expressive and powerful are the masterpieces of Dante, Michelangelo, and Beethoven. They pin their audiences down with images (literary, visual, narrative, musical) of sublime power, images which call up feelings of sublime terror. Since here the chief idea is that of divine power, there are no merely human feelings, no tenderness, and even no fear of pain. Pain is a divine infliction which cannot be averted, so that there can be no fear, only lamentations. Pain and joy are given facts which you accept, which you have no choice but to accept.

The emotion inspired by them is one of fearful awe, a sense of grandeur arising from terror at man's inconsequence before the Omnipotence of the Divine Being coupled with the stern pride of having risen above consideration of any meaner ideas.

Release from this state (arising again from either weariness or fatigue) leads to a pleasing and intense sensation of sweetness, since almost everything in the normal world is sweeter and gentler than the sublime awe with which you were oppressing yourself.[1]

The sublime effects make the audiences feel the power of the idea of God, the sweetness of being released from terror they are meant to

---

[1]Again, Plato's genius for fiction being limited to rhetorical ideas, he could not manage to produce works that lead to the second level.

identify with the love of God, which seems to fill the world, but in itself cannot be seen or understood by the senses or by reason.

Anyone can see that Michelangelo, Dante, and Beethoven produced very great masterpieces. Everyone is at least struck by the affectations of Rembrandt, Proust, and Wagner. Jean Arthur is ten times more difficult to recognize as a great genius, and is therefore understood a hundred times less than any of them since she requires of her viewers a much greater effort of the soul to know very lively pleasures that are known to few people. Moreover, since Correggio and Jean Arthur rely little on effects of fear, or on affectations of vanity and cleverness, they forfeit the chance of being deeply admired and respected by a great number of fools.

Chapter XI

This essay is neither a manifesto nor a work of art. The reader will not derive from it any of the pleasures he expects from either. I want to describe as exactly as possible certain phenomena that occur in the heart, but this has turned out to be a much more difficult task than I had imagined. Have I managed to strip myself of all personal feelings and state only the truth? I think I record facts, but I may be producing a worthless catalogue of feelings. We can see everything clearly but ourselves.

Chapter XII

Of Friendship

Whoever has been given a noble and sensitive heart by nature soon perceives himself or herself to be prone to harm at the hands of those who are less sensitive, and who have the double advantage of being capable of malice and of having the power of superior numbers.

From whatever caprice, nature grants few men and women the weakness of being moved deeply by noble acts, thus rendering them so far impractical as to make them occasionally forget their own best interests. Sooner or later, they arrive at the conclusion that they must hide their true feelings from the notice of the wrong people. Conversely, they develop the habit of judging the greatness of heart of everyone whom chance throws their way.[1]

They look for simple and natural manners in others, paradoxical though this sounds.[2] Not that artlessness ennobles, but it is found where nobility of sentiments is. I do *not* speak of the awkwardness that springs from ignorance, naivete, lack of society, etc.

Alicia L.-, one of the most spirited and nobly proud women I have ever met, many years ago, during her youth, used to take the greatest delight in the company of a highly amiable and amusing young man. This handsome fellow had many notable qualities, but what struck one most was a note of utter sincerity in everything he said or did, to the point that he would on occasion seem too blunt in expressing himself. Sincerity is not sensitivity, but it is difficult to say whether Alicia could see that he lacked the latter.

The liveliness and depth of expression visible in Alicia's countenance and movements when she was seen with this delightful but somewhat insipid young man could have persuaded even an intelligent onlooker that they were in love. But what chiefly convinced most people of this fact was the alternatingly lighthearted and tender mood that would take hold of him.

She was considerably more restrained with other men. This reserve was not lost to any. It provided fuel for many a merry jest. She was supremely indifferent to the voices of rumors.

The amusing end of this story is that Alicia finally got over her infatuation, and later grew to slightly despise the man who had been the delight of her youth. He, on the other hand, never quite overcame her suddenly leaving him one fine day.

I have met and know well both of them, and I can say in all truth that the nature of Miss L.-'s soul was formed of an infinitely nobler mold than his. She had taken his vivacity and enthusiasm to be reflections of a sensitivity he did not possess, and he did not greatly wish to disillusion

---

[1]Joe Gargery in *Great Expectations*.

[2]Ophuls was delighted after four years of neglect to find in Mr. Douglas Fairbanks Jr. someone who wanted him to direct a film. Later he recalled with amusement that the actor would habitually invite him to his place for weekends, which they would spend seeing the silent films of Fairbanks Sr. What would Ophuls have thought of Mr. Fairbanks had he met him for the first time in the 1950's? Betty Grable, who made one film with Mr. Fairbanks, at first looked forward to a friendship with him, but was soon disappointed by his character.

her on this score even when he was able to overcome his vanity so far as to be able to see the discrepancy.

Friendship is a great bore when accompanied by affectations and little falsehoods, yet most friendships have only these charming qualities to sustain and recommend them.

Those who love have no real friends.

There are at least two types of friendships, those that arise simply out of shared worldly interests, and those that arise out of common pleasures.

People who have nothing to express, even to those people whom they know well, can nevertheless derive a mild pleasure from *acting*. Besides, it gratifies one's vanity to have a listener.

Once during a long drive, my friend Frederick explained to me that while he was away in the army for a year or two (I cannot remember exactly), he had been thrown in with a group of coarse young men. Since they were not given leave to divert themselves in any manner outside the barracks, he had perforce to content himself with the company in which he found himself.

To be aloof was not practicable, and, in any case, he soon congratulated himself on having found one man with agreeable enough manners, as well as original though not too intelligent thoughts. They were soon on very friendly terms.

Frederick is a remarkably shrewd man, but it took him three months to discover that Mark was only occasionally sincere in what he said, and had the most cavalier attitude towards contradicting himself.

If he had not been so desperate for some diversion in the kind of life he had chosen in an ill-hour, and which he was planning to quit as soon as possible, he may not have allowed himself to be so completely fooled.

From the moment he discovered that Mark was often being merely clever, he descended to acting and affectation himself. The necessities of life are such that even this noble-hearted man had not the courage to throw over the friendship entirely.[1]

Friendship, like all other matters of the heart, is generally stronger and deeper among women. This fact is easily explained when you remember that men, as a group, and especially among themselves, tend

---

[1] I have the greatest faith in his good sense, and so I could not keep myself from asking why he had not done so. He was a little surprised, as it turned out from his reply, by the folly of my question.

to be more insensitive to the finer feelings. Besides, personal vanity is a greater, more intense passion among women, and it contributes to the strength of their friendships.

[Chapters XIII and XIV omitted]

Chapter XV

Of the Tastes of Men and Women in the Late Twentieth Century

I begin a chapter which will be of no worth as a description unless I succeed in stripping myself of all personal feelings in order to be able to describe facts.

In this chapter, I ignore the ambitions of a Napoleon, or even those of a Richelieu, which have degenerated to the hypocrisies of twentieth-century dictators. But what about the ambitions of the soul?

Today all of the arts are dead and have been so for about three decades.[1]

The death of the arts, or of a particular art, is not a new phenomenon. For at least a thousand years before Masaccio, the art of painting had been all but forgotten in the West. Only a dreary symbolic art remained, which, it is not surprising, is more highly esteemed today than it has ever been since the Renaissance. We have again forgotten the art of painting in the present century, which has again forgotten the art of painting in the present century, which has not produced a single great painter. The best was perhaps Matisse, but what was Matisse compared to Rubens, let alone Veronese? The most famous, Picasso, was very talented but expressed nothing more than what a second-rate post-Renaissance illustrator such as Tiepolo could, although it may take several centuries for the general public, guided for the large part solely by coffee-table books, to see this fact. Where it used to be courts that

---

[1]Television comedy has perhaps provided one or two exceptions. *Get Smart* and *Jeeves and Wooster*. The British series *Red Dwarf* will almost certainly be amusing audiences two hundred years from now.

made mediocre painters like Van Dyck, Reynolds, Boucher, and even the modestly talented Velázquez famous in the first place, since the beginning of the nineteenth century, it has been critics who have established the fame of David, Ingres, Cézanne, Picasso, and other even more mediocre painters.[1] Their wages and their own fame depended upon making reputations.

The cry of the artist for attention became shrill in the nineteenth century, when some European nations and the United States had advanced to the extent of permitting ART to become, in some quarters, an esteemed creed,[2] so that it began to be taken more seriously than it deserved. The French Revolution brought about a distinct change in taste among the most talented artists, though it took many decades before the new taste, and its many branches, became generally accepted by their public. Rousseau's claim for the dignity of the individual seemed justified and true to many after the American and French Revolutions, and it changed the character of nearly all the most esteemed works produced since then.

Democratic taste and political power raised the esteem in which the arts and artists were held in most societies.[3] But this was a transitional stage. The more clever artists saw very soon that the judges had changed, but the rules for success remained the same. Having become accustomed to seeing themselves thought of as of consequence to society because they displayed its best qualities, though, they could now look upon popular taste with surprise, dismay, and, finally, contempt. The cry for admiring attention was in fact a death rattle, and was last made among the generations which passed away by the end of the third quarter of the twentieth century.

---

[1] Klimt, Klee, Kandinsky, Mondrian, Modigliani, Pollock, Kline, Wyeth, O'Keefe, de Kooning and scores of others.

[2] Only Renaissance Italy was sensible in the place and consequence it gave to the arts in society.

[3] Raphael and Michelangelo were held in great esteem by their contemporaries, but it was not of the same type as that of Voltaire. But Voltaire was still only a great wit and philosopher; only with the Revolution did he become a national hero. Nineteenth-century France gave Hugo a heroic and national esteem which was perhaps greater in magnitude though less in elevation than that enjoyed by any of the other names I have mentioned. The esteem granted by their contemporaries to Beethoven, Wagner, Brahms, and Verdi was of another order from that granted to Handel, Gluck, and Haydn. In the twentieth century, Sartre was perhaps the last Frenchman who could achieve equal prestige. The belief in the great artist as a public hero has died with the likes of Sartre, Cary Grant, etc.

Those born later grew up when the transitional stage was past and the arts were beginning to be seen again for what they are: an agreeable pastime, and no more.[1] The absurd claims made for it by artists, critics, and taste-makers since early in the nineteenth century now inspired suspicion. Simple utility had become the only mode of judging worth. With such ideas dominating, even ambitious artists implicitly accept (often without knowing it) that no greater passions exist than those commonplace ones they themselves have felt and of which they have seen the outward manifestations in others. They are not capable of rising to intensity, or even liveliness of sensations because of ingrained suspicion of the exaggerations and opinions of earlier generations, and because of the lack of contemporary examples of intense passions in real life; to make up for this defect, and because audiences today are jaded and bored through over-exposure to amusements, they emphasize technical effects, violence, oddness (what is called *surrealism*), obscenity, vagueness (affectedly called *ambiguity*), bizarre and deliberately displeasing subjects—anything that will produce an effect of novelty or excess.[2]

Our pleasures today are so much milder than of those of the past six hundred years that the arts had to die through decadence (i.e., extremely exaggerated affectations), for in popular art of even the most fantastic genres are found only *concentrated* and idealized versions of the ways in which happiness is pursued in a society.

A strong faith (by which I mean one that its possessor does not think *conceivably* assailable) in anyone is not compatible with both scientific and democratic opinions, and it was generally a fervent conviction about something or the other that inspired the passions and masterpieces of the great artists of the past.[3] Of artists today, the works of how many will

---

[1]The trend started earlier, but became almost universal among writers born after 1915 (excepting Mr. Robbe-Grillet and his many imitators), and among filmmakers born after 1935 or so. Painting and music are dead arts today.

[2]It may be argued that a true genius can create masterpieces even in such unfavorable circumstances, so that if there are not any being produced, the reason is simply that no man or woman of true originality has appeared in the past few decades. Social and political circumstances in the West today allow a greater number than ever of those who wish to to step forward before the public as artists; and since everyone who wishes to can also step forward as a guide of taste, the smallest degree of affectation or seeming novelty is dubbed "challenging, subtle, powerful, intriguing, devastating, profound, brilliant, etc.," strokes, and the work judged a great one. This mechanism began in late seventeenth-century England, and has become more affected with time.

[3]Even those, in the West and in the Third World, who hate the ideas of democracy and

produce pleasure in men and women three hundred years hence? There is less desire for unattainable beauty today than is required for art of lasting appeal, and no passion at all.

But it is always possible that the audiences' knowledge of pleasure will continue to diminish to the point that even the works of today will continue to be praised. It is more likely that they will be forgotten and ridiculed in favor of a later crop. Only the special power of expressing vividly their very strongly held opinions keeps the works of Rembrandt, Dante, or Bach alive today.

A period of the past is like the body of a great leader lying publicly in state. The visitor knows that once the corpse had life and movement, and that many bowed and scraped before it and paid court to the personality it housed, and many others feared the powers it wielded. But once it is dead, it has no importance save as a symbol.

There can be no revival of the arts so long as society keeps moving in the direction it has in the last two hundred years. This fact is perhaps not to be regretted, as the choice between material prosperity and the arts is an easy one, especially for the man with a commonplace soul. It is those who oppose most energetically the direction that industrial societies have taken who produce the most dull art, full of gloom, petty self-pity, and puerile comedy.

Putting aside all personal feelings on the matter, I take the representative example of Nabokov. This Russian, easily the greatest writer of his time, who, along with Mr. Robbe-Grillet, wrote the only literary masterpieces since those of Lernet-Holenia, Faulkner, Yeats, and Proust, has not had the universal acceptance granted to lesser, and sometimes downright mediocre, writers whom he rightly ridiculed.[1]

Like Joyce and Proust, he is little read outside the academy, and much less understood, but he has the additional disadvantage of being disowned equally by all the nations.[2]

---

science cannot wholly ignore the steady and irreversible tide of historical developments. So much of the energy of talented men like Iqbal, Picasso, Hemingway, Mr. Antonioni, Fellini, etc. was spent in impotent fear and hatred of rational ideas, which they feared would lead to the drying up of the wells of sentiment, that their works are spoiled by the very aridity they despised.

[1] E.g. Céline, Hemingway, Camus, Mann, Sartre, Beckett, Borges, and others born later.

[2] Much greater respect will be paid to his art when Russia has freed itself from the yoke of Communism.   Jan. 1990

Two years later, the Soviet Union is a thing of the past. The Russians, though, are not

The case of Hawks speaks even worse about taste today. Though not the most sublime of artists, he has the inestimable merit of not entirely lacking in liveliness.

Giotto, Rubens, Rabelais, and Chaucer fared better because art in their days was not taken so seriously as to be ignored, and when something truly unusual was put forward, it had not yet become customary to ignore it. But for all practical purposes, Hawks is not a known quantity to most Americans.

I have taken some representative examples only to describe the fact that since the degree of habitual exercising of the imagination has declined generally, even when a few geniuses do appear, they attain incommensurate fame. This sort of thing always used to happen, but generally as an exception; now it is the rule, and there is a reason for it.

I see at least two manners in twentieth century tastes that reflect general fashions of the century. The first is the love of the primitive, born of having governments that operate along lines purely of utility and reflected in all the arts, in literature, painting, music, and films, and in time, reflected in the manners and words of most people in the West. It was born about the 1910's, the first of the two great transitional decades of the twentieth century, although the old European manners and passions had not passed away entirely. Even the opinions publicly trumpeted by communist regimes in their early years were primitive in color—everything else was capitalist or feudal, and decadent—though the communists found the primitive tendency in artists like Stravinsky and Picasso decadent.

In the West, primitive opinions triumphed during the second transitional decade, the 1960's, when popular rock music became the dominant art form that influenced all society, and all other popular arts, especially the second most popular, films. There is not much appeal to the imagination and the passions, but only to immediate physical hopes and fears garnished with a layer of petty vanity.

The second general trend is the appeal to the imagination of scientific discoveries. I do not mean the romances called science fictions, although their popularity is based upon the same appeal. The discoveries of, as well as the abilities of astronomers, physicists, chemists, engineers,

---

yet at the stage that the French were in 1789, and it is doubtful that much is to be expected from them. Taking aside the reactionaries, they are too intent upon imitating the United States.

surgeons, physicians, geologists, bioengineers, etc., inspire the imagination of men and women today as religious miracles and outlandish and insipid romances used to of people centuries ago.

Much in today's physics, astronomy, chemistry, biochemistry, bioengineering, medicine, engineering, etc., inspires that sense of admiration and a sense of mystery which are exactly the stuff that poetry and art are made on[1]; we have come a long way since the age of Locke and Newton, when science was popularly though erroneously thought to cool the imagination *entirely*.

Science, even as it dries up the heart and makes it unsusceptible to beauty and art, itself leads us back to poetry, albeit of a dry type.

The affectation of being scientific has entered into nearly every field of interest and knowledge, and is a product of a class of very mild vanity unknown until recent centuries, and not general until the middle of the nineteenth. It arises solely from this simple idea, "How very rational I am." Previously, those who felt pleasure in being rational did so because they felt themselves to be superior to the rest of mankind, who were easily duped and confused, and the pleasure was therefore greater.

The works of pedants today are largely the consequences of this pleasure of mild vanity having been grafted upon the pleasures common to pedantry everywhere:

1) the pleasure of conversation, or rather of inconclusive and unending conversation—the same pleasure that women derive from gossiping, the pleasure of never lacking for a topic or activity;

2) the wish to impress others by means of obfuscation and jargon, which leads to the pleasures of cliques, a matter of gratifying petty personal vanity through collective vanity.[2]

---

[1] E.g., the Superstring Theory of Mr. Schwarz, with its eight or ten dimensions and shadow matter.

[2] E.g., a man announces that he has discovered the existence of an entirely mysterious something called the unconscious which is of a nature that cannot be known by our thinking and feeling mind, but is very real nevertheless, and then proceeds to take upon himself the heroic task of explaining to the rest of us not endowed with equally transcendental organs of perception the intricate workings of this unconscious. Since this discovered entity has the advantage of being superior in power and unknown in nature to the thinking and feeling mind (which is all that those not transcendentally endowed possess), this man is free to say anything and seem a discoverer. He finds followers who enjoy the pleasures of cliques. In time, some of these discover that they are endowed with more powerful transcendental organs of perception than the master, and proclaim some new deep truths arrived at by twisting a few ordinarily known facts into seemingly novel

When societies were taken up with the rhetoric of religion, pedantry took on the affectation of examining religious and metaphysical truths. When enough advances in logic had been made to breed some skepticism, pedantry took on the affectation of examining and discovering transcendent truths through reason. Now that the sciences have become the most esteemed subjects in society, pedantry naturally affects the rhetorical colors of a love of facts and a suspicion of the word *truth*. Thus the scientific manner of always skeptically questioning every result and conclusion leads to the pleasures of vagueness among literary pedants.

The motives of pedants who have produced those incredible theories about language, literature, culture, and theories that have appeared since 1945 are the same pleasures that led to the production through history of works proclaimed by other pedants at the time of publication to be immortal foundations or developments of knowledge, and whose popularity sometimes lasted as long as thirty or forty years.[1] Given the fact that the colors of modern pedantry are those of the sciences, which for the greatest part are pedantic professions, as was the clerical profession in some cities in the Middle Ages, and the fact that pedants, universities, and journals feel obliged, because of the utilitarian principles of modern Western societies, to prove that they are no more indolent and useless than members of other more really necessary professions, it

---

shapes. Equipped thus, they set up shop, and the process begins again. This was the manner of Plato, Aristotle, Abélard, Aquinas, Rousseau, Kant, Hegel, Schopenhauer, Cousin, Marx, Husserl, Heidegger; nothing has changed.

What about the systems they make? Novelty of ideas is not a pedant's strong suit. Freud, for example, simply grafted Hahnemann's idea of chronic diseases, which must have been well known to him, onto the superstitious notions of exorcism and dream interpretations, and added some of his own private reveries: the pedant typically at work. Hegel grafted the idea of conflicts and wars onto a history of pedantry, among other things. Plato took an inventory of all things that seemed to be true because perceived by the senses and then proclaimed the opposite to be true and good, for this seeming novelty allowed for the pleasures of pedantry, the poor man's strongest passion. This class of men can never afford to clearly acknowledge the actual idea that makes for their own happiness. They are by nature dishonest, and in this respect are the exact opposite of the greater artists.

[1]The German philosophers of the nineteenth century, on the heels of Kant. Without them pedantry today would be less general. Nietzsche wrote once that wherever Germany goes it spoils culture. Unfortunately, his own books are little better than the other German poems in prose, being spoiled, in spite of the comic tone, by the same love of puerile exaggerations. I except that great poem *Thus Spoke Zarathustra* and the autobiography. Like Dante, Nietzsche became a pedant as soon as he stopped expressing his strongest pleasures in explicitly poetic form.

follows of course that competitive publication will be demanded of all pedants, for the sake of appearing productive and useful to society. It further follows that glory will be the province of those who appear the most novel and difficult, and there will sometimes be considerable wealth to go with the glory. So it should come as a surprise to no one that we have entered another age of scholasticism and schoolmen.[1] This time, though, the schoolmen have been joined by schoolwomen, and their boring exegeses are not on theological, moral, rhetorical, etc., works, but on social, political, journalistic, media-related, propaganda, artistic, theoretical, psychological, multicultural, interdisciplinary, ideological, ethnic, feminist, statistical, economic, etc., works.

Whenever a school of pedantry succeeds and finds financial patronage (i.e., it is said to exist), there is always someone whose personal interests are being served in promoting it. Since science and engineering have paid such great dividends of wealth, physical comforts, glory, and power, neither politicians nor journalists are willing to risk being thought of as cranks by asking any *foolish* questions, and neither, for the most part, are common citizens whose thinking is limited to the fear that, to use journalistic clichés, "a drop in education standards will result in competitive disadvantages in the global marketplace." Anyone who can claim that he or she is scientifically uncovering facts (no one is permitted to ask of what use precisely to society), and persuade a sufficient number to believe him or her, will not be sent back unrewarded. No one would want to stop public funding of *promising* enterprises, and private institutions also know the glory that comes with having as members famous men and women. Interest, promotion of career, is the motive for pedants today as it has always been, and those

---

[1]Freud, Jung, Wittgenstein, Heidegger, Husserl, Lukács, Sartre, Camus, Benjamin, Barthes, Foucault, Bakhtin, Jakobson, Saussure, Mr. Gennette, Mr. Fish, Mr. Derrida, Miss Kristeva, Miss Cixous, Mr. Levi-Strauss, Althusser, Lacan, etc., and their many followers. In order to succeed they are forced to disavow the mercernary motives that guide them— Molière's description of pedants in *Les femmes savantes* is exactly true to nature. The author should confess that he never, not even in his youth, passed through the stage when he wished for the solace of a community engaged in literary matters, whose products, strangely enough, are always direct or indirect expressions of self-praise. He lists names not in censure, but merely to complete the description of a class of happiness as it is to be found today. A man has no choice over what gives him pleasure, making all censure or praise equally ridiculous. All adjectives (e.g., inane, great, etc.) in this treatise are merely descriptive, not evaluative, and are used to concisely describe the number of ideas of pleasures in a given case relative to the number that the heart can know.

who are successful gather young followers by showing them what to profess and what to promulgate for like success. Once certain fashions are created, they inevitably survive by the inertia of conservatism until some changes in social manners and thought brought about by changes in political and economic fortunes make new fashions possible, and a new breed of pedants and experts moves in, and the cycle repeats itself.

With every change, since it is a replacement motivated by interest, those of the past become objects of ridicule: an inevitable fact that no one on the crest of a wave has time, imagination, or modesty to remember.

The laws regarding tastes are exactly the same, whether you are speaking of politics, pedantry, philosophy, or clothes.

We laugh less today than ever. Think of those considered comical today; but Proust or Cervantes, even Smollett, *laughed* infinitely more, and more deeply and powerfully, than do any today, and Proust was a puritanical and hypocritical idealist. Has our age then declined so much?

[Last page of the chapter omitted]

Chapter XVI

Of the Love of Glory

So far in dealing with the classes of vanity, I have examined chiefly the manner in which the arts are involved, for the simple reason that the other varieties are simple, and have already been well described. Greatness in any form is almost always the result of love of glory, and the great artists, philosophers, leaders, and scientists have all been driven by this common factor, with only the field in which glory is sought differing;[1] but what these are is beyond the power of a man to decide, since they are largely determined by his internal makeup and by

---

[1]Chance has much to do with any great achievement. But that the opportunity was exploited is a credit to him who did. And though reputation of greatness is often a product of popular ignorance and a lazy disregard for truth, such reputations do not last a long time. Even after the passage of several centuries, it is clear that Alexander and Galileo deserved the great fame they won.

opportunities which depend to a great degree on chance.[1] All that is needed is that circumstances and state of society not actually condemn, forbid, or effectively negate their ambitions.

Whatever the role of chance, true greatness is always the result of a protracted and intensified love of glory which motivates a man or woman to enter deeply into the passions that lead to greatness in his or her chosen field of glory.[2]

Love of glory is only the most powerful and passionate manifestation of the general desire for esteem. Vanity can only be gratified if you believe that those you esteem esteem you in return.[3] Those who are esteemed may be imaginary beings, or images of some great men of the past.[4] That talented pedant Milton has written:

> Alas! What boots it with uncessant care
> To tend the homely slighted Shepherd's trade,
> And strictly meditate the thankless Muse?
> Were it not better done as others use,
> To sport with *Amaryllis* in the shade,
> Or with the tangles of *Neaera's* hair?
> *Fame* is the spur that the clear spirit doth raise
> (That last infirmity of Noble mind)
> To scorn delights, and live laborious days;
> But the fair Guerdon when we hope to find,
> And think to burst out into sudden blaze,
> Comes the blind *Fury* with th'abhorred shears,
> And slits the thin-spun life. "But not the praise,"
> *Phoebus* repli'd, and touch'd my trembling ears;
> "*Fame* is no plant that grows on mortal soil,

---

[1] A man begins to enjoy whatever it is that he feels he has great talents for. Caesar would have despised the pleasures of James Joyce, as Joyce despised Caesar's. The sense of achievement provides half the pleasure, the hope of glory the other half. Talentless people often derive pleasure from thinking of the greatness of their heroes and heroines, because they feel that admiration entitles them to association with them, or at least to share in some of their glory. This is the reason why many leaders are able to attract a fanatically devoted following.

[2] To paraphrase Helvétius.

[3] So that it is an unfailing test and indication of whom a man or woman esteems when the lack of reciprocating esteem produces bitterness, regret, anger, affected contempt, or misery.

[4] There is no true happiness unless the admirers are both numerous and contemporaries.

Nor in the glistering foil,
Set off to th'world, nor in broad rumor lies,
But lives and spread aloft by those pure eyes
And perfect witness of all-judging *Jove*;
As he pronounces lastly on each deed,
Of so much fame in Heav'n expect thy meed."

Love of power is the result when a man puts the delights he expects to enjoy in the expressed esteem and fear of others over all other delights, and acts accordingly. This love rises in virtue in proportion to a sincere desire to equal or at least approach the merits and reputation of a great and popular man of the past.[1] In terms of the heart, the love of power in a statesman, soldier, or demagogue is equivalent to the love of fame that inspires the artist, philosopher, scientist, performer, etc.; their vanity is greater than that of those content with the tepid esteem only of the people with whom they are in everyday contact.

The great poet Nietzsche once wrote,

"'The will to power' is so hated in democratic ages that their entire psychology seems directed toward belittling and defaming it. The type of the great ambitious man who thirsts after honor is supposed to be Napoleon! And Caesar! And Alexander! —As if they were not precisely the great *despisers* of honor!

"And Helvétius demonstrates to us that men strive after power so as to possess the enjoyments available to the powerful: he understands this striving for power as will to enjoyment! as hedonism!"[2]

Nietzsche, in his only reference to a specific part of Helvétius' book that I know, fortunately attacked one of its three or four weakest chapters, for elsewhere Helvétius speaks of Caesar's love of glory, not honors. Caesar was motivated by a more lively and proud love of glory than the average tyrant; but to set up some vaguely defined poetic idea in place of love of glory is the sort of pedantry which spoils most of Nietzsche's books and is responsible for his popularity among pedants and men of letters generally.

---

[1]From Hobbes, who writes that love of virtue arises from love of praise. This is the reason that a great nation is often seen to have a succession of admirable leaders over several centuries, whereas other nations are condemned to one villain after another. In the latter, the appearance of one Parnell often does not correct the general corruption of morals. See Helvétius' *De l'esprit*.

[2]Translated by Mr. Kaufmann. The reader will no doubt have noted by now that many ideas in this treatise are borrowed from others; in fact, it would not have been possible but for the contributions of many women and men, both living and dead.

The difference is only in exactly what lay glory for Caesar, and in what lay glory for that buffoon Napoleon III or for Indira Gandhi. Nietzsche's "will to power" is nothing more than his emphatic term for one of the two chief classes of passions known by men (and the only one he knew), vanity. It is the German poet's manner of describing, from *inside*, ideas concerning vanity.

Helvétius, the greatest philosopher of the masculine heart as far as vanity goes, described exactly and in a dispassionate manner, and thus expressed the truth more exactly. At this point I would have preferred to insert a footnote directing the reader to his *De l'esprit* (literally *Of the Mind* (or *Spirit*), translated into English in the nineteenth century and given the title *Essays on the Mind and Its Several Faculties*); and to refer to chapters XV and following of the third essay as both minutely accurate and generally true descriptions of how love of glory and power operates upon the soul. The reader could, if he so wished, read the essay at his own convenience.

Helvétius is almost unknown today in the English-speaking world (and little read even in France). The reason for this neglect and ignorance is not difficult to discover. Had he lived in a more liberal nation and age, he may not have been forced to be as discreet and mild in his expressions of his ideas regarding man and society; if his liberal and far-reaching ideas had been stated more emphatically, he would have greater fame today.[1] Though he tried to tread as gently and politely as possible, his book was condemned by state and church, and he was forced to apologize publicly for it. Unfortunately, his book became notorious for the scandal it inspired and not for its great merits, and fame won in that manner usually dies in a generation or so.

The difficulty of access to his book will, I hope, excuse my quoting him at great length. I cannot hope to improve upon his anatomy of the subject. Perhaps in the future, if there are any future editions of the essay you are reading, there may be no need for the extended quote.

I quote from the early nineteenth-century translation of chapter XVI of the third essay in *De l'esprit*.

---

[1]How great would the fame of Hobbes ever have been had he stopped at chapter XII of the *Leviathan* instead of proceeding to the very artistically exaggerated thirteenth chapter, which forms the center of his book and spoils it as philosophy? Hobbes was of the bilious temperament (as described by Cabanis), and Helvétius of the sanguine, and so the power of their expression was necessarily different. The bilious temperament is forceful, and even a dull man cannot avoid heeding its expressions a little.

"To determine whether the indifference of certain nations with respect to virtue depends on nature or the particular form of government, we must first know man; penetrate even into the abyss of the human heart; and recollect, that, being born sensible of pleasure and pain, he owes, to the physical sensibility, his passions, and that to his passions he owes all his virtues and vices.

"... we must at length examine whether the same passions, on being moulded by different forms of governments do not produce in human beings the opposite vices and virtues.

"Suppose a man to be so much in love with glory as to sacrifice to it all his other passions; if, by the form of government, glory be constantly the reward of virtuous actions, it is evident this man will be always under a necessity of being virtuous; and that to form a Leonidas and an Horatius Cocles, there needs no more than to place him in a country and in circumstances like theirs.

"But, it is objected, that there are few men who raise the passion to this height. To which I reply that none but the man who enters deeply into this passion can penetrate into the sanctuary of virtue. This is not the case with respect to the men incapable of lively passions, and who are called honest men; if the latter be kept in the path of virtue at a distance from this sanctuary, it proceeds from their being constantly held there by the fetters of indolence, which they have not the strength to break.

"With respect to the men of strong passions, it is evident that the same desire which, in the early ages of the Roman republic, produced such men as Curtius and Decius, must have formed a Marius and an Octavius in those periods of trouble and revolutions, when glory, as in the latter times of the republic, was only connected with tyranny and power. What I have said of the passion for glory, I apply to the love of esteem, which is only a diminutive of the love of glory, and the object that attracts the desires of those who cannot arise to fame.

"The desire for esteem must in like manner produce, in different ages, opposite virtues and vices. When interest is a surer path to preferment than merit, this desire makes of men intriguers and flatterers; when money is more honored than virtue, it produces avaricious men, who seek for riches with as much avidity as the first Romans fled from them, when they were ashamed to have them in their possession.

"I shall observe, by the way, on this subject, the difference there is between the ambitious of glory, and the ambitious of high positions or riches. The first can never be otherwise than great criminals, because great crimes, from the superiority of the talents necessary to the commission of them, and the extraordinary advantages united with success, can alone impose so far on the imagination of mankind as to extort their admiration—an admiration founded on the inward and secret desire of resembling these illustrious criminals.

"The most exalted virtue, as well as the most shameful vice, is the effect of the greater or less intensity of the pleasure it affords us.

"Thus we can form no exact idea of the degree of our virtue, until we have discovered, by a scrupulous examination, the number and degrees of those pains which a passion, as for instance, the love of justice or of glory, may enable us to support. The person to whom esteem is everything, and life nothing, will, like Socrates, submit rather to suffer death, than meanly to beg for life. He who is become the soul of a republican state, in which pride, glory, and self-esteem render him passionately desirous of the public welfare, will, like Cato, prefer death to the mortification of seeing himself and his country submit to the yoke of arbitrary power. But such actions are the effect of the greatest love of glory. This is the highest pitch to which the strongest passions can attain, and here nature has fixed the bounds of human virtue.

"In vain we would deceive ourselves; we necessarily become the enemies of men, when we cannot otherwise be happy than by their misfortune. It is the pleasing conformity we find between our own interest and that of the public, a conformity generally produced by the desire of esteem, that gives us those tender sentiments that are rewarded by their affection. He who to be virtuous must always conquer his inclinations, must necessarily be an evil man. The meritorious virtues are never certain and infallible virtues. (In the harem, it is not to the most meritorious virtues, but to incapability, that the Grand Seignior entrusts his women.) It is impossible in practice for a man to deliver himself up, in a manner, daily to war with the passions, without losing many battles.

"Being always forced to yield to the most powerful interest some of that love for esteem, we never sacrifice any great pleasure to it, but those it procures. If, on certain occasions, sacred personages have sometimes exposed themselves to the contempt of the public, it is because they would not sacrifice their salvation to their glory; and if some women resist the solicitations of a prince, it is because they believe that his conquest would not recompense them for the loss of esteem.[1]

"The virtuous man is then not he who sacrifices his pleasures, habits, and strongest passions to the public welfare, since it is impossible that such a man should exist (If some men have seemed to sacrifice their interest to the public welfare, it is because, in a good form of government, the idea of virtue is so united to that of happiness, and the idea of vice to that of contempt, that they are hurried away by a lively sensation, the origins of which is not always to be discovered by them, and from this motive perform actions that seem contrary to their ostensible interests.); but he whose strongest passion is so conformable to the general interest, that he is almost constantly necessitated to be virtuous.

"Caesar was, without doubt, not the most virtuous among Romans; yet if he would not renounce the title of a good citizen without taking that of the master of the world, we have not, perhaps, a right to banish him from the class of honest men. In fact, among the virtuous, who truly deserve that title, how few are there, who, if placed in the same circumstances as Caesar was, would refuse the scepter of the world, especially if, like Caesar, they thought they had those superior talents that secure the success of great enterprises? Less ability would perhaps render them better citizens, and a moderate degree of virtue, supported by a greater anxiety of success, would be sufficient to deter them from engaging in so bold a project. Indeed sometimes a want of talents preserves us from vice; and frequently to the same defect we owe all our virtues.

"We are on the contrary less virtuous, as less powerful motives lead us to the commission of a crime. Such, for instance, is that of some of the emperors of Morocco, who, solely from the motives of making a parade of their dexterity, would, with one blow of a sabre, in mounting a horse, cut off the head of the groom who held the stirrup.

"If pleasure be the only object of man's pursuit, we need only imitate nature in order to inspire a love of virtue. Pleasure informs us of what she would have done, and pain what is forbidden, and men will readily obey her mandates. Why may not the legislature, armed with the same power, produce the same effects? Were men without passions, there

---

[1]And the loss of self-esteem, Helvétius should have added.

would be no means of producing a reformation; but the love of pleasure is a bridle by which the passions of the individuals might be directed to the public good....

"I might conclude from what I have said, that the love or indifference of certain nations for virtue does not arise from nature, but from the different constitutions of state; and in order to obtain a more accurate knowledge of the subject, I shall examine what motive it is that can excite in man such unbridled lust for arbitrary power as is felt in the East."

Two hundred years and more have sometimes not changed even the particular applications that can be made of the facts Helvétius describes.

That the exercise of power has become a thing of open general suspicion in democratic countries is a fortunate fact for the happiness of the vast majority of their citizens. Glory is the province of those leaders whose motives are deemed virtuous, i.e. conformable to the wishes of the majority of the people; the reputations of Washington, Jefferson, Lincoln, Gladstone, Disraeli, Roosevelt, Churchill, etc., are not less than those of any figure in history.

In other nations, those colonized or brutalized by previous governments, the liberators are apotheosized, unless the governments which they themselves set up are considered oppressive *and* toppled in time.

Danton and Gandhi are still revered; but what has become, or will become, of the reputation of men like Lenin, Stalin, Mao, etc., when the dust has settled on Communism seventy years from now? These men believed in their cause and had an interest in promoting the general good, no doubt, but so did Hitler;[1] love of virtue was deficient generally in their societies, and the fact that governments they toppled were oppressive and incompetent swayed to them the masses (always ready to be swayed by the loudest proclaimers). In a state of chaos and change, it is often the man who takes the most extreme and uncompromisingly ambitious steps who emerges victorious—e.g., Lenin's exploitation of a political blunder by rival parties in 1917 to get rid of them.

It is impossible to state *as a fact* whether what a great man with an ambitious plan pushes a nation into when he sees that his plans have a chance to succeed is a virtuous action or not.[2] Does he see more than

---

[1]Hitler had the house where his father was born demolished when rumors started spreading that his father was half-Jewish.

[2]Which is why Rousseau's notion of the "general will" is worthless, asides from its

others, or is he leading his nation into moral or practical disorders? Is the sacrifice he demands worth the changes he brings about?[1]

When nations are divided, chaotic, or simply weak due to economic problems, there sometimes seems no other way but to allow a dictator or monarch to arise.

> Ahi gente che dovresti esser devota,
> e lasciar seder Cesare in la sella,
> se bene intendi cio che Dio ti nota,
> guarda come esta fiera e fatta fella
> per non esser corretta da li sproni,
> poi che ponesti mano a la predella.
>
> *Purgatorio*, VI[2]

Dante placed Brutus and Cassius with Judas at the center of Hell not only for the crime of treacherous murder *per se*, but because they had happened to betray and murder the man who was in the midst of establishing the Roman Empire. His Italy was not to be united into a nation until the nineteenth century, but was not the Italian Renaissance the last great age of Europe (with Dante's own age marking the transition point to it)?

By the early nineteenth century, Italy was in steep decline, but what claims to greatness can it make since it was united by Garibaldi and Cavour? If oppression, religious and political, had suppressed the genius of the Italian people, it had also created some strong generations.

Those who praise or censure a strong central power most vehemently usually have their own personal interests in mind rather than the general interest.

It is doubtful whether that government could exist that would encourage the men and women of greatest passions and abilities; you cannot get rid of disagreements and envy.[3]

---

poetical value.

[1] The theme of Shakespeare's *Julius Caesar*, where, for once, Shakespeare was as interested in ideas *per se* as he was in dramatic pleasure. But, now that I think of it, there is another play in which you see the man, *As You Like It*.

It is impossible to come to a factual conclusion because politics is a matter of conflicting interests.

[2] Ah, people that ought to be obedient and let Caesar sit in the saddle, if you rightly understand what God notes to you, see how this beast has grown vicious, through not being corrected by the spurs, since you did put your hands to the bridle.

Mr. Singleton's translation.

[75]

So what one is left with, at best, are governments that are constantly under pressure from the people themselves.

Having power means that one is able to enjoy that many more of the pleasures that are generally allowed, and often many that are not; the desire for such unusual degrees of pleasure as well as love of glory lies behind ambition. But greatness requires a great opportunity to match the greatness of soul.

Opportunity made possible a Napoleon as well as an F. D. Roosevelt.

Whereas beauty is the chief ingredient in the production or enjoyment of art, and vanity only comes later and stays, power offers gratification only to a man's vanity, and is thus a much less inly inspired a phenomenon, and its pleasures are of a lesser variety, being limited to a love of glory, and, at best, a conviction of contributing to the general good or to the glory of one's people. Intensity (a product of fear) may be there, but the rarer and most lively passions are not.

Only rarely is the pursuit of power taken up with the most noble ideals in mind, as it was in the case of Washington. In these cases, the love of glory was identical with the love of virtue, and those nations are very fortunate whose institutions and manners promote the success of such men.

Many leaders lead by appeals to commonplace passions alone. They know how to appear to be the redeemers and saviors of their nations. Their degree of virtue depends upon the degree of virtue present in that society. Thus the differences between [ ], Gandhi, and Khomeini.

Machiavelli wrote the most famous treatise on the facts regarding power under a despotic government; Helvétius described passions and society more generally and universally, but he also came to the conclusion that unless love of virtue is the only path to success in a given society, a very great man in politics cannot but be a great criminal.

The Aurangzebs usually succeed, because of their wholehearted and shrewd adoption of what are today called Machiavellian ideas. Aurangzeb was one of the several sons of the Mughal emperor Shah Jehan. Upon hearing that their father was seriously ill, all the princes, who were each governors of the various parts of the empire, became

---

[3]Fortunately, Lorenzo de Medici proved me wrong five hundred years ago. But, then, the literary and philosophic products of that court were of the safely vague and diffuse Platonic kind.

involved in schemes for the throne. The most cunning and vicious of the lot was Aurangzeb, who manipulated, tricked, and finally killed all his brothers and imprisoned his father in a tower with only a daughter and an insolent eunuch as companions. He was also by nature a very religious man.

It is true that unlike Aurganzeb many of these great criminals were also far-seeing statesmen who saw that the greatness of their nation or empire redounded to their personal glory, e.g., Augustus, Charlemagne, Suleiman, Lorenzo de Medici, Akbar, Tokugawa, Richelieu, Catherine, Frederick, and Bismarck. They rarely had as brilliant successors, and the ultimate good that some of them made possible they had not aimed at, and would have been amused to know they had indirectly caused. But the solidarity and strength of a nation are the first criteria for great accomplishments of its citizens.

Very few men could accomplish great historical advances without there having already been considerable progress before them. Each generation must develop upon what has been accomplished before. One of the few exceptions to this rule was [ ] ....

Tacitus and Saint-Simon, the greatest historians, knew that character is revealed only in and by actions. They describe only actions and motivations: being accurate in such matters requires a rare talent.[1] Both were oligarchs describing states in which oligarchy or feudalism had been succeeded by tyranny exercised by one man, and so they had the advantage of being in a position that allowed them to describe both actions not restricted by any considerations but that of pleasure or the fear of this privilege being taken away by assassination, military defeat, or loss of imperial or royal favor, and the systems of flattery and intrigues by which courts operate.

A relatively uncorrupt and bland democratic government provides a historian largely with actions dictated by a desire to please the masses: i.e. only one type of flattery would be found in the age, a type usually found in a modified way even in the worst tyrannies.

---

[1]Livy still remains the greatest poet among historians. Suetonius, though he provides amusing anecdotes, lacked acuteness of mind. Plutarch, it is true, rivals Tacitus and Saint-Simon at times. The dour Thucydides was the first academic historian; Gibbon, Burckhardt, Taine, Toynbee, Braudel, Foucault, Miss Tuchman, etc. belong to this tradition. The academic historian is a little in love with the subject itself.

Chapter XVII

The ancient world recognized two great military geniuses, Alexander and Caesar, and the modern world has produced one, Napoleon. Though numberless scribblers and filmmakers have romanticized these men, this does not mean that there was nothing exceeding the commonplace about them.

Racine, Voltaire, Goethe, Balzac, Whitman, Conrad, Mann, Musil, etc., were vain about their works, and Dante was vain about his. Who would say that Dante's pride is of the same stamp as theirs? The pride of Milton and Joyce was merely that of a very clever pedant. The degree and purity of Dante's pride are relative matters. You only see what makes it stand apart when you consider how many of the pleasures of petty vanity it rejects.

Love of glory can be of a hundred shades, but rarely is the passion raised to the degree it was by the three greatest military geniuses the world has seen.[1]

Among civilian statesmen, there has been at least one such proud seeker of glory, Jinnah.

Jinnah, who had no religious faith whatsoever, and who despised the masses, was pushed off the center of the Indian freedom movement when Gandhi, with his saintly affectations, became overnight the most powerful man in it, but he came back onto center stage fifteen years later and ended with a political victory which was a personal victory of sorts for he was defeated in his original aim, an implausible one of erasing *through politics* the deep prejudices and mutual suspicion and hatred among the followers of the different religions. This victory lay in the division of the subcontinent into two large nations. In the last stage of his career, Jinnah had three groups of opponents: rival Muslim politicians, Gandhi and the Congress Party, and the British rulers.

The first was the most difficult to deal with. Jinnah had learned from Gandhi that only by appealing to the most primitive passions could the masses be moved to any action whatsoever. He had overestimated their intelligence early in his career, losing the leadership to Gandhi for this error.

---

[1]Needless to say, though they were characterized by a rare degree of energy all three made a good number of ridiculous mistakes (e.g., Napoleon's conduct in the Russian campaign).

The Muslims politicians who mattered were rallied behind him chiefly through rhetorical and paper politics, which later graded into exploitation of mass passions.[1]

By rejecting Gandhi's Quit India campaign, Jinnah got Gandhi to want to hold talks with him. This was the second political victory, and on Gandhi's own ground. Gandhi, with his usual hypocrisy, maintained that he spoke only for himself, but at the same time affected the tone of one who spoke for the Congress Party and its constituents. It was this kind of double talk with which he had revolutionized the exploitation of the media, his greatest contribution to politics.

For the first time he found himself outwitted at his own game, for Jinnah was able to put his cause forward in the view of the whole world through Gandhi, a media celebrity. The meeting put the stamp of official Congress recognition of the singular consequence of Jinnah to Indian politics, although by this time, Congress leadership was not in Gandhi's hands.[2] On this occasion, Jinnah deflated his rival's importance by insisting on the truth of the false position Gandhi had taken of not representing anyone, and by utterly refusing to budge from the rigid demand that the Muslims being a separate people should have a separate nation. By this time it was clear that independence was imminent, but by a stroke of pure media exploitation Jinnah had made in what manner and shape it was to take place seem to depend entirely upon him.[3]

I go into details because the facts are little known in the West. Jinnah is glorified in Pakistan as the father of the nation and vilified as an egotistical opportunist and British tool in India, and in the West as well, where Gandhi is looked upon as a saint. Jinnah simply used the British as he used the Muslims and the Congress after his experience that virtuous motives had failed to produce any results.

The Muslims would respond to Islamic slogans, and he felt that he could count upon the Congress Party to be shortsighted and blindly

---

[1]It was not in the interests of the Muslim politicians of the four provinces that mattered (Punjab, Bengal, Sind, N.W.F.P.) to support Jinnah, and they did not until forced by internecine rivalries, and later, by the changing passions of the Muslim masses.

[2]He had never held any office in the party, but his power had been the greater for this clever decision.

[3]Tolstoy saw Napoleon as a puppet who thought he controlled the destiny of Europe when he was only playing the minor role of the *apparent* agent who was the cause of the wars. It may similarly be said that Jinnah was only ostensibly the cause of partition. But the Napoleonic wars would not have taken place without Napoleon, and neither would the subcontinent have been divided were it not for Jinnah.

ignorant of its long-term interests. The British were only too happy to find Muslims resisting Congress policies as this slowed the independence movement, especially during the delicate years of World War II. Jinnah knew that he could become the pivotal force in Indian politics by exploiting the situation. The British did not want a separate Muslim state. They were in fact set dead against it.

Pure opportunism runs through Alexander, Caesar, Napoleon, and Jinnah, and in this respect they were commonplace men. None of them had any interest save personal glory.[1] Everything else only mattered insofar as it could be used to advance it. Virtue they had a modicum of, if you compare them to a man like Lincoln, but it was yet more than what most of their contemporaries possessed.[2] I have but to think of the reforms that Caesar and Napoleon introduced, and I must admit that they succeeded in doing their nations some good.

They had the talent and the good fortune to outwit very clever and intelligent enemies, otherwise we would never have heard of them. But the difference between them and commonplace tyrants lies in what gave them the greatest pleasure. They had their own petty pleasures as much as the next man does, but true happiness for them lay only in acquiring, not in the acquisition, for they did not believe in anything but themselves.[3] They sought in the main neither a greater portion of the common pleasures available to the more powerful men in their respective societies (though they would not deny some when offered) nor the reaching of some abstract ideal.

They had not the talent to keep what they had won. Napoleon is the proof of this. If there was no action of glory or great difficulty to perform, there was no pleasure in power.[4] Any long-term planning was

---

[1]For Jinnah personal glory was only to be won by rising to the role of the initiator and leader of an independent, parliamentary government dedicated to advancement of general interests of a people at the cost of superstitious, sectarian, provincial, etc., interests. He had little respect for the masses, his greatest fear was of anarchy and mob rule. He felt himself to be capable of higher ends than any other man of his age.

[2]Cicero was a better man, morally speaking, than Caesar, and Nehru than Jinnah, but they were also lesser men, driven by more tepid passions.

[3]So that there is no resemblance between any of them and Genghis Khan, Timur, or Hitler, who desired only to repay their people's strict obedience to their every wish with loot to keep them happy: theirs were organized crimes on a grandiose scale. There was nothing of the sublime in their souls: even their acts of cruelty were mean and petty, not acts of passion.

[4]Against all reasons, Napoleon was convinced a few years after Tilsit that Russia meant

hateful to them when it did not mean a continuous series of action. It was perhaps fortunate for Alexander, Caesar and Jinnah that they died at the heights of their careers.

Augustus, Richelieu, Akbar, Tokugawa, Kublai Khan, Maria Theresa, Frederick, Catherine, Lincoln, and Bismarck had abilities Alexander, Caesar, Napoleon, and Jinnah lacked. Bloodshed is part of everyday life until a society has become stable, and even then the state must be defended. The violent crimes of Augustus and Richelieu, even Bismarck, had their compensating point. Without strong states, there are savage contests and rather aimless violence between strongly motivated small nations. On the other hand, it is doubtful whether the ordinary Italian, Frenchman, German, and Indian was any the happier for the strongarmed methods of Augustus, Richelieu, Bismarck, and Akbar. On the other hand, they made possible the idea of nationhood that has been of advantage to some of these nations.

Unfortunately, the state that is united under absolute monarchy (or its equivalent) reduces its citizens to the role of slaves fawning over their affected rulers. In this respect, Lincoln was fortunate to have found himself in the role of the defender of a united republic, since his political genius was therefore at the service of his country.

It was their perpetual desire for action that gives Alexander, Caesar, Napoleon and Jinnah away as types. This restlessness was accompanied by a proud assumption of their obvious and complete superiority to the common run of men. They could only employ their great intelligence and imaginations to outwit their enemies, and to find new grounds upon which to fight them.[1] Their abilities failed them in all else, especially in their judgments concerning those close to them. Their vanity never tolerated independence of thought or action in their followers or rivals.

From the point of view of world history, their goals seem pure luxuries, for looked at in that manner they were nothing more than admirable expressions of great energy. The motives a leader gives his

---

to attack him. The spineless Alexander I was under pressure from his nobles, but he was not capable of any courageous action. Instead of patiently waiting (there was no immediate danger) Napoleon, who perhaps imagined and perhaps deliberately exaggerated the threat England posed for the Empire, insisted upon the necessity of immediate action. See the memoirs of Caulincourt, Napoleon's emissary to Russia during the important years from Tilsit to the invasion.

[1]The usual adventurer has not the acumen to be successful, even if fortune favors him: Richard the Lion-Hearted, a fool, or Charles XII.

followers are advancement of their interests, and safeguards from dangers. To accomplish great changes he usually has to call upon great collective motives, ideas of patriotism, religious causes, moral ideas, the lure of increased wealth, etc., and counter these with images of anarchy, terror, loss of property and official retribution. They have to portray themselves as necessary agents. In doing so, they naturally exaggerate, in the manner of artists and petty lovers, but more than most leaders, Alexander *et al.* were luxuries which the world can seldom afford.

Alexander led the Greeks, after his father had been assassinated, to a series of conquest in the known East, until his troops forced him to stop by refusing to cross the Indus.

Caesar's birth gave him great advantages, and he fully exploited every one of them. Before he received the command of the legions in Gaul, he had used every device, no matter how dishonest, to increase his influence and power in the republican politics of Rome. His many conquests, especially the glamorous exploits against the Gauls, could be looked upon, as indeed they were, the glorious triumphs of Rome, though they did not require a great deal of military genius. But when he crossed the Rubicon, it was clear that only Caesar mattered. The old oligarchy he wished to replace with dictatorship. Caesar merely made his personal glory be, for all practical purposes, the glory of Rome.

Napoleon was fortunate throughout his early career. He was especially fortunate in being able to use the rhetoric of the Revolution for his own advancement. This, plus the need for defending France, gave him further opportunities to display his greatness as general, opportunist, showman, and, most important of all, as *symbol*. And unlike Caesar's, Napoleon's early victories were against nations and armies equally advanced in military knowledge.

Napoleon made it possible for France to be glorious. But France, unlike Rome, had no tradition of glory. Their Henrys and the Louises had never sought to appeal at any level above that of affected petty vanity, and though the Revolution had given birth to a new spirit among many Frenchmen, it was this Italian soul who added to it the aura of immortal glory.

By the beginning of the twentieth century, the engines and form of warfare had become such that it is impossible for a Caesar or a Napoleon to appear again. Besides, the love of glory through military triumphs is looked down upon in rich democracies.

When this much cannot be understood, Jinnah must remain an utter mystery. The author of an excellent recent book[1] would have it that Jinnah, who had initially made his name in Indian politics as the "Ambassador of Hindu-Muslim Unity," never deflected from this aim, and that the so-called Two-Nation theory[2] was a bargaining tool whose effect backfired when popular sentiment became so passionate that it tied Jinnah's hands. Jinnah may have been a little foolish at the end of his career when he thought that something good could come from uniting the least civilized parts of the subcontinent, but he was too experienced a politician not to have seen from the beginning of his support of the Two-Nation Theory that it would pose a credible threat only if it gained the unanimous support of the Muslim masses, and that then it would not be possible to ignore it. For Jinnah, a man without religion, his last entry into Indian politics as the leader of the Muslim League which called for a separate Muslim state must have been a pure gamble, something he got into without worrying too deeply about where his actions would take him and the subcontinent.

The reason why the works of almost all commentators of and on the period cannot begin to describe the historical feat of Jinnah is that there is no logical connection between his apparent opinions at different points of his career, and because there seem to have been no specifics in his demand for Pakistan that truly give away his motives.

Helvétius said that in different types of governments and situations, different paths to glory seem open to men. For a man of Jinnah's genius and background, absolute integrity and respect for law were the basis for all political actions.

Parliamentary democracy and the making of political changes by constitutional means force a rational and coldly logical temper upon political actions.[3] This temper Jinnah, in a greater degree than any other world leader in history I know of, possessed. But in having it, he outdistanced his own people even more than Alexander, Caesar, and Napoleon did theirs.

---

[1] Miss Ayesha Jalal, *The Sole Spokesman.*

[2] According to which the Hindus and the Muslims made up two distinct nations in the subcontinent, and which ignored the followers of other religions altogether.

[3] Men are ruled solely by their passions. You cannot have a true and working democracy until the citizens of a nation as a whole are *relatively* cold and prudent men and women.

Military glory is a passion everyone understands, irrespective of his personal opinion about wars. But the highest glory possible in constitutional democracies needs a more delicately tuned imagination to understand it, and remains general glory no longer. Compare the direction in which Jinnah wanted to take the subcontinent in 1916 to that which Gandhi, Nehru, and Patel took. Was it Jinnah who was the narrow minded megalomaniac? Or was he merely impractical about peace between ignorant men, as he was about nation-building in his last years? Like Alexander, Caesar, and Napoleon, he went too far at the end, and did some foolish things, but as was the case with Napoleon's tyrannical and blind side, Jinnah's blind and unreasoning side was, I suggest, the result of a noble mind brought low by the sense that the undying enmity of inferior men was occupying itself with means of destroying him and his goals.

I doubt that Jinnah could have been a greater phenomenon had he been born in a Western democracy. Politics can never be an entirely rational affair since it consists merely of the conflicts and compromises of conflicting interests. The rarified sphere in which Jinnah liked to work simply does not exist for less brilliant men and women. When he saw this, he played upon passions he despised.

A man who holds the most dispassionate and rational opinions is always willing to compromise judiciously for something in return in order to go on, since he holds amicable survival of all to be the highest good. But such a man who also desires for himself a leading role in his people's politics is bound to please no party, since he is thought a partisan of none. This is precisely the position Jinnah drove himself to, but since his ruling passion was the desire for glory, he proceeded to exploit whatever interests and desires he was in a position to.

His representative importance is great. He is the proof that the type of virtue that parliamentary and liberal democracies most exalt is the very thing that will be most condemned and feared, and least understood. He has won little glory based on his true merits in a land where politics is wholly determined by birth and connections, where no one is forced to look above immediate personal gains. I doubt he would have had more where the opinions one professes to hold sometimes count almost as much as birth and connections.

Chapter XVIII

Of the Representation of the Passions in the Arts

I have increasingly come to feel, the more so in recent months (I write this on January 12, 1990), that if faithful reproduction of the passions is taken as either the criterion or goal of the arts, then a great deal of injustice has been done to the human heart. The passions of Hector, Aeneas, Camilla, Swann, and Natasha are *painted* passions.

In neither Tolstoy nor Homer, Balzac, Dostoevski, Molière, Ariosto, Guido Reni, Rembrandt, Verdi, Jean Renoir, etc., was there an excessive concern for exactness of description. Certain ideal effects are desired, and the artist focuses upon how to produce them.

The disadvantage of depicting things as they are is that a work of art as a result tends to lose in terms of its *effective rhetorical power* (if you ignore for the moment the question whether the capacity to see the truth existed in the first place in the artist).

What a man wants from a story, picture, song, etc., is a pleasing effect on his soul. Little importance is given to the exactness of the representation, since few men and women attempt to see either the world or themselves with such over-exactness. There is pleasure so long as the artist's ignorance or hypocrisy apparently matches theirs.

Perhaps the only occasions when depicting the passions exactly and as they are becomes pardonable is in the case of the strongest passions. What is then lost in terms of the effect on the senses will be gained by the advantage of letting the audience compare these passions with those they themselves have known, and only thereby being able to feel them. Certain passions are then not disbarred from expressive art. But you run the risk of being understood by none. But where would the world be if he or she who would move others by painting the truth were to be generally understood? It certainly would not be such an *efficient* place.

Chapter XIX

Of the Dramatic

Aside from rage, envy, joy, desire for revenge, hatred, love, suspicion, modesty, and some shades of pride, fear, hope, etc., I include the following among dramatic passions:

1) The desire to be respected, esteemed, or feared.
2) Fear of others and the desire to please.
3) The desire to be thought worth pleasing.
4) The desire to comfort another, or to increase the grief of another.
5) The desire to exploit another, or to be of use to him.
6) The desire to inspire gratitude and friendship, or to inspire hatred.
7) The desire to repay past kindnesses.
8) The desire to be envied.
9) The desire to delude, or to confess.
10) Curiosity regarding the true motives and actions of another.

Etc.

The term *expressive power* when speaking of dramatic works[1] is nothing more than a work's dramatic effect, its ability to make a man feel one or more such passions as if they were springing up in his own heart in actively involved responses to events and circumstances in his own life. The dramatic illusion is perfect at those irregular moments when this expressive power overcomes the inclination to disbelieve or feel ideal passions.

In dramatic works, besides the purely dramatic effects there are ideal effects that occur in the following order:
1) You must for the time being allow yourself to derive pleasure from a work of art. Coleridge called this phenomenon the "suspension of disbelief."
2) Something must have convinced you of the nobility of the passions, scenes, etc., being described, or of a few of the characters in the work, or at least of their being admirable in certain respects. There are a thousand reasons why admiration is or is not born. Perhaps you dislike all Venetians, perhaps you cannot resist a spirited young lady who is fashionably dressed. You may like a sensitive, inquiring man. The artist

---

[1] I do not mean plays.

may have convinced you of the nobility of a character by stating it explicitly, or by the nature of the actions or words he or she assigns the character, etc. This conviction regarding the nobility of a few characters adds a poetic tone to the dramatic representations of passions. The effect of music is naturally ideal, since it recalls to mind agreeable ideas, people, places, situations, etc.

3) The dramatic situation and action must be such that the nobility that was seen in the character(s) is brought out, heightened thereby, and shown in clear relief.[1]

If any one of the three is missing, the process stops, and there is no great pleasure from the ideal aspect of the work. It is this aspect that initially has the effect of beauty. Mozart, for example, whose non-operatic oeuvre is naturally ideal in nature as all non-vocal music necessarily is, has little of this ideal or poetic overlay of effect in his operas, and it is the sense impact of the accompaniment which produces the ideal pleasure. Shakespeare and Madhubala produce it by idealizing towards perfection a few of the characters.

Most plays rarely survive many centuries because they rely completely upon ideal or poetic effects (which include the pleasures of curiosity, i.e. love of suspense), and the nature of theatrical drama is such that all save commonplace ideal passions are very difficult to express in it.[2] The Greek and French playwrights are still read because they used poetic language as effectively as other famous poets. Verdi keeps up a skipping pace in order to keep his audience interested in that dull opera *Il Trovatore*.[3] Rossini's humor keeps him alive. How long the works of Ibsen, Chekhov, Shaw, Strindberg, Pirandello, Brecht, O'Neill, Williams, etc., will survive is still uncertain, but, unless kept alive by solemn pedants, they are likely to pass out of favor in another century or two, so long as a new fashionable batch replaces them—as they replaced the British and Italian playwrights of preceding centuries.

---

[1]Nikolai Rostov's suddenly kissing his father's hand in shame moments after having asked him in the coldest and rudest manner to pay off his enormous debt to Dolokhov—*War and Peace*, Bk. II, Pt. One, Chpt. 16. An example of this process when only ideal effects are produced, no dramatic ones, contrary to popular opinion.

[2]As opposed to that of novels, paintings, films, and operas, in the latter two of which it is easier for the artist to embellish the skeleton of actions with touches of rare ideal pleasures without clogging the narrative pace displeasingly.

[3]For the sake of example I choose this Verdi opera here, instead of some others which show his genius better. *La Traviata* and *Otello* are ideal works of genius, but poetic not dramatic ones.

The more lively your imagination, the more likely you are to be deeply moved by depictions of passion, sometimes even when you know that there is more exaggeration and triteness than truth in the depiction. Cold natures are less likely to think anyone worth their esteem who does not have the power to affect their future happiness.

I know people who find Iago more interesting than Othello. They are not moved to tears by the most powerful play ever written. Since they cannot feel the passions that Othello and Desdemona felt, they enjoy the grim and sour humor of Iago,[1] or else divert themselves with vague discussions on evil and grace.

A strong dramatic situation will always inspire sympathy in generous-minded audiences, so long as they do not feel manipulated, which would be too insulting. A beautiful woman in distress, for example, will always produce an ideal effect.[2]

The more strongly convinced you are of the nobility of the character, the more will the effect of the dramatic situation be felt as pleasing, beautiful, ideal.

The woman in the commonplace melodrama concocted by a hack will not move some men and women as much as Anna Karenina does; and depending upon one's sensibility, Anna's fate will be more or less moving than Cordelia's or Desdemona's.

Dramatic effect can only to a certain degree be said to be contained in a work; like all pleasures, it is a matter of the imagination, of feeling something to be pleasing. Paintings, sculpture, and related art forms have less ability to inspire dramatic effects than literature, music, or the cinema.

All dramatic art lies on the outer edge of the province of ideal art, since unlike that of pure (i.e., poetic) ideal art, the sensation of the dramatic entails that you feel what the characters are feeling in active encounters with each other. Men and women are much less inclined to fall into the folly of considering someone in front of them sublimely noble; there is much greater resistance from vanity here. Simple

---

[1]Because they do not even feel what he does, falling short thereby of what Shakespeare's works demand of his readers and audiences.

[2]See the dictum of that vulgar genius Poe. There are others today who will develop a livelier interest in an ugly old woman who is overworked by an oppressive and uncaring employer. A wholly vulgar character may arouse our sympathy because of his or her situation, such as, for example, Lolita; Nabokov did not want to inspire easy pity where the one who pities does not feel great pain.

admiration may come easily enough, but envy is more likely to arise than deep admiration.

Simple admiration implies that the admirer does not consider the attainments of the admired one absolutely necessary to his or her own happiness; or, he feels that they have already been attained by himself, and then he admires another who is like himself and not superior. Envy or jealousy must not come in at this point.

A man admires a successful young woman for her beauty as well as for her talent; but he will envy and hate her if she succeeds to an executive position he has coveted for the last five years, and upon which he had set all his happiness. From the moment that he even suspects her as a rival, the sight of her always strikes him as painful, and he has bitter words to say to himself, and if he is careless, even to others, about her beauty and reputation as a woman of talent.

Chapter XX

Shakespeare, Mozart, and Madhubala

In her best performances,—in *Mr. and Mrs. 55*, *Ek Saal* ("One Year"), *Phagun*, *Mehlon ke Khwab* ("Dreams of Palaces"), *Raj Hath* ("The King's Stubborness"), *Nirala* ("Unique"), *Boyfriend*, *Half-Ticket*, *Barsaat ki Raat* ("A Night of Spring Rain"), *Howrah Bridge*, *Gateway of India*, etc.— Madhubala was working with scenarios that were commonplace enough. You can edit out of her films (as you can out of those of Nargis, Hepburn, Arthur, Miss Bina Rai, Meena Shorey, Gable, Grable) all scenes in which she does not appear, and not lose anything of great worth.

Even in a film such as *Chalte ka Naam Gaadi* ("That Which Runs is a Car"), where her role is limited, the expressive power of all the scenes in which she does not appear arises from their association with her, comic genius though they possess. The other characters and the situations become dramatically effective to the degree that they occupy the thoughts of the character she plays.[1] This transmitting of sensations by

---

[1]Needless to say, when the script was very mediocre, even she can do little to enliven scenes.

conduction is an effect found only in the films of the very greatest actresses and actors.

She had an unrivalled genius for expressive power, she could express the most powerful as well as the most delicately fleeting moods in her acting, the most elusive dramatic passion in its purity; the *expression* was forceful and pure. It did not matter what she was expressing, the effect was usually light and graceful if seen as an example of ideal art. When this kind of expressive power is united with the talent to seize dramatic opportunities, you have the art of Madhubala and Shakespeare.

Truth in matters of plot, development, characterization, the movements of the soul, these were matters of little consequence to her. What mattered was that the dramatic passions possible in the scenes and situations be expressed exactly, and that she made good use of the most intense dramatic passions the story offered her the opportunity of as a whole.

It was when she was most *directed* and controlled by scenarios and directors—as she was in *Mahal* ("Palace"), *Amar* ("Noble"), or *Mughal-e-Azam* ("The Great Mughal")—that she gave her least successful performances.

Shakespeare did with words what she did by the actress' art. His best dramas were always built upon the most improbable situations and developments conceivable, and the characters were conceived, developed, moved about, and transformed with sovereign contempt for plausibility and truth (so long as the expressive power could be maintained).

Those great plays, *Two Gentlemen of Verona*, *The Taming of the Shrew*, *Much Ado about Nothing*, *Romeo and Juliet*, *As You Like It*, *Twelfth Night*, *Henry IV, pt. 1*, *Antony and Cleopatra*, *Othello*, *King Lear*, *Cymbeline*, *The Winter's Tale*, and *Macbeth* are entirely implausible so far as the stories go, but lose by this fact no advantage that goes with being true to nature.

The man of great courage, honor, and generosity who has killed his wife out of gullible folly and unbearable jealousy, and in a manner which shows a noble pride more than love (*pace* his own opinion of himself), moves me deeply when he kills himself out of grief and remorse only because I am made to feel *fully and precisely* what he feels at the sight of the corpse of Desdemona lying in front of him and what he feels in relation to the officers of the law who have put him under arrest.[1]

---

[1] I use the first person here for the sake of convenience and brevity only.

Shakespeare wanted the most extreme dramatic contrasts. Without his genius for the expression of dramatic passions, *Othello*, along with *King Lear* the play in which the most intense dramatic passions are expressed, would have been nothing but a brisk and amusing melodrama, a Spanish play, something by Calderón.

Madhubala does much the same thing, but in a different manner according to the nature of her medium: the sequence of passions felt by her characters, the manner in which she shows us these, and the startling mannerisms that surprise the viewer produce the dramatic effect. These are matters of mediums. In Mozart, the emphasis is on the expressive power of the melody of his songs, and on the use of sudden changes in dramatic situations.

In Shakespeare, people seem to speak better than anyone in life could, and Madhubala shows in her characters more variety, energy, and wit than can be *seen* in anyone in life; but the aim of art is to idealize, and they express the stronger dramatic passions only, the dramatic passions of those in whom experience or an ardent soul has supplied the heart with numerous ideas

The only writers who can compare in the expression of the highest reaches of vanity with Shakespeare: Dante, Cervantes, Fielding, Stendhal (of the 1826 *Rome, Naples, et Florence*), Nietzsche.[1] Take the following lines from the *Inferno*:

> Quivi sospiri, pianti e alti guai
> risonavan per l'aere sanza stelle,
> per ch'io al cominciar ne lagrimai.
> Diverse lingue, orribli favelle,
> parole di dolore, accenti d'ira,
> voci alte e fioche, e suon di man con elle
> facevano un tumulto, il qual s'aggira
> sempre in quell'aura sanza tempo tinta,
> come la rena quando turbo spira.
> E io ch'avea d'error la testa cinta,

---

[1]Austen, like Shakespeare, expresses lively feelings felt in the course of actual life. Neither discovered new beauties, and in this they were unlike Dante, Cervantes, and Fielding, who show us pleasures not to be found anywhere outside their works. These pleasures, capable of being produced only by works of ideal art and not seen in life may be found in slightly varied forms in other artists only.

dissi: "Maestro, che e quel ch'i' odo?
e che gent' e che par nel duol si vinta?"

(Canto III)[1]

This is an effective description of the horror and darkness of the scene, as felt by the pilgrim Dante. In the passage from *Macbeth* below, Rosse is telling Malcolm and Macduff about the miserable state of Scotland under the tyranny of Macbeth:

> Alas, poor country,
> Almost afraid to know itself! It cannot
> Be call'd our mother, but our grave, where nothing
> But who knows nothing, is once seen to smile;
> Where sighs, and groans, and shrieks that rent the air
> Are made, not mark'd; where violent sorrow seems
> A modern ecstasy. The dead man's knell
> Is there scarce ask'd for who, and good men's lives
> Expire before the flowers in their caps,
> Dying or ere they sicken.

Dante's lines produce the illusion of darkness, terror and solemn grandeur as imagined by a reader alone with the book in his hand or with the words in his memory. In Shakespeare, such an effect is not so strongly produced; instead there is the dramatic sensation: Rosse's words make me feel what he is feeling, i.e., *both* the speaker's passions with regard to his listeners as well as the effects of the terrible scenes he has witnessed on his soul. The genius (i.e., power of expression) of Dante is as great as that of Shakespeare, only the class of sensation is entirely different.

I am trying to be as dry and exact as possible here, but the subject is a very difficult one, and perhaps I have not the talent to overcome the difficulties I face.

---

[1]"Here sighs, laments, and loud wailings were resounding through the starless air, so that at first they made me weep. Strange tongues, horrible outcries, utterances of woe, accents of anger, voices shrill and faint, and the beating of hands among them, were making a tumult that swirls unceasingly in that dark and timeless air, like sand when a whirlwind blows. And I, my head circled with error, said, 'Master, what is this I hear? And what people are these who seem so overcome by pain?'"

Mr. Singleton's translation

There is nothing of what is called *good writing* or *good acting* (i.e., beauty of style) in the dramatic works of Shakespeare and Madhubala, respectively. What is thought to be so (in the case of Shakespeare, anyway, since concerning Madhubala's genius there is almost absolute ignorance) is, if I may speak here with more regard to truth than to the customs of politeness, the product of a man's or woman's ignorance of the nature of dramatic art. In Mozart's two dramatic operas, his accompaniments (not the songs) do possess great stylistic genius, and his ideal effects arise from them.

The genius of other artists enables them to express perhaps one or two ideal (i.e., idealized) passions faithfully, and it is in the matching of those one or two passions with some of those which their audiences consider to be pleasing that their successes and failures lie. It often takes a century or more for the audiences to catch up with an artist, sometimes they never catch up.

The genius of Shakespeare and Madhubala lay in the expression of many of the stronger sensations that more than usually intelligent and sensitive men and women often feel in the midst of actions involving others. The terrors and joys they feel without anatomizing them are inspired by the works of these masters—such passions as laughter, malice, love, anger, pride, resentment, gratitude, remorse, suspicion, fear, curiosity (regarding others), boredom, weariness, ambition, hatred, affectation, etc., etc.[1]

The expression usually does not define or describe the sensation being expressed. I can give innumerable examples from Madhubala, but it will be easier (i.e., for the reader) to give one from Shakespeare. The entire play bearing the Moor's name for its title was, it seems to me, designed by Shakespeare to express all the possible dramatic sensations that a man of Othello's character can feel when he is in love. All the other characters and their dramatic sensations are needed, in as much as

---

[1]Only pedantry will lead one to make the claim that this is all they do. Madhubala must follow the conventions of the Indian cinema of the fifties and early sixties; Shakespeare has occasionally to describe or explain details in order to fill in the story, scenic background, etc.

In any case, it would not be possible to follow every nuance of emotion that is expressed during one of their works. It is only now and then that it is actually possible to feel the full effect of one of their great works. You cannot change from one emotion to another (often opposite) emotion at the drop of a hat. Mozart spoils passages of *Figaro*'s fourth act by ignoring this fact.

they provide the narrative situations and changes, to attain this primary aim. Othello's character is that of a physically very brave and morally very honest man incapable of even slightly involved thought, and so of one who can only see things in the simplest manner, in blacks and whites, so to speak, and who can only *act* in relation to the circumstances he finds himself in. Now, to proceed to a specific example. When (in Act I, Scene ii) he says to both his own men and Brabantio's, "Keep up your bright swords, for the dew will rust them," the dramatic expression is of the sensation of such a simple and honest man of action whose instinct of the moment is to fight and kill the men he sees before him, but who is restraining himself, not out of prudence or respect for the law, but because of the image and thought of Desdemona. But the literal meaning (in context of the literal meaning of the earlier lines he speaks in this scene) of this line that Shakespeare has him utter has nothing to do with this dramatic sensation; further, Othello's character is such that the making of a poetic conceit regarding dew rusting the sword should be alien and even unintelligible to it—he could neither have imagined nor understood such a conceit. Shakespeare here, as usual, sacrifices meaning and plausibility to expression. The mind merely has to imagine a man speaking to others (the background and circumstances are in themselves inconsequential in this regard) in these words; that is to say, the sequence of the contents (not meaning) of the *verbal thoughts*, when combined with the simple idea of a man attempting to express his thoughts to the world around him and its inhabitants, produces an exactly dramatic sensation. It follows then, that the apparent and literal meaning of the lines he says can at best have a merely indirect relation to the dramatic sensation being expressed.[1]

---

[1]So, in *Twelfth Night* Shakespeare expressed the dramatic sensations possible in a man not altogether lacking in a capacity to dream of happy love a little, but incapable of real sorrow on account of it: Malvolio's. The dramatic sensations vis-à-vis his beloved, acquaintances, and himself (i.e., the sensations that form the act of addressing thoughts to yourself in words) consequent to slight but reveries-accompanied crystallization (which sensations are dramatic even though they include the element of a little crystallization, for a little crystallization does not violently withdraw the soul from the real world) are expressed by Shakespeare through Malvolio's words. But the apparent meaning of the words that would express them so that audiences which have equally mastered both the motions of the soul and the expressive capacities of language will feel those dramatic sensations arising in themselves is such that any man who utters them must seem a pompous fool; and, therefore, to make for the *appearance* of plausibility, must be shown as such. But there are not sufficient number of different dramatic sensations possible in such a man in relation to

One or more of the characters in the best plays seems noble to the audience who cannot understand dramatic expression (Duncan, for example, in *Macbeth*, or Cordelia in *King Lear*), and thus the ideal pleasures. Each of Madhubala's greatest characters expresses a wide range of passions, so that in, say, her characterization of Banani in *Phagun*, there are as many nuances (though fewer different passions) as in the whole of *Antony and Cleopatra*. Sympathy, in the case of the films of Madhubala, can only go to the character she is playing: you need not choose between an Othello and an Iago. Her expression of what Anita herself feels in *Mr. and Mrs. 55* covers the entire range of passions from

---

love to supply a five act play of the length that Shakespeare and his contemporaries were used to, and, besides, a play of the Jonson or Molière type would, by its concentration on apparent ridiculing, make the dramatic expression weaker, or at least more difficult to fall under the spell of. The apparently foolish character (Malvolio) must then be pushed into a subplot of a play whose main plot would also, to prevent it from spoiling the dramatic effects, have to be about love. The dramatic expressions of the other characters are those of petty vanity, but if read or heard as ideal art, they would seem to be about idealized light crystallization. Shakespeare must have thought it fortunate that he could play with apparently Petrarchan ideas (and satirical parodies of them), which would further please his Elizabethan audience and ensure the play's success, and which, as it turned out (for we see the proof in the play as it stands) could be phrased so that they would express the dramatic responses of petty affectation and petty vanity to some circumstances possible in love with dramatic exactness.

In *As You Like It, Antony and Cleopatra*, and *Cymbeline*, the apparent meaning of the words that would express the class of dramatic sensations he wished to express were such that Shakespeare had to give these words to women (Rosalind, Cleopatra, Imogen) though the sensations are distinctly masculine ones. (This picture of Shakespeare will seem unlikely but it must be remembered that no man is free not to do what gives him pleasure, and since Shakespeare felt pleasure in expression, he would naturally adapt his wishes to what would make for practical success, without which he would not have the opportunity (or time) to indulge in this pleasure.)

An art of this nature will naturally produce works whose profusion of verbal invention will seem bewilderingly extensive, patterned (because each work describes a certain single class of dramatic passion in its various nuances many words will be repeated, forming patterns of literal meanings that are of no importance to the expression, though they often do hint at the class involved), and difficult to reduce to simple literal meaning for each play. Such an art will also naturally impress and delight pedants for it answers to their needs perfectly; the pedant and the general reader alike is free to see in the works nearly anything he or she wishes. (Madhubala's and Mozart's respective arts not being verbal, they are that much less susceptible to such treatment, though even here Mozart's is more than Madhubala's.)

What not only pedants but all other readers will say in good conscience of this chapter may easily be anticipated. I repeat what I have said earlier in this essay: I seek no converts, no followers, for pleasures cannot be taught. If you did not already understand (in this case) Shakespeare before reading this chapter, you really cannot upon doing so, *even if you desired very much, if only out of curiosity, to understand him as he is described here.*

admiration, jealousy, painful moral contempt for someone once deeply admired with innocent and complete faith, pity, to renewed and increased admiration and love that Othello feels. There are no feminine equivalents in the film of Iago's passions, for a good reason, but there are for all the passions that his words and actions inspire in Othello, except the desire to kill, for pride in an extremely simple and honest soul operates in a different manner in the two sexes.

The difference between Shakespeare and Madhubala is not due merely to their different mediums. The souls of men and women are different, and the manner in which they feel, think, act, produce art, and derive pleasure from to it is bound to be different.

Neither Madhubala, Shakespeare, nor Mozart gives us passions as they in fact arise, increase, and die in the heart. If one is at all points expressing dramatic passions, one cannot simultaneously afford to be interested in factual causes.

The audience must have *some* knowledge of the dramatic passion being expressed, enough to recognize its specific nature. The direct effects of the situations in which the characters are involved is the easiest to come under. These, along with the seeming beauty of their styles, form the common pleasures that most men and women derive from their works.

Most characters of Shakespeare, Mozart, and Madhubala are considered *pleasing* by audiences, without regard to their moral or passionate nature. This is a purely a matter of opinion, and the result of the charm that the most admirable characters cast upon the rest, and of the wit of the rogues and villains, when the works are enjoyed ideally instead of dramatically.

Cosi fan tutte, the operas seria of Mozart, *Love's Labour Lost*, *A Midsummer Night's Dream*, *The Merchant of Venice*, *All's Well that Ends Well*, *Julius Caesar*, *The Tempest*, all of the English history plays (excepting only the character of Falstaff in the first part of *Henry IV*), *Badal* ("Cloud"), *Noble*, *Kala Pani* ("Life Sentence"), *Jaali Note* ("Counterfeit Bill"), *The Great Mughal*, *Insaan Jaag Utha* ("The Human Awakened (Aroused)"), and many others are non-dramatic ideal works, and of a more commonplace stamp than the dramatic works.

Shakespeare and Madhubala are identical in every respect, as are Nietzsche and Miss Bina Rai, Austen and Helvétius, Correggio and Arthur, Cimarosa and Meena Shorey, Fielding and Grable, and Stendhal and Hepburn: the exact same type of genius and moral makeup as found in the two sexes. This fact tells us something about the differences between men and women—see chapters XXXVII-XXXIX and LII below.

Taking into account these differences, there are exact correspondences between the works of Shakespeare and Madhubala (which cannot be discovered between those of either and Mozart's) in terms of the chief dramatic passions expressed.[1]

Romeo and Juliet — Unique
As You Like It — Dreams of Palaces
Twelfth Night — A Night of Spring Rain
Much Ado About Nothing — The King's Stubbornness
Othello — Mr. and Mrs. 55
King Lear — One Year
Pericles — Phagun
Cymbeline — Half-Ticket
King Henry IV, Part One — Howrah Bridge
Macbeth — Passport[2]
The Winter's Tale — Boyfriend
Antony and Cleopatra — Gateway of India[3]

So far as the contrast between Shakespeare and Madhubala is concerned, what appears to me to be the most important fact I suspect will make even the few who have been willing to put up with the ideas of this essay throw it aside in astonished contempt. For it seems to me

---

[1]I translate the Hindi titles of Madhubala's films into English except in the one case where it is eponymic—some of the titles are already in English.

[2]By about 1960, when she was in her late twenties, the organic disease of the heart she suffered from had advanced to the degree that Madhubala was rendered an invalid. *Passport*, like *Half-Ticket* seems to have been unfinished when this happened, for there are occasional snippets of scenes from earlier films inserted into both these films at points where the storyline demanded her presence—as well, there is an obvious stand-in actress who is always shown from the back, etc.

[3]I state facts, but in order to do so without causing excessive boredom in the reader or myself, I eliminate many interconnecting details. The reader ought to fill in these himself. *Mr. and Mrs. 55* and *Othello* will seem to have nothing in common if you do not know the dramatic passions expressed in either or both. The cause of the remaining differences is the different nature of the two sexes. Similarly, both *Passport* and *Macbeth* express the entire range of dramatic passions relating to danger and fear in a brave woman and man (as opposed to those in a weak woman or man, the entire range of which (and not merely the fear of criminals or of abandonment by a lover) is expressed in *Gateway of India* and by the lines of Cleopatra in *Antony and Cleopatra*).

that with only a few exceptions Shakespeare never portrayed any feminine dramatic sensation with any degree of truth to nature, and neither did Mozart. You only have to compare the dramatic passions inspired by the language or songs of their women to what Madhubala expresses to see the difference between the dramatic passion a woman actually feels and the manner in which she feels it and those that Shakespeare and Mozart attribute to them. Shakespeare, it is true, at least managed to express the element of purity as conceived by a woman in his most successful women, Juliet, Desdemona, Cordelia, Imogen, and Hermione.

For the rest, to my sorrow, taking aside the obvious references to narrative circumstances, it has always seemed to me that if a man were speaking the lines of Rosalind, Viola, Cleopatra, Beatrice, Goneril, Lady Macbeth, nothing will change so far as the dramatic passion that is being expressed. On the other hand, Olivia and Hero express ideal art sensations, like the women of Mozart, even Susanna and the Countess. So far as what is similar in men and women, Shakespeare and, less often, Mozart, express dramatic passions true to nature in their women, which is why the Countess' terror[1] at being discovered is to a great degree true to nature.[2] But all the dramatic passions that are specifically feminine, arising from their different manner of loving, and from the principle of feminine modesty and pride, they could not express since they had no knowledge of them from experience, and could not imagine the sensations that differences between the nature of the sexes made foreign.

Even Desdemona, *et al.* do not express only feminine dramatic passions, but rather ideal art effects of purity, but there is a little of the naturally feminine about them. For the rest, the dramatic sensations, exactly speaking, of Shakespeare and Madhubala are mutually exclusive, one being limited to masculine ones, and the other to feminine ones.

(In this respect Guercino is a mystery. Shakespeare, Mozart, and Gable express dramatic sensations of men, Madhubala of women. You would expect Guercino to follow in the pattern in some general manner but he does not.

---

[1]I wonder how many lovers of Mozart feel what he expressed, instead of a pretty sensation. But even this is perhaps much preferable to what a fool of a solemn pedant makes of the works of Shakespeare and Mozart.

[2]But compare this to the truer expression of Madhubala in *A Night of Summer Rain* in those scenes where Shabnam and Aman are fleeing from the police and parents. It is true that in one it is a violently jealous husband and in the other a brutal father who is feared, but the terror is similar enough to make this comparison valid.

His male figures are excellent ideal art productions, but his women are dramatic. In the earlier paintings that I know, there are only a few whose female figues have dramatic expression: *The Madonna and Child in Glory with Saint Pancras and a Female Saint in Religious Orders* in the parish church in Renazzo di Cento, *The Mystic Marriage of Saint Catherine* in the Staatliche in Berlin, *The Assumption of the Virgin* in the Church of the Rosary in Cento, and *Queen Semiramis Receiving News of the Revolt of Babylon* in Boston's Museum of Fine Arts. But most of those painted after 1630 that have figures of women are dramatically expressive of the situation and character, and these are his masterpieces.

Why could he express the peculiarly feminine dramatic sensations and not masculine ones remains, as I say, a mystery to me. The range of his work is vast, closer to Shakespeare's and Madhubala's than to the less vast range of Mozart and Gable. But the nature of painting means that he could only express isolated dramatic sensations and not draw forth of all the nuances connected with a given class of dramatic sensations. So, in this respect, he is like Mozart, and unlike Shakespeare, Gable, and most importantly, Madhubala. This limitation to isolated dramatic sensations also means that Guercino is like Mozart, and not the others, in that he can only express the dramatic passions of ordinary souls. Finally, I do not know a work by him that is of a melodic nature; I should admit that I have not seen *The Burial of Saint Petronilla*, which Stendhal thought was akin to *Hamlet*, and which may be a melodic work.)

In *As You Like It* and *Dreams of Palaces*, Shakespeare and Madhubala expressed the dramatic passions of domestic life they personally held most dear in life. In Mozart's case, the equivalent work is *Die Zauberflöte*, which expresses his love of art (music), the awe-inspiring grandeur of rituals, and tender vanity love. The number of other passions exactly expressed in other works shows the *dramatic* nature of their genius. It was perhaps inevitable that they would produce the melodic art of *Don Giovanni, Tomorrow is Ours, Hamlet.*

Chapter XXI

I was first awakened to the melodic side of Shakespeare, Mozart, and Madhubala by Valmère, the story of whose unhappy love we were all familiar with. One evening, which he had for the greatest part spent wrapped in silence, while we were engaged in a conversation about men and manners that had veered onto the subject of Shakespeare, he all of a sudden spoke up, "I must tell you, my friends, of how I have come to discover the beauties of *Hamlet*. All of my prejudices and opinions have changed lately. I look for reflections of my thoughts in everything chance throws my way. It seems strange to me today that there was a time when I was above this weakness, and ridiculed it in others. But today, my favorite passage, perhaps, in all of literature is the last one hundred lines of a canto in Dante's justly celebrated poem, though you know how strongly I dislike that great poet.[1]

"When I am very unhappy, nothing can lift my spirits; but when I have met with some heavenly kindness, I can take up books with some pleasure. I have found that Shakespeare alone has the power to sustain reveries solely by virtue of the power of his language and ideas, but even among his plays, I have found this power in *Hamlet* only. Many of the other plays are extraordinary, no doubt, but in *Hamlet* he seems to have been little concerned with the kinds of dramatic effects that he usually sought, though, sadly, this fact seems to escape most admirers of the play."

I replied, "Do you know that Stendhal once wrote that what the French enjoy in Mozart is the musical accompaniment, not the originality of the *songs* of *Don Giovanni*? You know of my great admiration of the art of Madhubala; but what popularity she had, and what fame she still has, is due to her great beauty—she is known as the Venus of the Indian screen to those who pick up all the ideas they have in their heads from journalism."

"I am, alas, not familiar with the Indian actress, not knowing the language of the country, but the comparison with Mozart is well taken."

By this time we were all astonished to see how much excitement was reflected in the features of this unfortunate man. "You are all surprised and incredulous I see," he went on, "but let me return to *Hamlet*. I have

---

[1]Valmère, a most deceptive man for a fatally sincere lover, loved to throw his friends' speculations off-track by quietly offering them red herrings.

found that when I read this particular play, coming to it after an hour or two of happy sensations, the drama is ten-fold more perfect than it ever is otherwise, and its perfections have nothing to do with solemn nonsense about philosophy, character, and the 'tragedy of life.' Rather there is something in it which can heighten the sensations that are already present in my heart. Admittedly, this only happens occasionally in the course of the whole play, and never more than for a few seconds, but after you have gone through the whole thing, the sensations by virtue, it would seem, of their accumulated momentum prolong themselves for up to several hours. If you pay too close an attention to the matter that you read, you will not feel the sensations I am speaking of. *Hamlet*, I think, is a most undramatic play; it is in the unfolding of the verse and prose melodies that the miracle lies. I can see no explanation for what I am claiming, but then there is no explanation why certain sounds or scents are pleasing, and others not."

"Do you know, my dear Valmère, you will be laughed out of the room were you to say all of this to anyone but your closest friends. Have you never read or heard what people have to say of *Hamlet*?"

"You may not understand me fully if you say that. If a man or a woman who reads *Hamlet* has only petty ideas, and has no knowledge of any happiness or pleasure but of the most petty and mean kind, why what can you expect but that he or she will think that the play is solely about introspection, philosophy, revenge, fear, irresolution, ambition, guilt, etc.? This kind of person is deeply grateful to Shakespeare for having blown up into grand philosophic dignity with the power of his art his or her own petty ideas or at least the ideas he or she would like to pretend he or she has.

"No, say what you will, *Hamlet* still has the special hold it does on audiences because it can make you feel more keenly than usual the beauty of whatever it is that you already think beautiful; but this only happens if the object of beauty is already very much in your thoughts. Otherwise, whatever other object occupies the mind or heart will appear in the most attractive light it can possess. Yet with me, the happiness I feel after half an hour or more of paying attention to the play is always less than that with which I had started it."

Betson, who had not been paying attention for the last minute or more, said, "*If* what you say is true, then it is possible that many enjoy *Hamlet* for all the wrong reasons, but *for them*, those are the right reasons, and that is all that matters. Is it not possible that many enjoy it as you do, but have not understood the pleasures they feel? They must then suppose themselves to be enjoying the play exactly in the manner that they have heard it ought to be enjoyed."

But Valmère had again lapsed into silence; it was only much later, after I had thought about his extraordinary outburst for some time that I for the first time saw how great a grief was his.

Restricting myself to what he said about *Hamlet*, I suspect, though without any evidence, that Valmère may not have been as ignorant of Madhubala as he claimed to be; certainly he loved Mozart. The more I thought about his ideas, the more convinced I became that such a clear and distinct understanding of Shakespeare (as it now seems to me he has) could perhaps not have been possible but by his being able to compare the effects on the heart of *Don Giovanni* and *Tomorrow is Ours* to those of *Hamlet*.

Beauty is that powerful passion which is inspired in the mind by some pleasing object when you come to see its pleasing qualities, and which persists anywhere from a few minutes to a day or two. You feel as if you are in a trance of pleasure, and whatever you think of is transformed by this feeling of pleasure. The object is not necessarily, not even usually, in the forefront of your thought, but merely to think of it again reawakens the pleasure; but dwelling too single-mindedly on it actually reduces it. The sensation of beauty cannot last for more than a few days (except in love, where new reasons are continually being discovered to keep it alive), and it is almost never again inspired by the same object.

If a work of art is to have beauty as its chief effect, you must bring some amusing or tender thoughts you have been having to it. It cannot rely upon memory, it is not a work of ideal art. It cannot provide your imagination with representation of objects and passions and still produce sensations of beauty every time you go back to it.

Chapter XXII

Raphael and Ophuls

The effect of the best works of Ophuls and Raphael is exclusively that of *maximum* beauty. For this reason, Ophuls and Raphael are less understood than Shakespeare and Mozart. (I do not include Madhubala here only because she is not yet generally esteemed.)

I fear that this chapter, even more than any of the preceding (if that is possible), will be deemed unintelligible by many, perhaps most, readers. But there are many things far stranger than what I am about to describe. I advise the reader who finds the existence of strange and powerful passions unbelievable to skip this chapter altogether.

Whereas *Tomorrow is Ours, Hamlet,* and *Don Giovanni* can inspire sensations of beauty in some, the best works of Ophuls and Raphael can inspire a series of such sensations, each greater in intensity than the last, until you reach the sensation consequent to imagining near-absolute beauty. But you must know such sensations from previous experience in order to derive this degree of pleasure from their masterpieces. If you feel that there is nothing more than rococo prettiness, and at best, purity and elegance of form in the works of Ophuls and Raphael, you cannot have crystallized greatly in any of your loves.

What can be said to clarify the art of these two great men?

The suspension of disbelief that makes for ideal art is entirely absent in their chief works—even the dramatic geniuses retain some ideal effects. In watching the films of Ophuls or the paintings of Raphael, you must respond to the women and men you see as you would to people in life. But this is a more difficult thing to understand than may at first appear; and, unfortunately, it cannot be explained to someone who does not know the difference. I state this beforehand because it makes nearly worthless my description of the phenomenon even before I attempt it. But this is the difficulty of writing about love in general.[1]

---

[1]The present editor has reconstructed this essay from Rollefort's scattered notes. The editor has invented the "I" who speaks throughout this chapter and the entire essay for the sake of convenience and continuity, and to shorten as much as possible the length of the essay. He claims credit only as the editor of the manuscript, and has felt none of the sensations described therein.

When you begin to look at the work (no matter how many times you have seen it before), you see it in a conventional manner, i.e. by suspending your disbelief, etc. This is the way that the heart reacts to painted passions.

It takes some time for what the viewer sees to become something more, a *perfect illusion*. He reacts to what he sees as if it were not a fiction but something in his own life.[1]

This corresponds to simple admiration changing into love when hope spurs the imagination on to delight in pictures of happiness.

The greater the vanity of a man, the less likely he is to make this all-important transition. You must be able to feel the effects of sublime beauty without immediately wanting the happiness it promises for yourself; you must have *respect* for the woman who inspires those extremely pleasurable sensations if you are to feel love as anything but a commonplace passion; and no one who cannot love like that can derive great pleasure from Ophuls and Raphael.

The difference between them is largely one of temperament: Ophuls' was melancholic, Raphael's sanguine.

They are visual artists. Love is chiefly inspired by what you see; the other senses are all important, but less so. You will never have fully inspired love in a society in which the purdah is strictly enforced unless chance has led a man to see the woman at least once. Otherwise he will give an imagined picture of perfect beauty (which he has made up out of images of feminine beauty he knows and out of the associations that her gait, height, voice, etc. inspire in him) to her name, and love that picture.

A man sees a woman very differently from the manner in which a woman sees a man.[2] As feminists never tire of telling everyone, women are usually seen as beautiful objects to be looked at, and the vast majority of them enjoy such admiration. Throughout most of history, a flattering portrait of a man was supposed to emphasize heroism or strength, not mere physical beauty;[3] portraits of beautiful women were a different story.

---

[1]Dramatic effects are entirely absent in the non-ideal works of Raphael and Ophuls. The perfect illusion I mean here is that felt by the sensitive man as he idealizes the woman portrayed. In dramatic masterworks, the production of perfect illusion entails complete identification with the character, the viewer assuming the character's passions and responses to his or her circumstances.

[2]See chapters XXXVII-XXXIX below.

[3]The chief exception that comes to mind is the age in France and England between

Even today, magazines designed for men will often have a picture of a lovely woman on the cover; and so will a magazine designed for women.

I need not add, perhaps, that there was never a need for enforcing purdah on men; women are not so easily tempted by the mere sight of a man.[1] If men in some societies felt that they had to lock away their women, it was because experience told them that women usually put affairs of the heart over everything else. Their desire for happiness guided them, not their visual tastes. In any case, the effects desired by Ophuls and Raphael are not simply a matter of liking the personage portrayed (i.e., they are not ideal artists).

Not being a painter, I cannot explain what were Raphael's *techniques*. I merely study how his art affects the heart. Raphael's best paintings are the portraits of young women such as *St. Catherine*, *St. Cecilia* and many of the Madonnas—the frescoes and the large paintings such as the *Entombment* and the *Transfiguration* are admired by those who find his other paintings too simple, as they find nothing in their hearts that responds passionately to them.

His genius lay in his knowledge of the first crystallization, but speaking in purely painterly terms, it is most easily to be seen in his use of light.[2] Leonardo, Rembrandt, and Caravaggio were masters of effects of chiaroscuro, but their beauties are those which we note physically in their paintings. But the beauty of Raphael's effects is not a prettiness of visual effect. After a quarter of an hour of watching one of his masterpieces, everything in it becomes blindingly invisible, and one is caught up in the most delightful of sensations.

How can I know whether this is not a response peculiar to me? I cannot; but the women of Raphael do not inspire in me any specific memories, and the effect of his canvases I do not find in any painter but him: I therefore conclude, for better or for worse, that what I feel is the result of his art.

Louis XIV's ascension and the French Revolution, when effeminacy was as admired in some quarters as manliness was in others. The idea of *refinement* so admired in those days was often taken to be identical with effeminacy and prettiness. The effeminacy of men in the West today arises on the other hand from the influence of the opinions women like to state openly and *publicly*, though not necessarily their true ones.

[1]Here, as usual, I state the general case. There are always exceptions. Those who used to be called women of easy virtue (i.e., women whose favors are easy to obtain) are obvious exceptions in this case. And also, their response to a man of the Gable kind. It would be tedious to always point out the exceptions, since the reader can note them himself.

[2]I.e., the way in which his figures are lighted.

The painting is completely out of focus, but the most divine sensations of beauty, of love, pass through the soul. The woman at the center of the painting is the only object you can fix upon as the cause of the sensations.

The whole thing is a duplication, in art, of the process of first crystallization. Raphael can make you feel the maximum of beauty and pleasure that this phenomenon affords.

But all the ideas are the viewer's; everything depends entirely upon him. I doubt that even the most sensitive woman can be as deeply affected by Raphael; on the other hand, his portraits of men are admirable, too (those of Agnolo Doni and Bindo Altoviti, for example), although I doubt that they have the power to sustain deep first crystallization in even the most sensitive women.[1]

The heavenly sensations do not arise because of the beauty of the women portrayed; the effect of sublime beauty cannot be contained in an object since it is a motion of the soul.[2] What Raphael allows his viewer to do is to bring all the ideas of beauty, of *nobility of heart* that he knows, the most sublime happiness that he can imagine, to his best paintings. Whatever he thinks beautiful, admirable, and noble, he will be able to discover reflected in them.

The *art* lies only in the production of that which a man's eyes can rest upon as a sight which proves to him that for the most sublime feelings that arise in him there is an object that fully justifies their existence, and therefore crystallization is redoubled. Raphael knew *what exactly* were the mechanics of first crystallization.

---

[1]Feminine modesty will prevent a sensitive woman from crystallizing about them. Further, crystallization in women is a matter of imagining the pleasures of being loved, so an art of portaiture is ruled out. This is the reason why there will never be a female artist who belongs to this class of artists. But there has been a Jean Arthur so I may be proved wrong by history. An actress of this class of artists would, I would think, express the consequences of deep crystallization on the soul of the woman.

[2]In the paintings of Leonardo, Titian, or Rembrandt the expressions and physical charms of the young women are brought out vividly. The expressions of women of Raphael are muted; their sweetness and purity are generalized. His countless imitators, even the famous Ingres and Renoir, imitated him in this respect, and never arose above prettiness because they had not the slightest inkling of the chief quality of Raphael's art. Unlike the other great painters of women, he avoids giving a particular charm to his idealized women, which even that deftly witty portrayer of generalized feminine perfection van Eyck cannot help doing. As a result, their expressive and physical charms are to an infinitely greater degrees than those of the women of other painters *springboards* for the imagination.

I say the same thing about Ophuls, who was a narrative as well as a visual and decorative artist. The nature of his art is the same as Raphael's. His films, it has been noted by many, are very complicated formally, but it would be an utter waste of time to disentangle or explain with affected *insights* their "structural and thematic complexities." Motifs are used by him only to facilitate the birth and progress of crystallization, they can only be understood in this manner.

Each new detail, each twist of the plot, each mistake or noble act of the chief characters, is a fresh stroke of beauty, each arouses a more pleasing and violent sensation than the last.[1] Ophuls, who knew how great an artist he was, once said with typical wit and modesty, when asked about the feeling of purity that one of his films inspired in some viewers:[2]

"I cannot explain it to you. The *theme* of purity may not be immediately apparent in a subject, but the story can develop towards that conclusion. A conclusion that has no explanation, that certainly has no explanation in real life. Perhaps it is dangerous to want to judge oneself, but I am sure I am not a moralist. Perhaps I am always looking for that beautiful purity even without knowing it. It is the most wonderful thing when you find it."

He could discover it in novels and plays where it did not exist; but when he made them into films, they were entirely different works. When Ophuls says he is not a moralist, it is not out of vanity that he speaks, as other artists who say the same thing do. He simply means that he is not chiefly an ideal artist.

Neither Ophuls nor Raphael went beyond expressing the sensations constituting deep first crystallization. Ophuls did not describe the actions and motives of women and men in love; his interest was in effects.

The neglect and contempt that Ophuls' works generally suffered and still suffer from reflect the social manners and passions of our time. The twentieth century honors nothing but affectations (of sincerity, honesty, sympathy, indignation, deepness, pessimism, anger, cynicism, complexity), power, and wealth. Even if Raphael was not understood by his age and the next ones, he was esteemed as a great ideal artist.

---

[1] A mistake that one of his heroines makes only raises the crystallization to a more serious level by making it less of an easy pleasure.

[2] Who later went on to become overrated filmmakers: Truffaut and Mr. Rivette. The watercolor sentimentality of Truffaut is as intelligible to most people today as the deep passions of Ophuls are not.

Raphael left the time element entirely in the hands of the audience, but Ophuls had to control that also. In speaking of the great Balzac's vulgar and boring *La lys dans la vallée*, which he would in all likelihood have turned into a masterpiece, Ophuls said,

"In that novel there is a dose of realistic detail which is splendid, musical. When Balzac talks about Napoleon, etc., realism plays its true role. It upsets and slows down the dramatic flow. You have to concentrate your forces to touch the heart; it is there, between that desire to touch the dramatic nerve-ends and your emotions; and it slows things down. It is its only dramatic function and it is splendid. When you dare to use it like that, you get an unbelievable control. It is as in a symphony, when you separate emotional truth from the truth of life."

I suggest that the reader think about this for a few moments. If he can understand what Ophuls is saying, he can no doubt understand his films, since his idea of the mechanism of effective art can be seen as a fact in them, and not in Balzac's novels.

Ophuls made two masterpieces, *Madame de* and *Letter from an Unknown Woman*. *La Ronde* and *Le Plaisir* are witty and precise treatises on some aspects of love.

The crystallization that Ophuls wanted to inspire in his viewers is not that of first, innocent love. It is the love that surprises one who has grown very suspicious with its suddenly opening vistas of purity.

The admiration that one can feel for a character of narrative literary art is *moral* admiration; sometimes a man or a woman falls in love with some character, but in these cases he or she uses his or her memory, and substitutes, in making a mental image to love, for the character's physical description a woman or man he or she has known or seen who does not contradict the description. But, for any man or woman who has ever fallen in love, there can be no mistaking between the first crystallization that occurs in life and the weakness one sometimes feels for a character in a work of art.

You cannot fall in love with a woman you have never met, but about whom you have heard the most admirable things.[1] At best, you may be predisposed to fall in love. If you have heard her voice (on the phone, or, in some countries, through the purdah), there is a greater chance that you may begin to love, but still no deep crystallization can begin. What does begin is the general dreaming of the pleasures of love.

---

[1] Or at least this is extremely rare, since I would not be surprised to see the madness of crystallization taking even this direction.

Painting has this limitation, that even the greatest genius cannot represent the passions in movement. From the appearance of the woman, her gestures, expressions, etc., as well as from the narrative situation in which she is placed (if any), and color and chiaroscuro, the viewer derives the moral tenor of the work.

If the woman painted is physically charming, other thoughts also come in. This was part of the intended effect of not only lascivious painters like Bronzino, Modigliani, Renoir, Picasso, Ingres, and Boucher, but of such great masters as Titian, Rubens, Matisse, Leonardo, Veronese, Correggio, Tintoretto, Guido Reni, Guercino, Rembrandt, and Goya.

Raphael's method was to paint idealized portraits,[1] with some of his Madonnas idealized to perfection. But what sort of perfection? There is moral purity, a certain moral gravity, reflected in their expressions, and grace and tenderness in their carriage, but there seems to be little else. For these reasons, Raphael is not a painter for twentieth-century tastes, but for the same reasons his paintings were considered exemplary for several centuries after his death. All this is in the way of viewing his paintings ideally.

The object of Raphael was to produce a painting,[2] the colors and forms of which would be a suitable (i.e. justifiable) resting point for the eyes as the imagination is engaged in crystallization. The idealized women of Raphael are not meant to *induce* crystallization, or even to inspire any marked admiration, at first. Rather, a viewer brings to the painting his own personal knowledge of love.

What the painting allows him to do is to concentrate his attention upon it as his imagination soars in all directions. But this is only possible because Raphael does not want him to scrutinize the painting. And he does not give immediate pleasure to the senses (as Veronese, Correggio, and Michelangelo do in their very different ways, for example). The moral content, the ideal aspect, in other words, is also unimportant. The painting has only to hold a man's gaze.

The violence that Raphael does to the nature of the art of painting in the demands he makes upon it and upon viewers is so great that as acute an observer as Stendhal, though he understood Cimarosa, Shakespeare,

---

[1]Idealized, that is, to bring out the *general type* of the man or woman being painted.

[2]If I wanted to use the popular cant of modern art criticism, I could have said instead "visual field of action," or something along that line.

Mozart, and Correggio, the deepest souls of the past who had left any record of their ideas, besides lesser men, did not understand Raphael fully. This is not because what Raphael expressed was unintelligible to him, for the reveries inspired by *Don Giovanni* can often coincide with it, a fact which a chapter in the *Histoire de la Peinture en Italie* shows that he seems to have seen, but not in his habitually clear manner. Rather, I think that if you have not seen and understood Ophuls it is nearly impossible to understand Raphael, for in the cinema such an art does not go against the manner of the art form as it does in painting. But once you understand Ophuls, it is impossible to see Raphael in an ideal manner.

This is the only means by which an artist can hope to reproduce the pleasures of first crystallization. In ideal art, an object or idea must directly inspire thoughts of the pleasure it promises.[1]

In cinema, the actors, the camera work, the mise-en-scène, the script, all have their effects. The works of great directors are closest to the instrumental works of great composers. There are the elements of literary narrative art, theater, music, painting, and dance, which are as the different instruments are to a composer producing a symphony. Fortunately, even in this only century of its existence, the cinema has produced a number of very fine films, and even a few masterpieces (of direction and ideas): Ozu's *Late Spring* and *Tokyo Story*, Renoir's *La grande illusion*, *The Golden Coach*, Mr. Kurosawa's *Sanjuro* (and perhaps *Yojimbo* as well), and even *La régle du jeu*, Hawks' two best films, as well as Mr. Antonioni's *L'avventura* and *The Passenger*.

What sets Ophuls apart is that though he sought to inspire a strong effect, in no way is a man supposed to identify with and feel the passions of any of the characters, except in error which he soon recognizes—this error and its correction parallel the self-criticism consequent to a sensitive lover's beginning to take the beloved, whom he hopes to someday make his, too lightly, without enough respect, by ascribing commonplace motives and passions to her. Since there is no identification, there is no question of vanity arising.[2]

---

[1]Thus, idealization can never take on the intensity of a perfect illusion in ideal art. At its most intense, the response to ideal art cannot go beyond the relatively mild pleasures of the first few moments of first crystallization. The best works of Raphael and Ophuls can sustain pleasures of far greater intensity.

[2]That silly idea of Brecht's called epic theater, still admired extravagantly by some, makes for pure ideal art of a commonplace stamp. The pleasure is one of joining the *soi*

Long passages of the films consist of a series of what Ophuls called "dose of realistic detail," which are used symphonically, in other words—what amounts to the same thing—they play the part of dialogue in an opera.[1] Then there are the scenes where the effect is that of renewed and thus intensified crystallization.[2] The heroines are idealized in the mind of a man (to the degree that he can), but the distance between them remains absolute. But this is what happens only in crystallization, when the object of love begins to seem so perfect that the thought of possessing it in any way is painful. The increasing sense of beauty is a phenomenon purely of the imagination.[3]

In *Letter*, the script was happily full of clichés useful for the purpose Ophuls had in mind, which was to provide justifications for the overcoming of cynicism with proofs that you see before your very eyes, as it were, of every idea of beauty and nobility that may be imagined. In this respect, the viewer is put in a parallel position to Stefan himself. Those who do not know what is being expressed will very justifiably censure the change that was made in Zweig's rather sentimental story. Neither Hollywood nor the scriptwriter need be blamed for it. If the story had had no greater influence upon Stefan than self-congratulatory melancholy, the idea of all possible justifications of cynicism having been overcome would vanish, and the film would lose its final effect.

After this film, Ophuls (perhaps very naturally) seems to have wished to produce the same effect, but without an equivalent of Stefan, whose

---

disant elect among mankind, the Marxists in this case, in seeing the truth, in this case about class conflicts and false social opinions. Mr. Godard, Fassbinder, and others fall in the same category—I exclude *À bout de souffle*, *Le mépris*, *Pierrot le fou*, minor harmonic works.

[1]This analogy should not be taken any further, as only confusion will result from thinking of Ophuls' films as vaguely operatic.

[2]E.g., in *Letter*, the scene when Lisa waits in front of Stefan's home, when she asks him to talk about himself, when Lisa and Stefan return to his apartments at the end of the evening; the moment when Lisa, with the roses in her hand, steps off the curb on to the street as she looks up at the lighted windows of Stefan's apartment near the end of the film. Or, in *Madame de*, the third meeting of Madame de and Donati, at the diplomatic ball, the sequence of the dances, Donati's unexpected visit as Madame de is preparing for her trip, the beach scene, Madame de tearing the letter she has written; her hiding the earrings in one of her gloves, the last meeting of the lovers.

[3]Of the ideal masterpieces of Raphael and Ophuls, such as the Stanzas in the Vatican, the cartoons, *La Signora di Tutti*, or *De Mayerling à Sarajevo*, little need be said. They were meant to be enjoyed in the ordinary ideal manner. The great intelligence and purity of feeling of these two great men were bound to be reflected in their best ideal works, although their lack of interest in describing nature faithfully makes these works very much lesser achievements than the masterpieces, which are made around purely imaginary ideas.

inclusion the entire art of *Letter* demanded. His first attempt was to put together, on the practical and financial side, a project for the filming of Balzac's *La Duchesse de Langeais*, and when it fell apart, he returned to France, where after two more films (including his only popular success after *Liebelei*, *La Ronde*) he returned to the same plot in the Vilmorin novel he filmed, *Madame de*. The character is the exact opposite of Lisa's, given to trivial pleasures, lacking sincerity, and most importantly, lacking the moral gravity of Lisa; the important thing was that this character change in a matter of instants to very nearly that of Lisa—the scene of the embassy party when Donati asks Madame de who gave her the jewels. The nature of her feelings, her own real moral nature, so to speak, she learns in an instant, *when it is too late*, this inevitable loss being necessary if the first crystallization is to reach maximum intensity (in the earlier masterpiece, it was Stefan who bore the weight of this knowledge). This is a very unnatural and implausible development in itself, but Ophuls had arrived at that stage as an artist where his mastery of his medium was such that he could suggest ideas through the barest of nuances[1]; in this manner they have been accumulated sufficiently to make the central scene (lasting only a few minutes) not merely plausible, but fully developed in ideas and implications. From a little joy there is a jump to deep crystallization. The stages are not set out, but the effect is now isolated and arises only from the central character, who though never herself rises as high as Lisa. In the earlier film the expression is direct, in the latter it is taken for granted, implicit, and the barest nuances suggest the ideas expressed. I think that the second work had its inspiration in more than merely the desire for the effect to be derived from a single character; in addition, there was the desire to make it arise even when the woman is not perfect, since this is what actually happens in crystallization.

Raphael perfected his art in 1505 or 1506, and the works of Raphael corresponding to *Letter* are the *Madonna del Granduca*, *Small Cowper Madonna*, *Madonna del Belvedere*, *Madonna of the Goldfinch*, *La Belle Jardinière*, *Canigiani Holy Family*, *Bridgewater Madonna*, *Tempi*

---

[1]In their melodic works, Shakespeare, Madhubala, and Mozart had reached the same stage, as had Cimarosa and Meena Shorey in their chief works, and Miss Bina Rai, Nargis, Hepburn, and Stendhal in each of their last masterpieces. The reasons why they reached this stage were different, according to the class of art they produced, and the mechanics of each was also thereby different. I am recording only the similarity of stage.

Madonna, St. Catherine, Aldobrandini Madonna, Alba Madonna, Sistine Madonna, and *St. Cecilia,* which was painted around 1514 or 1515. Raphael's second stage consists of two paintings that go together: *La Donna Velata* (1516) and the figure of the Madonna in *La Spasimo de Sicilia* (1517). These two together express the same order of ideas as the first and second parts of *Madame de.* Obviously, Raphael could not hint at this fact directly, considering the fact that the second one needed the background of idealized Christian myth (just as Ophuls needed an idealized capital of grace and culture in his masterpieces).

You must bring to *Hamlet, Don Giovanni, Tomorrow is Ours* thoughts of what gives you pleasure. This may be the thought of a board room meeting where you have acquitted or will acquit yourself very well[1], or the thought of a trip to Paris or Florence or a nearby ski resort, or any other object or situation. All of these pleasures will be less than those that may be derived from Ophuls or Raphael, but if you are thinking of a woman the thought of whom always gives you deep pleasure, the pleasure will come closer to equalling Ophuls' or Raphael's. However, even if you are in love with the woman, the feelings that melodic works can sustain are not, in comparison to what Raphael's and Ophuls' masterpieces can, very deep—they are more or less equal to the degree inspired by the time a viewer gets to the scene when and right after Lisa rejects her young military suitor, or to the middle of the scene of the second dance that Madame de has with Donati, or to the equal degree of crystallization in front of a Raphael Madonna. As soon as higher stages are reached, he discovers that there is nothing in the words, songs, or acting that corresponds to and supports these higher ideas, and this is because Mozart, Shakespeare, and Madhubala reached their limit of knowledge of happiness at this stage.[2]

---

[1]Fear or doubts prevent one from deriving any pleasure from these melodic works.

[2]Stendhal, whose soul was much deeper and more extensive in its ideas than Mozart's, put into *Don Giovanni* more than it actually sustains. In *Henri Brulard,* when he speaks of his love of this opera, he says he thinks that he loves it for the genius of its musical expression, not for the memories it inspires (of Milan, i.e., of Mathilde), but he confesses he cannot be sure of this matter. Cimarosa is a greater composer in terms of expression than Mozart, and although Stendhal felt this, the art of Mozart being of the nature it is, after Milan it was inextricably associated in his mind with the object of passionate love, and therefore he could not feel it to be lesser than Cimarosa's. When he speaks of his love of Mozart's opera being so great that to hear it he would walk through mire etc., it should not be forgotten that the deepest and most powerful love inspires absolute respect, which in turn inspires unaffected modesty of expression regarding it. Cimarosa's music, which itself,

Chapter XXIII

Nietzsche and Miss Bina Rai

Nietzsche and Miss Bina Rai were makers of portraits. They resembled Raphael and Ophuls in that nothing contented them but maximums—maximum vanity in their case, not beauty.

Nietzsche's great character portrait is Zarathustra; there are certain hints in his later writings that he meant to write a work in which another, very different portrait would be given to the world, but this must remain only a conjecture.

Miss Bina Rai's two great character portraits are the heroines of *Anarkali* and *Ghunghat* ("The Veil").

Nietzsche sought knowledge of all possible ideas of beauty, nobility, etc.; he possessed the genius (that bugaboo of mediocrity) needed to succeed. To express in a work of art the maximum self-esteem a man can possibly have, he invented Zarathustra.[1]

In his lesser works, Nietzsche used ideas and opinions of others and studied their origins in the mind, but more often than not he distorted facts into symbols: this is what he does, for example, with Plato, Socrates, Christianity, Caesar, Greek tragedies, Napoleon, Goethe, Schopenhauer, Wagner, etc. I speak of these lesser books only because as a describer of nuances of vanity, as well as a poet who wished to express his own passions, he needed such symbols. They were useful to him in producing his own ideas in *Zarathustra*.

For Miss Bina Rai ideas expressed in words, history of ideas, and history itself held little importance. To display a woman who can have the greatest, most self-knowing self-esteem: that was her aim as an artist.

The difference between Nietzsche and Miss Bina Rai defines exactly the difference between the souls of men and women. What women or men of commonplace abilities *affect* may be anything and is a reflection only of the then current fashions; I speak of the nature of their minds

---

rather than any memory associated with it, inspired such love, Stendhal would not speak of with the note of boasting that he could of Mozart's, about which he appears in consequence to be more enthusiastic.

[1] I must speak the language of poetry in order to describe it—this is a fault, but one which I do not have the talent to correct.

and hearts, how and in what manner they operate.[1] As a rule, no woman whose soul has fire in it can rest content with a cold consideration and understanding of even the most passionate subjects. She desires only to *feel* deeply, and nothing can match love in intensity.

For obvious reasons it is easier to discuss in words Nietzsche's art than Miss Bina Rai's.

The "will to power" is only an emphatic phrase denoting vanity. Hobbes described it in the seventeenth century with clarity and precision as the chief human passion; Nietzsche merely put his conclusions into poetic language, and described, as Hobbes did not and as Helvétius did, the subtle nuances of the many forms in which it is seen in the world, but Nietzsche did so consistently from the point of view of his own chief passion, which was a very different shade and intensity of vanity from Helvétius'.

He calls the expression of vanity the dionysian expression, the "tragic" expression, of the soul—but Zarathustra is also a "dancer." This tragic character is not simply the consequence of the practical difficulties of life, but also of the fact that experience shows a man that his desires add up to nothing more than futile vanity.[2] But even with this knowledge of futility, he still has only vanity to gratify. The dionysian is praised; vanity should be expressed with the greatest energy and joy possible. Only then does the idea of appolinian restraint become important.

The "eternal recurrence" idea is the most demeaning to one's vanity; even extinction with death does not reduce the pleasures and pains of an individual to the kind of mechanical inconsequence that this idea does, if

---

[1]Readers will note that I do not flatter the fashions of the day. Will I incur the anger and hatred of feminists, fashionable intellectuals, etc? Whoever wishes to know the truth must harden himself or herself; it is always only vanity that makes us resist truth when it stares us in the face.

[2]It was this part of his thought that made Nietzsche feel what he called a spiritual affinity with Dostoevski and Schopenhauer. For Dostoevski, vanity, or "pride" (as he called it) was the greatest source of unhappiness for men and women, for it led to a feeling of moral emptiness. He felt the pain of humiliation to be less painful than the pleasures of petty vanity, and for this reason recommended utter humiliation, and preferably public humiliation, to all as the only true path to happiness.

Dostoevski himself was perhaps not an extremely unhappy man for most of his life, and according to all accounts a very vain one. His talent was for mild expression, not honest thought; the unintentionally comical ranting in his *Writer's Diary*.

true.[1] In combination with the pledge to oneself to gratify every instinct of vanity, the eternal recurrence idea produces the greatest intensity of vanity, equalling Dante's, Michelangelo's, and Beethoven's severe pride.

The overman is the man[2] whose vanity is gratified by the "eternal recurrence" idea (taken as a fact) more than it can be by any other fate; he restrains the dionysian enthusiasm he is naturally given to with the apollinian coolness that he must develop in order to thrive in a world which he knows to be governed by the principle of eternal recurrence.

By such self-overcoming, he is filled with vanity at the thought of his own utter inconsequence: Nietzsche logically and in detail worked out the most contradictory form of vanity possible. Vanity arises from knowledge or imagination of one's consequence. Nietzsche saw that to intensify its pleasure to the maximum degree possible, he had to overturn the mechanism; since all consequence is imagination of consequence, and the intensity of the pleasure of vanity is directly proportional to the difficultly felt in trying to imagine the nature of the consequence, the maximum intensity would be logically and scientifically reached by first defining utter inconsequence of a man (eternal recurrence), and then deriving all consequence from that utter inconsequence, the most difficult idea of consequence for the imagination to form, and therefore the most intense.[3]

All of the above must be understood in terms of feelings, by appealing to one's pleasures and pains.[4]

---

[1]Nietzsche killed two birds with this one stone. It was partly the repetitive, *mechanical* aspect of the eternal recurrence idea that mattered to him. There was also the fact that if everything recurs eternally, then all idealisms will be proved doubly false, and the overman, knowing that the universe eternally recurs, lives with the constant knowledge that all paths to happiness followed by men are based on unsupportable and unjustified lies, but that he must live eternally in a world full of weak liars mechanically repeating every action and thought, with only seeming freedom of the will behind all these lies, and that he must derive his greatest joy from this fact.

[2]This maximum vanity possible in a man very naturally denies women any moral worth. To give a woman any worth would be to bring down the extreme intensity of vanity a few degrees.

[3]This maximum degree of vanity constituted happiness for Nietzsche. He expressed (as opposed to describing it) this happiness most clearly in the famous "Drunken Song" near the end of *Thus Spoke Zarathustra*, as the contradictions become absolute: midnight too is noon, pain too is a joy, etc. There is nothing masochistic or religious (i.e., Jonathan Edwardian or Dostoevskian) about Nietzsche's happiness.

[4]On occasions, Nietzsche liked to pretend that he was above pleasure and pain.

Exactly the same as what I have said about Nietzsche may be said of what Miss Bina Rai expressed, except that in her case you must judge and understand the ideas by an exact knowledge of what actions, looks, way of talking, etc. convey about ideas, feelings, opinions, etc. The scripts of the films are in themselves trivial, as is usual in the works of the greatest actresses and actors, except as providing an opportunity for the artist.

The more imagination and intelligence a man possesses, the more he becomes passionately interested in ideas regarding fate, time, destiny, justice, ethics, politics, history, beauty, memory, love, etc.,[1] and interested in them in order to derive conclusions of a general nature, for this gives him great pleasure. He supports his vanity with ideas far removed from the concrete world around him, often gladly sacrificing intensity of feeling for the cold pleasures of abstractions. These interests, when expressed, need not be expressed in words.

Women of great imagination and intelligence are far more sensible; their deepest interest lies in feelings only—other things matter less; and it is only a very strong interest that discovers new ideas. Only the vanity of being admired for the same reasons as men inspire them to discover great pleasure in the ideas of general history, fate, metaphysics, etc.[2]

---

[1] Or in questions of mass, velocity, force, solubility, electrical fields, DNA, etc.; or in problems of space, color, chiaroscuro, types of models, etc., etc.

[2] I.e., commonly, though not universally, the motive is envy of the rewards men receive for such conceits. Women almost never rise above personal fears and hopes, and they therefore excel in domestic matters, business, and politics; the penchant for making sweeping generalizations about the race is naturally foreign to them (save in the form of coffee-table conversations), and it only develops in those societies or situations in which they feel they must *prove* themselves (to other women and, more importantly, to men) to be as rational as men. There can be an Emily Dickinson; but there could never be a female Dante, Milton, Blake, Dostoevski, Kant, Plato, etc. What kind of a mess a woman ends up with whose vanity drives her to attempt so-called great themes or stylistic or ideological abstractions in the manner of men can be seen in the works of George Eliot and Gertrude Stein. In mathematics, the theoretical sciences and the arts (save for acting), they are not in their element. They do well so long as the thought does not become too abstract (e.g., Mme Curie and Lise Meitner, both of them great scientists). In the arts, they can imitate men so far as to achieve a surface obfuscation; i.e., they can achieve the level of abstraction of a commonplace male scholar. When a woman begins to philosophize in print, you can be sure, on account of the principle of feminine modesty, that she is clever, but not intelligent, affected and without deep feelings. Stendhal put the matter more succinctly than I can: "Dès que les femmes entreprennent des raisonnements généraux, elles font de l'amour sans s'en apercevoir." ("As soon as women attempt general observations, they are making love without knowing it.")

Upon reading the paragraph I have just written, I am tempted to delete it out of

Miss Bina Rai described states of maximum feminine vanity in her chief performances. In both *Anarkali* and *Ghunghat*, she plays women who love far more than they are loved. Her characters are driven by the desire for self-esteem, and this they can only secure through love.[1]

Here you have the chief distinction between the minds of men and the minds of women: This desire for complete happiness through excess of love parallels the "will to power" vanity of Nietzsche. The basis of Anarkali's happiness is her great vanity at the thought of the great worth of her love.

She comes to feel that the object of her love does not return her love equally; and finally that he is not worth the love he inspires,[2] which means that her own feelings, whose growth, in spite of herself, she cannot put a stop to, are themselves utterly worthless.

This knowledge in Anarkali is parallel to Zarathustra's awareness of eternal recurrence in that from it derives the idea that is most injurious to her sense of vanity.

Yet she derives the greatest joy of the pride and vanity of loving her prince from the very fact that her own love is worthless ("meaningless" in the poetic Nietzschean vocabulary), because fixed upon a shamefully unworthy object. As in Nietzsche, there is an utter contradiction of logic; this manner of joy is the form that maximum self-love in women takes, the form in which they find the greatest possible idea of self-esteem.[3]

---

politeness. I leave it as it is as I think that no sensitive and spirited woman will be angry at my words upon rereading them.

[1] I speak of what this great woman expresses, not of what is in the scripts, which are no more works of genius than are the libretti of Mozart's operas. I speak only of *Anarkali* henceforth in this chapter.

[2] The respective responses of Miss Bina Rai and the underrated actor Pradeep Kumar when the lovers in *Anarkali* are sentenced to death. He expresses very vividly a simple though strong joy ("How wonderful it is that we will die for love."); it is a matter of a fine effect very well executed. Miss Bina Rai expresses a much more weary and deeper pleasure, "I am happy that I am sacrificing my life for an object utterly unworthy of my undying love." It is no wonder that she looks so stricken and aloof at this point. What could possibly be more demeaning to a woman than to love better every day a man whose soul strikes her as being beneath hers in every way, and more so every day?

[3] There is a great difference between the chief pleasure of the two great Bina Rai heroines and that of Ophuls' Lisa, who continues to idealize Stefan in spite of everything. It would be even a greater error to put her portraits next to, say, the women of Mr. Bergman and Mr. Antonioni, who are merely smug, and, in fact, as commonplace as the men in the films. They enjoy the pleasures of petty vanity in condescending to speak to, and sometimes forgive their misguided lovers; they are not *proud* of the fact that *their own feelings are utterly inconsequential*, as Anarkali is.

These states of highest pride are not immediately reached; Zarathustra and Anarkali must pass through many stages and shades of vanity to get to them.

There is always pain when something that has gratified one's vanity no longer seems to be of much worth, and, for this reason, pain is so commonly expressed by them as their characters continue to rise through different opinions and degrees of vanity until they reach the limits ordained by nature. They must pass through (i.e. consider temporarily) every general type of vanity (save petty vanity, since it holds not even the most momentary attraction for the nobler spirit).

Life can afford little contentment to any spirited woman if she does not feel strongly, and the pride Miss Bina Rai describes is a very intense sensation.

Their desire was only to find the maximum attainable happiness through maximum vanity in a man or woman who is very intelligent and very skeptical, as well as one who has been granted by nature a temper that refuses to permanently fall prey to disappointments or despair of any kind.

Needless to say, the knowledge that your actions are motivated solely by vanity is likely to wound your vanity if you are hypocritical, and you will not take great delight in Zarathustra and Anarkali.

Nietzsche, Miss Bina Rai, Shakespeare, Mozart, Madhubala, Raphael, and Ophuls had each exact and complete knowledge of *different* types of sensations, all falling within the class of happiness arising from vanity and beauty.

In their great masterpieces anyone may see his or her ideas of vanity/beauty/first crystallization reflected, and nothing more. *All* that is expressed by their works cannot be understood by any save those whose knowledge of the heart equals theirs, for what you do not already know from experience you cannot understand when expressed in art.

Chapter XXIV

Helvétius and Jane Austen

There are two writers who have described *exactly* most of the subtle nuances of vanity in men and women, respectively: Helvétius and Jane Austen.

The difference between the two arises from the inborn differences between the sexes, which include that of the different manner in which they accept received ideas.

Women of intelligence, like men of intelligence, are interested in ideas, but a very intelligent woman (not merely a very clever one, intelligence in women being inseparable from a capacity for great feeling) is little contented with remaining in the domain of ideas. Only feelings matter to her.[1]

Helvétius wrote books of philosophy; Jane Austen wrote novels, because they appeal finally to feelings, albeit through application of reason.

Nietzsche and Miss Bina Rai describe a particular state of intense vanity which coexists with the greatest skepticism about their own worth. Everything in them is subordinated to the expression of this state.

The central ideas in Helvétius are the following:

---

[1]The woman who has thought of happiness and its many forms and stages *for herself*, without having merely imbibed the commonplace ideas of her day and set, is likelier to have the strength of character which makes her tender expressions that much more prized by the man who adores her, if he be sufficiently intelligent to understand her. It is this type of woman in whom vanity and susceptibility to the tender passions increase proportionately to each other. Women like Gertrude Stein or Simone de Beauvoir were clever women driven by their lack of beauty and the set of opportunities open to them to seek approval of literary circles; their petty vanity prevented them from having any capacity for tenderness. The former affected indifference to this sort of weakness altogether, the latter's feelings for Sartre arose from weakness, the need for his praise. Since 1970 it has become fashionable for a woman to write boring books that express self-pity and petty anger disguised as "analyses," and written in involved and turgid styles. Once this fashion was born, and thus it became socially a respectable thing for a woman to express self-pity and petty anger, and *this* became the received opinion, nearly all educated women began to adopt and express the same ideas. Their writing an increasing number of books shows not that women by nature are passionately interested in verbalized and abstracted thought, but merely that the latest fashions have even more of a tyrannical sway over their actions than over men's.

1) All human actions and sensations arise from the pursuit of pleasure and the avoidance of pain. All thought is reducible to sensations and feelings.

2) Pain is felt more strongly than pleasure because pleasure *must* be imagined whereas pain usually arises automatically.

3) We can know nothing except through our senses. Even the most abstract scientific, moral, and poetic ideas are finally but the results of comparison of different pictures produced in the mind when comparing the pleasures and pains we feel in the presence of different natural objects.[1] All our ideas of immaterial phenomena are drawn from objects that strike our senses.

4) A man is under the necessity of esteeming (or even understanding) in others only himself, his own ideas, etc., because what is not in himself he cannot begin to put in relation to what is, except erroneously. Esteem is dicatated solely by interest.

5) The passions are all the results of this desire for pleasure and avoidance of pains, and must be understood then by studying how different types of government and institutions encourage and discourage different passions.[2] Legislators should know how exactly laws affect what passions are to be found in a society.

Helvétius was indebted to Hobbes and Locke, but he described and anatomized these ideas much more minutely and generally than either of the British philosophers. To have been able to accurately and fully describe all the different nuances which the principles above lead to required not only intelligence but also unerring knowledge of the world. However, it would be pedantic to say that he is not sometimes a bit off, but only in his examples, not in his descriptions of motives and passions.

He had no illusions concerning how vanity has to be gratified, and that is by general esteem. The more consequence you know yourself to be thought to have, the more respect you know you command, and the

---

[1]E.g., Einstein felt pain when an attempt to formulate some aspect of a theory seemed to him to contain an illogical or false element. Conversion of that pain to pleasure was possible only by the discovery of a more logical and experientially valid explanation. Led by the unalterable law of pleasure and pain, he directed his energy and thought until he revolutionized physics for all time with the General Theory of Relativity.

[2]E.g. The differences in the aristocracy that existed in the reigns of Tiberius, Charlemagne, Elizabeth, and Catherine; the court of Louis XIV vs. that created by Napoleon; the leading families of New England. The difference in the power that well-born women had in various aristocracies.

greater the number over whom you exercise command or respect, the greater will be your happiness.[1] Helvétius was simply indifferent to the more extreme or sensitive forms of masculine vanity, and to the distinctive nuances of feminine vanity altogether. His interest lay in describing the passions of the majority, as well as in trying to define what virtue (i.e., moral good) is from a dispassionate angle.

Unfortunately, he himself had only moderate fame. Voltaire, Rousseau, and Diderot, men who could not rise above triviality in their ideas were the leading literary lights of his age; in England, Hume was famous, and by the end of the century, Kant was the rage of Europe. Helvétius was little read, but famous because his book had been condemned by church and state.

Yet this great man must have known the reason for the relative neglect of his works, even among philosophers.[2] To his trivial and affected contemporaries, his ideas were too simple, and his love of personal fame contemptible. They were simply not honest enough to want to see men as they are, and although clever in little things and producing *bon mots*, they had little knowledge of the heart.

The province of intelligence is the study of nature, of things as they are; to be clever is to have the talent to impress others with your ideas and talent.

What drove Helvétius to abandon Paris for ten years and write the greatest book of cold philosophy in world literature were not only the desire to point out the mistaken assumptions in his friend Montesquieu's *Esprit des Lois*, and a wish to establish political philosophy on a sound foundation by describing human passions and motives accurately. He

---

[1]The man who cannot rise above the pleasures of vanity-beauty, and who puts out that he desires a fit audience, though few, secretly desires the whole world to praise him, loudly though he denies this to others, or even to himself.

[2]His comparison of the relative effects that the speeches of Demosthenes and the axioms of the Lyceum had on the Athenians, in Essay III, chapter IV of *De l'esprit*.

Fame in philosophy is the result of the topicality of the ideas presented or of the degree to which they seem to justify flattering reveries. Locke is given credit for the discoveries (such as the tabula rasa and association of ideas) that Hobbes had already made in a more forceful, accurate, but politically perilous manner. The fame of *Leviathan* sprung from the topicality of the authoritarianism Hobbes advocated. Locke belonged to the enemy party, but his *Essay Concerning Human Understanding* is a more prolix, popular, and inexact version of the first section of Hobbes' masterpiece. It seems very different because of his manner and emphasis. A pious and vain man, Locke denied ever having read the *Leviathan* before writing the *Essay*.

also wanted glory, and being gifted with uncommon mental powers, he must have felt that he could only win glory as a great philosopher.

Hobbes prized the security of civil unity and stability above everything else, so he was willing to describe the heart of man as it is. By knowing man, he hoped it would become possible to control man's passions and guide him to a peaceful commonwealth under a strong sovereign. Locke escaped into the pleasures of knowing facts for the sake of knowing them (though he slips often), as much as for the improvements that knowledge brings.[1] Helvétius lacked the pedantic spirit, and he thought that to teach men public virtue with good results was not impossible.[2]

The consequent desire for contributing to this improvement led him to study the heart coldly. The greatest good for the greatest number, that was Helvétius' idea of virtuous thought and action, especially in the public sphere—an idea later taken up and vulgarized by Bentham and the utilitarians, who reduced to an economic idea Helvétius' more general idea of interest as pleasure of the soul consequent to pleasure of the senses.

In spite of this vulgarization, his definition of a virtuous public action (the first and only one which was exact and precise, and not merely

---

[1] By concentrating upon an inquiry into the origin of ideas, he managed to gently obscure Hobbes' discovery that love of pleasure, and thus, vanity, or the increase of power, was the governing principle of all human thought, feeling, and action. Having ignored the central idea of Hobbes, the one that created political headaches, Locke instead put emphasis on the fact that since a man is born into the world with a minimum of prejudices, the moral makeup he comes to have depends entirely upon experience. The idea of *improvement* then becomes logically inevitable and politically desirable: Locke's critical advance over Hobbes was not in psychology (i.e., study of the heart), but in political thought, though a confused and minor one, but it led to Helvétius' book. He was as less of a political thinker than Hobbes as he was a psychologist, but in paragraph 13 of the second *Treatise of Government* he at least pinpointed one logical weakness in Hobbes' reasoning: is man necessarily happier under a bad government than he is in the natural condition, or, what amounts to the same thing, how do you insure that governments promote the interests of their citizens? The rest of the work is a fine piece of idealistic political propaganda in favor of liberal and generous principles, and important for its call for change and improvement in governing institutions. Still, the question posed in that paragraph pointed to the need for a more thorough anatomy of the heart and of manners, following in the footsteps of Hobbes, which, to give him his due, Locke in his mild and inoffensive manner tried to undertake. But it was Helvétius who provided a rigorously logical and general theory of human passions, manners, institutions, and governments, and Montesquieu who provided a set of guidelines for republics.

[2] His idealistic notions are expressed in his second and last book. In this pattern he is like Austen and others.

rhetorical) was implicitly adopted by the United States in its Constitution, and later by all other nations which claim to have popular forms of government. It was this implicit rhetorical adoption of the Helvétian idea in American politics that was largely responsible for the benevolent turn (as far as the vast majority of the middle class is concerned)[1] that capitalism finally took in mid-twentieth century. The struggle against the industrial and financial barons was long and bitter, but the historical turn of events made up of the Depression, the New Deal, and World War II led to the perfect merging of Adam Smith[2] and Helvétius, two of the three moral thinkers upon whose principles the United States was formed, only two of whom are given their due at this point in history.

The Helvétian solution works, but only when the natural passions of a people have been cooled to near refrigeration. Helvétius knew that the cooling of natural passions must be taught, and therefore the chief subject of his philosophy became education;[3] an education that would make people think more of their long-term interest and change their ideas concerning wherein glory and greatness lay to a more public-spirited sphere. To provide a proper background of knowledge for the change, he wrote his second book *De l'homme*, published posthumously out of fear of persecution at the hands of the church and state. Whatever the idealistic faults of his educational theory, he was evidently going in the right direction. A democracy that claims to be following in its aim the public good becomes a ridiculous shadow theater where the passions of the people have not yet been cooled: England in the 18th century (the situation has improved very slowly over the last two centuries); the years following the French Revolution; India and Italy today.

On the other hand, the Helvétian ideal has to a degree been produced in Sweden and Switzerland—which proves that rigorous and heavily industrial capitalism is not absolutely necessary, so long as geographical and geopolitical factors are not unfavorable.

---

[1]Though much decried by gloomy and disappointed armchair men of letters and minor artists.

[2]That other great philosophic descendant of Hobbes. From the Boston Tea Party until the triumph of the Federalists, the United States was involved in harmoniously merging Montesquieu with Adam Smith.

[3]Even on this subject Helvétius is unaccountably unknown, whereas Rousseau's feebly reasoned and very boring *Émile*, with its romantic opinions regarding children, has provided the rhetoric of progressive education its most commonly used ideas. Helvétius notes somewhere in *De l'esprit* that thought requires effort, and man is by nature indolent. The principle of inertia.

This refrigeration of the soul is the paradoxical end of the Helvétian program for establishing virtuous governments by appealing to the lively passions. Perhaps this is the only solution that is practically possible and generally beneficial. Helvétius' ideal was closer in some particulars to some of the Greek states, or the early Roman republic, where men were motivated to great actions of use to the nation because the idea of immortal glory lay therein, than it is to modern democracies, but generally his dream has come true.

Helvétius does not describe the chief passions of private life in any detail, so that he must seem unbearably tedious to most women.

Intelligent and sensitive women shun fame and public attention as instinctively and avidly as clever women seek it.[1] True happiness is a strictly domestic affair for them, and they would rather be esteemed by a lover than by the rest of the world, though they fear the world's contempt as much as their lover's.

In speaking of Jane Austen, you cannot ignore the clichés that always are relied upon by those not granted the gift of thought. I have avoided speaking of the influence of their societies on Raphael, Ophuls, Shakespeare, Mozart, Madhubala, Nietzsche, Miss Bina Rai, and Helvétius only because their genius is not explainable by them. I take it for granted that for its successful expression, *any* genius (not only of expression) requires fortune, propitious circumstances, and a society advanced enough and ready for the genius. Shakespeare would not have written a play if he had been born a quarter of a century later, and he could probably not have written the kinds of masterpieces he did if he had been a compatriot and contemporary of Molière.

I have no doubts that had Jane Austen been born into an upper middle class English or American family in this century, she would have written novels which are as limited in the nature of actions and characters shown as hers are. Only the specific rules by which courtship is conducted and the general manners of the characters would be different.[2]

---

[1]That is to say, they do not like to have their true innermost thoughts publicly known. Those who lack sensitivity love to broadcast them, almost always wholly out of personal vanity.

[2]If I may make a comparison, the difference of society and era would have merely changed the arithmetic, but left the algebraic equation intact.

The vanity of a sensitive woman is gratified by her knowledge that she is thought to be of great consequence by the people among whom she lives. Her family, her friends, her social circle, and especially her lover are all that matter to her *personal happiness*. For all the rest of the world, she can have deep interest and sympathy, but it does not affect her heart very deeply.[1]

The social and political subjection as well as the lack of education that women throughout most of history have had to suffer usually resulted in intelligent little girls growing up to be very silly women. They were never taught, indeed rarely allowed, use of reason. Once given the opportunity they show themselves to be the equal of men in many fields, especially the practical and the non-scientific. But a woman is a creature ruled by her heart, and the most remarkable women have exact knowledge of the vagaries of this organ.

In her last four completed novels, Jane Austen described the various types of feminine temperaments, and the different means by which these can attain happiness. Those who think her novels cold, unnatural, and artificially though very cleverly constructed as novels fail to see that all of her plots and plot developments, as well as the distribution of different temperaments among the characters in each novel, are governed solely by the desire to draw an accurate picture of the heart of her heroine; everything has to be brought out so that the reader understands with absolute clarity what is happening in the heart of Elizabeth and Anne.

Her two masterpieces are *Pride and Prejudice* and *Persuasion*. These works occupy the same respective positions in her oeuvre as *De l'esprit* and *De l'homme* in Helvétius', *Letter* and *Madame de* in Ophuls', *Anarkali* and *Ghunghat* in Miss Bina Rai's.

In the works of the first group (i.e., *P&P*, *Letter*, *Anarkali*), each of the main stages of vanity-beauty that the central characters go through until the highest is reached is described in sequence and detail.

The second group consists of masterpieces in which the artists attempt to inspire the passions *ideally*. These are, consequently, in a sense ideal works of art, because the audience is expected to feel the passions for the central characters, and there is no attempt to systematically describe their development and changes. The heroines of

---

[1]They become distraught over the plight of strangers who are in the news because their imaginations are often very active in picturing horrors as if they were happening to themselves.

these works do not reach the heights that their counterparts do, but the audience does since it has to force its imagination to work more intensely. It is the nature of the passions inspired by the works of this second group which are different in kind (though still within the class of happiness from vanity-beauty) from those of ideal art.

For any woman to be susceptible to sensations of deep happiness, she must be convinced of her own inner and secret worth. I mean, this necessity is felt much more strongly among women than among men. In order to describe a character going through the universal stages of vanity until she finds happiness in the highest one possible within the course of a normal social life, Jane Austen chose in her two masterpieces women whose sense of their own worth is hardly ever shaken even momentarily. She herself was such a woman.

Elizabeth Bennet has to learn much in the course of the novel, but it is Darcy who requires the true moral education. Elizabeth, for Austen, has worth in herself, but we come to know of Darcy's worth only through knowledge of how deeply he is struck from the beginning by Elizabeth, and how increasingly much he is willing to do for her. His moral education consists of learning to follow that course in life which his admiration of her forces him to. Elizabeth's passions are described with exactness and truth to nature. When, at Pemberley, she wonders whether she wishes Darcy to come in to tea or not, she feels *yes*, until he does. Only when a day or two later in despair she tells him about Lydia and Wickham does she feel the pangs of regret about what she let go, and the rebirth of love, now a deep form of vanity love. In time, with doubt coming in to accelerate the process after the elopement of Lydia, her love is intensified, and even more so when she discovers with gratitude Darcy's role in the patching up of the problem. It is taken for granted that Darcy is intelligent and even amiable behind his austere appearance and demeanor; otherwise he would never have fallen in love with Elizabeth in the first place.

Since Anne Elliott's great error took place years before the point at which the novel begins, we are allowed to see neither the details of what happened, nor the scenes of regrets and remorse. We are merely told that it took her a year or more to overcome her grief at the loss of the man she loves. All her growth of spirit and mind has taken place before the novel opens. The question is merely how long it will take Wentworth to recognize the true worth of the woman he still loves in spite of himself. He has to resist the weakness of wounded pride.

Even after he is on the right path, he fears the consequence of his attentions to a girl he only singled out because there was no one else. To the end, Anne is assumed to have been right in having allowed herself to be persuaded against accepting Frederick seven years before they meet again. Austen silently passed over the fact that only the final happy developments of events justify her initial rejection under pressure, and that these took place was a stroke of incredibly good fortune for the lovers.

The heroine of *Emma* is a woman who can make the most silly mistakes and yet is not held contemptible on that account. It is because of the silent admiration that Knightley (who is Darcy sans the need to learn anything) never stops having for Emma that the novel succeeds in showing off to charming advantage a potentially intelligent and witty heroine who usually falls prey to silliness and pettiness. Knightley has no illusions about Emma, yet he truly esteems and loves her. It is the nature of her as yet dormant (but for all that, to Knightley still all there) feelings and the liveliness of her nature that he loves, for in terms of accomplishments and moral conduct Jane Fairfax is clearly her superior. Emma is the young woman in whom Austen most clearly described what a woman secretly wishes to be: her silliness is shown in great detail to express to readers how silly by common and public standards a woman may be, and yet be a superior creature, i.e., worthy of being loved by the worthiest, most clear-sighted, intelligent, and handsome man. In fact, she can think herself very worthy, because in spite of every element of her character that speaks against her, she is still the chosen one.

The fact that Emma of all the Austen heroines is the one women almost invariably prefer is, as Edmund Wilson once said, a reflection of the self-image that most women like to have.

For the same reasons, Fanny Price is the least popular heroine among them. Men are often bored by her, but I have read (or heard) few feminine responses written in this century which do not show impatience with and anger at poor Fanny. Women reject her so passionately because Fanny is exactly the type of woman no woman today wants to be. Eighteenth- and nineteenth-century societies, and especially the middle classes, encouraged women to be meek and passive by praising them when they were so and holding up the ones who seemed most so as models for others. Fanny was popular enough with the early women readers, and probably anticipating that this would be the case, Austen felt it not unnatural to name her after her favorite niece; but women today resent being thought of as defenseless and weak.

Mansfield Park was written to describe the nature of the happiness attainable by a woman of Fanny's temperament and circumstances, the *exact opposite* of Emma's. The grim, overbearing, and very English moral tone of the novel was necessary because Fanny had to be shown triumphing against great odds while retaining her passive, gentle manner. The crises had to be orchestrated in such a manner as to seem the results not merely of faults of upbringing and prejudice of the other characters; they had to be shown to proceed from the same moral shortcoming from which arose the error of not recognizing Fanny's great virtues.

For in spite of her extreme shyness, she desires recognition and attention throughout the story, but recognition of the great worth of the passive soul in her. She feels herself to be superior for having such a soul. Although very jealous of the fatal attraction that Mary's lively spirits and conversation have for Edmund, she never wishes herself different.

In her minor characters, Austen drew men and women of weaker characters and moral natures than her heroes and heroines, focusing upon those parts of their characters that were of interest to a sensitive woman.

Helvétius sought to describe ideas and facts about the mind and about societies, and he limits himself to describing these.

Austen sought to describe the nuances of feminine self-esteem in the course of a finally happy love, so she had to invent sets of characters and situations in which they could be fully described.

She based her characters on her own acquaintances, exaggerating and idealizing (i.e., generalizing) their most notable characteristics and peculiarities in the manner of all competent ideal artists.

Her caustic, charming wit was a product of her unshakable, though tender, pride.

Chapter XXV

Of the Greatest Possible Vanity Happiness

The manners in which the highest degree of vanity happiness has been attained may be restated in brief as follows:

1) The imagining of the most potent force imaginable, and then seeing all merely human joys and pains in light of that superhuman force and in full sympathy with it: the vanity happiness of sublime character, reached, so far as I know, only by Dante, Michelangelo, and Beethoven.

2) Knowledge of the purely imaginary delights of the reveries of love in the abstract (not crystallization regarding any real person, but that of ideal art), along with intimate knowledge and close study of the exact happiness of a great majority of people, most of which is seen as slightly or deeply comical or ridiculous, often for purely imaginary reasons; the vanity happiness of alternately comical and tender (though more of the latter) character, reached, so far as I know, only by Fielding and Grable.

3) Knowledge of the exact dramatic passions of men and women, and consequent sure vanity of both ability and number of pleasures; the vanity happiness of dramatic character, attained, so far as I know, by Shakespeare, Guercino, Mozart, Gable, and Madhubala only.

4) Logical rise to maximum vanity by using its mechanics though not fully understanding the mechanics; the vanity happiness of logically maximum character attained, so far as I know, by Nietzsche and Miss Bina Rai only.

5) Conscious knowledge of the exact nature of the mechanics of vanity; the vanity happiness of commonsensical character attained, so far as I know, by Helvétius and Austen only.

6) Conscious knowledge of the exact nature of the mechanics of nature; the vanity happiness of scientific character attained, so far as I know, by Hahnemann, Kent, and Einstein only.

Such very intense pleasures are known only consequent to knowledge of intense grief. It is so as to overcome unhappiness from purely imaginary causes (from some other cause than petty vanity) that a man or woman is forced to discover purely imaginary reasons for happiness, thus producing the stronger and more intense degrees of happiness.

Take the example of masochists like Dostoevski or Edwards. This class of vanity happiness, which perhaps came into being in the West only with Christianity (though known in India even earlier), is obviously related to the happiness not only of Dante *et al.* but also to that of Nietzsche and Miss Bina Rai. The difference in genius (i.e., of degree of pleasure) arises from the fact that Dostoevski and Edwards had never known any unhappiness that did not arise from petty vanity, the evils and miseries they imagined having arisen from a sense of injured petty vanity—e.g., the thoughts, "Am I deserving of God's love?" "Is the pride I feel at perhaps being deserving of salvation sinful and deserving of God's displeasure?" "Have I really humbled and humiliated myself sufficiently to merit salvation, for it is on salvation that I, unworthy though I am, have set all my hopes and which I intend to teach the human race the way to?" "How can God allow such and such evils to exist, of which were I the victim, I would be miserable?" etc.

But for Dante, Michelangelo, and Beethoven the great universal force (God) was from the beginning to be thought of as the only important entity there was, with nothing else mattering in the least. So all human joys and miseries, including their own, were of no consequence in comparison, and it was this thought of a purely imaginary nature having nothing to do with petty vanity, "God is everything; I and everyone else are nothing; I must love God for this," that must have made them unhappy at some point of their life. But to be weak enough to feel so was to disrespect the all-important universal force, which being the only important entity there is, should be loved for making the world in the manner it has over all other possibilities.[1] Therefore they had to invent entirely imaginary justifications for happiness at the felt-truth of the idea of divine omnipotence (or in Beethoven the omnipotence of the universal force) and the logical result of the inconsequence of all feelings of mere mortals. They were thus able to raise a rather commonplace medieval passion found not only in Dostoevski and Edwards but St. Francis and many others to the maximum degree of stable vanity happiness possible.

A related class of ordinary pleasures of vanity is that which arises from a pretended love of selflessness and hatred or contempt of selfishness (e.g., the Buddha, Schopenhauer, Beckett); this class has been

---

[1]The relation of the happiness of Dante *et al.* to Nietzsche's and Miss Bina Rai's should be obvious from this idea.

raised to the highest level of vanity by Ozu, who was not made unhappy by the thought, "Selfishness is mean or worthless, therefore I must attempt to attain selflessness to the degree possible," but by the thought, "To will anything, even a supposedly selfless state, feeling, or act, is to be self-oriented, and therefore not noble; to do otherwise is impossible even as a possibility." Now, where utter selflessness appears most to at least exist is in the feelings of a parent for a child, at least in the best of cases; this, because the mechanics of the imagination makes the parent think of his or her child as of the self, but since this is not in fact true, the love for a child, in the best cases, appears to be a selfless love which asks for nothing in return, not even the desire for some sort of requital or acknowledgement. Therefore Ozu's imagination concentrated on family relations, and in *Late Spring* he rose, by means of ideal art, utilizing narrative and cinematic exaggerations, to a level where a selfish series of acts acknowledged to be such is equated by the imagination with selflessness.[1] In *Tokyo Story* where he pushed the idea into a new apparent shape, the selfish person who is unselfish is now made into a daughter-in-law; here, as in many such second equivalent masterpiece by an artist of the higher reaches of the imagination, the barest nuances of style carry the weight of ideas.

A singular case is that of Rumi. A poet of thoughts, he seems to have had a peculiar nature: he had the proselytizing spirit without any real pleasure from converting or persuading others to a faith. There was the pleasure of being connected with (in the language of poetry, being one with) God, common to mystics, as well as the proselytizing spirit, also not uncommon, but no real pleasure from converting, though conversion was desired. What made him unhappy most of all, "Faith in and union with God is everything, but all thoughts and words even about this are nothing, so to speak or think of this subject, to myself and others, is all-important but worthless." This unhappiness was overcome by the imagination's conceiving of the necessity of expression, and therefore of poetry and thoughts, and then not deriving any happiness from the expression, which though is simultaneously regarded as imperative from God's point of view, as bringing more people to God. The pride, then, is of being one with God in this mission, since one is, in the end, indifferent to it, and this maximum vanity happiness, expressed

---

[1]Ozu's happiness, like that of Dante, Michelangelo, Beethoven, Nietzsche, and Miss Bina Rai, consisted of making the process of vanity as contradictory as possible.

in the *Mathnavi* ("Spiritual Couplets"), is that of the supreme confidence of knowledge, of knowing all, because the illusion is that one is one with God and therefore knows all. The conventional mysticism of being lost in God (or "the Eternal") in the self, or being all composed of Love, etc., found in all religions, and in men and women such as Kabir, Eckhart, Teresa of Avila, Lao-tzu, Attar, Tagore, Novalis, Dickinson, Whitman, Ramakrishna, Lurian, etc., is raised in intensity and number of ideas in the case of Rumi into the unique intense pride of *knowing solely* with God. In a strange way, the maximum vanity happiness of contradictory selflessness is here combined with that of identifying with the conceived omnipotent force.

For Fielding and Grable the idea that produced the greatest unhappiness was: "Experience and examples tell me that when you feel something there has to be something that justifies that feeling; however when I try to justify the feeling of love and tenderness that often takes hold of my soul for what seems no reason at all, the only result is that it vanishes." Their response: Examine what justifications others have for their happiness; seeing that for the very large part these justifications are hypocritical, affected, self-ignorant, or venal (or a combination), they found in them objects of a never bitter laughter; but, further seeing that the best of justifications are not infallible guides to happiness, they were able to feel much more confidently and intensely the feeling of serious and tender love in the abstract, not unjustified any longer because the ridiculousness or shortcomings of justified alternatives are seen all too clearly. The comic tone of the two has its cause in the fact that everything but that degree of love and consequent virtue strikes them as either slightly or deeply ridiculous.

Shakespeare, Mozart, and Madhubala in their melodic works provide something that justifies reveries of beauty; this requires an extremely ornate and even barbarously ornate use of the medium, that, when it operates upon the soul with an essentially insignificant backdrop of narrative events and themes, frees the imagination from thoughts of happiness to allow it to dwell upon whatever comes to mind as *possible* reasons for happiness. You think upon anything that already gives you pleasure and feel that the happiness it promises you seems to increase even as you continue to think of it as the melodies flash upon your soul.

I think that their ability to feel a great number of dramatic passions so strongly must have led them to unhappiness over the thought of their final indifference to each, and subsequently to their exploitation of their nature to produce dramatic art, and finally to the level of happiness where one's own character or wishes are insignificant, and the reveries of beauty the only thing of consequence. Though their secondary works are dramatic, they discovered their greatest happiness (and produced their greatest masterpieces) in a sensation that has nothing to do with active interactions among people.

Not so the case with Gable, also a dramatic genius. Being made unhappy by the thought, "Sensitivity leads, practically speaking, to failure and unhappiness; impudence, which has the drawback of finding no object to be of any worth, thereby producing no real happiness, leads on the contrary to practical success and what the common run of people generally think is happiness," he could only attain happiness by a study of the heart that allowed him to affect impudence that contained all possible ideas, to the degree of utter self-containment, self-assurance, self-contentment, and self-love. This was an affectation, an act, and he knew it. The unwitting result of this dramatic genius, which surprised Gable himself, was that women saw in the manner that he played his roles a man of an astonishingly strong character (the masculine quality they admire most), plus, what made him stand apart from all rivals and leave them behind, a man who seemed to be able to see to the depths of their own souls unsentimentally and derive pleasure from what he saw there—this second part of the unwitting result arose from the fact they did not at all comprehend that the impudently assured self-containment, though utterly natural once attained, was a deliberate and conscious affectation to avoid imaginary unhappiness on the part of an all too sensitive man.

In addition to the ones described already, there is at least one more manner by which an equal degree of vanity can be attained, that of Cervantes. This one has the curious appearance in as much as only pleasure is expressed, and very little of the pain that must have preceded it.

In all these cases where the highest level of vanity happiness is attained, in the process of knowing these new pleasures, a man or woman ends up making an intimate study of the heart, for these pleasures are of too novel and curious a character to be known and understood until sufficient mastery of the workings of the heart has been attained to allow him or her to clearly mark all the nuances that distinguish them from ordinary pleasures.

Don Quixote is a record of Cervantes' discovering this highest degree of vanity happiness by means of extreme idealization regarding the possibility of dreams that are known to be impossible, that is to say, of ideal art. What Proust stated, and Renoir and Titian (in his non-harmonic paintings) expressed was limited by the fact that none had suffered himself to fall into the folly of inventing reasons for unhappiness out of thin air, reasons having nothing to do with petty vanity, as Cervantes did. Instead of being made unhappy by the thought that "If life had such and such a quality it would have been better or perfect, but unfortunately it does not," Cervantes was made unhappy by the thought, "I like only what is not real, not because reality is poor and what I imagine to be perfection better, but only because one happens to be true and the other not." Having allowed himself this folly of the imagination, but not content with remaining unhappy only for this reason, he was in a position to rise to the highest degree of vanity happiness.

First, beginning to see in a clearer light other people's happiness, he found much to laugh at their love of illusions, at their self-delusion (e.g., the priest in *Don Quixote* during the book burning scene). But that most people and their passions were laughable was not enough; by being able to laugh at his own special unhappiness, vanity was more keenly and fully recompensed for the very imaginary unhappiness that he suffered from. These two factors having come together when he began to write *Don Quixote* his vanity was sufficiently gratified for him to feel a little happiness and indulge himself by prolonging the work of art, a description of what never happened and so something that had not the drawback of being real. This new happiness, consisting as it did of purely imaginary delights, and sharpened further by exact knowledge of many other people's happiness, and the limitation of those, is equal in degree of pleasure, of imagination, to Fielding's or to that of the Mozart who wrote the music of *Le Nozze di Figaro*.

This is as high as the passion of ideal art can go.

If, instead of Cervantes', the idea that produced the most unhappiness in an artist who happened to have a talent for painting was, "Everything painted is pretty, and nothing real is so; and this not because there are no beautiful things in life, but merely because in the former case, everything is imagined, while in the latter, it is real," he will be driven to paint with extreme liveliness of sensations in order to find a deep pleasure that can overcome his unhappiness. He will delight in colors and figures to an extreme degree, and this newly discovered happiness will in turn lead him, because he wishes to be able to explain its nature to himself, to a deep study of the heart. In the faces and gestures of his figures will then appear the result of this knowledge. But for him this will still not be perfect happiness. In his feminine figures he will be able to abandon himself to pure love of prettiness raised to a sublime degree by having adduced to it knowledge of lower pleasures, and then mostly when the situations wherein they are described are touched by a sense of pure enchantment, when they are set in imaginary gardens of delight. This is what you will find in the mythological paintings of Veronese, a painter who has been surpassed only by Raphael and Correggio, and equalled only by Guercino and Michelangelo.

The masters of the irrational logic of reveries, Raphael, Ophuls, and the Shakespeare, Mozart, and Madhubala of the melodic works, for some portion of their lives at least were not content with the stable level of happiness at which Beethoven, Cervantes, Miss Bina Rai, Betty Grable, etc. arrived, because the unchanging level of happiness consequent to intense movements of the soul, though very great, does not produce the illusion of perfection as do sustained tender reveries, in which every moment is a discovery seemingly for the first time of the promise of what one suspects is perfect happiness.

Chapter XXVI

Correggio and Jean Arthur

The chief merit of Correggio's painting is generally said to lie in the chiaroscuro effects, and the manner in which they heighten the amorous subject. But that may as well be a description of Leonardo's genius, with only the shade of amorous effect differing.

George Stevens called Jean Arthur one of the greatest comediennes of the screen; Capra said that she was the greatest actress he ever worked with. No one else of note has had much to say about her,[1] yet those are

---

[1] When I wrote this I did not remember Hawks' disappointment with her. He directed her in his trivial melodrama, *Only Angels Have Wings*. Jean Arthur, he later said, was the

sufficiently high praises. But what do they tell us of her art? If you did not know whom Stevens was speaking of, you may think, "Oh, of course, Carole Lombard."

Correggio and Jean Arthur expressed in their best works all the various sensations of first crystallization that occur in love which has met with requital; the pleasures of the imagination during intimacy.

Ideal and harmonic artists can only show pictures of love that are exaggerated according to the specific arts. So, Rembrandt's Bathsheba, Renoir's Camilla, Tolstoy's Anna, Nabokov's Ada express beauties that are products of painterly, cinematic, and literary exaggerations and not the exaggerations of love, and so cannot equal the intensity of the sensations called up by the latter.

Leonardo is an exception. His greatest happiness seems to have been inspired by physical love, and it is its pleasures largely that he sought to express in most of his paintings.[1] But physical pleasures are just that, physical. All that can be expressed in art is limited to the crystallization of physical love, and the pleasures of the imagination during the actual possession of a woman.

Leonardo succeeded in expressing the latter. Having talent as well as genius, he devised a manner of making his women seem physically present in a manner that no other painter even approaches. Further, he put them in misty and desolate places, to suggest the idea not of sadness but of solitude, of being away from intruders. If other figures besides the central female one were required, because his age demanded that the most successful painter produce Madonnas or other religious figures, they are described with great physiological exactness.[2] They thus do not distract in the manner of ideal art from the feeling of a secluded niche far away from people but endowed with the worth of the whole world— they are purely ornamental presences, and do not take away the eye from the Madonna.

---

only actor or actress he had ever worked with whom he felt he had not helped in any way.

[1]One of the anecdotes he loved to repeat as forming a good argument for the superiority of painting over all the other arts concerned a man for whom he had painted a beautiful saint. Some time after the painting had been delivered to him, he came back to Leonardo begging him to repaint the picture, only this time leaving the figure unclothed, for he had fallen in love with the woman and did not wish to be reminded of the apparent religious subject. Can any other art form have an equally great an impact upon the soul, Leonardo would ask.

[2]By which I mean that he gives them a studiously chosen temperament.

In all of the portraits of women, including the Madonnas, Leonardo carefully gives very precisely observed physical details that are natural to real women—he approaches the subject as a scientist, not an ideal artist. The impulse that drove him to put the thing down on canvas and fix the image is that of the imaginative side of physical pleasure, the pleasures *of the imagination* that arise in the course of possessing a woman, and this is what you feel when you see the paintings.[1]

Kate Chopin and, in our own age, the actress Miss S— have expressed the pleasures of imagination in the course of intimate physical love in women as fully and successfully as Leonardo did those in men.

Physical crystallization at its most intense has been expressed by Annibale Caracci in the Farnese Palazzo frescoes and by Emily Brontë in *Wuthering Heights*. This is purely the pleasure of dreaming of physical pleasure.

No doubt there is some intensity in physical crystallization, but the imagination being limited to mental ideas of pleasure deriving from the sense of touch and sight sans moral ideas, it cannot compare with crystallization of a more deeply passionate character[2] where the most extreme ideas of moral worth are put to use as well. Too much beauty in a woman hinders crystallization because the first impression can never be surpassed. Correggio and Jean Arthur express the maximum number of ideas of pleasure that happy love knows.

Raphael and Ophuls expressed the maximum intensity that the first crystallization produces. Intensity in love is a product of doubts, doubts concerning the beloved's true merits, her love for you, and your own ability to maintain the appearance of an attractive or at least proud self-respect; doubts concerning all the circumstances that prevent a closer intimacy with her, etc. When crystallization continues at a rapid pace simultaneously with these doubts, the intensity increases exponentially.

They express that aspect of vanity love which is torn by doubts and fatal despair consequent to irreparable loss.[3] Unhappy love alternates

---

[1]The effect of those paintings where the subjects are men, such as *The Last Supper* and *Saint John*, is more tender, perhaps because constant dwelling upon thoughts of physical love, and its frequent gratification, led him often to feel the sweet languor of the aftermath.

[2]I do not speak of the second crystallization of passion here, but of deep first crystallization.

[3]This is why Ophuls said that the effect of purity (i.e., maximum crystallization) that he attempted to express had no explanation in real life, for any thought of action would dispel it.

between unbearable grief and sensations consequent to the imagining of *perfect moral beauty* when you are able to ignore the truth and fall back upon imagined solutions.

The works of Correggio and Jean Arthur inspire less intense sensations because they call up the tender reveries of deeply affectionate intimacy.

Let us say, for the sake of clarity and convenience, that the degrees of perfection that one can find in the object of love ranges from the minimum of one to a maximum of eight. Raphael and Ophuls give you the pleasure of feeling the perfection to be eight, but this is only possible because at no point do you stop exaggerating with your imagination the pleasures possible. This is still not absolute perfection, for what is felt is still moral beauty as opposed to passion, but it is as high as the ideas of moral perfection can go. Raphael and Ophuls could express these because they single-mindedly follow the logic of unceasing crystallization during an unhappy love.

If, on the other hand, when crystallization has proceeded until the stage when six degrees of perfection are felt, and then full requital and intimacy ensue, the resulting happiness that will be felt is what Correggio and Jean Arthur express in their greatest works. The loss of a sense of perfection is made up for by the pleasures of certainty of happiness. So, the sense of beauty is not perfect, but the sense of secure vanity happiness is.[1]

---

[1]Stendhal described the matter as follows,

"On pouvait peut-être désirer encore [apres Michel-Ange, Giorgione, Titien, Raphaël] quelque chose de plus doux et de plus attrayant.

"Le Corrège parut, et sut réunir à des formes plus grandioses peut-être que celles de Raphaël, quelque chose de suave et de tendre que la peinture n'avait point exprime avant lui. Il éloigna de l'âme tout ce qui pouvait la blesser, même le plus indirectement....

"Le Corrège fut le premier qui peignit avec l'objet de presénter aux yeux une réunion de couleurs agréables, une opposition de lumières et d'ombres qui leur offrît un doux repos, et par ce plaisir physique pénétrât jusqu'au coeur....

"Ce grand artiste voulait toucher les coeurs et s'en emparer d'abord. Il a connu les secrets de la séduction....

"Mais, quelque grand que soit le Corrège, je suis loin de croire que Raphaël doive lui céder. Quoique les peintures d'Allegri soient plus égales dans l'exécution et plus exquises, il n'a pas possédé au même point que Raphaël l'expression des mouvements de l'âme, dernier objet de la peinture, à l'égard duquel tous les autres ne sont, pour ainsi dire, que les moyens. Du moins il n'a surpassé Raphaël que dans les expressions de deux mouvements de l'âme: l'attendrissement de la *Madonna alla scodella*, de la *Madeleine devant saint Jerome*, et la volupte des âmes si profondement sensibles.

"Le peintre d'Urbin n'a rien fait dans ce genre, tout comme le Corrège n'a pas laissé de

Whether the pleasures of these reveries are preferable to the ones of perfect beauty that Madhubala, Shakespeare, Mozart, Ophuls, and Raphael inspire, or the reverse, who can pretend to say? On the one hand you have more intense sensations and the other more gratifying ones. Whether intensity is preferred or gratification depends upon your temperament.

In regard to the control of the time element, the same difference exists between Correggio and Jean Arthur as between Raphael and Ophuls. Correggio had perforce to leave all the succeeding stages up to the viewer;[1] Jean Arthur described these by relying upon the developing plot.

The chief problem faced by them was the same that faced Raphael and Ophuls as artists, How do you inspire the birth and deepening of

---

têtes d'apôtres comparables à celles du tableau de la *Transfiguration*, ni des figures de femmes qui aient l'expression sublime de la *Madonna alla sediola*....

"En voyant un tableau de Raphaël, l'âme sent plus de ce que les yeux voient; dans le Corrège, les yeux sont plus enchantés que l'âme n'est touchée...."

"One could perhaps still desire [after Michelangelo, Giorgione, Titian, Raphael] something sweeter and more attractive.

"Correggio appeared, and could unite to forms more grandiose perhaps than those of Raphael something sweet and tender that painting had not expressed before him. He eliminated from the soul all that could offend, even very indirectly....

"Correggio was the first who was painting with the aim of presenting to the eyes a union of pleasing colors, a contrast of lights and shadows which offers them a sweet resting-place [or rest, tranquility], and through this physical pleasure penetrates into the heart....

"This great artist wished to touch hearts and take possession of them at once. He has understood the secrets of seduction....

"But, however great Correggio is, I am far from thinking that Raphael must yield to him. Although Allegri's paintings were very equal in execution and more exquisite, he did not possess to the same degree as Raphael the expression of motions of the soul, the highest aim of painting, in comparison to which all others are, so to speak, nothing but means. At least, he did not surpass Raphael except in the expression of two motions of the soul: the tenderness of the *Madonna all scodella*, of *Madeleine before Saint Jerome*, and the voluptuousness of profoundly sensitive souls.

"The painter of Urbino has done nothing in this genre, just as Correggio has not left behind heads of apostles comparable to those in the picture of the *Transfiguration*, nor figures of women who have the sublime expression of the *Madonna alla sediola*....

"When seeing a picture of Raphael, the soul feels more than what the eyes see; in Correggio, the eyes are more enchanted but the soul is not touched...."

Although Stendhal saw Raphael less clearly than he did other artists, out of no lack of abilities or faults of his own, the difference he draws between Raphael's expression of motions of the *soul* and Correggio's manner of touching the *heart* is nevertheless perfectly accurate and precise.

[1]Though he could express different nuances of happy vanity love in different paintings. Thus, his Madonna now at the Louvre has a very different effect from his Io.

crystallization in your audience when everyone dreams of different particulars?

The answer was identical. They aimed at producing what, to those who have known some great happiness in love and who want to revive those reveries, will be a suitable resting place for the eyes.[1]

In themselves, the great Madonnas of Correggio and Jean Arthur's performances in *History is Made at Night* and *A Lady Takes a Chance* have no power to inspire any reveries. The draughtsmanship of Correggio often seems crude, even ugly on occasions, especially in comparison with that of the Florentines, while Jean Arthur rarely seems to rise above the expression of pretty sentiments.

Their effects are produced by the very casual appeal to the soul of the viewer.[2] The effect is offhand, and like the happiness of requited and intimate love, it cannot be traced to its source in the mind without destroying the sensation—and when that happens, the source, whatever it was, ceases to be of any consequence.

------

[1] Happy love in their case.

[2] Even in a film like *The Devil and Miss Jones*, in which there is no love plot worth speaking of, the effect of Jean Arthur's acting is roughly similar to that in *History is Made at Night*, though the degree of crystallization expressed is less. Similarly, those paintings of Correggio where the subject is more directly amorous as well as some of the lesser Madonnas. Even in his most amorous paintings, Correggio retains some moral ideas of pleasure. He never expresses solely the delights of physical crystallization in the manner of Leonardo or Annibale Caracci. The lack of sobriety and of evenness of temper in those paintings prove that he did not feel love in the manner of Leonardo—it is that sobriety in the latter that produces the tinge of melancholy that is associated in his paintings with solitude. Similarly, Jean Arthur in *The More the Merrier* in comparison to Miss S- in a number of films, or *The Awakening*.

BOOK TWO

"Why does she laugh with them?" He was not sure of anything anymore. He did not know what he was doing, nor why. "What mad folly has brought me back here? Could I be more unhappy if I left forever?" Thus the evening passed.

Rojas

Chapter XXVII

Of Love

Stendhal divided love into four classes, passionate love, mannered love (*amour-gôut*), vanity love, and physical love, a classification that cuts across temporal and geographical boundaries.

Mannered love is very rare today in the United States, but it survives in the uppermost classes of some poor countries. It is the most insipid and affected form of love.

By far the greatest majority of people love from vanity. At best you may expect to find a good dose of physical pleasure mixed in with vanity, but even this is rare.

Physical pleasure is to a great degree unknown among women outside the United States and those nations and classes most influenced by American opinions. Even among men, universally speaking, it is much less common than you would at first think. Physical desire is the most common thing in the world, and only a little less common is its natural denouement. But physical love has its crystallization, an advanced degree of which is rarely to be met with, except in the warmer southern regions.[1]

Deep physical crystallization is for the large part unknown in the northern nations where the general population is constantly hard at work, originally out of dread of hard winters, though today this fact, which still exists, is obscured by the general prosperity of the West. The imagination of such people is ossified through too habitual practice of petty self-interest. They cannot afford a more cavalier attitude towards life. And the six months of very cold weather is enough to cool the physical passions to the degree that they need some time in the spring before they begin to become lively again. Therefore the relative coolness of physical passion even among the aristocrats and royalty of past ages.[2]

---

[1]This, unfortunately, is not a glib generalization. Why is there a rejuvenation of the animal spirits in the spring?

[2]Except in a few individual cases (Henry VIII, Catherine the Great) wherein promiscuity was not a mild passion, as in Casanova or Charles II, but these exceptions

Passionate love is very rare today, and has been so through all history. I mean true passion, for vanity will often pretend to be the grandest of passions. Societies need not be ascribed the entire blame for its rarity. In his description of passions Helvétius made only one error. He was convinced that every healthy man is endowed with equal and identical nature at birth. No wonder he had nothing to say of passionate love, which is a delicate flower of mysterious birth.

Chapter XXVIII

Of the Birth of Love

Love is born with the hope of being loved.

You may have met the woman whom you will one day be madly in love with without having conceived for her in all that time any feeling above that of tepid admiration, if even that. What is even more strange is that even warm admiration does not in itself lead to love until you begin to hope, and then it does not matter whether any admiration preceded it or not. In fact, too great an admiration before the birth of hope is a serious disadvantage since hope will then not result in as violent and unexpected a thunderbolt of pleasure from crystallization. Only thoughts of a conquest can then arise.

Until love is born, the beauty that you see in a woman is a general estimate, and rarely considered too curiously. After its birth, her beauty (i.e. physical plus moral elements promising happiness) is greatly exaggerated by the lover, the degree of exaggeration depending upon the liveliness of his temper. A cold and vain person cannot crystallize too much; a woman's physical charm, her wealth or position, her being coveted by men by whom he seeks to be envied, etc. will lead him to exaggerate her worth a little, but not too much. Any excessive idea of her worth would strike him as ridiculous. He fears wounding his self-esteem.

The pleasures of crystallization arise from imagining to yourself how much happiness the beloved will give you. Since every perfection the

---

stand out so clearly that they prove the general case has been the opposite. And Italy, Spain, and Greece are not northern countries.

lover endows her with increases his pleasure, he ascribes to her all the perfections he can think of. The limit is his sum knowledge of beauties and perfections. It has nothing to do with the qualities of the woman he has fallen in love with, so long as these do not strike him as repulsive nor blatantly contradict his illusions—even in this latter case, a man of lively passions will, given a little time, produce for himself justifications, extenuating circumstances, etc., that vindicate her entirely.

The initial intoxication is often so great that the lover can easily imagine the beloved to have perfections absolutely incompatible with her true nature.

Although common in both sexes, this sort of misjudgment occurs perhaps more among women. For a woman of any spirit and imagination at all, love is always something divine and heavenly. When she begins to love in earnest, the newly felt pleasures are so keen that she will often not bother to consider coldly and logically the true character of the man she has fallen in love with. Careless of matters of prudence, she will generously ascribe to him all the tenderness and sensitivity that she herself possesses, as well as exaggerate the most attractive masculine charms. Only experience teaches such a woman coldness, but by the time she has learned to be suspicious, she may be afraid of loving again, or if she is prouder, be contemptuous of the folly of loving. Pride and caution lead her to withhold her heart even when she gives herself up to a man—until she is absolutely certain of his true feelings.

There is another kind of misjudgment, a more affected kind.[1] This is when a man tells himself that he is very much in love when he is not. This leads to the most ridiculous affectations, and there is not much pleasure to be had. Such affectations are the lot chiefly of those who love only because they do not want to left behind. Left to themselves, without the examples in society, history, books, and films that they know, they would never waste their time in dreams of love, but content themselves with its commonplace forms and declarations. Petty vanity dominates their hearts.

It can be stated mathematically that if the quantity of beauty, nobility, etc., that a man knows from memory is, say, x, then sooner or later the beloved will be thought to be the only being in the universe

---

[1] Madame Bovary and Léon. I use literary examples only as illustrations known to many.

who possesses x (the maximum possible to the one in love) amount of worth, and hence will be that much lovable.[1]

Not only do all known virtues and lovable qualities appear to belong to the beloved; what you thought tedious or ugly may become suddenly a lovely thing when it is linked to your beloved by chance or by herself. She tells you that she loves to ride horses, and all your hatred for the country disappears in an instant. You can hardly wait to take riding lessons, you dream of her leading you through to competency in the sport, step by step. You overhear her telling her friend that she always wanted to be in the advertising business. Suddenly you no longer have utter contempt for the vulgar banalities of advertisements. You begin to see how much nobility one must have to be fascinated by advertising in the first place, and, truly how much charm there is in the whole business.

Crystallization only continues in this manner so long as the lover is not absolutely sure of success. The moment he is sure he is loved, especially if he imagines intimacy to be just around the corner, it stops for the time being. At first, the mind is agog at the prospect of the physical pleasure that lies ahead. Vanity comes in next when crystallization resumes after intimacy, and he congratulates himself on the happiness that is now his: every perfection that has delighted him is now enjoyed out of vanity, for the knowledge that it is his.

For maximum physical pleasure, the interval between hope and intimacy should be minimum. The crystallization of physical love is a matter of memory. As the interval increases, the portion of the sum pleasure that arises from vanity also increases. Attachment and fidelity are also bound to increase, unless the crystallization continues to consist of anticipations of physical pleasures only. It is up to the woman (in whom love develops more easily into a serious attachment) to ensure a more lasting attachment. It is no wonder that delaying tactics, coyness, pretended indifference, false anger, pretended interest in other men, etc., are the stocks-in-trade of women's responses.[2]

---

[1]Countless poets, both those who have celebrated the physical aspect of love and the more mystically inclined, have stated this fact explicitly, e.g., Shelley's *Alastor*, *Epipsychidion*, and his short essay *On Love*.

The cold or vain man is what he is because he lacks ideas of pleasure. Imagination acts solely upon perceived objects, so that the pleasures of self-love depend upon how highly you esteem those whose admiration you seek.

[2]Women whose favors are easily obtained have little hold upon their lovers. Only his

After intimacy, crystallization resumes its course, and continues so long as love does. The happiness that he has found in the arms of his mistress inspires gratitude, which leads him to further exaggerate her worth. He convinces himself that no other woman could have given him half as much pleasure. In this manner, the pleasures of intimacy and vanity together in turn inspire further crystallization, and his love deepens, though the intensity of vanity love levels out as soon as gratitude for tender intimate pleasure is born.

Crystallization may stop at any point due to accidents of circumstance, the lover's discovering that he has made a mistake, or because something she does, or does not, wounds his vanity.

Chapter XXIX

Of Hope

To hope is to notice in a woman a weakness for yourself.

It *always* leads to curiosity. For at least a few seconds, the man pictures to himself what pleasures the woman can give him.[1] At this stage, the imagination *automatically* exaggerates these as much as it can with respect to her, and depending upon the intensity with which this happens, and upon the thoughts regarding the disadvantages or inconveniences of loving her (e.g., she is less than beautiful and insipid after all, her father can have you thrown into jail, she has a very revengeful lover already, you run a risk with your own present love, or because pursuing her will interfere with the time you can give to your career, etc.), crystallization continues, or ends at this point.

---

fear of being ridiculed (i.e., the fear of having it thought that she left him), or his general lack of confidence with women can guarantee such a woman that her lover will not be unfaithful. In a society like the United States', where love has been made easy, infidelity is very common among both men and women. In more repressed societies, the cause of infidelity is that men and women make their selection of a marriage partner on the basis of the wealth and security that will result from the connection. It is from fear of ridicule that the Italians and the Spaniards used to lock away their wives, as the Arabs and the Indians still do. In tolerant societies, infidelity arises when some sort of love or the other has brought the men and women together in the first place.

[1]*Much Ado About Nothing.*

There is only one exception to the rule: When the object's ugliness is so keenly felt that hope does not inspire even curiosity. So it is as much the proud man or woman who begins to love with difficulty as the cold one.

There is no limit to the duration of this phenomenon where you exaggerate to yourself the pleasures a woman can give you. It may all be over in an instant, or it may last a lifetime.

There is no difference between hoping and loving.

The birth of hope is simpler and more common among women, not only because their imagination is more preoccupied by the subject, but because a man makes no effort, except in the rarest of cases of extreme vanity, to hide his admiration. In this matter of the birth of love, as in almost everything to do with love, a woman's situation holds greater possibilities of an uncertain or unhappy end. She has therefore to always be cautious and restrained both in accepting the attentions of a man she has not positively decided against yet, and in attracting the attention of the man she prefers.

Women generally suffer less from doubts of whether they have succeeded in inspiring a lively interest in a man they want to attract, but they have more reason to doubt the sincerity of the men who profess to love them. A man does not doubt the sincerity of a woman who has glanced a little more than casually at him several times, although he may doubt the liveliness of the interest.[1]

I am speaking of serious love, love based upon *dreaming*. So far as easy love is concerned, women have it much easier. Even mild prettiness goes a long way.

A society tolerant of love develops institutions to bring young men and women together in an air of gaiety and amusements. The birth of love is greatly encouraged when they can come together in situations public enough for them to risk love without having to face those they met for the rest of their lives. On the other hand, intensity of crystallization is discouraged, and the general blandness of love further discourages intensity by example.

---

[1] The younger the woman, the more likely she is to be playing at love, and the more suspicions there should be about her sincerity. The desire to shine in the eyes of her friends usually takes precedence over love before she is eighteen. Later, unless she is using a man to inspire jealousy in a lover, a woman gives hope to a man only when she is sincere. The exceptions are when she is desperate to marry or find a man who will pay her bills, or when she needs the aid of a man to promote a matter in whose development she has an interest.

Otherwise, very few dare to love (for loving requires great *courage*) until they are sure of being loved in return, and this is triply true of women. Certainty can only come with time and experiments, and the lover can never rule out the possibility of a half-hearted rejection. He must have sufficient vanity to be able to bear this easily, and this is why women in societies that lack such institutions know better than to follow their hidden wishes for happiness and begin to love in return.[1] They fear that they cannot afford to trust in the good intentions of any man not approved of by their parents.

Fear hinders the birth of love, and makes all but impossible open declarations of feelings to the object of love.

There is always the additional fear of being humiliated by the story of his failure getting around. Every stage of love is a more difficult undertaking then, but there is possibility for passion to develop should the first few stages be successfully passed. The development of passion, though, depends upon the nature of the man and woman.

In countries whose government and societies are very corrupt, to the degree of general dishonesty,[2] passion never develops among men no matter how great the obstacles overcome. The reason for this is that their wish to find a mistress arises, at best, from petty vanity; generally, though, they are interested in nothing more than physical pleasure, and to be able to boast to other young men. They can never be unsure of that woman's love who is flying in the face of all the pieties she has been taught, all the caution and fears that have been instilled in her—at best there is gratitude, which is much preferable to the common forms of love that are found in such countries. But due to this very abandoning of caution, women who wander outside socially accepted circles have nothing to live for but love. The highest passion nevertheless rarely develops even among them since their greatest fear is that their lovers will give in to family and social opinions and to the idea of interest, and abandon them. This fear prevents crystallization to the point of absolute perfection.

I can distinguish at least two types of hope:

1) A man deduces from the words, glances, etc., of a woman that she has

---

[1]Their minds are generally trained from their early years to esteem only social rank and look down their noses at love. They give all their attention to acquiring fashionable affectations.

[2]Many third-world countries today.

a weakness for him. If he begins to admire in return, or if he already admires her, he instantly finds many reasons for loving her.

When she begins to love, a woman often feels the need to resist the pleasure of dreaming once she has given the name of love to her reveries. She doubts the wisdom of giving the man too much encouragement at first—something she knows she could not prevent herself from doing if she begins to love—especially if she is sure of him. If not, she fears giving her heart to the wrong man, which for a woman of a sensitive and loving temperament is a mistake fatal to her happiness.

Wherever love is held in low esteem, even men may feel ashamed of the thoughts that arise once they begin to love in earnest. A sensible man[1] only resists the pleasures of newly born love when he already has a mistress.

2) Something causes a man to reflect on the greatness of soul of a woman he has just met or of one he has known for some time without having singled her out in any way. Even though he is uncertain whether or not she has conceived any favorable ideas concerning him, he begins to love because he hopes she has.[2] But even this is not necessary: he can show her his interest, and love is born.

He thinks, "That woman has a sublime soul capable of the most noble love. How much pleasure there must be in being loved by such a creature! Perhaps she will come to love me. She is worth every sacrifice." At this point he is in grave danger, and unless he exercises great caution and restraint, he loses himself in reveries. In this fashion are the greatest (and generally unrequited) passions born, so it is necessary that he control himself at the earliest stage if he wants to avoid years of misery. The problem is that no man falls into this kind of folly unless he is already sick of worldly pleasures, and so he does nothing to curb his imagination from conceiving pictures of heavenly happiness.

The woman has been seen in a sensitive moment (or so the lover tells himself), i.e., a *weak* moment when she does not appear immovable,

---

[1]He who is free of superstitions and venal fears, and has the logic and intelligence to know of and distinguish clearly between the different paths to happiness, and to know which one is for him, and why.

[2]I speak of those whose experience of life and love is great. In teenage years, or whenever the opportunities for love first arise, both men and women are apt to fall in love without the slightest degree of hope out of curiosity regarding love and the desire for greater self-esteem. After a few years of experience the birth of serious love in this manner becomes nearly impossible.

distant, and utterly indifferent, and in his imagination the lover only gives importance to this moment, and to other similar ones. The pleasure of believing in what these seem to say to him is too great to resist with cold logic.

He feels he has good reason to hope, for the nobility and capacity for tenderness reflected in everything to do with the beloved must mean that she will love him once she knows his true feelings. This is only the first of many false leaps of logic that a passionate lover deceives himself with.

There is already less vanity to begin with among such lovers.

They begin with a great practical disadvantage. There is a general and well known rule in love: the more happiness you expect from the love of the beloved, the less effective will you be in obtaining it. In other words, the more you love, the more unhappiness you should expect as your lot. I frankly do not know whether a clear knowledge of this general rule is of any use to the lover. What can it do but encourage him to fall back upon his vanity, a ridiculous response.[1] Fortunately, no one who is capable of passionate love listens to wise counsels when he or she falls in love. The fact is that he cannot connect the idea of unhappiness with that of the woman he loves, and so is blinded to logic.

Second crystallization, or passionate love, is likely to develop in these cases of purely imaginary hope, unless the beloved removes all doubt at once.

When her imagination leads her to set her entire hopes on a man who has not shown any interest in her, a woman is beyond help. She may be able to attract his attention and admiration easily enough, but she will find it difficult to inspire passion since this can only be done by sowing seeds of the strongest doubts in his mind. She must play the game very cautiously, encouraging but rebuffing him in such a manner that he despairs but continues. What makes this very difficult is that she fears, and generally with good reason, that he is not as deeply in love as she. It is then a very tricky business for her to persist any considerable length of time without the fear of losing him altogether getting the better of her. A less than passionate love on his side is better than not having at all the man she loves to distraction.

---

[1]That of those disappointed or humiliated in the past, and bitter as a result. Much vain philosophy (poetic and cynical) is born in this manner, sometimes producing great fame. Eliot, Sartre, Byron, Schopenhauer, Hitchcock, etc.

It is absolutely imperative that a superior woman have the most astute judgment, and a complete knowledge of the ways of the heart if she is to find the kind of happiness she has been seeking since the age of fifteen. Weakness or ignorance in these matters can only result in a life of misery. This fact is so clearly impressed upon their minds that they go to the other extreme, and tend towards overcaution by the time they are eighteen. You will find that intelligent young women possess greater knowledge of themselves, of men, and of the varieties of happiness that exist than do young men, who commonly thrive upon the most dubious ideas born of blind self-esteem.

Another result of this second type of hope: A woman has assured the lover with the most blatant marks of favor, but he has not the courage, vanity, or plain intelligence to think himself so fortunate as to be already favored by her. He will love her deeply in spite of them, because he does not see them for what they are. He hopes that once she is persuaded of the sincerity and purity of his love she will *begin* to love him. But these inspired cases are very rare.

Chapter XXX

Of the First Crystallization

It helps, though it is not necessary, that a little admiration precede hope.[1]

A woman who finds that the unhandsome face or appearance of a man who has thrown himself at her feet, so to speak, prevents her from loving him may not crystallize at all to begin with. However, it is not impossible that in two weeks she will consider him quite passable, and in a few days the handsomest man she has ever laid eyes upon. Such is the madness of crystallization. But one must have time to dream if crystallization is to occur.

Today, when love is generally a tepid enough affair, and passionate love almost unknown, much of what follows may not only be completely

---

[1] The art or science of physiognomy is universally derided today, but it is used by everyone all the same, not only during the birth of love, but during later stages of it, too. In the birth of friendships, even of the most casual variety, physiognomy also comes into play.

unintelligible, but seem, insofar as it is comprehended, utterly untrue to nature. But I assure the reader that I have not the genius to invent anything.

The first moments of hope combined with admiration fill the mind with such pictures of possible happiness that everything else pales in comparison. The temptation to give in to these delicious sensations is too strong to be resisted absolutely.

At this moment, love is born.

The lover delights in discovering perfections in his beloved; and the pleasure of doing so acts as the motive for continuing to love. In other passions, beauty is a transitory sensation that vanishes in a few hours or days. In love, the sensation is reborn every few days, or every few hours, as the lover discovers something new, something unknown in his beloved to admire and dream of. These sensations seem to him *to intensify* in time as he begins to doubt his chances.

It is necessary that success of any type not come too quickly or easily; and that is why *dating* is deadly for the growth of love. The more unsure you are of even catching the glance, or putting in a word in her presence, the deeper will be the pleasure felt, because there is more time and necessity to *imagine* the probable happiness that will be produced by success, and thus greater opportunity for exaggerating it.

Let me try to describe the madness that seizes upon the heart in love.

You are going about some everyday affairs, when, as you turn left at a major intersection, you think you notice his red coupe on the other side. Suddenly your heart is going at a dizzying rate, and it is a few seconds before you are fully aware of just what has happened, it is all over. It is only a few seconds after this delightful but taxing shock that you discover with a pang that you made a mistake, and that it was not he. But fifteen minutes later you are still reeling from the imagined encounter. What happened was that the shock violently restarted the crystallization process.

As summer comes around, the lover notices a thin scar a few inches above the right elbow of the woman he loves. It inspires the most tender reveries in him. The very thought of such a scar is soon enough to transport him to heaven.

He sees on television or reads an account of some bloody period of a distant nation's history. The cruelty and barbarity of some of the personages are proofs of the nobility of his beloved. The heroines of the account seem to be dim and lackluster versions of her. He reads of a trade treaty or a taxation policy, and that is a further impetus to crystallization. He thinks how lovely it would be to live in that country if he could live there with her. He fondly tells himself, "With what heroic simplicity she would always act in the most perilous of situations—what happiness it would be to die with her if it came to that."

As soon as intimacy is attained, the pleasures felt are those of vanity, of knowing how much happiness is yours, and although crystallization continues, it is a much less heady and more sluggish phenomenon after it. The pleasures of tender intimacy can make up for the pleasures of hope-inspired crystallization.

Chapter XXXI

Of Vanity Love

You cannot know during the very initial stages of love to what heights of passion it will develop.

The type and intensity of love can change at any point. Initial thoughts of tenderness may dissipate as the beloved fails to live up to expectations, but physical pleasures may compensate for its dissipation. The opposite often occurs.

Every little nuance of word, gesture, glance, action, etc., of either lover, every accident or new circumstance, can change in an instant the entire character of their love.

No change is permanent, the heart keeps revolving from one to another sensation. That is why love, unless it is utterly affected, is never boring.

Even hatred has its crystallization. Neither of the lovers can become wholly indifferent to each other, until years after everything has ended, if then.

The qualities that are felt as perfections of the object of love are as individual as individual temperaments. For the birth of love, some admiration, hope, and a certain weariness with the *common pleasures* of the world are all equally necessary conditions.[1] The absence of any one of these makes for the insipid passions which can only be called love by default.

The more a man or woman loves out of excess of feeling, and the less out of physical desire, weakness of character, and fear of solitude or ridicule, the more intense are the sensations of love.

The initial impulse is that of simple physical love. One thinks how wonderful to be able to touch her, kiss her, hold her, etc. The slightest hope that she does not dislike you and may give you a chance is reason enough to hope; but when there is a great deal of vanity, the lover wants to be sure of his being favorably received before opening himself to the never far-from-the-mind possibility of a humiliating rejection.

About beauty, Stendhal said that it is an aid in the birth of love. It is not necessary that it be felt initially—so long as ugliness is not present as an obstacle. By ugliness I mean either the lack of perceived physical beauty or the perception of moral blemish, both matters purely of opinion. The fact is that when love is born, whether he suspects as much or not, the lover can see nothing ugly or unbecoming in the beloved anymore, and in a few days he is at a loss in trying to discover anything in her which falls short of perfection. It is only when a physical or moral blemish becomes so transfixed in his imagination that he cannot think of the woman without recalling it that love is stifled before it can manage to turn one's head. In such cases, even if there is some initial sympathy and pity involved, these are replaced by hatred if the perception of this sympathy emboldens the other to unwelcome importunities.

A man or woman will naturally be displeased by unwanted attentions which inhibit his or her own natural manners.[2] This is the reason why a lover who is having difficulty obtaining the love of a woman must exercise great care in how he persists in his efforts to soften her heart. It is only too easy to lose even the little respect he may command in the most secret corner of her heart.

Women lose even more through blatant aggression, to which even gentler sorts are led by despair.

---

[1]The more the weariness with ordinary pleasures, the more violently the first moments of love take hold of a man's or woman's whole being. A content heart has no motivation for inventing new and perilous enchantments.

[2]I.e., even when pity or sympathy has existed heretofore, unwanted advances inspire painful thoughts of loss of freedom and finally, hatred.

If you believe that the one you love is an extraordinary and noble creature, you must be content with seeking a sympathetic understanding of mind and heart, and let fate do the rest. You must act and speak with restraint, and let passion be seen through the whole pattern of your manner. This course of conduct should not be too difficult if you trust the judgement and character of the beloved.

If there is even a little love on the other side, judicious inspiration of doubts alternating with sporadic shows of weakness is the best device. Women commonly use this strategy, and we ought to learn from the mistresses of the subject. I do not think this a cynical advice. The lover is no longer his own master, his whole fate depends upon the kindness of the beloved. All means are permissible toward attaining his end, save false promises and force, both of which inevitably cut off the strongest feelings, and reduce love to a pallid pleasure. When you try to inspire doubt, you will yourself doubt of success, and crystallization is thereby accelerated.

Once love is born, even ugliness appears to be beautiful. A woman notices that her lover, who has just returned from a war, has a hideous scar across his left cheek; or he has lost his hand in an accident. The most tender feelings are inspired by these deformities, and she finds great pleasure in taking care of him, and showing him how much she still loves him. If the injured party is not a creature of vanity, he will be not too displeased at the disastrous loss, in spite of all the inconvenience it otherwise causes him, especially if he feels that her love has only increased greatly as a result.

The birth of love is hindered when one or both feel that there are too many ingrained differences of background or character between the two. These are felt as ugliness.

In these days of racial, ethnic, and cultural stances, affectations, and conflicts, the topic of love between people of different backgrounds, races, etc., is not irrelevant.

Here is what happens when the possibility of love is felt for someone who *seems* to belong to another world: There is either admiration (of one or more qualities that do not seem ugly), or hope, but almost never both at the same time. The differences convince him that no true and deeply felt requital of the admiration is possible. Hope produces suspicion or triumph (depending upon the relative worth ascribed to the two backgrounds, races, nations, etc.). E.g., a woman thinks she is considered an easy catch, he does not respect her, or that she has him in her charming net. It obliterates for the time what admiration there was. The birth of love, which makes the one who loves convert everything regarding the other into dazzling moral perfections, is thus ruled out, and only simple vanity is left.

I doubt that an Indonesian man, for example, will prefer a pretty blonde over a dark-hued beauty. Physical love for the former means nothing, and although his vanity may be gratified by making such a woman his mistress, more tender feelings are unlikely to arise. No matter how keenly the outward charms affect him, all those beauties and moral opinions that depart from his ideas of perfection will at all moments be too strongly impressed upon his mind to allow crystallization. It is only when the woman has thoughtlessly given him too much hope that he is motivated to overcome his hesitations, but in such a case, passion is ruled out. I choose a random example here, it could have been a Swedish man and a Hispanic woman, a Japanese and a Zambian, etc.

It is always merely a matter of prejudice and vanity when one group thinks itself superior to another.

The birth of love is a matter of finding in someone everything that you already think beautiful; this must occur before you begin discovering novel beauties.

An Italian who spent part of his early youth, and feels absolutely at home, in America will be as likely to fall promptly in love with an American woman as with an Italian. A Japanese who has never been abroad will not find the most beautiful Frenchwoman or an Indian mistress as pleasing as a moderately beautiful Japanese mistress, even if he has taken the time to learn French or Hindi. If the most beautiful foreign woman he feels can give him three units of pleasure, the most charming Japanese woman will seem to be able to give him eight. If this man has traveled and lived abroad a good deal since childhood or adolescence, or if he has a more than common power to acclimatize himself to the all the nuances of social manners and prejudices besides those of his own countrymen, if he is mad about France, etc., then only is love possible, since perception of differences will not prevent it.

Because of modern films, music, journalism, television, radio, etc., similar fashions and affectations crop up around the world today. This has encouraged love between very different men and women. There are few barriers to the development of love in the United States. Only the blacks are still out of the picture regarded as a whole. There are more barriers in Europe, even more so in Japan, and so on.

Once love is born, few things can immediately kill it. Annette H.- , a young woman of very great beauty,[1] and of equally great delicacy of mind and temper, once told me she was fed up with having to repeatedly reject men who would not give up. I was an old friend, who moreover had the misfortune not to have ever fallen in love with this charming creature. After thinking for a while, the only thing I could think of saying was, "The only absolutely certain method of ridding yourself of an unwanted but untiring admirer is to heap a host of undisguised personal insults in the most unceremonious manner upon him in public. This will humiliate and anger him, and better, may make him think you coarse. The most strongly worded private rejection cannot kill love. He will not believe you, or he will endeavor to forget your words. He will not be able to forget you or give up, unless he has nothing but vanity in his soul. Both polite and rude private rejections will merely make it impossible for him to conceive of happiness with you, without thereby making it seem that there is less misery in staying away."

In such cases, crystallization stops, but the unhappiness of unrequited love continues for an indefinite time.[2] If the initial impulse of love was

---

[1]The reader may not take my word for this claim, so I give the following inventory: Beauty of the British variety: slim, good-figure, tall, small round head, thin pert lips and small nose, very lively blue eyes, very fair complexion with just a touch of faint blush of pink, reddish hair, changeable and lively temperament (the other British type of beauty is the cool, elegant, immovable, unapproachable woman). Altogether different from the affected pertness of expression and manners of Frenchwomen; the soulful eyes and manners of beautiful German women (the other type is the masculine German woman); the eager and soulful earthiness of broad-boned Slavic beauties; the passionate temperament of a strong Italian woman whose beauty lies in her character; the sensual temperament of Spanish women reflected in their glances, gait, and carriage; the long-haired, round-faced, dark-eyed beauties of India the greatest part of whose lives revolve around social affectations, prudery, fear of poverty and scandal, and secret wish for physical pleasures; Japanese women who think themselves beautiful when they make themselves up into pretty, elegant, and delicately decorated dolls. This kind of classification is only useful when talking of nations as a whole. Individuals exhibit infinite variations: the study and pursuit of beauty and happiness are as much an art as a science.

[2]Darcy's reactions to Elizabeth's rude rejection vs. Collins' to her polite rejection, in *Pride and Prejudice*. Darcy is immediately humiliated, Collins persists, his vanity blinding him to the fact that she despises him. It is not in Darcy's power to cease to love Elizabeth, although he at first tells himself that he hates her, and then deludes himself with the thought that she means nothing to him anymore. Collins forgets her immediately.

strong, all sincere attempts of the object of love to convince the lover of his utter lack of hope will only add to his conviction that she is most worthy of love, and that only she can make him happy. He feels that he is only too aware of his present state of happiness to be mistaken in this regard—this is the absurd delusion of this disease called love, but it also produces the greatest happiness that can be known on earth.

Love, once born, survives more easily among women. Once a woman has in her own heart given herself to a man, only the most abject stupidity on his part can make her feelings change. Even then, she is more likely to repent having fallen in love than to positively stop loving him. Thus, love is doubly dangerous for her.

The more fiery the imagination and warmer the sensibility a man possesses, the more easily love is born. Given a man and a woman of more than common though roughly equivalent warmth of imagination, the birth of love will *probably* (this is only a conjecture) be a more violent and disturbing conflagration in a man, because he will not try to resist in any manner whatsoever the sensations arising within his heart. For this reason, love endures more easily among women. When a woman feels the first violent effects of love, she is divided between giving in to the delightful new reveries, and exercising caution and restraint before the impending crisis. Deep passion, at its birth, is felt by a woman as a secret pleasure that she does not want to fully acknowledge even to herself, let alone to the man who has had the good fortune to inspire it. She may show him marks of favor, but gently, and never exhibiting the true degree of her weakness.[1]

Once crystallization has begun in earnest, everything is adduced to its continuation. It becomes impossible not to find the object of love increasingly enchanting and perfect.

For a cold person, crystallization is not a violent seizure of the feelings; there is little discordance and astonishment, because there are for such a person no series of lively impressions that take control of the heart.

Love, even more than other passions, is absolutely independent of the will, which is why it is so perilous.

Both Aguecheek and Roderigo are rogues, but the latter in his own foolish manner is desperate about Desdemona. Aguecheek is easily turned away.

[1]The comparison I make in this paragraph is not valid when love is purely physical.

Chapter XXXII

Of Passionate Love

The first crystallization consists of all shades of feelings that arise between the point of thinking "She is admirable," and that of thinking "She is perfect, and she is/is not mine."

The simple pleasures of the senses are magnified in the mind of the lover by his imagination. Let us say that the beloved can give him 10 units of pleasure of the senses. He may begin by thinking it will be 8 or 10 units. Six hours later, it is 14, soon it is 16, 6, 24, etc. Depending upon his sensibility, and the duration of hope, this can go on until she seems almost absolutely perfect. After intimacy, which stops this process temporarily, it resumes again. He has his imagination to thank for these surplus units of pleasure.

As she begins to approximate absolute perfection, the keenest transports of love are short-lived, because they are products of extreme nervous energy, and endanger the health of the lover if prolonged too long.

The entire process is purely a matter of beauty and vanity: every fresh stroke of perfection makes the lover happier. His mood is gay and light in the early stages whenever he thinks he is likely to enjoy those perfections. The intoxication is so delightful and novel that it drives out all other thoughts. He begins to set his success in this matter far above that in others, and seeks the love of his beloved in every way he can. This sort of intoxication can lead women to give in too soon.

Unhappiness arises whenever the thought, "She is not/never-will-be mine," takes over. When hope revives, or when he forgets himself and begins to remember the perfections of the beloved, delight and joy are felt again.

The thought, "She will never be mine," poisons the life of the lover as much as does the thought "I will never be a lawyer, statesman, success, etc.," the lives of other men.[1]

Intensity of love depends upon the degree of doubt. The degree of pleasure or pain always depends upon the expected degree of either. For

---

[1]In Japan, students occasionally commit suicide when they have failed to secure the high marks needed in the qualifying examinations to enter those universities on which they have set their hearts.

a few days after he falls in love, the lover has been lost in thoughts of undreamt of pleasures. The time draws near when he shall be in the company of his beloved again. He believes he has reasons to hope for a kind reception, otherwise he would not have been crystallizing at the mad rate he has.

The longed for hour arrives and he stands before her. She on her part ignores him, or treats him as she would any other acquaintance. His distress is immediate. Several hours later, when he has had the opportunity to ponder over his situation, he is in a state of grief beyond words. What is worse, when he tries to think of a means to escape his misery, nothing offers itself. He tries to throw himself into his habitual pleasures, only now they are utterly insipid. He resolves to try to forget her, but he cannot, etc.

Now, in the next meeting, he may find more grounds to hope or despair. When everything seems to be going well, he dreams of her perfections, and of the happiness he will know with her. When things are not going so well, he shuttles back and forth from despair to imagined solutions and happiness. He cannot find any happiness except in being sure of her weakness. He invents long, intricate conversations during the course of which he and the woman he loves come to a *perfect, tender understanding.* He imagines her in his arms, protesting her love for him.

Doubt operates in strange ways. It can poison a lover's happiness even though his beloved has received him with kindness. It can vanish even though she has not. It is nearly impossible to trace its repeated births and deaths to the true causes.

One or two remembered details from his meetings with the beloved are isolated, and only they are given any importance. All the facts that contradict the conclusion regarding whether he is loved or not he has just arrived at fail to seem true to his imagination. But those one or two details that seem important produce either doubt or hope, and the lover continues on that path until, without any warning, he suddenly recalls a contradicting detail with special vividness. It overturns all his old convictions, and he falls into the opposite convictions. Now the details that previously had such great persuasive force seem trivial, and certainly to not be proofs, only the new details seem to give a true picture of where he stands in the heart of the beloved.

First crystallization may go on for any length of time. When hope is followed by doubt and then despair, the first crystallization is intensified. If you obtain all you want at this stage, no matter how prolonged your ordeal has been, passion will not develop, although great doubts after intimacy, whether they be imaginary or based on only too factual foundations, can still lead to passion.[1]

The period that must elapse between the first and the second crystallization is open to all variations. There are no limits in either direction, although it generally consists of several months at least. The exceptions are when 1) the lover is very weary with commonplace pleasures; 2) he fears that either his own or the beloved's death is imminent, and that he has no time to lose; 3) a permanent separation is imminent.

No logical answer exists as to why second crystallization occurs.[2] It is a natural phenomenon, though a very rare one. I doubt whether more than an insignificant fraction of the people of any age or country have ever known it.[3]

First crystallization can persist for any period of time in both favorable and unfavorable circumstances, but the intensity of love (i.e., the degree to which the mind is *actively* engaged in crystallization and in fearing unhappiness) diminishes inevitably in time. A prolonged series of disappointments intensifies love for perhaps a year or two at most, and generally much less.[4] After that love may not die, but it is a less intense and exclusive passion. The pain that results is partly due to mortification, and partly to regret, the exact proportion of each depending upon the lover's vanity.

When and if you obtain the favors of the beloved, your imagination no longer remains actively engaged in rendering her perfect. Instead you set about proving to yourself how happy she has made you. Vanity love is the end of almost all happy cases of love.

---

[1] I speak of men only in this sentence.

[2] When I wrote this, I thought so. The mechanics, at least, seems clearer to me now, and I describe it in the chapter on Cimarosa and Meena Shorey.

[3] It may be that you are born either with or without the soul than can know it. This is merely an opinion, and I am not sure whether there is a reasonable basis for it. [Later addition:] For reasons explained in the previous note, this opinion seems to me more of a fact than when I wrote the last sentence.

[4] Dante continued to crystallize throughout his whole life about the perfections of his Beatrice with undiminished intensity, although other loves punctuated the crystallization. A proof of the durability of first crystallization even when the beloved has been seen only a few times in the course of twenty-five years.

Here is how Stendhal described the second crystallization:

> "Alors commence la seconde cristallisation produisant pour diamants des confirmation à cette idée: Elle m'aime."[1]

Several related events constitute the second crystallization:

1) The beauty and perfection of the beloved seem to increase a hundred- or thousand-fold in degree beyond even the near-perfection felt during the most intense stages of the first crystallization. This illusion arises because an entirely different type of pleasure is being felt. The beloved is felt to be *absolutely* sublime, the *only* source of happiness that the world has ever possessed. This exaggeration of her worth is accomplished at the expense of the amount of happiness that the rest of the world and its pleasures promise.

2) The lover loses all sense of vanity with regard to the beloved. She appears to be so sublime and awe-inspiring that in thus exaggerating her worth, the lover underrates his own. This occurs during first crystallization, too, but to a very much less degree. By virtue of being in a position to judge her perfections, he still retains an all-important tinge of self-esteem. By the time the second crystallization is well under way, she is everything and he and the rest of the world nothing. To feel the need to prove to himself that she is a divine creature is to insult her and act in a manner utterly unworthy of her, etc.

3) The desire for possession is replaced by the desire purely to be loved.[2] The lover's mind, which was formerly engaged in extracting from every fact that it could proofs that his beloved was worth loving, that she was astonishingly perfect, now is as completely engaged in discovering proofs of this one fact: She loves me.

---

[1]"Then begins the second crystallization producing as its diamonds confirmations of this thought: She loves me."

[2]For those who have never felt passion, these words will hold no meaning, unless vanity leads them to assume that they have. In vanity love, the thought, "She loves me," is a *symbol* in the mind for the fact that you can at long last know the happiness you had promised yourself; it is rarely recognized for being what it is, but this is a merely a matter of lack of self-knowledge, and it does not alter the fact itself. In passionate love, happiness arises *solely from the knowledge* that you are loved by the object of love; no other wish exists. The only important question is, "Does she love me?" But in ninety-nine percent of all cases, this question is merely a matter of the vanity, and, as I have said, a symbol of the true question that is being asked, "Is he/she mine?"

For this reason, passionate love has much less to do with pleasures of the senses than the love of first crystallization. The wish, to be sure, is still to be as close, in every sense of the word, to the beloved as possible, but in vanity love this is so as to delight in her physical and moral perfections (and the greater the tenderness and less the vanity that makes up happiness, the less concomitant share that the idea that she is delighting in yours has in your happiness), and in passionate love so as to be absolutely sure that she loves you passionately also.

The passionate lover, having no vanity, is *constantly beset* with doubts, although he has absolute and unwavering faith in his mistress.[1] But it is this very doubt that prevents him from tiring of his mistress after intimacy. The intensity of love cannot slacken when doubt always stirs it up, especially when there is no true reason for doubt. Such is the happiness of passionate love.

Passionate love is a full-time occupation, not a part-time hobby.[2]

To know that you are loved, this is a symbol in vanity love (which in the end is always very sensible). It means, "She is mine." In passion, everything and every idea but the thought, "She loves me," is a symbol for the truth or lack of truth of that one thought. With its birth, the lover begins to believe in all seriousness that with the exception of being loved by his beloved, no other form of happiness exists or has ever existed for him or for anyone else on earth: for him this is a simple fact of nature.

Most people whose pleasures are not exclusively those of petty vanity have fallen in love once or more in the course of their lives, but few have known passion, which arises from excess of spirit and not from a need for approval, companionship, and physical pleasure.

A sensitive and passionate soul always hopes to meet someone who will seem to him or her worthy of adoration. He or she finds little or nothing of true worth in life until such a lovable object is found.

As soon as the slightest interest begins to blossom into love, a passionate man instinctively contrives to see every perfection in the

---

[1]He will wager his life that there is not a shred of insincerity or falsehood in her, and yet doubt whether he is loved or not even though she has just whispered into his ear the magic words, "I love you," after having gazed tenderly into his eyes for half a minute—and when in the opinion of any rational man she has not given him the slightest reason for doubt.

[2]For this reason it was not possible among savages. It requires leisure, and time to dream in relative physical security.

woman. Too keen a sensibility is a practical disadvantage, his fate may be an unhappy one: he often loves more than he is loved. Still, the beloved for him remains completely lovable.

After many happy or unhappy loves, this man happens to meet a woman who is seemingly truly sublime and intelligent, and capable of the greatest passion herself. He is astonished and delighted by his discovery of the perfections peculiar to this woman. All his previous loves suddenly appear to him a very different light, and affected. In comparison to what he now feels, they seem trivial. He begins to dream of a happiness of an altogether different order than any he had earlier imagined the existence of. The earlier *contrivings* of perfections in his previous loves now appear to him to be nothing more than the promptings of vanity. He has too much respect for the woman he has met to let the slightest taint of vanity infect his reveries about her; he wants absolute truth where she is concerned, since the perfections he can contrive or distinguish he feels to be absolutely below this woman's true perfections.

If she does not requite his love after he has persevered for a very long time, to the point of having lost all hope, he may be driven to console himself with other loves,[1] not because he has stopped loving her, but because his love makes solitude insupportable. He returns to his earlier contrivings of perfections, to increase the pleasure he gets from these new loves, but now he adds (as much as he feels the new mistresses can contain) to these perfections the sublimity he had come to know in the one passionate affair of his life.

He may have known great doubts and suffered a great deal in most of his loves, but the fact is that he knew passion only once: second crystallization only occurred with that one woman concerning whom his thoughts were *entirely* free from vanity.[2]

No one can fall passionately in love more than once in his or her life.

Even in vanity love, there is often one who has inspired more love than any other.

There has been much talk recently about a young lady of middle class family who caught the eyes of a very wealthy, very handsome, and not too young millionaire, who, for some chance reasons difficult to discover

---

[1]The alternative is to shoot himself. Stendhal's fate with Mathilde Dembowski.

[2]So that first love, in which one is always comparing what is happening to preconceived ideas and borrowed notions, is never passionate.

at this remove, lost his head and fell in love with her. She found nothing ridiculous in him; they were seen together everywhere. It was naturally assumed that they were lovers, and would marry one day, since the man seemed to be the one who was more in love. Her pride was equal to her beauty; she was kind to him, but he had his work cut out for him. Being very taken with her, he found her very charming in every way. But do what he would, she would not marry him, arguing that marriage would only spoil their love. "What will remain of our love when we cannot *allow* ourselves to be tempted to pursue other pleasures than those which we can give each other?" she would ask him with a mock-innocent expression in her eyes that he could not resist.

One day at a rather exclusive party, she was introduced to a short, stout, thirty-five years old man of average means whose friendship with some rich old member had introduced him to a higher social circle than his own. Being an utterly natural and unaffected creature she met him with her usual amiability.

She kept running into him for the following months at other parties and smaller affairs as well, and as they had many common interests, there were always topics enough for making conversation.

Not suspecting in the least any weakness in herself, she did not refrain from dwelling with pleasure on the latest meeting, and looked forward with perilous eagerness to the next. Unfortunately, the pleasure she found in his company always exceeded a little the pleasure she had expected, so that she did not begin to tire of her reveries. The whole thing seemed only an innocent friendship.

Her friends noticed that she was madly in love, a fact that surprised them the more since he was rather awkward in elegant surroundings, which did not stop him from sporting a sullen, proud air. They thought him a rather insensitive man, if anything, who though he now and then circulated among their set, had not the slightest respect for wealth, not even enough to be ironical about it.

The millionaire, who had so far been secure in the assurance of at least not having a rival, soon got wind of her madness. He was not a little annoyed, and wondered whether he ought to feel insulted. After all, there had been an understanding between them, etc., and she had never carried any other infatuation so far. All of this was too much to bear, and he confronted her with her unbecoming conduct, only to be astonished to find that this action forced her to acknowledge to herself for the first time (as she openly admitted to him) where she stood. He had been dismissed from her heart, and was about to be dismissed from her presence. He protested the unjustness of her conduct, but found himself being shown the door by his absolutely calm and unmoved mistress.

She had found the perfect excuse even as she was forced to acknowledge her passion to herself, which, hard as it is to believe, she assures me, too, that she had not yet. Although aroused to the most furious and revengeful jealousy, her lover could do nothing more than spread the most scandalous stories about his rival, in which he had the misfortune to color him too darkly to be believed.

It had ironically been the very insensitivity of his rival that had led to his winning a place in this young woman's heart. Her stolid hero was utterly unaware of what was going on. She was convinced otherwise about his soul. She thought she could read the hidden truth in the only attractive physical feature he had, his uncommonly fine and expressive eyes. Not having met any man yet who seemed to her to possess the great spirit that she thought he did, she had never before taken the trouble to find out with too great a curiosity what it was she wanted from love or life, but now she could think of nothing save the fact that she now knew.

Never sure whether his amiability during conversations about rare species of flowers or European history extended to a more secret passion, the more she thought about it, the more she was driven mad by uncertainty. Soon after she had confessed to herself what now ruled her heart, she found herself unable to face him on the old footing, in fact, she found herself altogether unequal to the prospect of meeting him calmly.

Even after her passion had taken such complete possession of all her actions as not to remain hidden from anyone (although she herself knew not what to do except to hide it from everyone, especially from the man who had inspired it), his natural stolidity prevented him from showing too much joy at his great fortune of having won the heart this very beautiful and proud woman.

Wearying of her unhappiness, she was soon reduced to casting out hints, going so far as to talk in general terms of marriage in as much of a tone of a scientific description of this ancient social institution as she could manage to give to her seemingly carelessly thrown out words. But he, who out of vanity did not wish to let his indifference become all too plain, was far more eager to discuss orchids.

One evening he took advantage of her weakness, and received all the favors that this lovely and desperate woman could bestow. The seeming alteration of his feelings came as a surprise to her, and if she did not respond with intelligent caution, or least according to the dictates of feminine pride, it was because she knew she would lose him altogether if she resisted. The outcome of her gamble was that he lost what little interest he had in her. He still visited her privately, but did not long trouble himself with hiding his indifference. Not knowing what means to use to inspire his love, she was at a loss as to how to spend every hour that passed, each of which reminded her of her unhappiness.

Soon his visits ceased. She heard from her friends that he was marrying a woman he had known for years. Unable to hide her unhappiness, and beyond the stage of caring what others thought, she dropped out of the set that her earlier lover had introduced her to and moved to a distant state where, according to a few sketchy accounts that have been circulated, she lives largely in solitude. Those who had known her for years prior to this secluded chapter of her life assumed she could not bear the humiliation.[1]

The pleasures of non-passionate love depend upon how admirable the object of love has become to the one in love. The pleasures of vanity love then are as various in shade and intensity as are the individuals in their makeup. We are interested in passion, where there is no such diversity: the pleasures of all who love passionately are *identical*, only the degree to which they are loved leads to what difference there can be in the happiness felt.

---

[1] I change *all* the background details in order to keep the identities secret.

Chapter XXXIII

Continued

For a passionate lover, everything he sees, meets, thinks about, etc., becomes colored completely by the soul of the beloved. She is always in his mind, and everything else that passes through it merges with her, and, strangely enough, all such things confirm and strengthen his conviction of her perfections. There is a reflected glory in everything: everything reflects the absolute perfection of the beloved.

The lover finds the strangest things to have the power of giving him the most violent transports of happiness.

Only the thought of something that acts as a brake to his crystallization (a rival, social obstacles, a pressing business arrangement etc.) is painful, because it stops crystallization.

In the earlier stages of love, during the first crystallization, the lover tends to idealize the beloved, exaggerate her merits, and endow her with every perfection under the sun. Those particular things which acquired reflected glory at this stage may be sentimentally recalled at a later period, when the headiness of the original passion has vanished. Their memory still gives pleasure.

But when crystallization is still going on, these particulars (e.g., her friends, her car, her handbag, her social background, her hobbies, the characterizing idiosyncrasies of her gestures, speech, dress, gait, etc.) acquire so much importance that the thought of them can drive him into mad happiness or mad grief, depending upon how much hope he has at that moment. The name of the city where she used to live, when it is mentioned in an otherwise boring book he is reading, makes him forget the book and all other thoughts as he loses himself in tender reveries.[1]

The reaction is as strong, and of a more physical nature, making his heart gallop, when he unexpectedly runs into someone who looks like the woman he loves, or is wearing very nearly the same dress as he once saw on her, or has the same cut and color of hair, etc. The same thing happens if a woman has a way of talking like hers, or wears the same perfume.

------

[1]What Duboc used to tell me he felt when he came across a mention of RE; Fernando has a similar reaction whenever he hears someone casually mention M—

April 16, 1991

Doubt produces passion; but in the greater number of cases love accompanied by the greatest doubts does not lead to *passion*.[1] Thus doubt, by itself, is not enough to explain why passion arises. You could be driven mad by uncertainty, and violently desire the exclusive favors of the beloved, and yet be as far as you can be from knowing passion. So how does one describe what passionate love is? This is a great problem, one which, to tell you the truth, I am not sure I can solve.

When a man of a lively and romantic temperament falls deeply in love, the less he feels he has reason to hope of success, the more he must resort to his imagination to produce pictures of happiness, and the more the beloved is transformed by it into the most desirable object in the world. When hope is minimum, the lover desires a favorable response from the beloved so strongly that were he to obtain it there and then, he would in all likelihood know not what to do. She hardly exists for him apart from his imagined picture of her.

Crystallization here has been limited to pure idealization with no other desire in mind. It is still the first crystallization. This state is rare, but it is essential that it occur at some point if passion is to develop.

Passion can arise at any point, even after intimacy, provided a sufficiently great revolution in *both* circumstances and feelings has occurred since intimacy which has destroyed all that had been produced in the milder form of love that existed during intimacy.[2]

The lover derives little happiness from the woman as she is. He is well past the stage when he could feel happiness at the mere thought of her beauty, charms, nobility, etc. At first, he knew almost nothing about her. His imagination supplied him with all the details he wanted to know, and he made sure that he only ascribed perfections to her. Everything that he did not know had to be as perfect as the little that he did.

The part that this kind of imagination plays diminished with time, as the lover was able to observe, study, and gather information about her, and to let his mind dwell at leisure on what he had discovered. Although her sight may not leave him cool and unmoved, and may, in fact, leave him with little presence of mind, he still has progressively decreasing need for imagining her responses, gestures, motives, etc.

---

[1]Doubt leads the doubting lover to make demands similar to those of passion upon the other lover, but the happiness he or she enjoys when not in doubt arises from vanity.

[2]This is the case with men. Women rarely pass onto the second crystallization before intimacy.

If at any point his hopes increase, he begins to delight in thinking of the pleasures he feels he is about to know. The mind then begins to estimate the nature and degree of the anticipated pleasures; and, thus, a farewell to passion.

This is what happens when passion is born: If he continues to have little hope, or almost no hope, the lover in his imagination transforms the beloved into a woman seriously in love with him; he holds conversations in his mind that could only come about if she were so. When he cannot produce imagined solutions, crystallization stops and he is miserable. Thus, *facts* become for him anathemas. He lives purely in the imagination. This is why the happiness of passion is the greatest known to humans. In his mind, then, he arranges it so that it would be the greatest unhappiness for the woman he loves to feel uncertain of his passion. His imagination constantly supplies him with different scenarios of the utterly transformed beloved. The woman as she is disappears behind this imagined version of her who is *absolutely* sublime, and who loves him; and so on.

As time goes by, imagined solutions do for him less and less. His unhappiness at not being loved becomes greater as he comes to feel that he is only deluding himself when he is happy in thinking of her. This is the stage at which the *worst grief* known to man is felt.

Only at this stage does true, lasting passion arise.

If the beloved has given herself to him before this stage, passion rarely arises. But by this time, to think her absolutely sublime, and to think of her love as the only thing in the universe worth anything, have become habits of mind. He would be hard pressed to remember the type of man he was before he met this particular woman, to recall to himself what sorts of pleasures he pursued then, etc.

Later, after years have passed, he may recover sufficiently from his protracted mental disease to be able to resort yet again to his imagination, but until then his life passes in utter misery. Everything reminds him of his unhappiness, everything reproaches him for deluding himself into thinking that any happiness could ever exist for him, that there is anything in this world but unhappiness.

If the beloved gives herself up to him before passion is born, though crystallization had been of an intense and doubting kind, and has been going on for some time, only the most intense prolonged doubts after intimacy can lead to passion. The later the birth of these doubts after intimacy, the more the whole process leading up to passion must start from scratch. If the very next morning you are convulsed by jealousy and doubts due to some chance remark by your mistress, it will seem as though you did not enjoy her true favors at all the previous evening. You will be more desolate than you were a week ago, when you did not expect the good fortune that was in store for you, since now there is no demand or proof that you can ask for that will *entirely* settle your doubts.[1]

The only way to observe passion and distinguish it from vanity love is to observe the different types of happiness that love gives rise to in individuals, which can only be done by examining exactly whence they arise. All unhappy lovers may behave or talk similarly, but it is the moments of happiness that give the passionate soul away.[2]

Before the birth of passion, all known perfections, and others that were becoming newly discernible, were ascribed to the beloved. Afterwards, only the beloved is perfect, and only when some thing or idea seems to be a dim reflection of her does it possess any pleasure for the lover.[3] The phenomenon of indiscriminate reflected glory of the earlier stage of love, where the process is the opposite to that of passion, dies with the birth of passion.

Passion takes at least several months of uninterrupted crystallization to develop. It is the curious fate only of excessively sensitive and spirited

---

[1]This experience is very common among women, which is why passion arises in them after intimacy. Since love is a generally more important affair for them, this is also the reason why passionate love among them is more common.

[2]"It is only by observing and comparing the pleasures and pains of others that you can understand what you yourself feel, and until you can understand that you cannot begin to advance to greater pleasures. So it is in your interest to study all forms of happiness. This is the only excuse I have for writing this otherwise useless and rather ill-organized essay. I try to make clear to myself what I observe in others. This cools my mind, and makes it less illogical in its proceedings. By writing down my observations and conclusions, I leave a record of them not only useful to me as a guide, but which others may use as a point of departure and comparison for their own pursuit of happiness. If they can find even one nuance truly described herein, that is something."

These words are scribbled on the side- and bottom-margins at this point in the manuscript by Rollefort.

[3]Falconetti finds in the face of a child in a famous Titian painting depicting a Christian rite a delicate echo of the appearance of Clara; his soul lifts to the heavens at the sight of that out-turned face—even when he sees it in a cheap reproduction of the painting. It matters little to him, he told me, that those eyes and the noble angle of the cheek he admires so much, because these remind him of Clara's, belong to a very young boy in the painting.

souls. You always know it when it is passion, because it is unnatural to find yourself unconcerned with beauty, unconcerned, except momentarily, with the idea of joy, and because the object of love is so violently transformed by the imagination that you even wonder if you are truly in love with the woman in question. This, although it is the only kind of love worthy of the name.

The passionate lover desires to be as close as possible to the soul and mind of the beloved, which is not an easy task since he is looking for symbols and not for any particular set of actions. He is only happy when he feels his love requited *with equal passion*. To be in her arms and not feel that she loves him as much as he does her is a torture only exceeded by that of seeing her lost in dreams of another or thinking of her in the arms of another. Strange as it may appear, this folly of his does not arise from vanity, which he is in fact very far from feeling where she is concerned.

The lover's being wholly possessed by the thought of being loved by the beloved so far as to have become blind to all other pleasures, after the initial curiosity regarding her has been completely dispelled, is the keynote of passionate love.[1]

There is a world of difference between the pleasing transports that arise during the birth of love, and what is felt in passion. At the latter stage of this madness called love, the beloved is the arbiter of all merit, beauty, nobility, worth, etc., and she alone in the universe is felt to possess these. Everything else in it is felt to be beautiful or even acceptable, only insofar as it reflects her. *Absolute awe*, then, is the note of passion. He stands before the beloved as before God. He has been so reduced by his misery and hope for sublime happiness that he cannot so much as imagine (he, a creature who lives almost entirely in his imagination) any longer that any happiness exists but that of being loved by her.

The irretrievable loss of the beloved at this stage is the greatest misfortune that can happen to a man. It empties his world even of the possibility of happiness.

---

[1]I am speaking of true passion, not the false romanticizings of hacks, mediocre artists, as well as those of most good ones. Vanity very often leads to the affectation that passion is being felt.

Chapter XXXIV

Continued

In the highest form of vanity love, the love of the beloved is desired because the lover feels his happiness will never be complete without this greatest of pleasures. If he is loved, the tender pleasures he feels lead him to love her more. Increase in gratitude and love follow each other. In this manner, vanity increases love and tenderness, as do physical pleasures when enjoyed in a spirit of tenderness more than rapacity.

Affectations aside, the loss of the beloved hurts more in vanity love than the loss of her love.

Fear of losing each other often leads a pair of lovers to convince each other and themselves that their love has all the joy it initially possessed. There is also the wish not to appear ridiculous in their own eyes.

Before the age of twenty, members of neither sex know their own hearts sufficiently to rise above the lower rungs of vanity love. For one thing, at that age they are too uncertain about the position they will occupy in the world, too taken up with hopes and fears. A young person, man or woman, is bent upon proving his or her consequence. The pain of discontented vanity stings so much in these years that it is no wonder that cold men and women think that the unhappy love they knew during adolescence was the height of passionate abandonment to love.

Vanity plays a large part in all first loves since the lover is keenly aware that he or she is for the first time enjoying a passion universally regarded as the greatest pleasure, which has been denied to him or her heretofore. There is a greater desire to impress others. This is perhaps the one stage in life when both masculine and feminine self-esteem depend equally upon success in love.

Passion can only come later, when a much greater suspicion has developed regarding all forms of happiness, including those of love.

As the second crystallization proceeds, the stage comes when the beloved is felt to be so absolutely sublime that the lover dares not even to entertain the thought of trying to rudely approach her person, so afraid is he of profaning what is now holy for him. Such hesitation arises partly from the fear of incurring her displeasure. The thought that she will not believe his earnest claim of having absolute respect for her makes him wince. In addition, the mere thought of any action which sullies the purity of his feelings he feels almost as a disabling physical blow.

If at this extreme stage of passion the beloved is not kind and relenting, there is little chance that he can do anything to dispel his unhappiness, let alone to insure his happiness. Every time he sees her, all his thoughts and motions freeze, and he comes across as a stiff bore. He loves not at all the beautiful woman he sees, but the sublime creature he imagines her to be. There is no way he can respond sensibly to the woman he sees.

A certain amount of cold and calculated behavior is therefore *necessary* for complete happiness in love. It is usually in these moments of coldly motivated actions that true practical progress towards happiness is made. But in doing so, the lover must inflict an injury on that sense of delicacy which permeates all his thoughts concerning the beloved. Afterwards, when he is in the position to enjoy the love of the beloved, or when he is alone thinking of the past meetings, and planning the next one, he can return to his passionate self.

The only problem with this fine manner of facilitating conquests is that the more passionately he loves, the less is he able to be calculating (even for an instant) in anything concerning the beloved. You cannot convince this man to risk offending the woman he loves. He would rather suffer for eternity the state of being unloved rather than give the slightest cause to make his beloved think him a Don Juan, someone who regards her lightly. He does not have the presence of mind to inspire *doubt* in her mind, without which *she* will never come to conceive for him that passion which he so much wishes her to feel.[1]

In fact, the lover acts and thinks like a madman where his beloved is concerned. He does not see clearly anymore, no matter how much he tries to, and no matter how much he thinks he is succeeding in doing.

---

[1]He has lost his vanity to the point that he absurdly disregards the importance of inspiring in her admiration for himself, admiration which can only be born if she thinks him worthy of it, i.e., if she can see in him some tangible proofs of inly rooted pride and strength of character (masculine virtues that women admire most). Without the birth of lively admiration, love is ruled out. The passionate lover's great blunder is in assuming that her imagination will make up for everything—he forgets that it was some tangible proofs of pride, inner strength, and sweetness of temper that made him fall madly in love with her. Without that initial impression, his own imagination would not have been called into play.

Even the smallest thing concerning her will not be seen by him as it is. Every such thing makes him either much happier or much unhappier than he was before he perceived it. Detachment, then, is out of the question.

Never ask a man in love to talk of his beloved. For one thing, only the vain man talks about the woman he loves easily. The passionate lover, if he can bring himself to talk about her to some especially supposed good friend, or to an accomplice or a friend of hers, will talk so that he will be doubly removed from her as she is. He, when he is forced to, will only utter what he does not think. He will carefully avoid expressing his true thoughts. When he praises, there is always a grain of falsehood or exaggeration in what he says. The amusing thing is that, in truth, he cannot see the woman as she is to begin with. His words are nothing more than an amazing farrago of nonsense.

A sensitive woman will waste away from unhappiness merely because an insensitive man, with respect to whom she committed the entirely pardonable folly of having fallen in love, is unfaithful.

I remember once hearing a shrewd and hardheaded but seldom solemn Latin American businessman speak quietly of a newly acquired mistress to his friends. He was well known among them as a lady's man, and he felt it to be wiser to own up to his newest conquests than to vainly deny them and risk their witticisms. This clever man's words were polished and smooth, but his heart being involved by this love as it had only been once or twice before, he came across as much less lucid, and much more ridiculous to his audience than he thought.[1]

The happiness that a passionate lover feels when he finds his efforts, his days and nights spent in hoping and despairing, etc., crowned with success cannot be imagined by those who have never known them. The beloved gives herself over completely to her love for him. The hours he spends with her surpass all others, making everything else seem inane, worthless, and painful to think of going through again. However, perhaps because this happiness arises from the fulfillment of very delicate and imaginary possibilities of happiness that he had dreamed of earlier for a very long time, those moments of perfect happiness leave no trace of memory behind them.[2]

---

[1]And he only loved out of *vanity*. However, in most circles, as in his, the appearance of too much love in the actions or words of a lover inspires ridicule, which only those who lack pride fail to note.

[2]As Stendhal was the first to note.

You remember you were happy, but you cannot remember at all what you felt. This fact makes every new transport of passionate love seem novel; memories of past reveries do not dull the keenness of the present transports.

The happiness a passionate lover finds in the arms of the woman he loves arises from sensing her love. The fact that she is in his arms, that her eyes are gently fixed upon his, and that her words are full of tenderness and solicitude, are symbols for him that she has abandoned herself completely to her love for him. It is this last that is directly responsible for the happiness he feels. But it is only in cases of vanity love that a lover can discern even vaguely what she is feeling at the moment. In passionate love, this effort is impossible, since his imagination is engaged otherwise.

It is only in periods of great uncertainty or outright jealousy that the passionate lover makes the error of beginning to think that his happiness lies in the procuring of the symbols themselves; he forgets that they are only symbols.

Of a pair of lovers, the one who loves more makes greater demands for proofs of love upon the other. The other, if he or she is not very deeply in love, can easily be displeased by these demands. To be the object of a passionate attachment when you do not return the feeling is always tiresome in the long run, even if vanity is a little gratified initially.

When passionate love exists on both sides, it does not carry the two away to reveries at the same time; sometimes one feels its effects, sometimes the other; the one who does not feel it at a particular point ought to respond with eagerness in order to ensure the complete happiness of the other. Unless he or she is distracted by some momentous problem, or in an absolutely cold mood at the time, passion will soon revive.

It is impossible to feel the reveries of passionate love at all times. Such expectations in those temperamentally incapable of even a moment of true passion leads to a sharp disappointment with love, and makes them suspicious of love altogether, a circumstance much more common among women. Think of all those articles you see in popular magazines of women in which the rarity of a man who is never disappointing is described in a sour tone.

The love of a man who is sure from the beginning that he is loved will never develop into a passion. This is not true of women since for them the first crystallization consists of imagining the pleasures of being loved, and the second (i.e., passion) arises from doubts born after intimacy. To know that a man is desperately in love does not make passion absolutely impossible, so long as she does not find the idea of being loved by him very displeasing, and so long as she nevertheless has reasons to periodically doubt the earnestness of his *expressions of love* and the permanence of his present feelings.

But if a woman wishes to be loved by a man only because she knows herself to be *capable* of a little love for him (i.e., she either wants nothing more from love than a mild gratification of vanity, or she fears solitude, poverty, old age, ridicule, etc.), she still is more likely to *sympathetically* tolerate the demands that excess of passion may lead him to make than a man who feels only a little love will those of his mistress. This is because the gratification of vanity at having secured a passionate admiration is a passion among women, though almost unknown among men.

There are, of course, women who are as little under the influence of the tolerant kind of vanity as most men are. I speak of those who are capable of true kindness on occasions at least.

Sinha was telling me recently how he almost hated himself for the love he felt for Rita H.—, since she positively disliked being loved by him. She had not disliked him to begin with, she had been friendly enough, but as soon as he told her he loved her, she grew averse to his company. He told me that he knew she did not positively dislike him, but she found his attentions distressing in the extreme since she pitied him but could not love him. This pained him, and for her sake, in moments of blackest despair and gloom, he wished he had not fallen in love with her four years ago, since when he has known mostly unhappiness.

It was in a moment of rare honesty that he admitted to me that much as he suffered and even regretted at moments that he had fallen in love, he could not but consider all the amusements and ambitions common in the world worse than ridiculous.

We were walking down a quiet rural street late at night. Since he was silent, I did not want to disturb him with trivial conversation. He was apparently lost in thoughts that too often lay uppermost in his mind. A few minutes later, he suddenly exclaimed how wretched and hopeless his life was, and astonished me by breaking into tears. But he stopped as suddenly as he had begun, and with a curt word of farewell, he turned around and walked away before I could say anything, leaving me in a state of great amazement. I was at an utter loss to explain his conduct. I have not seen him for these past five months now. Is his state to be envied or pitied?

He has in the past told me about the utter happiness he feels every day at least once, a happiness that arises solely from thoughts of the woman he loves, and which he haughtily told me was of a nature that I could never even dream the existence of. He was deeply sorry that this was so, for I was his best friend. But later that same evening, when I called upon him to see if he wanted to join us at the theater of a nearby city, I found him disgusted by life and full of thoughts of suicide. But that, he told me, is a matter complicated enough. I could see that he half wanted me to leave him alone, and half was afraid that I would. I felt great pity for him, and as I left, I thanked my stars that I have been spared this fatal disease of the soul.

Chapter XXXV

Examples

I illustrate the difference between vanity love and passionate love by comparing two famous unrequited love affairs: Yeats' passion for Maud Gonne and Stendhal's for Mathilde Dembowski.

Both fell in love with proud women engaged in revolutionary politics. Both were refused by the woman they loved. Stendhal's "Métilde"(Mme Dembowski) had children, and was separated from her husband when he met her. Yeats' "Helen" (Maud Gonne) shocked him by marrying a brutal officer, Major John MacBride, in 1903—they separated two years later. Stendhal's was passionate love, Yeats' vanity love of a relatively exalted type.[1]

Yeats was driven by his despair to write many poems describing his love. In "Adam's Curse" he tells his beloved and her lady friend of the difficulties of composition. The beautiful friend replies:

---

[1]Vanity love in ascending degree of crystallization: Catullus, Goethe, Pushkin, Petrarch, Yeats, Hölderlin.

"To be born woman is to know—
Although they do not talk of it at school—
That we must labour to be beautiful."
I said: "It's certain there is no fine thing
Since Adam's fall but needs much labouring.
There have been lovers who thought love should be
So much compounded of high courtesy
That they would sigh and quote with learned looks
Precedents out of beautiful old books;
Yet now it seems an idle trade enough."
We sat grown quiet at the name of love;
We saw the last embers of daylight die,
And in the trembling blue-green of the sky
A moon, worn as if it had been a shell
Washed by time's waters as they rose and fell
About the stars and broke in days and years.
I had a thought for no one's but your ears:
That you were beautiful, and that I strove
To love you in the old high way of love;
That it had all seemed happy, and yet we'd grown
As weary-hearted as that hollow moon. (1902)

This is a faithful expression of the weariness that now and then attends vanity love at an advanced stage (whether requited or not, so long as self-complacency does not cancel the desire for absolute happiness). Crystallization resumes in spite of everything: Eight years after "Adam's Curse," Yeats wrote "Words" and "No Second Troy."

WORDS

I had this thought a while ago,
"My darling cannot understand
What I have done, or what would do
For this blind bitter land."
And I grew weary of the sun
Until my thoughts cleared up again,
Remembering that the best I have done
Was done to make it plain;
That every year I have cried, "At length

My darling understands it all,
Because I have come into my strength,
And words obey my call";
That had she done so who can say
What would have shaken from the sieve?
I might have thrown poor words away
And been content to live. (1910)

NO SECOND TROY

Why should I blame her that she filled my days
With misery, or that she would of late
Have taught to ignorant men most violent ways, ***?
What could have made her peaceful with a mind
That nobleness made simple as fire,
With beauty like a tightened bow, a kind
That is not natural in an age like this,
Being high and solitary and most stern?
Why, what could she have done, being what she is?
Was there another Troy for her to burn? (1910)

The difference between Stendhal's love for Mme Dembowski, and Yeats' for Maud Gonne made them respond to rejection in different ways.

Othello's love was vanity, Desdemona's passion (deliberately misreading the play ideally for the moment). This I say because of what each does, and how. Since he had never known passion himself (he would not have been the great dramatist he was if he had), Shakespeare expressed it in his usual manner. His Desdemona is a noble and pathetic victim.[1] If she were passionately in love with Othello, she would have either felt no regrets that she was about to die at the hands of the man she loved; or, recognizing too late that she had made a dreadful mistake about his worth, she would have proudly and disdainfully pointed out to him his grave and ridiculous error, and fought every inch of the way, but even this would be the result of the fact that her love rose out of vanity.

But there is something noble in her attempt to cover up Othello's

---

[1] I take Othello and Desdemona as examples because they are figures known to all literate people, i.e., because they can be seen and judged by everyone. As I have said, I would not look to Shakespeare for a description of passionate love true to nature.

crime. Othello's wounded pride is excusable considering the images that Iago paints for him, and his revenge noble and immediate, but no lover who loves his mistress passionately would have acted as he does. Once he is passionately in love, nothing short of ocular proof, or a confession to the effect by the beloved, can convince a man that she is capable of anything false, let alone of infidelity. But at the very moment before death, Desdemona, to go solely by her act, rises above vanity to passion for once, though Shakespeare's expression is not that of passionate love.

Neither Duc de Nemours nor the Princesse de Clèves rose above refined vanity love.

Héloïse's love was passion, Abélard's vanity.

The examples I mention above are all such that one can speak of one way or the other. But could passion have developed among the affected courtiers of Louis XIV? Saint-Simon tells us that perhaps it did on occasion:

"Les mémoires publics de cette princesse[1] montrent à découvert sa faiblesse pour M. de Lauzun, la folie de celui-ci de ne l'avoir pas épousée dès qu'il en eut la permission du Roi, pour le faire avec plus de faste et d'éclat. Leur désespoir de la rétraction de la permission du Roi fut extrême; mais les donations du contrat de mariage étaient faites et subsistèrent par d'autres actes. Monsieur, poussé par Monsieur le Prince, avait pressé le Roi de se rétracter; mais Mme de Montespan et M. de Louvois y eurent encore plus de part, et furent ceux sur qui tomba route la fureur de Mademoiselle et la rage du favori, car M. de Lauzun l'était. Ce ne fut pas pour longtemps: il s'échappa plus d'une fois avec le Roi, plus souvent encore avec la maîtresse, et donna beau jeu au ministre pour le perdre. Il vint à bout de le faire arrêter et conduire à Pignerol, où il fut extrêmement maltraité par ses ordres, et y demeura dix ans. L'amour de Mademoiselle ne se refroidit point par l'absense: on sut en profiter pour faire un grand éstablissement à M. du Maine, à ses dépens et à ceux de M. de Lauzun qui en acheta sa liberté. Eu, Aumale, Dombes et d'autres terres encore furent données à M. du Maine au grand regret de Mademoiselle; et ce fut sous ce prétexte de reconnaisance que, pour élever de plus en plus les bâtards, le Roi leur fit prendre la livrée de Mademoiselle, qui était celle de Monsieur Gaston. Cet héritier forcé lui fut toujours fort peu agréable et elle était toujours sur la défensive pour

---

[1]Mlle de Montpensier, known as the Grande Mademoiselle, then the richest woman with a private fortune in Europe.

le reste de ses biens, que le Roi lui voulait arracher pour ce fils bien-aimé. Les aventures incroyable de M. de Lauzun, qui avait sauvé la reine d'Angleterre et le prince de Galles, l'avaient ramené à la cour. Il s'était brouillé avec Mademoiselle, toujours jalouse de lui, qui même à la mort ne le vouloir pas voir. Il avait conservé Thiers et Saint-Fargeau de ses dons. Il laissait toujours entendre qu'il avait épousé Mademoiselle, et il parut devant le Roi en grand manteau, qui le trouva fort mauvais. Après son deuil il ne voulut pas reprendre sa livrée et s'en fit une d'un brun presque noir avec des galons bleus et blancs, pour conserver toujours la tristesse de la perte de Mademoiselle, dont il avait des portraits partout."[1]

This same Mlle de Montpensier was actively involved in the Fronde, and the Duc de Lauzun desperately sought again the favors of the King long after her death. Was passionate love conceivable among such people? Yet how did they at times act with respect to one another, at least when apart? Can mannered love among two very spirited persons sometimes vaguely take on the appearance of passion?

---

[1]"The public memoirs of this princess reveal her weakness for M. de Lauzun, and the folly of the latter in not having married as soon as he had the King's permission, in not having done so with the greatest speed and pomp. Their despair at the retraction of the King's permission was extreme, but the donations of the marriage contract had been made and were confirmed by other acts. Monsieur, urged by Monsieur le Prince, had pressed the King to retract his permission; but Mme de Montespan and M. de Louvois had once again the greatest part in it, and were the ones on whom fell the fury of the Mademoiselle and the rage of her favorite, who M. de Lauzun really was. This was not so for long: more than one time he forgot himself with the King, and yet more often with his mistress, and gave fine chances to the minister to ruin him. It ended by his being arrested and conducted to Pignerol, where he was extremely maltreated by his [M. de Louvois'] orders, and where he remained for ten years. The love of the Mademoiselle did not cool at all in his absence; it was turned to profit in order to make a grand establishment for M. du Maine,* at her expense and that of M. de Lauzun, whose liberty was thus bought. Eu, Aumale, Dombes, and the other lands were given to M. du Maine, to the great regret of Mademoiselle; and it was under the pretext of gratitude that the King, to elevate his bastards more and more, made them assume Mademoiselle's livery, which was that of Monsieur Gaston. This heirship was always very little agreeable to her and she was always on the defensive regarding the rest of her estates, which the king wished to wrest from her for his beloved son. The incredible adventures of M. de Lauzun, who had saved the queen of England and the prince of Wales, brought him back to the court. He fell out with Mademoiselle, always jealous about him, who herself until her death never wished to see him. He had kept Thiers and Saint-Fargeau from the donations. He always let it be understood that he had married Mademoiselle, and he appeared before the King in a great cloak, which the King took very ill. After his period of mourning, he did not wish to resume his livery and assumed from then one of nearly blackish brown with white and blue galloons, to preserve forever the sadness of the loss of Mademoiselle, whose portraits he had everywhere."

* One of Louis XIV's sons by Mme de Montespan.

Chapter XXXVI

Of the Temporary Death of Love

All unhappiness in love (in other words, the worst unhappiness known to man) arises from a single event: for whatever reason, crystallization stops. For example, you think you will never enjoy the happiness you have been promising yourself; or jealousy is inspired by knowledge of a rival. Some matter of worldly affairs intrudes upon your attention by the nature of its extreme urgency, a matter of survival. Or, you are too sure of being loved. Crystallization is nothing but dreaming of unspeakable happiness.

It is difficult to write about passion because the feeling dissolves if one attempts to describe it. Reasoning about passion destroys the *simplicity* without which there can be no passion. For this reason, it is hard to keep up the reveries of passion for a long time away from the beloved. This is also the reason why, though passionate love is a phenomenon of pure imagination, it is necessary that the beloved is there with you, returning your love; otherwise all the energies of the mind are expended in imagining those two facts. This may give a not negligible degree of pleasure for a few months, but the mind soon tires, and crystallization stops.

How do you describe the feelings of unhappiness that arise when crystallization has stopped? From the feeling of everything conspiring to show you your happiness, everything mocks you for your unhappiness. The reveries of happy love are so intensely delightful and heavenly that *everything else* revolts the spirit. The trouble is that although the lover wants nothing but to somehow return to the state of the earlier reveries, the more he tries, the more chimerical and forever departed they seem; and the more desperate and unhappy he becomes.

To not be able to feel the passion that you felt is fatal to your happiness. You note that earlier when she did this or that, you went off your head with happiness, but now it does not move you at all. This thought makes love seem a very wearisome duty, even the thought of love is mentally tiring. What is happening is simply that crystallization has stopped, and unhappiness, feeding upon itself, renders the revival of crystallization increasingly more difficult.

Remember that once crystallization stops, you fall back immediately upon vanity.[1] You would like to feel the happiness you knew earlier, and the seeming impossibility of being able to feel it leads to the unhappiness of ungratified vanity.

The lover looks upon anything or anyone whom he has identified as the responsible agent for his unhappiness with keen hatred; it is a powerful feeling that can get the better of even the most gentle souls. I know of sweet tempered women who, when they are with the men they love, lose all their sweetness upon hearing that a friend, neighbor, or relation for whom they used to have the most cordial and warm affection is going to pay them a visit. Everyone who can hinder the pleasure of loving and being loved is looked upon as a mortal enemy.

When the beloved has subjected the lover to unjustified humiliation, such as, for example, by making cutting remarks about something which he knows she knows he likes, for no other reason than to pain him, the lover can easily, without the least vanity, be overcome by the feeling that her words were unworthy of her noble soul. Crystallization stops; but the unhappiness, as all unhappiness in love, arises because he cannot love her as much as he would like to.

When crystallization stops because of satiety, there is at first a pleasing sense of freedom. The passion that had been at the center of your life seems now to be a stifling burden. You suddenly see again how many different pleasures the world has to offer, how many amusing things there are to do; the beloved seems to be very sublime still, but this is only a rhetorical idea at this point, not an imagined idea taken for the truth. However, soon all those seeming pleasures pall; next they seem insipid and inane; finally hateful. Crystallization restarts, if he is fortunate; if not, he wishes it would.

When crystallization has stopped, the lover not uncommonly begins to descry imperfections, sometimes very grave ones, in the woman he loves. Decidedly less common is the birth of penitent self-contempt a little later. The fact is that the lover is unhappy, and every fresh thought that comes to him he feels makes him even unhappier, and he is as much lacking in logic and the ability to see the truth about the beloved and himself now as he was during crystallization when he thought her perfect; it is simply the reverse side of the coin. For a general law can

---

[1]It was this fact that led Stendhal to originally call his autobiography *Souvenirs d'egotisme.*

formulated: the degree of happiness that love can give a man is always proportionate to the unhappiness it has been the cause of.

A woman especially is overcome with self-contempt and remorse when second crystallization stops. Love is the all-embracing affair of her life. When she is forced to fall back upon vanity, she blames herself for having given in to passion to begin with—this is a generally true fact, I think. For no woman who is not very superior can feel passion, and it is the fate of a superior woman to be very susceptible to the restraints of feminine pride and modesty. She feels she lost her head and did not pay adequate heed to signs of danger. Remorse follows; she might also be tortured by thoughts of having lowered herself forever in the eyes of the man she loves—for she continues to love, although she may not want to admit it to herself, but love now produces only pain.

Love increases in its hold upon the heart, even to the degree of becoming an exclusive passion, by *overcoming all resistance to itself,* whether imposed by outside circumstances, or arising from vanity. Each time crystallization stops, it has a chance of starting again with greater force, and the object of love thereby obtains a stronger and more durable hold on the heart, until the stage comes when even when crystallization has stopped, the lover goes on loving from habit; the alternations from crystallization to the cessation of it, and back again, do not then seem so sudden and alarming.

Chapter XXXVII

Of the Passions and Moral Makeup of Women

In earlier ages in all nations there were three classes whose feelings had to be spared at all costs: the aristocracy-royalty, the clerics, and the military.

In our own democratic age, we must spare the feelings of every group that calls itself one. Start stating facts about liberals, conservatives, whites, blacks, women, men, etc., and you are likely to get into trouble with them.

What I say in these chapters on the passions and moral makeup of women will no doubt stir some of them to produce vehement accusations of prejudice, ignorance, etc.;[1] no doubt some feelings are entirely closed to me as a man. I am merely an observer whose sole intention is to describe the facts as exactly as possible. We all have our idiosyncrasies, but epistemological skepticism regarding the most obvious facts is only a mask used too often to respectably hide one's ignorance. As you can see, I do not intend to flatter anyone, woman or man.

The imagination of a woman is constantly focused upon considerations of her immediate happiness. It is as strong and powerful as a man's, though it usually does not range as far afield, unless disillusionment has driven her to put her pride in attaining success in other occupations and subjects than her personal sphere.[2] Even the most sensitive and intelligent woman will ultimately be only interested in those matters which bear directly upon her happiness; although this may include whatever subjects they think becoming them to take an interest in.[3]

Thanks to today's feminist inspired changes, women have taken up employment everywhere (although still for the large part unjustly only in the lower ranks). Many of the feminine characteristics make them excellent managers and accountants.

A woman is generally ruthless in managing money, and in making the most shrewd and sure investments. Even intelligent women are usually sticklers for rules, especially if they feel that they are being constantly compared to their male peers.

It follows that women are less *original* as managers, their imaginations being deployed in producing new combinations (often very clever ones) within existing set of ideas.

They can be excellent financial dealers, politicians, etc., but there are rarely great theorists or inventors. We have had a Catherine of Russia and a Madame Curie but as of yet no female Hahnemann or Einstein.

In the domestic sphere as well as in the public, they possess the same hardheaded attitude towards attaining goals.

---

[1]Which should surprise no one who remembers their chief passion, *personal vanity*.

[2]The birth of a bluestocking. The Mary Bennetts grow into Mrs. Westerns if they have any intelligence. These are the kinds of women you may respect a little from far-off but find difficult to admire close at hand.

[3]French salon hostesses for nearly two centuries took great interest in all intellectual developments. What France did, the rest of the world ultimately copied, whether they admitted to the fact or not.

The Japanese, being fanatically efficient, have two main roles for women: clerical or assembly-line work and a housewife/mother. The Japanese husband hands over his entire salary to his wife who then gives him his spending allowance. He habitually gets drunk with his friends in the company of professional female entertainers, and comes home to find his wife ready to pull of his shoes, produce his slippers, draw him a hot bath, and tuck him into bed. I am sure this state of affairs will change considerably in fifty years.

To explain what I mean by imaginative directness of women, I illustrate the phenomenon with the help of a diagram. Let X be the feeling of happiness consequent to a man's or woman's having obtained his or her chief wishes, and let A, B, C, D, etc., be the different pleasures felt at the possession of different desired objects and different attained aims, so that $A + B + C + D + \ldots = X$. The two basic types of configurations that can arise are:

$$1) \quad \begin{matrix} A \\ B \longrightarrow X \\ C \end{matrix} \qquad\qquad 2) \quad \begin{matrix} F - A \\ E - D - B \longrightarrow X \\ C \end{matrix}$$

The first case is that of direct vanity. Here A, B, and C, (such as, for example, the knowledge of your beauty, wealth, the esteem of Mr. So-and-so and Miss So-and-so, Mrs. So-and-so, etc.; or, in more admirable cases, some proof of the worth of one's character when measured against someone great, some proof of one's generosity, courage, prudence, etc.) directly lead to X.

In the latter case the person may think that it is E and F that please him, whereas it is A, B, and C.

Hume was a clever man who wished more than anything else to be a famous author, and his talents seemed to point in the direction of philosophy. To be taken for a great philosopher, he produced the theory that every man and woman is a collection of selves,[1] and attempted to

---

[1]Montaigne had also given exaggerated descriptions of the universal phenomenon that different nuances of vanity constantly succeed one another in his "Apology for Raymond Sebond," and Proust was to do the same later. Exaggeration in this matter makes for philosophical skepticism which in turn makes for lack of concreteness, for vagueness, and

prove that the idea of causality is purely an opinion and does not necessarily correspond to the mechanics of the universe. He passed silently over the fact that he was led to this conclusion by means of causal logic. Hume's was a case of petty vanity, yet he also needed to be able to justify to himself the pleasures of vagueness by means of cold and fancifully complicated abstractions, and he thought he partly derived his happiness from the beauty of those abstractions, the fact that they lacked simplicity and were therefore of a more than commonplace stamp.

El Greco produced paintings not only to pay his bills and to win for himself the reputation of being a genius, but also because his religious sentiments could only be gratified by such means. He deceived himself a little less, for his was not as petty a moral nature as Hume's, but the vanity of both men worked indirectly.

Most men are simple, and being so, are perhaps not very different from women in the way they use their imagination for practical matters. In fact, it is for this reason that women are so often much more intelligent, shrewd, and determined in everyday affairs. *Some* men are capable of the more involved and indirect forms of vanity, but women almost never are.[1] A woman's pride leads her to put a high worth on abstracted conceits far removed from anything having a direct effect on events in life because it is fashionable to do, and so gratifies vanity *directly* (the case today), or because not having any alternative to winning praise (direct vanity again) than by appearing to be very different from other women they pursue what women were taught not to (the general case in the past).[2]

Men of great moral genius belong to the second class, but due to this fact they are less susceptible to true passion which demands simplicity on all levels. Simpletons, on the other hand, often are more faithful lovers, and are not infrequently more loved by the most intelligent and spirited women. It is rare when a man of great moral spirit and pride is willing

---

without lack of clarity and exaggeration there can be no minor poetry. La Bruyère also expressed a similar conceit, probably deriving from Montaigne in this case, but his motive was to appear witty to his contemporaries. I have been told that even A. France has this idea. When Montaigne exemplifies his idea in his essay on experience, he seems an amateur in comparison to Rumi, who, five centuries before Montaigne, had subsumed it rather totally in *Fihi ma fihi* ("In It What Is In It").

[1]I know of very few exceptions: Marie Curie, Emily Dickinson, Willa Cather, George Eliot, Lise Meitner, etc.

[2]Aphra Behn, Mme de Staël, Mary Cassatt, Gertrude Stein, Virginia Woolf, Georgia O'Keefe, Miss Iris Murdoch, Miss Doris Lessing, Mary McCarthy, Miss Steinem, etc., etc.

to sacrifice his vanity at the altar of his beloved. Most such men at best glorify their mistresses to increase the pleasures they will feel in their arms.

The opposite is true of women. The more spirit and the greater moral genius they have, the more likely they are to find in passionate love their only happiness. But men fall so far below them in this respect, and they themselves are, in spite of their intelligence, so completely blind to what makes for moral superiority in men that they do not necessarily find men who are worthy of them. But the greater the soul of a woman, the more she is likely to find delicious pleasures of pride in the fact that she loves.

An ability universal in all *intelligent* women, even those who have cold hearts, which I do not think I have yet mentioned, is the absolute certainty with which they can in a very short span of time see with exactness the weakness of character of even the most intelligent and polished man—so long as a succession of weak moments has not made them fall in love before they do. They need not be motivated by any suspicion or hatred to be able to do this. A woman has a sense of personal vanity, much keener than men's, proportionate to her intelligence, and must thus know the weakness of others in order to protect her own sense of vanity. Thus her ability to see weaknesses is a reaction developed to the degree of having become an instinct.

One must know the ins and outs of vanity in order to be able to immediately perceive in what it is based in someone else, and how it may be undermined if needed. This talent comes in handy not only as a social ornament, or to deflate some pompous fool, but also when she needs to make an effective move of calculated cruelty against a lover whom she wants to punish for some offence, imagined or otherwise.

The more intelligent and spirited the woman, that is the greater her soul, the more she is apt to be tempted to such a display at some time or the other. She feels that otherwise she has impermissibly lowered herself; and now and then this thought, which is usually forced into the back of the mind, torments her sharply. Only in passionate love is such a woman entirely above this kind of display.

In this general chapter on women, I should, being a late twentieth-century man, say something about the movement known as feminism. It is a typically feminine phenomenon. Considering the ridiculous opinions regarding women that have until very recently held sway the world around, the feminist movement ought to be praised for its attempt to change the role and rights of women in society.

The greater proportion of women today around the world continue to live in a state of relative subjection. At best, they lead the lives of pampered pets or exotic toys who are given a free rein to amuse themselves with expensive trifles, if the masters of their fates are rich enough to afford them.

Lack of education, or of a properly rational education, can make idiots of whole populations. The undeveloped world, so-called, is full of women who hold the silliest ideas and whose lives are taken up with the silliest pastimes. The fact that this kind of treatment was universal through history in all nations until quite recently, with only rare exceptions, has only been possible because of the nature of women's makeup.

Maternal love and the desire for expressed esteem (i.e., personal vanity) are the two greatest forces at work in the hearts of most women.[1] About the former there was never any problem, and the latter could always be directed through custom, by allocating the praise for which they are so thirsty to certain manners,[2] to lead women to seek power that can be wielded through their sway over the hearts of men. It was under some monarchies that women had the greatest power.[3]

Women have much less power today, but a greater number of them have a greater freedom to do as they please. Feminism became a strong force in the 1960's, which was a time of great changes at all levels of society. Education was general among women in the West by this time, and, equally important, the chief nations in which the youth rebellion movements arose were all enjoying a level of general prosperity never seen before on earth. Since survival was not at stake for any part of the population, the new movements were not crushed as soon as they arose. They were not even dealt with too severely. The ideals of tolerance are only followed when they can be afforded.[4]

---

[1]From the late 1960's through the 70's, to be a mother was declared by some journalists an unfashionable thing in comparison to being employed, and fashion has a tyrannical sway over women. Those who wished to imitate these journalists followed this fashion, but maternal love being as strong a passion as it is, this fashion was vanishing by the mid-1980's.

[2]Just as today a woman wins praise by being liberal and ambitious regarding her career.

[3]A small number of women had a great share of the power in Europe in the middle centuries of this millennium. See the memoirs of various courtiers of France, Italy, England, Austria, Spain, etc. It was after Peter established a modern monarchy in Russia that women began to become powerful.

[4]It is for the same reason that the working class assumed a new degree of political

The facts of military survival made it impossible for women to share equal political power with men, but as war becomes increasingly technological in nature, women are getting an increasing share of the power. And even though at present this change is still limited since war is still only partially based on technological superiority, the first step in such a matter is of greater general consequence, so far as changes in manners are concerned, than the later ones.

Aside from the positive changes brought about by feminism, the great pleasure motivating the movement lies in its ability to gratify the petty vanity of a great number of women who would otherwise be at a loss as to what to do and say in today's societies. It gives them a way to keep their imaginations and hands occupied, and provides a topic of conversation that never bores because it bears a direct relation to their personal vanity.

True to their nature, most women discover an interest only in what immediately concerns them, and they cannot be bothered to extend their imaginations to abstract considerations only indirectly related with self-esteem, only in what is affectedly called *women's concerns*.

A few days ago, I heard a feminist on a public television channel telling her audience how the "intellectual quest" in her life *began* with her observing with anger (i.e., wounded vanity) that "objectivity" has always been thought a masculine "trait."[1]

Women are generally too sensible to get fascinated by ideas *per se*. Perhaps I am wrong, but I doubt whether any female Plato, Descartes, Rembrandt, Beethoven, Kant, Dostoevski, etc will ever appear.

But that is precisely the claims of feminists: that women are different and they ought to be judged differently, and why should men disagree? The great passion of most women is personal vanity or pride, and the whole of what is called feminism is a record of women's passion for this subject.

My experience in this regard (for what it is worth) has been dismal. I will anger many when I say that I have yet to meet a single woman who rises above the commonplace who bothers her head over the topic of feminism. All women in the West today are grateful for the changes of the last thirty odd years. But it seems to be a fate of affected, cold

---

power after the Depression. The infrastructure was already there in the U.S., the factories and knowledge were there; the stock market crash provided the opportunity for change.

[1]April, 1990.

women to become the champions of feminism. They think about the subject constantly, talk about it with other feminists, write articles, take educational courses, and bore their lovers with the subject. The lovers put up with these ideas by telling themselves that all women have their idiosyncrasies which men only slight to their faces at their own risk.[1]

Superior women rarely descend to pettiness, and for good reason. They would be mortified (for them the greatest pain there is) to feel that their pride falls short of that which does not feel the need to prove itself in any manner because it is natural to them.

> o dignitosa coscienza e netta,
> come t'e picciol fallo amaro morso!
>
> *Purgatorio* III[2]

Vanity being gratified in nearly the same manner in men and women (albeit women have greater pride in themselves than we do, a greater desire for expressed esteem and for being respected), it was inevitable that they would come to imitate each other in their speech, manners, and motives once a set of silly but universal ethical opinions regarding the passion of physical love, especially this passion in women, went out of fashion in the 1960's. It should not then be surprising that love today is generally taken to mean chiefly physical love, even by women.[3] But this is because of their love of imitation. Few women would risk being thought not to feel as all other women claim to, about which they learn from the media, or from popular feminist gurus—since their friends also imitate the same models studiously.

---

[1] A fact that these men have sufficient prudence never to let their mistresses discover.

[2] "O pure and noble conscience, how bitter a sting is a little fault to you." Mr. Singleton's translation. A description of Virgil. The character of Beatrice is sometimes censured by women of letters today whose vanity is grated upon by the noble picture Dante draws. I do not blame them, for her character is unintelligible to most women by virtue of the great imagination Dante gives her. Finding her very unlike themselves, they are prompted by their vanity to speak with contempt—they have no choice, for petty vanity never leaves any.

[3] I speak of fact here, not the false rhetoric generally used by women and men to make their lives seem prettier.

Chapter XXXVIII

Of the Birth of Love in Women

The birth and progress of love follow a different course in women from its birth and progress in men.

Admiration is an important element in both cases, but it operates in different manners. A man feels admiration, and begins to think, "How delightful to be able to talk to, touch, and kiss her." A woman who feels admiration for a man feels some of these delights about him, but the chief thought that arises is, "How delightful to be touched, kissed, loved by him."

From the beginning, love among women is one step ahead of the love of men: it starts with vanity dominating, whereas in men the effect of physical beauty dominates.

A man generally is startled into deep curiosity by hope (i.e., the imminence of physical pleasures) or a strong impression of beauty: ideally, he would like to receive a delicious hint from a beautiful and charming goddess. Particular attention gratifies the vanity of a woman in a way that is peculiarly feminine; but in inspiring admiration before the birth of hope, the heroic and the strong of character hold greater importance for most women than mere handsomeness. A man who has the strength of character a woman admires will immediately seem to have a pleasing face and address. A pleasing form and person are the most important considerations only for women who cannot love but physically.

Physical pleasure is always a tertiary consideration for a sensitive and loving woman. This is simply a fact based on physiological differences between men and women.

The birth of love in a woman of spirit is a divine movement of the soul arising from imagining the pleasures to be found in being respected and loved passionately by the man she admires.

The reasons why women begin to admire is a difficult thing for many men to understand or praise. At least women know what pleases men; but men, for whom love is a less important affair, rarely take the trouble to study the passions of women.

As Stendhal has noted somewhere in *De l'amour*, a woman rarely falls in love with a man on account of what she perceives to be his moral nature. There is rather some (to men) very unclear proofs of worth that a woman is looking for in a man, and unless he is seen to have them, a lover will have little chance of being loved by her (even if circumstances lead her to grant him her favors).

Some women admire men of great valor, fame, those with reputations of being leaders in state or business affairs, of being famous artists, sportsmen, etc., just as there are women who are willing to love men with money.[1] But the sentiments and actions that constitute moral excellence in the minds of men are not very important to a woman when she is discovering to herself reasons for loving a man. To put it simply, with all the differences of opinions and tastes that exist within each sex, there is a greater difference between the moral ideas each sex finds lovable: the lovable moral ideas that to a man constitute the soul of a woman are very different in *kind* from the lovable moral ideas that to a woman constitute the soul of a man.

The difference, I think, has to do with the difference in the wish that arise from admiration, which has been described above. When a man begins to love, and not merely to desire a woman physically, he pours into the woman he is falling in love with all the moral ideas he finds most noble and generous. A woman in love wants to be able to see in the man some symbol of those ideas that would make his loving her of most pleasure to her: depending upon her own moral makeup, these may be a special sensitivity to the secret corners of a woman's heart, passionate fidelity, emphatic faith in self, generally recognized merit of some sort, wealth, his being admired by women whom she admires, envies, or fears, dark and handsome looks, an appearance that cuts a good figure at a formal dinner party or at a beach, etc.

The difference is consistent with the fact that, aside from personal vanity, the other great passion among women is *maternal love*, which, unlike romantic love, does not consist of thoughts of the pleasure of being loved. In their friendships and loves, personal vanity is the chief

---

[1]The wives of Nabokov, R., and G., for example, had the greatest faith in the abilities and future fame of their husbands-to-be, and admired them for their superiority. Then there are the wives of Marcos and Mao, whose good fortune it was that their husbands ended up with great power. As for love of wealth, it is a universal passion. Even being the widow of X may not take away the temptation.

passion, and so being esteemed is the most important wish; only in maternal love do they love as men do. Since passionate love is only a little less rare among women than among men, we are dealing with the pleasures of vanity here.

As long as most women are sure of being loved by their lovers or husbands, they are content, but their hearts are not necessarily *actively* involved, and in this state a woman is always secretly a little bored. It is when uncertainty or the fear of losing the love of the man is felt that active love is reborn. Otherwise, their love often finds its objects in their children. Not that this is always the case. The fact, however, is that few women find men they are sure of *and* who deeply stimulate their imaginations and make them love them with an active crystallization for any considerable and uninterrupted span of time. Conversely, the commonplace woman feels the generalized need for what she calls love (i.e., the gratification of her petty personal vanity by the eager attentions of a man, preferably of one she finds admirable) so strongly that she often gives the appearance that she is capable of great love.[1]

It is rare for a woman not very much in love who yet is faithful to her lover for some other reason than fear of discovery to feel that he demands more passion from her than she is willing to give. Most women can get along fine with acting out a piece of passionate behavior to make happy a man; and most women of any intelligence are expert actresses.[2]

Women, justifiably,[3] are convinced that it is their physical beauty that is most likely to call attention to them and please prospective lovers, as well as to keep their lovers attached to them. Perhaps due to this habit of mind, they themselves are almost always inclined to prefer well-dressed

------

[1]So one would mistakenly conclude by thinking of the subject matter of all those women's magazines, popular fictions, and films that all women are passionate creatures pining for the right man to show up. This prettifying of commonplace passions is an affectation born of vanity—it is a matter of style.

[2]Very few women are truly in love with the men who are their lovers. They settle for whomever they have ended up with if they cannot find a more pleasing substitute. It is impossible for a woman to be faithful to a man *in her heart* if she meets another who seems to her more suited to make her happy. She will admire and love the latter with her whole being, whether she admits to the fact or not. It is impossible for her to keep herself from constantly dwelling on the merits and lovableness of the man she admires most. It is this fact that must make the heart of an imaginative woman never a tedious place.

[3]Justification born of personal and collective experience.

and fashionable men, given a choice.[1] Such a matter has almost a *moral* force for most women.

I know a very handsome man who is always receiving desperate encouragements from women, not all of them single (this man is not myself, incidentally). It is amazing how many strangers are willing immediately to be loved by him. He is a little elegant in the manner in which he dresses, which is easy in America where most men are very careless, but I believe he would stand out anywhere because of the proud superiority of his bearing which marks him out from both the commonplace run of men and from callow egotists.

As an experiment we asked him to wear coarse and roughly tailored clothes in public for a few weeks. Hardly a woman glanced at him.

Women will reply and say that it is the nature of what men want to see in them that forces them to support a huge fashion industry; and as I have said there is truth in this statement. But most women love prettiness for its own sake,[2] and find it difficult to excuse the lack of it in men who profess to love them.

Since I have said a few words about my very successful friend, I should add that De Silva denies being an uncommonly handsome man. He tells me that until recently women never noticed him, or if they did, they were very cold and aloof. One day, I finally succeeded in persuading him to tell me his secret. He excused himself for as long as he could, but finally agreed to tell me if I would be willing to put up with a recital which inevitably would seem ridiculously conceited.

"You see, I always had the greatest desire to succeed with women, but I had no idea how to do so. Their pattern of cool avoidance foolishly convinced me that whatever it was that they wished to see in a man, I did not possess it. Today, I can see that those things called handsomeness and amiability boil down to having a face, person, and manners which suggest ideas of physical pleasure to those of the

---

[1]In those circles (e.g., young Dead Heads, followers of an ancient rock music group called The Grateful Dead) where the opinion as to what constitutes being dressed pleasingly is very different from the general public's, the clique fashion rules. So also among high school students, etc.

[2]This, incidentally, is also the one of the reasons, besides that of their reserve due to considerations of modesty, that they never rise to sublimity in any of the arts except for acting. This is also the reason why they are almost universally passionate interior decorators and prettifiers of homes, especially after marriage when they feel that their tastes will be judged with some severity.

opposite sex. That is to say, the contours, lines, features, etc., of your face, trunk, arms, etc., and the way you carry yourself should instantly put into a woman's head the notion that you have innumerable and unimaginably delightful ideas concerning pleasures of physical love. This is how beautiful women and handsome men strike those of the opposite sex. Looks are more often deceiving than not, but how many are there who have the strength of mind to resist thoughts of very deep pleasures?

"The day finally came when I decided to attempt to understand my enemy; I began to study the heart of women; perhaps I never fully understood that I lacked a pleasing address. But I understood that to succeed in anything you have to give people what they most wish to possess.

"Since my goal was success with women, I attempted, and finally succeeded, in affecting an air of great self-assurance and pride; not extreme conceitedness which will make a woman suspicious, for her eyes and manners will then tell you, 'You do not impress me one little bit.' Instead, you want to give the effect that you are *inadvertently* expressing (as you go around your little everyday affairs) your absolute contentment at being shamefully successful all-round in everything you do, that you consider yourself a man apart, that you have gratified scores of women. This expression, if true to nature, and thus convincing, persuades a woman that you come certified to give untold degrees of pleasure. She begins willy-nilly to imagine how much pleasure she would have with you. But you must understand women to the depths of their heart before you can successfully have such an effect, because only then can you feel the superiority to them that makes them wish to make you the master of their fate.

"When I see a woman I find pleasing, I look straight into her eyes, the desired effect being to make her think that I am surprised and quite taken with her charms. The assurance bit is always there, so that she is flattered by the peculiar attention, even as she is put off by the assurance. But the conviction, incidentally never well-founded, that she has made an impression on me which no other girl has usually rallies her to the side of love. The glance has to express not only the self-assurance of a very successful man and a lively interest: it must also make her feel that in my imagination I already hold closed in my arms her more than willing person; it is my *easy* conviction that SHE *will* find this development very pleasing that makes this bold ploy work. It works because she believes, perhaps without having put the matter to herself in so many words, that I must be right, for otherwise I would not have the look of a man who knows that he has pleased innumerable women.

"The imagined pleasures are too intoxicating, my expression of absolute success tells her that she urgently needs to tempt and attract me, for she can easily lose me to a more audacious woman who has the brains to see how much I am worth. For this reason, I *never* have to beg for favors, not even with the proudest or most sensitive women. They fall at my feet begging for attention and love. To be successful you must at all points have the conviction that it is always the woman who wants to please you, never the other way around—which is a recipe for failure. Remember that a woman wants for herself a man who can take care of himself and her, who knows the ropes, so to speak, who can take charge, who knows how to give and command pleasure. Such is the secret hero of the dreams of most women. Because he is almost never met with in life, a woman will adore you if you seem to fit the bill.

"But then there are those innumerable cases where a woman I have not even noticed walks around to where I happen to be, and does something clearly meant to encourage me to accost her. In such cases, the only reason why this happens is that she must have associated pleasing ideas of physical love with my appearance. In fact, it is often a good idea even if you have seen a woman before she sees you to either not let her see you admiring her, or to make her think that she has not made much of an impression; this makes her wish to, and thus she begins hoping for a favorable reaction on your part. There is no distinction between this hope and the hope that you will proceed to possess her in good time.

"Physical comeliness is not all-important, for you can suggest a ten-times more lively idea of your being a purveyor of more untold pleasures than most physically handsome men, so that most women, who in my opinion are stimulated by nothing as much as by the thought of physical love, would prefer you when given a choice. You must on no account show too much weakness: just enough restraint and plausible modesty to flatter the woman deeply. She will never want to leave you then, and you can do with her what you please until you get bored of her.

"When you first speak with her, remember to eye her steadily, boldly, intermittently, (depending upon the type of woman she is, something which you learn only from experience) but coolly, as if eyeing a piece of very valuable merchandise to see how much pleasure it will give you versus how much trouble it will be. Be humorous and playful as with a child. Any action or word smacking of keen desire for her, if perceived by her, will cool her by taking away the motive for wishing *for more and more* while uncertain as to whether she will get what she wants. For the rest, wait for her to begin giving you those unmistakable signs, the feminine language of gestures, movements, intonations, stresses, the thrill in the eyes, and then she is yours. Oh yes, let them all talk about feminism and respect and sensitivity and honesty amongst each other and in public, but I tell you from experience that not one woman in ten thousand truly wants any of that bunkum. The most vociferous of them yield with the greatest melting compliance."[1]

He tells me to study the courtship manners among wolves, baboons, deer, lions, certain species of birds; the female chooses according to certain criteria of success in domination, which criteria, scientists today tell us, are not necessarily the ones most conducive to the survival of the given species, although it is possible that at an earlier historical age they may have been.

---

[1]He later told me —
What is pleasing to women of one age and nation is not so to those of another. But physical beauty is not necessarily the strongest impetus to physical attraction among women; rather, it is the suggestion of *certain ideas only* of independent masculinity that inspires maximum admiration. In those societies where women seldom, if ever, let themselves come to know physical pleasures intimately and without false shame, the bold, charmingly impudent style I described to you the other day will not be as effective as it is in the United States, though it will still stand out and make a marked impression, for physical pleasures are common to all, no matter how they try to suppress or disown them. Women in such nations are usually only taken up with ideas of reputation, praise, and security, anyway—and a very boring group they make.
When I asked De Silva for the name of someone famous who exhibits the qualities of masculine self-assurance that he claims are so universally noted by most women, and which please a good number of them to no end, he told me, "Clark Gable, most of all, almost in a purified form; in *Gone With the Wind* and *Soldier of Fortune*, to name his greatest performances. I am speaking here only of how women see things. Very few women would not find him irresistible if they met his Rhett Butler or Hank Lee in flesh and blood, as opposed to merely seeing him in a film. Also, Mr. Sean Connery's expressed ideas in *Thunderball* and *Never Say Never Again*—in the first three Bond films he had not yet attained full mastery, and his initial popularity among women arose as much from handsomeness. Gable in his very expressive, warm, and gracefully and comically impudent manner, and Mr. Connery in his much more subdued, colder, and biliously elegant one, produce that effect of easy assurance and masculinity that I spoke of. They express nuances of pride and strength of character that women immediately, before any time for reflection, find most pleasing and worthy of admiration, whether they admit to the fact or not; as Beethoven had a sort of pride that many men of letters find most admirable."

With De Silva's amused permission, I have included in entirety his impudent speech here, in spite of its extreme cynicism. Since I have myself seen women consistently prefer him to handsome, amiable, popular and richer men, there must be something to what he claims, something of a nature generally applicable, and thus worth recording.

But, to return to love among women.

A woman needs to feel proud of the man she calls her lover, since her self-esteem depends upon having made him fall in love with her. If she cannot, she will stop loving him. But it is not merely the soul and thoughts of the man that she wants to be proud of. He who gives her his arm in public must *seem* a good catch, someone for whom other women would envy her. Some men see their mistresses in this light as well, a fact less justifiable in a man, and one which unfailingly reveals the mean nature of his character. Women feel the flaws of their lovers to be their own which are being displayed to the world at large, and are cut to the heart by them—even the most sensitive women feel this.

Chapter XXXIX

The birth of love involves the total being of a woman as it never can in a man.

When he begins to love, a man, if he is at all spirited, feels immediately that the greatest pleasures that the world offers are opening up to him. A woman feels that the *only true pleasures* of the world are opening up for her.

The difference can be seen in the expression of their eyes, and in their actions. Desire for favors wells up in a man, and he forgets all other pleasures in imagining these new ones. When she sees that she is admired by a man who does not displease her to begin with, her whole being is immediately involved in the adventure. She instinctively feels everything in life but what she now feels is inconsequential and *a lie*. This is why all women develop the art of dissembling their true feelings, hiding behind masks of indifference or false pleasures.

Because of this total involvement of being, love is a greater affair in a woman's life than in any man's, no matter how sensitive and imaginative. But for this very reason, love is a more complicated matter for her, for she cannot afford to lose in this greatest gamble of her life.

She must be careful at every step, and not give in at the wrong time, or to the wrong man. This instinct of hesitation is what makes passion possible; it directly leads to the birth of passion in men, and indirectly in women.

A man measures the degree of love a woman feels for him by the degree to which she grants him favors. Does she let him talk to her, how friendly is she, how angry at any liberty he takes? A woman cannot do more for a man than to give herself up entirely to him; at this stage a man is sure of her love. Infidelity makes him uncertain, but it also makes him lose respect for her. The pain is then from vanity, not from absence of passion. But for a woman it is much more difficult to ascertain how deeply a man loves her. His love for her is by nature a more symbolic affair; he must assure and reassure by his words and actions that he loves her. Thus flattery becomes a key weapon.

Most systems of courtship take these matters into account. Such customs are absent only in nations where love is frowned upon. There, parents or guardians approved by society decide upon matches.

Women are ever unsure whether they are loved in earnest or not. This makes for great difficulty for a man who is too much in love. He has to distinguish his attentions from the kind of formulaic flattery he despises. This is all the more difficult if he loves her passionately, since her presence never fails to deprive him of his rational faculty. He has no choice but to hope that the intelligence and imagination of the beloved will enable her to understand him by the whole pattern of his actions, and to form a picture of his character and makeup true to nature.

They display astonishing patience in love. When absolutely secure in the knowledge of being loved by the man they love, they can often go for *years* without so much as laying eyes on him, or see him no more than once or twice a year.[1] To know that they are loved is sufficient if circumstances prevent them from granting favors. This admirable control over themselves is by no means very common, but never can I prevent myself from feeling a great admiration whenever I come across one who displays it.

If, however, a woman doubts the love of a man she unfortunately cannot stop thinking of, there is no end to her inner impatience, howsoever well she disguise this fact. She wants to see him standing before her eyes, she wants tokens, phone calls, letters, etc.

---

[1]True even today in long-distance loves. Such love is almost never passionate, I would think.

Since a woman of any spirit is much too proud to openly pursue a man who is not hers already, she is rarely reduced to awkward bashfulness the way a man easily is if he is of too passionate a nature.[1] She never lays down her mask of modesty even when she is flirting, for she does not have to make the direct verbal and active advances that may be curtly rejected. A woman is ruffled *only* when she is *surprised* in any manner by a suitor. Only then are her reactions unpredictable even to herself. Otherwise, she has always decided upon, or at least carefully thought of, a course of action for every contingency she can imagine, and she depends upon her gifts for acting and dissembling to carry the day.[2]

This inborn gift for dissembling that all intelligent women possess must lead them to have a sense of guilt very different in kind from ours. For a man to dissemble where his deepest feelings are concerned would wound his pride and self-respect deeply; he would never be able to forgive his lack of honesty.

But even the most admirable women are never deeply troubled by these matters of conscience. They apparently do not feel any contradiction between honesty and acting: their pride must not be humbled, their good name not sullied. And no woman can rest with the thought that a man with whom she may have a mind to fall in love does not esteem her very highly. Where her own entire happiness is at stake, a woman easily overlooks any qualms of conscience, and this is why women can be much more cruel and vindictive than men, more cruel in vengeance, but for the very same reason, their actions often move us so much more when they arise from love.

For once she loves, a woman very easily puts her whole soul into the passion. Pride, the dictates of which once told her to resist the subjection and helplessness of love, later makes her support the cause of love against every obstacle of circumstances or ethics.

With regard to the physical side of love, the importance given it varies from woman to woman.

---

[1] Inexperienced women who have never frequented society excepted, and their cases are similar to those of men who have lived very little in social circles.

[2] For many women (even for many who are not ruled by petty motives) the power they have over the men who admire them give them the greatest pleasures they know. But there is a great difference between the way a coquette enjoys these pleasures and they way a woman of great pride enjoys them.

Those who have weak wills desire little in the way of physical pleasures, just as they make few other demands upon their lovers, husbands, and friends.[1]

At the other extreme, passionate souls, always under the necessity of restraining themselves before others, learn to move about in the world protected by a strong conviction of their true but unknown nature.[2] When such a woman falls deeply in love, the physical aspect matters solely as a symbol, and not for its common pleasures.

The vast majority of women fall between these two extremes. Physical pleasures have varying degrees of hold upon them, depending upon their habitual methods of gratifying their vanity. Weariness with the pleasures that are allowed or available often inspires a desire for an intense, requited physical passion since it offers an escape from boredom without making too many demands upon the imagination.[3] Since the self-esteem of almost all women depends on their opinion concerning their success in love and the intensity of sensations derived from this success, this is an excellent and easy way to gratify their vanity when they have developed great though often secret contempt for what the other women of their social circle pursue as pleasures.[4]

Vanity is the ruling passion of both sexes; but although most men also derive what pleasure they obtain from love from vanity, in general, women derive a greater portion of the sum pleasures of love from it. Pure physical pleasure is secondary to such convictions as the thought of her extreme good fortune to have such an ardent admirer and excellent lover, admiration for the man, the thought that she has saved him from a

---

[1]Miss Bates in Austen, or even Charlotte Collins. Generally, in life, women of phlegmatic temperament. See Cabanis.

[2]Why this rare type arises only among well-to-do circles. Nargis portrayed the different stages that can be reached in *Jogan* ("The Nun") and *Mother India*. The social views and theories of the directors of these films (Kidar Sharma and Mehboob Khan) were not particularly shrewd, and are inconsequential to Nargis' portrayal. You watch her expressions in *Mother India* and ignore the fact that Radha was meant to be an idealized portrait of the poor peasant women of India. If this supreme master had herself been born such a peasant, she would never have reached the heights of knowledge concerning the human heart that she did. [Later note, added about four years after the writing of the above: Long experience has taught me that it is intellectually foolhardy to posit a limit to her abilities. However, I leave that last sentence of the original note as it is, as the idea expressed in it seemed to me to be the truth when I wrote it.]

[3]Emma Bovary.

[4]Unfortunately, most women around the world are still brought up to look down their noses at physical pleasures. It is only in a few nations for which this is not entirely true.

worthless existence, that she is envied or feared because of who her lover is, the charming idea that she is in possession of the greatest pleasure that life holds for her, etc.

Women who think of physical pleasures as an end of an ongoing love with even one man are never capable of more tender feelings with any.[1] This fact is not necessarily true in the case of a man for the simple reason that in neither tender vanity love nor in passionate love does a man ever feel the necessity of acting according to the peculiar dictates that characterize feminine modesty and pride.[2] The exception are all inverts, not only women but men also, for all of whom such dictates exist as strongly as they do for women generally, and the violence they must do to these in their mind by a confession of inverted love would be too great to be borne if these dictates were the product of pride that revolts at the thought of physical pleasures as an end. But they are not, for they are the products of hypocrisy and affectation only. Physical love is the only form of love known to inverts, the tenderness they display to a lover being born of the fear of wounded vanity, not born of vanity love. Since their collective vanity is bound to be wounded by clear acknowledgement of this fact, they equal the woman who loves men physically only in the degree of hypocritical outward adoption of what they think are elevated motives they feel called upon to assume.[3] For

---

[1]See the works of Kate Chopin, especially *The Awakening*, "At the 'Cadian Ball," and its sequel, "The Storm." She wrote as effectively as she did because she approached the subject of physical love in women in a scientific manner, aiming at precise description of the pleasures only. Jane Austen called these pleasures those of the *animal spirits*, and portrayed them as they are (as well as in what sort of women they are found) in Lydia Bennet. In our own time, Miss S- has expressed the different nuances of physical love in the films she has appeared in. All three women are in agreement that when physical passion takes precedence over vanity in a woman, she cannot feel any other type of love—which does not mean that she cannot fall in love, for physical love has its crystallization. So, the love of Lydia for Wickham is of a different character from Mary Crawford's for Edmund Bertram.

[2]The modesty of a man passionately in love arises from his conviction that he must not be unworthy of the woman he adores.

[3]From Plato's dialogues to the claims of modern writers, such as Mr. E. W. The only men to have described the love of inverts with even a modicum of honesty were Petronius and Proust. It is to Proust's credit that he did not shrink from describing how prevalent this form of love is, at least among men (though he exaggerated its commonness among women), and of the forms and manners it assumes—but even he did not describe the large group of men who are like Kryten in the episode "Dimension Jump" of *Red Dwarf*. Inversion does not necessarily mean that women do not also please, and this Proust describes as well, but in all cases where inversion exists at all, everything beyond the simple physical pleasures is merely a matter of rhetoric on the part of inverts. This is the reason

most women physical pleasure without the overlay of vanity would be a humiliating experience. Many dream of it, but very few are willing to risk it in life.

Such being the case, it is the greatest blunder possible to let a purely physical type of woman know that you have fallen for her in a deep manner. Such a thought immediately cools her blood, and since for her love holds no pleasure but in its physical nature the lover's expressed feelings make no impression on her imagination of possible pleasures. Worse, she sees the granting of the smallest favor (e.g., a ten-minute *tête-à-tête*) as a very major compromise of her professed self-sufficiency, and thus, as an impossible step. The lover is left without the smallest of encouragements or hope.

In every such case, even if he has made this mistake initially, it is necessary, if he still wishes her to love him, that the lover persuade her (gradually and convincingly if he is trying to redeem his earlier mistake of tactic) to believe that he is extremely indifferent to her in any high-flown romantic way, and that he coolly thinks of her only in terms of physical passion; and that if *she* refuses him, he will simply take his pleasures with the next pretty woman who comes along—herself being the only loser. If she believe this, she is more than likely his if he quietly and self-assuredly push hard enough once he sees that her feelings have changed and settled. The amused indifference and calm self-assurance are strong masculine beauties in her eyes. By being a little coy (not haughty and unapproachable as she used to be, when she had been approached in the wrong manner), she makes the man decisively prove his mettle by overcoming that coyness and possessing her; this triples her pleasure for it triples the crystals of pleasing masculine charms she builds around the man who she feels is about to possess her.[1]

Prostitutes, call-girls, courtesans, as well as those women who grant favors to a good portion of those who ask for them, are forced to console themselves with the expression of cynical opinions of the world, happiness, men, other women, etc., since for them love cannot contribute to their self-esteem. Another way of stemming the tide of self-contempt is to take pride in the length of their lists of customers or

---

why Proust, whose pleasures were closest to those of Rembrandt and Wagner, fell far short of even them in his knowledge of love, of which he had very little more than Schopenhauer.

[1]De Silva.

conquests. Lastly, they can persuade themselves that the material gains they have won more than make up for the wounded pride. They would like to affect that their pride is intact, because wounded pride seems contemptibly the lot of fools.

There are others who grant favors right and left to whomever they take a fancy to without a thought of remorse since no other pleasures exist for them on earth.

Chapter XL

Of the Degrees of Susceptibility to Love

Most women have dreamed of love from their earliest years. Men dream of women, women dream of love. There are years in boyhood when it is thought of as unmanly to show the slightest interest in girls or love. Since these are precisely the years when a boy desperately seeks to prove his mettle, he lives in constant fear of ridicule. Many a man never advances beyond these boyhood affectations, and though he feels no shame in pursuing a commonplace degree of physical pleasures, love continues to play a small role in his life.[1] He chooses a wife the way he chooses a car or his wardrobe.

There is never an age when love is unfashionable among women.[2] Sustained religious and moral warnings about the dangers and evil nature of love uttered by avaricious parents, schools, religious institutions, as well as lessons concerning modesty, only deter the imagination of the meek type of young woman. Give a woman a little spirit, and she will willy-nilly lose herself in thoughts of love, in spite of everything, if only to imagine the hearts she wishes she could break in the future. Since it is not uncommon for a woman to lack courage when it comes to public reputation, she stops short of carrying out her bold

---

[1]A relatively rare phenomenon in the United States, it is true, but common enough elsewhere. Where women are allowed to leave a man when they wish to, men have had to develop certain refinements of manners that will prevent such a calamity.

[2]It is only after the age of thirty that women who have had bitter experiences in love become founding members of little cliques where it is a *faux pas* to speak positively of men or love, or, when these cliques are of the Proustian type, of men and love. The pose of indifference among girls at twelve is a reaction to that of ten- to twelve-year old boys.

dreams in life unless a pose of indifference to public opinion is respectable among a sufficiently large part of society, as it is in the United States today.

Since the dreams of love of young women are not founded upon knowledge of the passion, the habit only results in a greater *predisposition* to love among them, not in a greater capacity.

This capacity depends upon the degree of susceptibility to reveries. A man who has not dreamed as often in his early youth as a woman commonly does of love may fall desperately in love when he is twenty five. But he must have dreamed of something with great intensity of imagination.

Such men do not reveal their true character until they fall in love. No one prior to that unfortunate event would have accused them of possessing a *feminine sensibility*, but let them only reveal their true thoughts after it to anyone; the friend would despise his feelings unless he himself is hopelessly in love with some woman. Any woman (especially his beloved) will think him absurdly weak-minded should he have the courage and foolhardiness (these are one and the same in all such cases) to reveal what he feels.[1]

Conversely there are men all of whose poetic dreams from early youth have consisted of love. They are simple men, the Germanic type, Werthers, very uncommon today in the West except among the youngest ages.

There is a difference of night and day between these two types. Those who have dreamed of glory and of doing great, heroic deeds are by far the rarer, and are a much stranger breed.[2]

Strangely enough such a man becomes truly heroic only when he has given over his dreams and ambitions, having been made so unhappy by a pair of beautiful eyes as to have forgotten everything that used to guide him before. Ask him now about his thoughts of his own glory and nobility, or better not ask him that. Fierce pride remains in him yet, but it is the pride of being worthy of the woman in his life. True, it is only a passing phase when his imagination is exhausted, for it never lasts long.

---

[1]Such a sensibility in a man is rarely admired highly by women. He must still possess the aura of strength and danger.

[2]To me, that is. I belong to neither, being only a scientific observer of bizarre phenomena.

Overexposure to opportunities reduces the intensity of love.[1] This is why for many their greatest, most headlong love occurs before they are twenty. At that age, love is unknown and even a dullard must rely on his imagination to supply him with pictures of what love must be like. This is being in love with love. And though this love is most poetic and enchanting while it lasts, it can never be very deep. There are simply not enough ideas in the mind at that age; women may have more about love than men, but they have little knowledge of life. The more knowledge of the world, and the more consequent weariness and disillusionment, the deeper is love when and if it is born.

A series of unhappy affairs leads a woman to adopt a cynical opinion of love and lovers.[2] She feels that it has not granted her any of the happiness that it had seemed to promise to her youthful heart. Her natural tendency to hesitate is heightened, all the internal movements of feminine reluctance to take a chance stand out then in bold relief. She puts up greater inner resistance to the feelings that may sweep her from rational and cautious conduct. Such a woman is capable of passion for the first time in her life, but it all depends upon how strong her pride and fear are, whether they will triumph or give way in the end when the right man appears, *if* he appear. At this stage, pride and caution prevent the birth of love, be the woman of ever so loving a temperament.

The protective instincts of feminine pride and modesty should on no account ever be overlooked when considering the course of passion in women. They make passion possible in the first place in both sexes.[3] As soon as she notices a man's interest in her, an element of self-observing enters into her thoughts and actions, its degree depending upon her own initial weakness for him. The more commonplace her passions, the more indistinguishable is this element of self-observing from affected manners born of the knowledge of being admired and gazed upon. Even when admiration is unwanted, every experienced woman knows that an unwanted admirer must be snubbed at once, and that cruelty is the best

---

[1]Houses of pleasure, beaches, parties, bars, and other so-called night spots are the places where love is most down to earth.

[2]Miss Joan F- is just one of the more charming of such women. Barbara Stanwyck at least pretended to something of this sort. At a remove, feminists; at another, women who have had to sell themselves, or forced by difficult circumstances, a weak will, or petty ambition, to surrender themselves to men they found displeasing, or were ill-treated by.

[3]Passionate love in men arises from doubt of being loved, and there could be no doubt were it not for feminine reserve.

medicine, the affected attitude of complete indifference (unaffected indifference does not feel the need to proclaim itself) and contempt.

The protective instincts are not sharply awakened unless he openly solicits her favors in some way, or unless she indulges herself in the perilous enchantments of the imagination to such a degree that the true state of affairs leaves her unhappy.[1] At that moment she may give the name of *love*, or sometimes, *true love* to her feelings, and the inborn instinct[2] (always a bit of a mystery to men) followed upon by education exerts its influence over her actions and words; even thoughts. A woman risks so much in love that it should not be wondered at that she becomes over-cautious as soon as she feels she is deeply involved.

For the coquette, being sought after is a great pleasure. The shy or inexperienced woman must fight her fear. The greater number defend themselves gallantly out of a respect for custom, so as not to lose the respect of others, their lovers, and themselves. In such, the more generous and elevated their idea of the love they feel themselves falling into, the more *earnest* and therefore more admirable—and ennobling in their own (and they think their lovers') eyes–seem the dictates of modesty and pride. They would rather lose the love, at this stage, than lose their lovers' or their own respect. I am not sure that all such women are keenly aware when this tendency becomes pointlessly burdensome to all concerned, and when slightly ridiculous through excess—but I speak as a man, and do not know whether this is more than a personal opinion.

In their reactions to love, women can be divided into four classes. This is not a hard and fast classification, but it is useful in considering how passion, the thing of interest to us, arises in some.

1) Women who are incapable of strong attachments, and who desires pleasures of different kinds. Without ever putting it into so many words,

---

[1]So that when he notices that a woman is beginning to think of him in a special manner, the lover should refrain from anything but the most casual and unmeaningful though amusing conversation, or he should merely be in the same room engaged deep in conversation with others while making sure that their eyes meet once every fifteen minutes —no more, no less. To make what she would consider to be advances will prevent crystallization for the moment—unless his charms in her eyes are breathtaking, and his mistake trivial and unfrightening, this may be the end of the whole thing, for some time to come at least.

[2]The difference probably goes beyond the physical differences. Being on the receiving end (no matter how forward she is) seems to dictate this development. The proof of this is the coquettish, sly behavior common among inverts as flirtation deepens, which Proust has described very accurately.

they expect nothing more than casual friendship and (perhaps naively) constancy from their lovers. Finally, there are some for whom physical pleasures suffice.[1]

2) Those who are incapable of strong attachments, their happiness in life arising from vanity inspired by social praise, wealth, rank, possessions, etc. The affected woman, the woman whose chief pleasure is cultivation and pruning of her beauty, so-called accomplishments, and affectations of manners.[2]

Such a woman hates to talk of her true feelings almost as much as does a sensitive woman, but out of fear and not pride and shame, and conceals everything behind a façade of inscrutable arrogance. In this group belong those who are practiced coquettes. They know how to make a man despair who has had the misfortune to have fallen in love with them; they do this coldly, with a studied aim.

3) Those who are by nature formed for strong attachments. They are gentle and sweet in disposition, and very much need to be loved. A direct and simple approach to love gives them away as types. When a man manages to come across as being truly fond of such a woman, so longer as he is not too displeasing to look at or think of as being regarded as her constant companion by her friends, she returns his feelings immediately, and generally does not take too long a time to let him know of his good fortune. They easily become fond of a man who has not shown any signs of admiration, but who seems of a loving and lofty temperament, or to whom they are in any way grateful. They are often deceived in love because of their natural simplicity. This is not to say that they do not on occasion put on an aloof air.[3]

4) Those who are by nature formed for strong attachments, but in whom extreme feminine pride and modesty, those forces of resistance, guide their conduct. Experience does the rest, so that by their twenties

---

[1]Their lack of pride is such that some are willing to admit as much on national television. This type is a modern invention, a product of the late industrial age whose incredible prosperity arising from the general exclusive love of utility has destroyed the idea of haughty pride.

[2]Such a woman is perfect for a man who wants a peacock for a mistress, who wishes to show her off as a gaudy asset. Lebruc finds such women amusing. This man tells me that the woman I admire is dull beyond patience. I find his charming mistress a very beautiful and lifeless doll.

[3]Such women are also apt to love, or at least grant favors to, more than one man at the same time, out of weakness. They cannot refuse a man who seems truly taken with them.

Desmoulins

[213]

(the exact age depending upon their intelligence) they are capable of passion, due to reasons explained earlier in this chapter. Their pride is a more severe version of the common woman's vanity, just as the idealizations of a great poet are nobler versions of the identical phenomenon of vanity-beauty that lesser mortals also know. The women in this group are haughty in spirit, not from affectation. They have great pride, too much of it to let them stoop to displaying it decoratively. A man must be keenly observant and perceptive to be able to distinguish them from the affected type.

It is only the fourth type of woman who is capable of passion. Such a woman needs to see in the man whom she loves a generous, simple, and heroic nature. When an admirer for whom she has some fondness does something amiss, something low, dishonorable, cowardly, or even something which in itself is not deplorable, but which will inspire public censure and disrepute, she is immediately cut to the heart. She will not hide from him that he has done something unworthy of his love for her. This woman finds it difficult not to feel ashamed of a lover who does not stand up to the most stringent tests of character.

I know a woman who was very fond of a certain young man who was little aware of her existence. It took her time and effort to find circumstances to take advantage of, but she finally succeeded in getting him to notice her. This man astonished her, and even more, himself, by promptly falling deeply in love with her. He declared his feelings, was rejected by the now suspicious lady. She had loved him for his independent and arrogant air, and it was precisely this which disappeared from his manners and expressions in her presence, although at all other times he still made the same impression.

After being rebuffed several times, he decided that it would be better not to be despised altogether by the woman he loved. He stopped begging her for kinder treatment, in fact, he assumed a completely cold, arrogant, even angered air whenever chance threw him into her presence. The strategy worked better than he had imagined it could. Not only did she stop despising him, but a new respect for him was born in her heart, so that she loved him infinitely more now than she had before. She now saw his abject weakness in front of her as a proof of nobility of heart and the purity of his love. The pleasure of thinking that this very proud man was sacrificing his independence and pride for her sake alone intoxicated her beyond anything she had known. Having in fact a very loving, if too proud, soul, she gathered courage, and casting aside her own pride, let him conclude that she was beginning to love him.

The problem with feminine pride is that the very women whom a passionate man is liable to fall in love with are those in whom this pride has the greatest influence. The more he loves, the more helpless he is in front of her, and the more reason she will have to despise this as a weakness. Women of little pride but warm feelings may be flattered by the helplessness of a lover so long as he reforms to a respectable degree soon, but the passionate man is generally too good a reader of character to fall in love where he will be made happy almost immediately. Thus, all great loves are thorny affairs, or as Shakespeare has said, "The course of true love never did run smooth."[1]

There is a reason why a man of passion and intelligence (there is never any passion without intelligence in either men or women, but there may be intelligence without passion among men) is rarely attracted to women who are not proud. But for the same reason, he is liable to place his affections in the wrong place, and fall in love with the merely arrogant woman whom his imagination transforms into a sublime creature.

The woman of a spirited and loving nature who has a nobly developed self-esteem and a severe and independent moral nature would be prudent to also develop a sensitivity to subtle signs of strength of character in men. But since most women, no matter how intelligent, become blind to the moral worth of a man as soon as they begin to think in terms of love and loving, such a sensitivity is very rare. A man who has not been provided by nature with what the woman he loves prizes highly is in a poor situation indeed. The fault lies with women.[2] They want to be loved, but they cannot see (or do not take the trouble to) the things that give away the type of man who can meet them as an equal in purity, pride, and intensity of passion. And so they commonly settle for less.

---

[1] I take the meaning out of context.
[2] Needless to say, I speak as a man.

Chapter XLI

Of Feminine Modesty and Pride

In the early years of this century it was a rare thing to catch sight of the pretty ankles of a woman in public except in some luxury beaches and nightclubs. Today the sight of much more is common enough.

In India where modesty is still often carried to the point of general hypocritical prudery, the sari even a century ago allowed a woman to go in public with her waist practically uncovered.

Among many aboriginal people women present themselves in public in a manner that would shock all civilized people, especially women themselves, even though the fashion of imitating them in this regard was born among a very small minority in the West.

If feminine modesty is a matter of social custom, why is it universal in almost all civilizations? The modesty of a Korean woman may differ greatly from that of an Englishwoman, but they will follow the conventions prevalent in their societies. Rare it still is that what is called a liberated woman will point-blank and very directly ask a man to share her company when she keenly wishes to: the stronger her wish, the more that even she feels restrained by modesty and pride.

For my part, I would not be surprised if the ideas of modesty and pride were invented long ago by men all around the world to keep their women in check. These ideas were probably born of the fear of abandonment and ridicule when savage life gave way to the first glimmers of civilization. Those early men must have felt that unless they fettered women by playing upon ignorant pride, most of them would always follow the lead of their hearts and live only for love.

Men become so enamored of women that they often forget what strange creatures they are. Governed by pride, they are creatures of conventions to a degree that is impossible for many men to conceive of. Your general dolt of a successful man is a conventional creature *par excellence*, but even the most intelligent woman will accept the conventional pieties regarding the rules of feminine modesty and pride.

We must take them as given facts. Their influence is general. Because this respect for conventions is found among women as a rule, a man should be prepared to look deep for the true reason why the woman he loves is willing to flout those conventions for his sake. Is it love or merely some other custom (e.g., that a woman without a man is a ridiculous object) that is responsible for her willingness to forget the dictates of modesty and pride. This utterly illogical proceeding is made necessary by the fact you are dealing with an irrational set of actions. The insincerity of a man is a simpler affair.

I do not think that this matter of modesty and pride is solely to be attributed to the desire to be respected by their lovers. There is also the fear of being despised by their social circles, especially other women. The tyrannical hold the opinions of other women (strangers, acquaintances, and close friends) have on the minds of most women is amazing. You will find the most intelligent women (especially the most intelligent women) utterly at the mercy of these opinions as far as all practical decisions in granting favors to their lovers are concerned.

It is difficult to say whether pride is more or less absurd than modesty since they are two aspects of a single governing principle of action.

Women very proud of their beauty and power over men, and who derive all their happiness from their beauty and sway, live a life of curious paradox. They must appear to despise those they attract, when the very basis of their contempt is the existence of that admiration they secretly seek. They want to strike their admirers as being difficult to please, and consequently, to keep up the fiction, they resist pleasures until this becomes a habit. Incapable of loving, they are then won by men whose excelling point is their cleverly varied impudence. They know how to flatter them even while they deflate their affectations of pride by ignoring these.

Their beauty is in fact a burden since it prevents the pursuit of happiness. If they allowed themselves a glimpse of the truth, they would see that the pleasures they know are exactly the same as those they originally despised in others, and which they had long ago determined to avoid. They too are pleased by securing the admiration of many directed solely at them; consequently they are equally at the mercy of the whims and tastes of others as the more amiable sort.

However, it gets even worse, for they commonly end up with either impudent men or fatuously admiring, docile, and (often) rich men. I think the more intelligent ones know this; they rarely have the glowing features of happiness. But who can say to what extent they acknowledge the truth? They must perforce assume a perverted pride if they tell themselves the truth, so that the unhappier they are, the more willfully proud their air and words become.

Feminine modesty makes of love a very difficult affair, and tricky as it makes happy love for men, I am inclined to think it makes it even more tricky and more elusive for women. A woman who has fallen in love with a man out of gratitude, or simply because to her otherwise boring life he brings a romantic note, cannot do more than cast out hints of her inclinations. The happiness that a man feels at having opened his heart to a woman is denied her. Even if he is rejected, there is a consolation of knowing that the beloved knows in all details the condition of his heart, and no lover who is seriously in love doubts her capacity for generous understanding.

The feelings of a woman who has been ignored or abandoned by a man she is deeply in love with are probably of a nature that no man can fully know. This is a difficult thing for me to understand or describe, being myself a man, but many observations, as well as descriptions by women of their feelings, persuade me to accept this as a fact.

It is to avoid this pain that many women instinctively apply brakes upon their crystallization until they are reasonably sure of being loved first. But this is an easier principle to decide upon beforehand than one to act upon when in danger. For most women, their self-esteem is inextricably tied to their knowledge of being loved. Unless they have made at least one agreeable man fall in love with them, they remain discontented with themselves.

To lose a man she cannot help loving to another woman, or to some other passion of his (such as his profession, hobbies, or ambitions) makes a woman feel either self-contempt, blind anger, or, more commonly, a combination of both. She feels she has no basis upon which to respect herself, and her anger and resentment at being forced to feel this pain she directs half at herself and half at her delinquent lover. At this stage, it is always a great source of consolation to know that there still are, and have always been, a good number of agreeable admirers. Only when seriously in love does having admirers make not the slightest difference.

The more pride she has, the more pains she will take to hide her grief from the world, especially from her lover irrespective of whether she feels that he does or does not love her. Women of a cold temperament will promptly take another lover, or at least begin to give another man great hope. Those who are not will busy themselves with some self-devised task, or get involved in some group affair (such as community or charitable work) in order to seem content. If a woman feels he still loves her as much as he used to, she will refuse to have anything to do with him unless and until she has managed to humiliate him in his, her, and perhaps even the world's eyes. Only then can she bring herself to take him back.[1]

There is a reverse side to this. Anyone guided solely by considerations of pride or vanity is susceptible to love only by its being wounded in the right manner.

The extremely vain woman who steadfastly refuses to be engaged by anything a lover says does not think of him at all when away from him—and when she is with him her only thought is to get away as soon as she decently can. But if he manages to insult her on her *own grounds*, under the pretence of merely telling her the truth regarding the differences between him and her, i.e., according to her own set of opinions and pleasures, she appears from the conversation the lesser of the two, she will think of him night and day in anger and resentment, but this is often the first step towards the birth of love. Her thoughts can take two directions, or both alternatingly. That he is better than she will lead to admiration, though she may take some time before admitting as much to herself. That he deserves to be insulted in return is the other thought. At any rate, she now cannot stop thinking about the man. If she humiliates him so effectively that she thinks she has seen the last of him, he is in great luck: for soon the triumph of successful revenge loses its first glow of joy. She turns to other things with eagerness, only to find that the pleasure to be found in them has vanished. All her old customary pleasures pall before the pleasure of revenge so recently and sweetly indulged in.

---

[1]Many women forgive their lovers of occasional infidelities, but the result is that their lovers take them for granted. This is why most intelligent women know that to forgive their lovers is to lose their respect. A woman *always* prefers to be loved, or least respected by a man even if she does not love him anymore; if she still loves him, she can rest content with the knowledge that she is loved. (This fact, incidentally, makes playing hard-to-get an unstressful course of action.) To know that in fact he loves her gives sufficient pleasure to her vanity to balance the pain of not being able to spend hours in the pleasures of shared intimate love.

She begins to think again of him, wishing that he would do something, if only to give her the opportunity of triumphing once more. She may even return to the thought of his statement of superiority with kinder sentiments. Without knowing it, she has begun to crystallize; soon she will be madly in love, for to her this newfound path to gratified vanity will seem to be the most intense love: She finds that his presence and cooperation are absolutely necessary to her happiness. "I cannot be happy without him," she tells herself. At this stage the lover must play his cards with reserve and coolness until she has begun to despair and has hinted to him as much, and even after intimacy he must always keep her at arm's length, so far as equality of worth is concerned. An effective caustic and sharply derogative (always only on her own grounds) remark now and then thenceforth will make her remain madly in love. Any too tender overtures will make her fall out of love, and if in a moment of weakness the lover has committed such a grave error, an act that humiliates her more than his common words may be in order.

Modesty carried to extreme lengths is prudery. Now, it is no exaggeration to say that prudery and the encouragement of prudery rank among the greatest vices of the human race. This idea is ridiculous until you consider how much happiness has probably been sacrificed at the altar of false modesty.

If for nothing else than for its eradication of prudery American society deserves praise. It is chiefly through its influence that in the rest of the industrially developed world prudery is a thing of the past. Love was easy in the society that existed when the nation was born because the old-world ideas of pride and virtue were being abandoned in favor of the idealization of wealth. So long as one was productive and thus of use to society, one was morally good. For a woman to give herself to such a man was socially beneficial, and for this reason encouraged. Prudery survived more in the South, because Southern society, supported by slave-labor agriculture, was built upon old-world social ideas.

Chapter XLII

An Example

The stories of two eighteenth-century European women, Lady Sarah Bunbury and Mademoiselle de Lespinassse, may serve as examples of different extremes of conduct that feminine modesty and pride can lead women to adopt.

The upper classes of both France and England had rigid rules regarding modest behavior that every well-bred woman was told to follow. Most such societies are puritanical, but pleasure was still too much loved then in France. The rules, however, did make women who loved to affect extreme modesty to inspire greater publicly expressed praise. The nature of modesty shows itself most clearly manifested in such a situation, since it becomes codified into rules of mannered love, which, however exaggerated they were, could not have been imposed in the first place unless they conformed in some manner to nature.[1]

Lady Sarah Bunbury, born in 1745 to an English duke, himself a natural son of Charles II,[2] married a Thomas Charles Bunbury (who was made a baron a few years after his marriage) without being in love with him. Bored with her husband, and longing for something more divine in life, she briefly took for her lover the French philanderer, aristocrat, and adventurer Duc de Lauzun. Lauzun declared his passion for her soon after meeting her at a dinner given by the Prince de Conti, and was politely but resolutely refused. Experienced in the ways of women, he did not entirely give up; a friend, Mme de Stainville, who was the

---

[1] The early Church or the Communist governments of Russia and China could not have survived for more than a few years were it not for the power constantly broadcast extreme ideas of moral worth have at some moments in history.

[2] See Dryden's amusing portrait of this pleasure-loving monarch in *Absalom and Achitophel*, an inept ruler who, though, possesses the distinction of having had the reign which, due to his own lax moral nature, and to the reaction to the preceding Puritan government, forms the only period in history when the ruling class of England were not sunk in gloomy and sour stiffness of morals. In their arts as well, the English then substituted cynical wit and the celebration of the pleasures of the senses for gloomy seriousness. The cruel Earl of Rochester may seem a monster to moderns with their bland palates and moral cowardice, yet how much morally preferable such a man is to the likes of solemn and dull pedants such as Malory, Spenser, Milton, Defoe, Bunyan, Pope, Carlyle, Tennyson, Lawrence, Auden, and a multitude of other men of letters.

mistress of Clairval, had deposited some incriminating papers with Lauzun that her husband discovered by breaking into Lauzun's apartments. Mme de Stainville was packed off to a convent, and when Lady Sarah questioned him about his despondency one evening, Lauzun replied, "I am as unhappy as it is possible to be, and I am losing, in a horrible manner, a very dear woman, and I shall never be anything for her whom I worship." Lady Sarah was immediately interested, and asked him for details. Someone soon interrupted them; she had only time to tell him, "I dine this evening at Mme du Deffand's."

I quote now from an old translation of the memoirs of Lauzun[1]:

"Although I had not been at this Mme du Deffand's for five or six years, I succeeded in having Mme de Luxembourg take me with her. The manners of Lady Sarah towards me were completely changed. Her eyes fixed on mine told me a hundred things which I dared not understand, and I thought her interest in me was solely due to pity. Her vivacity appeared moderated by a gentle languidness. Her abstraction had many charms for me since I had reason to consider myself the cause of it. When everybody had left Mme du Deffand's, she wrote a few words on a slip of paper, and said to me as she went downstairs: 'Read this on retiring.'

"One can readily imagine with what eagerness I returned home! I read these three English words: *I love you*... I did not know a single word of English. It readily occurred to me that these words meant the same as our *je vous aime*; but I wished it too much to flatter myself of its possibility. My night was spent in all sorts of reflections. At six o'clock in the morning, I hastened to go out and buy an English dictionary, which confirmed that I was beloved. One must have been as much in love as I was then to form an idea of my joy. I flew to Lady Sarah's as soon as I could think her awake.

"'I arose early,' she said to me with a charming grace, 'for I had no doubt but that you would come to breakfast with me. Let us begin having breakfast. Send away your cabriolet for I wish to close my door to everyone, so that we may be able to have a talk together without being interrupted. Sir Charles is at tennis, as well as Lord Carlisle, and they only return at dinner.'

"We had breakfast; she had her door closed, and the conversation which I am about to report began:

---

[1]Which is as amusing as the best novels.

'I love you, monsieur de Lauzun, and seeing you so unhappy, and so tender, I was persuaded that you loved me, and I was unable to resist the pleasure of relieving your troubles, by confessing that I loved you. A lover is ordinarily hardly an event in the life of a French woman; it is the greatest of all for an English woman: from this moment all is changed for her, and the loss of her existence and of her rest is commonly the end of a sentiment which in France has but an agreeable and but little dangerous outcome. This certainty however does not always stop them. Choosing our husbands it is less permissible in us not to love them, and the crime of deceiving them is never forgiven us.[1] I shall add to that real remorse of being so ungrateful for the kindness of Sir Charles, whose principal occupation is my happiness.[2] I have pleasure in telling you that I love you, but I am not the less convinced that we have nothing but misfortunes to expect from our love. Our nations are always separated by the sea, and often by war. We shall spend the three-fourths of our lives without seeing each other, and our destiny will depend always on a letter going astray or being intercepted. We have everything to fear from Lord Carlisle; he has been in love with me for a long time, and he is reasonable, because he believes it impossible that I should have a lover, but jealousy will enlighten him promptly, and will make him capable of anything. I must also speak of my character: I am naturally a coquette; I shall sacrifice my coquetry to you with pleasure, if that depends on me; but your jealousy could render us both very unhappy. I have too good an opinion of you to give any consideration to the risk of surrendering my honor and happiness to your probity and to your discretion; judge if I should, if I can have a lover!'

"We promised each other not to wander from the strictest circumspection and prudence, but our pledges were soon violated. Lady Sarah loved me very much and granted me nothing. Lord Carlisle began to suspect us but hoped she would soon forget me. The date of her departure for England approached, but her husband asked us to accompany them for part of the voyage. Finally, Lord Carlisle could no longer control himself and challenged me to fight on our return to Paris.

---

[1] English women until quite recently have had much greater freedom in choosing their own husbands than have had women on the Continent.

[2] See Chapter XXXVII above. The moral nature of women when it comes to love. Lady Sarah's remorse and regret may have been unaffected, but they had no force upon her actions. They were of almost no consequence whatsoever to her.

We separated at Arras. Lord Carlisle did not have the courage to leave a person so dear to him; he returned to England.

"She wrote me letters telling me of her love and of her remorse at having to deceive two men who loved her very much. Her letter to M. le prince de Conti so flattered him by her confiding in him that within two weeks I had leave to go to England. There I was received in a manner to increase my love, if such a thing were possible.

"The time I spent at Barton was certainly the happiest of my life. At the end of a few days Sir Charles was obliged to absent himself for three weeks, which I spent in *tête-à-tête* with his wife. She showed me the tenderest love but would grant me nothing. Finally, one evening she told me that I might come down to her room when everyone had retired. I awaited the long-hoped for moment with extreme impatience. I found her in bed and thought I could take some liberties; she appeared so offended and grieved at my conduct that I did not persist. She however permitted me to lie near her; but she exacted a moderation and reserve which were almost beyond me. This charming torture lasted several nights. I had lost the hope of its ever ending, when, passionately pressing me in her arms, she crowned all my desires.

"'I did not wish,' she said to me, 'that my lover should have anything by force, nor that he should owe it to my weakness or to his lack of respect towards me. I wished him to owe everything to my love. I give myself to you; yes, Sarah is wholly yours.'

"We went out riding together the next day.

"'Do you love me more than all else,' she asked me, 'and do you feel capable of sacrificing everything?'

"'I definitely do,' I replied without hesitation, and with the certainty of never repenting it.

"'Well!' she continued, looking at me with eyes that have no equal, 'do you wish to give up everything, leave everything, to come to Jamaica, to devote yourself solely to the happiness of your mistress? I have a rich childless relative there, who has love, indulgence, and of whom I am sure; he will receive us gladly.' And as I was about to reply: 'Wait,' she interrupted, 'I do not wish to know your answer before a week.'

"What Lady Sarah proposed to me was in truth what could render me most happy. I regretted none of the sacrifices which would probably have cost another so much; but I could not conceal from myself the fact that she was frivolous, a coquette. It seemed to me impossible that she should not cease to love me, that she should not one day repent so rash a decision. Lady Sarah, unhappy, dissatisfied, without occupation, without subsistence, at the other end of the world, might reproach me for being the cause of her ruin; it would have been a Hades, and such a prospect frightened me.

"The week passed. I confided my fears to her.

"'It is well, *mon ami*,' she said to me, somewhat coldly; 'you are more prudent, more provident than I; you are perhaps right, let us drop the subject.'

"Her manners towards me were the same. I however thought I saw in her something constrained, which gave her anxiety. Her husband came back and we returned to the city. Sir Charles had to go to Bath to take the waters, and I volunteered to accompany him. Lady Sarah promised to wait for my return and have her door closed. However when I returned, filled with the eagerness that a lover feels, I was dismayed to not find Lady Sarah in London, and to learn that she had left with Lord Carlisle, to go to Goodwood, to the home of the Duke of Richmond, her brother.

"All that fury and jealousy could inspire took possession of my heart. I wrote a letter to Lady Sarah, dictated by anger and hastiness; I sent it to her at Goodwood by one of my men. I told her that if she did not return to London at once, I should consider her the most wicked, the most false and most perfidious of women. I awaited the return of my messenger with inexpressible impatience. He returned at last, and brought back a gentle and even rather tender reply; some reproaches regarding the way in which I embittered all the charms of love by my violence. She promised to be in London in two days. I waited for her at her home until midnight. I saw my hopes rise and fall that day, perhaps the longest in my life. I returned to my rooms, and my whole night was spent in walking and in the most painful thought.

"At six o'clock in the morning, someone knocked at my door; I was the first to open it. Lady Sarah had just arrived and asked for me. I ran or rather flew to her. I thought her face was serious and composed: a table with all things necessary for a breakfast was before her, and several servants were in the room. More than an hour passed before we were alone.

"'Now,' she said to me, 'that I need fear no interruption, I must speak of matters which interest us equally. You know what charming qualities in you have won my heart. Even the excess of your jealousy did not displease me; that of your love being so great a compensation! Your anger, when you thought me a coquette, I bore with submission, without ill-humor, and I have never found it hard to ask your pardon when you were not always in the right. I wished to give Lady Sarah wholly and forever, her very existence, her reputation, the most absolute power over her. You have not had sufficient confidence either in your constancy, or in mine. You have not found me necessary to your happiness, and you did not care to have with me bonds that nothing could have broken. In crushing my heart, you have weakened your image in it; you have continued to be jealous and violent, after having lost the right to be: I now feel all the dangers of this. Nothing can make me forget them. If my brother had asked to see your letter, how could I have refused him? And if the Duke of Richmond read it, I was lost; and sacrificed for whom?... You have destroyed the sentiment which attached me to you; I no longer love you; but it was too tender for the impression, now painful, not to last. From now until a time perhaps far off, we could not meet with indifference; I therefore make bold to ask you as a favor to leave England, and henceforth count only on the tender friendship which I have vowed to you for life.'

"Struck as if by lightning by a blow so fearful and unexpected, I lost consciousness. She left me with Mme Joanes, sister of Sir Charles, who entered the room a little after I fainted. After I recovered my senses, I returned to my rooms seemingly quite calm. I attempted to follow her, but fainted again after a few miles on the road. I returned to London, and was ill for several days. Lady Sarah wrote earnestly asking me not to go away without coming to Bath to say good-bye to her. I could not resist the pleasure or rather the necessity of seeing her, and to have a last explanation. She received me with interest, with friendship; but she was so changed towards me that, far from thinking of prolonging my sojourn, I thought of hastening my departure. I returned to France very different from what I was on leaving it for England; nothing could divert me from a sentiment which made me so unhappy. Yet Lady Sarah wrote me regularly. I did not think she had a lover; but I had been loved by her, and she no longer loved me. My unsociableness was so great that nothing could diminish it. I learned that Lady Sarah was ill in London; nothing could stop me. I left immediately without leave of absence, without passport. She accepted this token of affection with pleasure and gratitude.

"'Leave, my friend,' said she, 'within twenty-four hours, remember that Lady Sarah is nothing more than your friend. Do not incur the risks for her which a longer absence might entail.'

"On my return I heard from her more rarely; and finally not at all."

I am afraid that the actions of the Baroness will seem implausible and incredible to many American and European women today. The charming torture Lauzun recounts would be to them a certain method of alienating their admirers. Women from other parts of the world, though, may be ready to censure her for being a harlot. It is a rule for virtuous women who do not themselves lead lives of any great happiness to paint in the blackest colors the character of any woman who dares to gamble her happiness and reputation upon the outcome of love.

It seems excessive and arbitrary cruelty for a woman to torture her lover as Lady Sarah did Lauzun after she has given him to understand that she loves him, but in point of fact, this is not very surprising considering the codes regarding modesty and respect for women existing then.

No woman who has not altogether given up on the possibility of being happy can be faithful in her imagination to her lover or husband if she does not love him any longer.

It was inevitable that the well-meaning but stolidly boring Sir Charles be deceived; his wife divorced him in 1776, and married George Napier six years later. The attentions of Lord Carlisle could not have inspired much above gratitude devoid of love, and it would be folly to blame her for this. A man looks for a tender and sublime goddess in the woman he falls in loves with; a woman commonly looks for a hero who cuts a strikingly fine figure in her eyes and those of the world, a man she can look up to and who spices her life up with a hint of dazzling danger. Lauzun for her possessed an air of danger and uncertainty that promised untold pleasures, and the tender concern of Lord Carlisle and her husband must have seemed pitifully uninspiring and unromantic in comparison.

But jealousy inspired by witnessing his dejection at the removal of Mme de Stainville to a distant and impenetrable convent was the decisive factor in the birth of her love for Lauzun. That after he had repeatedly told her that he loved her he could still feel tender sorrow at the departure of a female friend must have been mortifying; it changed the pleasing sensations of vanity which the memory of his professions of love inspired into a desire to secure his heart as solely her possession.

I do not think a proud woman ever falls in love unless she feels simultaneously both that her admirer cannot get her out of his mind, and that this man whom she admires, although he is capable of ardent and serious love, has a million other pleasures that he can sacrifice her to. Uncertainty magnifies the image of his worth as a lover; it deepens crystallization more in one hour than all the tender concern and solicitations of a Lord Carlisle do in a lifetime.

It was folly in Lauzun to have disappointed her in his answer. A lover must risk everything upon a single throw of the dice; otherwise love is the most wearisome of duties.

If he thought Lady Sarah a coquette, he should not have been ready to profess complete devotion; if he loved her he should not have hesitated to sacrifice everything *without giving a thought to consequences*.

The subsequent coldness of his mistress I confess I find admirable, though inevitable since she was following rules regarding what passionate lovers were supposed to do. She was too intelligent not to have seen from the beginning that the lover she was about to take was a handsome but vain fop; but, as I have described in an earlier chapter, rarely does even the most intelligent woman let ideas of moral worth guide her in love. To her imagination, he had sufficient perfections to make her forget her boredom and fears. The prudent reply to her suggestion of emigration to the New World had the effect of reawakening the pride she had sacrificed to her love when she gave herself up to him. Whenever this happens love dies. Was the fact that she took no pains to dissemble her disappointment and the death of love a proof of her sensitivity and superiority, or at least as much of these as a proud English aristocrat of the eighteenth century could have had? Or was it slavish imitation of the rules of mannered love?

Feminine modesty and pride make it almost impossible to proceed in a simple manner. Simplicity should rule between lovers, for a practical reason. There can be no happiness if you cannot speak your mind as soon as an idea arises without the fear of incurring immediate and deep displeasure.

The birth of a frown of displeasure or boredom on the face of the beloved causes (excepting the pangs of jealousy and utter rejection) the deepest unhappiness possible.

It is a rather unfortunate fact that the heart of a woman prompts her, out of pride, to reward love with grimaces, frowns, silences, and contempt even when it itself is moved to love. The lover must wait for intimacy before his mistress will condescend to act in a perfectly natural manner with him. What should have been pure earlier is sullied with small falsehoods.

Chapter XLIII

Another: Julie de Lespinasse

Mlle de Lespinasse, who had the misfortune to have fallen passionately in love, had all of what was admirable about her century and little of what was ridiculous. In fact, she is one of the exceptions to my theory that the woman capable of passion, or even the higher reaches of vanity love, dislikes moving in literary circles. Of all the women who have left some record of their feelings, only of Nargis and Hepburn can I say with any degree of assurance that they clearly surpassed Mlle de Lespinasse in greatness of spirit. All three held in equal contempt considerations of pride once they were passionately in love, but Hepburn and Nargis had the greater pride and the greater energy in their soul, and consequently greater depth of feeling and thought, but of that later.

I quote from a few of Mlle de Lespinasse's letters as they give a picture which cannot be improved upon of the proud feminine heart which has been reduced to misery by passion.[1] The heart is ever in motion in passionate love, a fact that prevents boredom from spoiling its pleasures. I choose three consecutive letters (written on Oct. 8 and 9, 1774) that illustrate the effects of passion, modesty, and pride in a woman most succinctly.

"Saturday, midnight

"First of all I must tell you that your ink is white as paper, and today it has really put me out of patience. I had ordered your letter to be brought to me at M. Turgot's, where I was dining with twenty persons.

---

[1]They were written to her indifferent lover, M. de Guibert, author of an *Essai du tactique* much admired in its day, and an affected fop.

It was given to me while at table. On one side I had the Archbishop of Aix, on the other the inquisitive Abbé Morellet. I opened my letter under the table. I could scarcely see that any black was on the white, and the abbé made the same remark. Mme de Boufflers, who was on the other side of the Archbishop of Aix, asked what I was reading. 'Remember where we are, and you will know what it is.' — 'A memorial, no doubt, for M. Turgot?' — 'Yes, just so, madame, and I wish to read it over before I give it to him.' Before returning to the salon I had read the letter through, and I am now going to reply to it—though I must do it hastily, for I am very tired with the great exertions that I made today. I have seen at least a hundred persons, and as your letter had done good to my soul, I talked, I forgot I was dead, and I have really extinguished myself. The truth is I had a 'great success' because I brought out the charms and the intellects of the persons with whom I was; and it is to you, *mon ami*, that they owe that pastime, so sweet to their self-love. As for mine, it is not intoxicated by your praises; I reply to you like Couci: 'Love me, my prince, and praise me not.'[1]

"*Mon ami*, keep yourself from ever having the kindness to set forth my blessings and display my gifts; never did I feel myself so poor, so ruined, so poverty-stricken; in estimating what I have, in making me see my resources, you only show me that all is lost. One means alone remains to me, —I have long foreboded it, I even think it a necessity — namely, to make total bankruptcy; but I postpone, I delay, I comfort myself with hopes, with chimeras; I know them to be such, and yet they sustain me a little —but you destroy all by the horrible enumeration that you make of them. Ah! what a deplorable inventory! if any other than you had attempted to console me, to reconcile me to life by these hopeless consolations, I should say to him, like Agnes, 'Horace, with two words, could do more than you' —but it *is* Horace who speaks to me. Oh, *mon ami*, my soul is sinking. What more will you invent to

---

[1]Compare this to Héloïse's begging Abélard in her second letter not to praise her for her supposed virtues and strength of character: another very independent-minded, courageous, passionate woman of the greatest possible honesty and generosity. The different reasons they gave for why they were ashamed at being praised by their former lovers are due to different circumstances, though in both cases inspired by the fact that their lovers were less passionate than they. Their pride revolted at such praise, and the consequent shame made crystallization all but impossible, making them think that they longed for an indifferent response rather than insincere praise altogether lacking in tenderness.

torture me? I shall be, you say, sustained, guaranteed, defended, etc. Well! never have I been all that; if you set your friendship at that value, I ask none of it. I have been weak, inconstant,[1] unhappy, very unhappy; I have feared for you; I have wandered in the wilderness; I have done wrong, no doubt; and it is one harm the more to dwell upon it. I have not an impulse, I never say to you, that does not cause me regret or repentance. *Mon ami*, I ought to hate you. Alas! it is long since I have done what I ought, what I wish! I hate myself, I condemn myself, and I love you."

"Sunday evening. October 9, 1774

"*Mon ami*, I have read your letter twice; and the total impression I receive from it is that you are very amiable, and that it is much easier not to love you at all than to love you moderately. Make the commentary on that, but not with your mind; it is not to your mind that I speak. *Mon ami*, if I chose, I could dwell on certain words in your letter which have done me harm. You speak of my courage, my resources, the employment of my time, and of that of soul in a manner to make me die of shame and regret for having suffered you to see my weakness. Ah, well! it was in my soul, of which no impulse can be hidden from you. When it was moved to hatred, I let you see it; but was hatred all that I allowed myself to feel?

"*Mon ami*, on reading again the recapitulation that you make of all there is on earth to keep me from destruction, I ended by laughing over it because it reminded me of a saying of Président Hénault, which is good. At a certain period of his life he thought that, in order to add to the esteem in which he was held, it would be well to become devout; he made a general confession, and afterwards wrote to his friend M. d'Argenson, 'Never do we feel so rich as when we move our belongings [que lorsqu'on déménage].'

---

[1]Mlle de Lespinasse had been in love for more than five years with another man younger than herself, M. de Mora, son of the Spanish ambassador to the court at Paris. They met in 1766, and he died in August, 1772. In September she met the Comte de Guibert, in fresh flush from the success of his book, and fell in love in spite of all the vows she had made to M. de Mora before his departure from Paris in August a few days before he died. Knowing how sincerely he had loved her, she was overwhelmed by guilt at how quickly he had been supplanted, and at the fact that her love for M. de Guibert was the greater one. Somewhere in an earlier chapter something has been said regarding: what is morally beautiful to women.

"I shall dine tomorrow with the Duchesse d'Anville. I like that house; it is one the more where I can see you; you live for what you love and for the gay world every evening; but will you not dine where I do? That will bring you into the society of those persons who are the most on your own tone. Fools and stupid people are never afoot before five or six o'clock; that is the time when I return to my chimney corner, where I nearly always find, if not what I should have chosen, at any rate nothing that I wish to avoid.

"How is it that I have never told you that I am urged, entreated, to go and re-establish my health in England at the house of Lord Shelbourne? He is a man of intellect, the leader of the Opposition; he was the friend of Sterne[1] and adores his works. See what an attraction he must have for me, and whether I am not much tempted by his obliging invitation. Admit that if you had known of this piece of good fortune you would not have omitted it from *my pompous inventory....*

"Your letter to d'Alembert is excellent; and as we are very communicative we gave it this evening to M. de Vaines, who was charmed by it, and desires to show it to him who could enjoy it without its alarming his modesty. You will never guess what occupies my mind, what I desire to do: to marry off *one of my friends.* I want an idea that has come to me to succeed; the Archbishop of Toulouse could be very successful in the affair. The young lady is sixteen years old and has only a mother, no father, and a brother. They will give her, on marrying, thirteen thousand francs a year; her mother will lodge her, and do so for a long time, because the son is a child. This girl cannot have less eventually than six hundred thousand francs, and she may be much richer. Will that suit you, *mon ami?* Say so, and we will act; it can be done without offence, because the Archbishop of Toulouse has as much skill as courtesy. Let us talk it over; and if this plan does not succeed I know a man who would be very glad to have you for a son-in-law; but his daughter is eleven; she is only a child and will be very rich. *Mon ami,* what I desire above all things is your happiness; and the means of procuring it for you will become the chief interest of my life. There was a time when my soul would have been less generous, but then it responded to one who would have rejected with horror the empire of the world. What a memory! how sweet, how cruel! Good-night; if I

---

[1]Her favorite author.

receive, as I hope, a letter from you tomorrow I will add to this volume. For the last two days, I have suffered less. I have reached the stage of two chicken-wings a day, and if that regimen does not succeed better than the others, I shall put myself on a milk diet."

"Still Sunday, October 9

"The adieu was very sudden, very abrupt, and you will readily understand that I have a thousand other things to say to you; for, if I am not mistaken, this is the last letter I shall write to you. As to this, I shall know tomorrow. You tell me that you are going to your regiment…. How I hope you are not mistaken, and that I shall really see you in two weeks. Fifteen days! that is a long way off; once I looked for a nearer coming. —Ah! I shudder! what a dreadful recollection! it poisons hope. Ah! *mon Dieu*! it was you who troubled and overthrew the happiness of that tender and impassioned soul; it was you who condemned us to an awful misfortune, and—it is you I love![1] Yes, we hate the evil that we do, but we are drawn to it. Without your consolation I would have died of grief, and now I am fated to live, to languish, to moan, to fear you, to love you, to curse life, and cherish it at some moments….

"Here I was interrupted: people came and proposed to me to go and see Duplessis. He is a portrait-painter who will stand beside Van Dyck. I do not know if you have seen the portrait of the Abbé Armaud painted by him; but, my friend, you must certainly see that of Gluck; it has a degree of truth and perfection that is better and greater than nature. He has put ten heads into it, all of different characters; I have never seen anything finer or truer in that respect. M. d'Argental came there, and showed us a letter he had just received from M. de Voltaire; I thought it so good, the tone so natural,[2] it brought him so near to us, that, without thinking whether it was discreet or not, I asked for the letter; I asked for a copy; they are now making it, and *mon ami* shall read it —that thought is at the bottom of everything. *Mon ami*, I must repeat and say, as Sterne to his Eliza, 'Your pleasure is the first need of my heart.'

---

[1]Sense of the comic of one passionately in love.

[2]In common with her century, she admired the inane writings of this witty and important Frenchman. It is impossible today to think of anyone calling Voltaire's style or tone *natural*—but then they were no more unnatural than those of many today considered natural. This admiration for Voltaire's tone makes me suspicious of her admiration of Duplessis, of whom I know nothing—and Van Dyck failed in his imitation of Rubens. But her description of the portrait of Gluck is not spoiled by affectation, which is saying much, considering what pedantic criticism commonly is.

[233]

"*Mon Dieu!* how difficult it is to begin a letter when one has to make sentiment with one's mind. But I must write to Mme de Boufflers. She has not once mentioned your name to me; I am not sorry, but how is it that people do not seize every occasion to talk of that which pleases them? There is, of course, a certain degree of affection which hinders; it is what prevents me from speaking to her of you, but she has never felt any such embarrassment, I am sure; she has nothing to do with loving—she is too charming!

"*Mon ami*, I know myself so well that I am tempted to think you are laughing at me when you speak of my successes in society. It is eight years since I retired from the world; from the moment that I loved I felt a disgust for such successes. What need have we of pleasing when we are beloved? Is there one feeling, one desire left that has not for its object the person whom we love and for whom we desire to live exclusively? *Mon ami*, you have no such desire, have you?"

I let Mlle de Lespinasse express herself, but I do want to state several facts that can be deduced from her letters.

About the waverings of feminine modesty, feminine pride, and remorse, I have written enough. What forms they take after passionate love has been born is clear from the letters of Mlle de Lespinasse, Héloïse, the Portuguese nun.

Crystallization causes the lover to not be able to see the loved one as she is. But as I have said in the first chapter of this work, in passionate love a woman can see that the man she loves is not in truth who she thinks he is, but still be incapable of regarding him as otherwise than absolutely perfect.

However, women, who love only with their hearts, are capable of deceiving themselves more than men who are passionately in love.[1] D'Alembert, the great mathematician and scientist, was in love with Mlle de Lespinasse, and finally came to live with her in her house—without thereby causing any scandal, since it was clear to all that theirs was what is called a virtuous friendship. She did not love him. Now, there is no reason why a woman's heart should be thrilled by the love of a man merely because he has made many original discoveries in mathematics and science. She wants the man who loves her to have an air of easy self-assurance, adventure, intensity, aloofness, etc., and not having studied

---

[1]See the third paragraph of Chapter XLV, below.

the moral makeup of men carefully and precisely enough, can too easily cast all her hopes of happiness in love on the wrong man.

I see nothing ridiculous in a woman's falling in love with a younger man, as Mlle de Lespinasse did twice. The ridicule attached to such a love reflects only the worst form of hypocrisy or envy,[1] and is itself a very ridiculous affectation.

She herself knew that she should despise him for having taken full advantage of her weakness, and then having told her he was incapable of loving her. There must have been something in the man capable of attracting a reasonably intelligent, but not pretty, woman with literary affectations: he was also the first lover of that influential bluestocking Mme de Staël, a woman of a much coarser moral nature and intelligence than Mademoiselle de Lespinasse.[2]

Mlle de Lespinasse did finally help in the arrangement of her lover's marriage. Consequent despair carried her off to a premature grave in 1776.[3]

Chapter XLIV

Of a Very Rare Class of Moral Actions

Of virtue Stendhal wrote,

"Moi, j'honore du nom de vertu l'habitude de faire des actions pénibles et utiles aux autres.

"Saint Siméon Stylite, qui se tient vingt-deux ans sur le haut d'une colonne et qui se donne les étrivières, n'est guère

---

[1]The former when men ridicule, both when women ridicule. That fool Sainte-Beuve's cleverly snide and condescending tone in his essay on these letters.

[2]Mme de Staël—the type described by Fielding in his *Tom Jones* in Mrs. Western, with the difference that Mme de Staël, though possessed of a commonplace heart, did not lack the vanity and affectation of self-knowledge to want a *grande passion* to spice things up. She could never understand why love never delivered upon its promises because she never knew it. Even that boring writer Constant did not deserve the hardships she put upon him with her jealous and affected demands. Like Mrs. Western, she was not an altogether unintelligent women.

[3]See Appendix One below, and Kent's lectures on the materia medica—on ignatia and natrum muriaticum in particular.

vertueux à mes yeux, j'en conviens, et c'est ce qui donne un ton trop leste à cet essai.

"Je n'estime guère non plus un chartreux qui ne mange que du poisson et qui ne se permet de parler que le jeudi. J'avoue que j'aime mieux le général Carnot qui, dans un âge avancé, supporte les rigueurs de l'exil dans une petite ville du Nord, plutôt que de faire une bassesse."[1]

Gandhi is thought to be a modern saint because he preferred political power to his dinner. His vow of absolute chastity and his amusing means of testing it by having (on the whole ugly) young women sleep in his bed are regarded as proofs of great virtue, apparently because he refrained from acting on his desires and taking hold of any of them. The pleasure of imagining the proximity of forbidden pleasures is often more intense than their enjoyment.[2] However when you parade a particularly dreary form of prudery[3] as rare virtue, you often get paid in the currency of others' high esteem.

In contrast to Gandhi, I think of that great and unaffected man, Martin Luther King, of whose character, it will be remembered, the worst that his enemies in the government and papers could say was that he had a number of mistresses.

Since I am on the subject of Stendhal, I may as well say that I regard Mathilde Dembowski to have been on the whole a virtuous woman. There can be no doubt that in spite of all of his blunders and indiscretions she was in love with him; why else would a proud and upright woman as she was have continued to let him see her once a

---

[1]"For my part, I honor with the name of virtue the habit of performing painful actions of use to others.

"Saint Siméon Stylite, who for twenty-two years sat atop a column and gave himself lashings, has but little virtue in my eye, I admit, and it is this that gives too free a tone to this essay.

"I do not esteem much more the Carthusian monk who neither eats anything but fish nor permits himself to speak but on Thursday. I confess I prefer General Carnot who, in advanced age, bore the rigors of exile in a small Northern town rather than commit a mean act."

De l'amour (Of Love), chapter LVII

[2]Samuel Johnson habitually went half-way with his wife's maid, but always refrained from possessing her though she was willing. Throughout his life he wrote solemnly on the virtues of chastity, and championed the great sentimentalist of his century, Richardson, for his tedious and contrived novels on the perils of giving in to pleasures of the senses. See James Clifford's biography.

[3]Prudery is the worst form of avarice—Stendhal.

fortnight? Vanity alone would have made her tire of him long before she laid that condition on him, and the quicker because of his very gently pressing her so often for more favors.

It was not fear concerning her reputation merely that prevented her from granting him any favors. Her involvement in the carbonari conspiracies, as well as Stendhal's nationality and, as it seemed to the Milanese, suspiciously ingratiating manner made happy love practically impossible for them; she could not tell him she loved him in so many words and then refuse to grant him anything, so she would admit nothing.

Her reproaches, though perhaps too strong, were quite justifiable for a woman seriously in love, and who thus could not be entirely sure of his true feelings. Her own actions very delicately conveyed to him her true feelings. However, she sacrificed her own highest possible happiness for the lower one of being faithful to her people and their cause. Therein you have a perfect example of the purest love and purest virtue combined in the same person.

It is no wonder that Stendhal went nearly out of his mind from grief at her outward coldness.

I have little else to say on this dangerous subject. We are all likely to think virtue exclusively our very own possession and be put out when told that it is not so.

A virtuous man does not always act virtuously, but he cannot fail to do so and not feel pain at the lapse.

Many who do not love can act virtuously, but it is the serious lover who is the most interesting in this regard. At first the beauty and perfection of the beloved make the lover wish to be worthy of her.

But in passionate love, the exclusive desire of being loved by an absolutely sublime being makes all thoughts of mere pleasure loathsome and very painful. The passionate lover, like everyone else, desires to be happy; but his happiness is at the opposite pole from that of the pleasures of vanity. Pursuit of his own pleasures is felt as a greater pain than it is by one whose chief passions are of commonplace nature.[1] He can do no more than humbly hope for kindness and tenderness from his mistress.

---

[1]It is this fact which convinces me, more than any other, that women can love more passionately than men, that is to say, maximum degree is greater in them. No matter how strong their love, they can bring themselves to sacrifice it to considerations of common sense and prudence if circumstances or the conduct of their lovers warrant the sacrifice.

Chapter XLV

The practical lot of women is not an enviable one, however you look at it. It is not merely the social injustices meted out to them of which I speak, but of the makeup of their souls as well.

Many women blessed (if that is the word) with cold hearts do well in the world given a fortunate birth. Oppressed societies always have rules for manners designed to appeal to their petty vanity and wish for security and respectability; following the strict and complete rules laid down for them keeps such women busy and happy. In more happily organized societies, they are given greater opportunities in society, and increasingly, in politics; though they have not until very recently had a very great influence but through their husbands or lovers.

Because most women have dreamed a great deal of a great love since the age of thirteen,[1] because most men are sadly incapable of loving in a manner that will keep crystallization going for a long span of time, these women are doomed to disappointments in life. The cheerful faces seen in society, in public, should not deceive you. They hide their true feelings instinctively; their pride would revolt at the thought of their misery, or even boredom, being known to others. Few women of spirit think more highly of their lovers than of themselves. This fact must have forced observant men who established the customs of nations (which survive yet in those societies less earnestly in love with the word *freedom*) to teach all women who were not born or sold into the employment of providing pleasures of the senses to men to esteem their duties to family and society as the highest and only virtues, passports to social respect and the kind of happiness that it promises.

Whatever may be hyped as descriptions of the nature of women in popular films and magazines in the late twentieth century, the simple fact is that for most women, happiness still lies in the attaining of love, respectability, wealth, and a well run household. The idealized portraits[2] of ambitious and fearless women doing and saying whatever they wish most to that hack writers and hack filmmakers continue to pour out please most women, but rarely inspire in them a wish to emulate in life

---

[1]Their *instantaneous* compliant attitude the moment they espy one who appears to be the ideal man.

[2]The happiness of women who write, act in, or direct these consists in putting them forward for public approval, and in seeing themselves in a heroic light for doing so.

their heroines. They commonly imitate the rhetoric of courage,[1] but that is about all.

Since women risk so much in love, it is perfectly justifiable for them to be cautious and slow in bestowing favors. It seems to me that the only four morally justifiable motives for such caution in the face of the birth of love are:

1) Doubt regarding the earnestness of the man.

2) The wish to inspire respect for herself by not appearing to be an easy catch, and thus of little worth to the man.

3) The wish to inspire passion through prolonged doubt.

4) Uncertainty whether he is that prince of her heart she has been waiting for all her life.

All other motives arise from prudery, fear of what others will say, or coquetry, and (except for the last) are rarely met with today in Western nations. In other nations, they make happy love the very rarest of phenomena, although they may intensify it. This is not a complete misfortune so long as social fears, affectations, and ashamed physical love are not the common motives and manners of the people, since when they are it is rare that *both* lovers have the greatness of soul to be entirely free of them.

I have said that a sensitive woman risks all her happiness in love. This fact makes her resist falling hopelessly in love if she can help it before she is absolutely sure of being loved in return.[2] Not that she will not give herself over to pleasing reveries concerning an admirable man. She simply thinks three times before gambling her entire happiness on the

------

[1]A fact that has great consequence for their lovers. See last chapter below.

[2]Mlle de Lespinasse is a case in point of the sufferings of a woman who has put her heart upon an unworthy object. It must have taken her a greatness of courage only dimly intelligible to a man to see in a cold light her feelings in those remarkable letters, and lay open all her heart to him, although undeceived in rare moments of clarity regarding his petty moral nature. A woman cares little for this lack in her lover once she is deeply in love. In the beginning, as well, it is generally of little consequence to her; the idea of her own power over him, or what she imagines to be such, matters incalculably more. Jane Austen (and several other superior women) would have disagreed with me. Certainly, they portray feminine love to be more moral an affair, but I am not sure that their loves in life were born chiefly from moral admiration. I would very much prefer to be mistaken here.

uncertain chance of being loved by him.[1] Passion proper only begins in a woman after intimacy has been attained.[2]

I have spoken sufficiently of the birth of second crystallization and passion in men in earlier chapters. In women, it is feminine self-esteem or pride that must be *entirely* overcome if passion is to arise. So long as she has not granted all, and so long as he has done nothing to make her think otherwise, a woman capable of rising to passion in general feels that she can assume that the man who, she is convinced, loves her in earnest and who possesses an equal degree of pride and strength as she holds her in the highest respect possible. What she fears is that upon granting him the privileges of a lover she will discover that she has fallen from the towering pedestal she had occupied until then in his eyes. The picture of the shared happiness of intimate passionate love is all but blocked out of her eyes by the thought of the steep plunge her own image in his heart is bound to suffer, and crystallization stops periodically for this reason. The more uncertain she is of the permanence of his love and deep respect, the less likely she is to concede any important point to him. Consequent unhappiness inspires her to discover justifications for not giving in to love even in her heart.

As in men, successive deaths and rebirths of crystallization increase exponentially the hold that the object of love has on the heart. The stage comes when she is so much beyond her power in love that she is willing to risk *all* for the chance of perfect happiness. It is impossible for her to see the man she loves as otherwise than perfect, but being constantly surprised by how much she loves him and to what excess of folly her imagination leads her in painting pictures of perfect happiness, she is ever in doubt of being loved as much in return. Thus, the moments immediately preceding, as well as the moment of yielding itself, are those of extreme despair, misery, and a blind hope that she herself regards as entirely illusory.

But once she has granted everything to her lover, her pride and self-esteem are entirely out of her hand, and in his, and she demands proofs that she has not fatally lowered herself. She is forced to discover reasons to justify her drastic move.

---

[1] The failure to do this is not uncommon, and is the chief cause of misery among women. A proud and intelligent woman for this reason protects herself by not allowing herself to indulge in too many reveries about the man she loves.

[2] Stendhal, to my knowledge, was the discoverer of this fact of the heart, as of many others.

But since what she wishes for is not a tangible fact but only a judgement made by interpreting actions, gestures, demeanor, and words, she can never be sure if her happiness is a fact, or merely illusory. "Does he respect me as much as he used to? Does he love me in earnest? How can I know?" these questions torture her now when she has given herself to him, and can withhold nothing from him anymore—when she has *nothing more to give*. At this stage, unless she receive an unending number of proofs of passionate love, the memory of the past, when her pride was her own possession, will cut her heart with remorse.

Passionate love is born in women only after this stage; when the hope and wish for happiness in the midst of her misery and shame make her forget beyond even the possibility of recall her sense of pride, modesty, and self-esteem. A different class of imagination must then be used to discover the happiness that derives solely from the thought of being loved by the man she now loves passionately, and whose perfection now appears to her to be beyond the absolute.

She thinks solely of the fact that she is known to him, that he has seen into her soul, and knows it:

"Whatever happens, *he* knows that I too lived, that my soul knew this passion, that I love without vanity. And if he but know this, it is enough, for then I am loved by him."[1]

I speak of passionate souls here. A vain woman, like a vain man, will think that she can please her lover; it will never enter her head to question her own powers to please permanently. Any cause for doubt will call forth a volley of protest, and even sometimes abuse. And if she doubts her power she will be unhappy because she feels she does not deserve failure, but deserves happiness.

Doubts lead to lovers' quarrels—even passionate love never arises without them. These are of the greatest benefit, as nothing deepens and makes more lasting love between lovers as quarrels arising from their doubting *passion* in each other.

Passion arises in a woman when prolonged doubts after intimacy stop inspiring resentment, a desire for revenge, self-pity, or self-contempt though love has not died.

It is only with the birth of passion that a woman capable of passion yields herself fully to her lover; happiness in passion is thus impossible

---

[1]The illusion that makes for the greatest happiness that can be known.

before this, since even a trace of false reserve—the least impurity in the abandonment to passion—dispels the purity of happiness.

Chapter XLVI

Before intimacy:—

The lover has been thinking day in and day out of the woman he loves, but when he meets her again, she is not the woman he has been thinking about. He wonders, "Do I truly love her? Or am I just making myself think I do?" He thinks about this new image he has of her for a few days, and is as much in love with it as he was with the previous one, which has graded insensibly into it. Again, after another meeting she is neither of the women he had been dreaming of with the greatest happiness (assuming hope is beginning to outweigh doubt).

What is happening is that crystallization so transforms the beloved that he cannot see her as she is. But every time he meets her, the encounter is so brief (in his opinion), and comes after a sufficiently long period of separation (a few days or more) so that he has not time enough to form an image of her that covers all the details he discovers. The beloved thus changes in appearance, beauty, and character every few days. For this reason, he does not begin to get bored with her.

With each new image, his crystallization is deeper than it had been with the earlier one—successive births of crystallization in connection with the same woman always increase exponentially the hold she has on the lover's heart. However, also with each he feels he has overcome his weakness, that he is no longer carried away by his passion for her, even as in fact it is deepening.

I frankly cannot tell whether crystallization in women follows the same course. I doubt that it does, at least not with the same intensity, because their sensations of beauty in love do not consist so much merely of what is seen as ours do, and are consequently more romantic once they have begun to crystallize in earnest. Thoughts regarding the state of affairs of a man's heart, the probable degree and seriousness of love she has inspired, occupy a woman's mind during her brief meetings with him.[1] This is just as well, for when a woman questions her earlier

---

[1] I speak in this chapter only of the stage after serious love has been born. Where much

convictions that greatly exaggerated his worth, further crystallization is seriously imperiled. She is quick and decisive when it comes to judging whether a man is worthy of being loved or not;[1] thereafter her heart takes over. Her mind only resumes its strict and cold sway if she stops loving him altogether, but not when crystallization has stopped temporarily due to jealousy or doubt, unless she is not in a forgiving frame of mind; even then it is the heart which has made her unforgiving of his faults.

Only some act, word, gesture, or manner of his that strikes her imagination very forcibly as a proof of some blemish of character she feels she must have overlooked earlier, I think, can make a woman in love seriously question the image she has formed of the man she loves.

Chapter XLVII

A Melancholy Affair

I am afraid that this chapter will prove to be unintelligible to the greater number of readers. I have deliberately put it off for as long as possible, in the hope that not many who have read so far will find it absolutely fantastical or chimerical. I assure them that I relate a story true in every detail.

If you have found this work scarcely credible so far, I can tell you that this is yet another chapter you will want to skip. It will only anger you by what it suggests:

> There are more things in heaven and earth, Horatio
> Than are dreamt of in your philosophy....
>
> *Hamlet*

Valmère was a foreigner, and the skeptic must rest content with the assumption that there are diseases only foreigners are susceptible to. In civilized as well as not so civilized countries today, a case such as his is

---

time has been spent conversing with one another during the initial stages of love, there cannot have been much crystallization, since for both vanity is constantly at stake.

[1]Although she may not press herself to decide until she is sufficiently sure of her power over him.

equally uncommon and out of the common. You will see a few pining vaguely for a great love, and many more who are pining for requital of their loves. But I have seen no case which rises so high above all considerations of vanity as did Valmère's love for "a noble lady" (as he liked to call the young woman) of his acquaintance.

Valmère could never bring himself to tell us the name of his beloved, calling her simply the Lady Margherita, or Margherita. Now that he is dead, we will never know her identity. How he had fallen in love with her, and the story of his failure are recorded in great detail in his private journals, which he started to keep after he met her. They abound in expressions of love and grief, and I hope they will be published in their entirety some day. I record some extracts from them later in this chapter.

Valmère writes only that he had seen Margherita four times before he fell in love with her, but never did he speak to her in those meetings. In fact, he writes that he had never given more than the slightest thought to her until the fifth meeting, when they happened accidentally to end up seated close to each other. Probably to protect her identity, Valmère does not specify in the least in what sort of place her met her, etc. I can only tell that he spoke very little to her that day in the course of two hours, but that he was deeply moved by the time they parted.

He says he could not tell in the least whether she was also beginning to love him though she was amiable in the extreme. It was enough that he could see she had a soul capable of the highest love.

The next meeting was equally laconic, and it equally filled him with what he himself thought were unreasonable hopes. The third time, he was fortunate enough to find himself alone with her for a few minutes. There was no one around. He hesitantly declared himself. He writes that at the end of the first meeting he had attempted to say something to her, but had found that he had lost his voice. The great confusion and lack of self-assurance were unprecedented. He had never known anything like them before. To counteract this fatal weakness, he had written a letter declaring all his feelings and hopes. She seems to have accepted his words and the letter with the sweetest of smiles.

But when they met again, there was an implacably hostile look in her eyes, and *extravagant* indifference and contempt were written all over her movements. He was struck as if by lightning by this severity, as he was sure that he had addressed her with the greatest respect, and that he had sincerely told her what he felt. He had expected a polite rejection, but she at first refused even to speak to him, and when she did, rejected him coldly.

When he had thought more on it, her response seemed to him his greatest reason for hope. If she were truly indifferent to him, she would have politely but decisively refused him, without the initial hostility. Her uncertainty and wavering hostility were perhaps better than anything else, for, according to him, they were the signs of her nobility of soul. He reasoned that she must have taken offense at the liberty of his expressions, and been insulted by what she took to be slick and easy professions of love.

He loved her for her pure and proud mind, and for the honesty and generosity of her soul. He used to say that he never regretted what had happened. He was sure that they were meant for each other, two hearts that stood apart from the rest of the world. I think he was mad enough to be grateful to her.

Unfortunately, she never did give herself to him. But he to the bitter end remained unwavering in his absolute admiration of her. He would often go off into long panegyrics on her virtue, depth of feeling, sympathy, kindness, etc., and we would have to pretend that we were not bored to death by the recital. He was very unhappy, but he would not have exchanged his unhappiness for the greatest happiness of any other man.

I had known him long before this sad affair. I honestly do not think I have ever met anyone more intelligent or courageous than he. He was not lacking in wit and amiability, when he wished to be sociable. This claim will surprise the reader who has in all probability conceived the lowest opinion of my dear friend.

He himself used to often tell us of the surprise he had felt when he initially fell in love. That he should turn out to be one of those who live and die for the hope of extracting a smile from a woman he had never expected in his wildest dreams. He had known many men who had suffered in love, but they were all of the naive and simple sort, and undistinguished in every way save their patient acceptance of grief. He had naturally associated extreme passion with sincere, simple, somewhat dull and phlegmatic natures, and had always thought himself safe. But he was beyond caring what was thought of him, his ambitions of glory were dead. He wanted only to be loved by the woman he loved.

In appearance, Valmère was extremely handsome. His bearing was noble. There seemed to be a great fire in him which pierced through his eyes and made him stand out in every crowd. Whenever I saw him in his last years, I thought of the lines:

> Guarda quel grande che vene,
>   e per dolor non par lagrime spanda
>   quanto aspetto reale ancor ritene!
>
> *Inferno*, XVIII [1]

The papers he left behind in my care show another side of him, the lover utterly prostrate before the mistress of his fate.

I quote now from various pages of his journals:[2]

"I am utterly at a loss as to how to spend the rest of my life without her. Every minute is a fresh torture, the pain of every moment seems unprecedented. I am afraid of taking permanent leave of my senses.

"I comfort myself with reveries about a happy life with Margherita, and for a few minutes I am almost happy. I try to tell myself that *I* do not matter, that it is ridiculous to think of myself and not her. If there is no God, and this is the only life we shall ever have, should I waste my time thinking of my own unhappy fate? If there is a God, will He not in His Wisdom see that justice is done, and that she will, sometime and somewhere, at least acknowledge that she believes I love her.

"What absurdities I am led into. I am not sure of anything anymore. I would not fear going to my death if she just once would deign to look into my eyes and tell me she loves me. It would be better than to live on in this wretched manner.

"In spite of my efforts, the thought that she does not love me comes back like a fatal disease, and cuts me to the heart. It is contemptible, but I cannot help the weakness of self-pity. The happiness that seemed so near at hand, and so heavenly, that very happiness in the hopes of which I live, seems to mock me bitterly for my unhappiness.

"I am unhappier when I see her than when I have not seen her for several weeks. Away from her I can think of her without hindrance; but in her presence, and later, due to the vivid memories of her every look

---

[1]   Look at that great one who comes
       And seems to shed no tears for pain:
       How regal an aspect he yet retains!

[2]The present edited layout is wholly mine, though more or less chronological. Valmère scribbled nearly illegible notes to himself, and dated them. He was little concerned with elegancies of transitions. The notes, in truth, make for very tedious reading, and are badly written to boot. I only retain them here for their nearly negligible value as a record of reactions of a man who loves passionately, as judicial institutions keep records of old court cases. I advise all readers to skip to the next chapter.

and word, all I can think of is one fact: *she does not love me*. If only I had the courage to leave her forever.

"Why do I lie even to myself? Is this falsehood worthy of her?

"If she does not think me worthy of her, than I must obviously not be so. But I *know* I love her with the purest passion. I can do no better. I wonder, will she ever find greater happiness than with me, she who was born to love and be loved passionately, who can never be happy but through love? Yet she refuses to grant me a mere *tête-à-tête*.

"In her presence I lose all my rational faculties. I look and act the fool. I trust in her completely, but she refuses to grant me acknowledgment of belief."

The next extracts are dated several weeks after the ones above:

"Thank god, she has at last given me some hope. So she is not entirely indifferent to me. Oh, sublime soul, how grateful I am that you have condescended to give me silent tokens of your love. I cannot believe that any lover has ever been granted as much happiness by his mistress' greatest favors as she has given me early this afternoon. What matters separation when hearts are joined as ours are?

"A week-long dream of continued happiness was shattered yesterday morning. I met with an unaccountably cold reception from her. Was my telephone call taken so adversely? Is she angry at the lack of discretion I showed, or at my presumption of being loved? Howsoever it may have happened, I cannot fault her for her anger. Absolutely prostrated as I was with grief at the unexpected disaster, this is better than the suspicions I had entertained earlier concerning her integrity and candor. Those few days when I wavered between thinking her unbelievably and startlingly perfect and thinking her a heartless coquette, were they not infinitely worse than anything I have felt in the last thirty-six hours?

"These past several months have completely altered my whole character. I used to be extremely proud and always convinced of my great superiority over the common run of men. I was convinced of a glorious fate, of immortal fame, etc., etc. How INANE those fancies seem to me now. What do I not owe her?

"I do not know anymore whether I am happy or not. Do I want to live? *Why* does she not show more kindness? I know her to possess the most generous of hearts, yet she grants me nothing. I must either believe she is playing false with me, or that something uncommonly important is forcing her to repulse the man she loves. The former conjecture is too painful for words. I would a hundred times rather be rejected permanently for the slightest fault of mine, however unfair this would be, than to have to think badly of her.

"How ironic it is that I am rendered speechless by her divine presence. And I have the temerity to ask her to love me. Why in God's name should she love me? What can she see in me that she can admire? In my folly, I want to be loved for who I am, yet I am always someone else in her presence than the person who loves her. As if that were not enough, I know I am not who I was when I first met her. Add to that the fact that whenever I meet her, I am surprised by how different she is from what I conceive her to be in her absence, and one begins to get some idea of what sort of a madness love is.

"For the first few weeks of love, I had the greatest doubts not merely concerning her love and character, but as well about whether I was even in love with the woman I used to meet once or twice a week. I would be in heaven in her presence, in the heaven of her mind, so to speak, and in this effort to be one with her soul, I felt that I was a million miles from the lovely creature who sat a few feet from me. Fool that I am, I admired, loved, and was silent when I most needed to say something amusing, and so advance my cause.

"I have noted a most curious phenomenon: After I have been with Margherita, all other women seem to me to be plastic dolls, without souls, utterly bereft of any charms. They strike my senses as would an anonymous brick wall: unnecessary ugliness. However, when I have not seen her for weeks, but have been thinking of her with gratitude and love, every semi-attractive woman attracts my attention. Each one seems to me worthy of being loved. Consequently, I arrive back at my rooms having fallen in love a hundred times that day.[1] This phenomenon bothered me for some time, until I saw that I was merely transplanting what I felt for Margherita into them, but that I would have been utterly

---

[1]In another much passage written a year or so after this one, on the other hand, Valmère wrote:

"It has been more than ten months since I last laid eyes on her. Nothing pleases me, nothing inspires the finer feelings. I keep returning to every memory of her I have, reliving happier days. But was I happier then? I do not know, but I would do anything to return to when I saw her regularly.

"No matter how much I try to reason with myself in my more rational moments, I cannot find any substitute for the happiness I would have had with her. All pleasures but those of the purest love seem to me inane; and every woman I see but reminds me of her soul, and I am plunged into reveries about the past."

bored, not to say, repelled, by their company.

"Earlier today I visited with a few friends a bookshop located a few blocks from where she lives. In the art-books section of the shop I found an interesting volume in which I pretended to be deeply absorbed. My friends were about me, but looking in other directions. Suddenly, from behind one of the counters, a middle aged lady emerged, followed by a pretty girl of about twenty. I looked up to see first one, and then the other. My casual glance froze as I saw the girl. I recognized Margherita's eyes in the girl's eyes. Her hair and face were similar, and she possessed the same type of beauty as Margherita's. For a moment I was completely bewildered, and did not know what to do, or how to look. I began trembling from weakness from the surprise, although by then I knew it was not she. The girl noticed my reactions, but passed on. I had not the courage to look at her again. At that moment, one of my friends came up to me and started talking about the book I was holding in my by now nearly lifeless hands. Fortunately, I managed quite well to hide the numbness of spirit and body which had overcome me, and which lasted for another five minutes.

"How much I envy, and have envied, everyone who is privileged with her society and conversation. So many have received her smiles in my presence, and I but once or twice. But I do not only envy them; I also despise them for not recognizing the immense privilege they are enjoying. Some very mediocre persons now inspire some very pleasant recollections in me, and I hope to run into them, and not into more intelligent and witty friends.

"The last few days have been horrible. Why do I let myself suffer in this intolerable manner? Reason tells me to quit thoughts which repeatedly leave me miserable. Is it not because it is a million times more painful, after an hour or so, to feel pleasure in something else than to continue to be miserable on account of her haughty demeanor?"

Chapter XLVII

Of Intimacy

Intimacy is the last stage but one in the long and difficult road to happiness through love.

The more the vanity of the lover has been battered in the course of his passion, the more complicated this stage becomes for him.

When only physical pleasures are involved, intimacy is a direct and immediately pleasing development.

When vanity is at stake, intimacy is a very satisfactory denouement to the periods of hopes and despair. It is a more symbolic event for the one who derives more pleasure from vanity than from the physical side of love. To a man, it proves that the woman is at long last his. To a woman, there is pleasure at having secured this happiness for herself, although at the back of her mind she fears that she will lose her hold on him now that she has given up everything.

At the higher end of vanity love, some pain is felt in the series of events that constitute the birth of intimacy.

A certain part of a man's mind is besides itself in expectations of exquisite physical pleasures. But if he has a sensitive heart, he recoils every other minute from the lewd ideas that suggest themselves to his mind. He labors to rise above them to a more tender and generous ideas regarding the soul and heart of the woman. But underneath it all, he is made very happy when he senses that the resistances of the beloved are quickly vanishing. The chief thing is to proceed carefully, and in a manner that will not alarm her. What hesitations there are arise from the fear of being thought a fool.

A sensitive woman who is finally letting herself succumb to the last stages of vanity love is in a very different situation. She is about to exchange the role of a queen for that of a slave. All her life she has lived by the codes of modesty and pride, and has seen no reason to censure herself for any reason whatsoever. Now suddenly she has decided to throw all caution and habits of mind to the winds. Finally, there is the fear that her lover will be disappointed in the quantity of pleasure he expected from an intimacy with her.

Everything is more complicated in passionate love. The lover's self-love has been battered beyond recognition by the aloof indifference of the beloved. He finds it difficult to approach her person rudely. He has been in the habit of regarding her as an unapproachable and pure goddess and angel, and the very thought of possessing her makes him wince. To top it all off, he further fears that his high claims of deeply respecting her will now be recalled, and he will forfeit her love if she comes to disbelieve them.

On the other hand, he fears angering her by untoward hesitations that he fears she may interpret as either a sign that he lacks strength of character or a sign of his lack of passion.

In passionate love, intimacy is merely a symbol for the lover's happiness. In itself, its birth is very painful. I advise the passionate lover who has happily reached the stage when intimacy is imminent to remember that his mistress is in all likelihood in even greater trepidation.

Love is a crisis in every sensitive woman's life. The moment of giving herself up to the man she loves is the most important of her life. She gives up all alternatives at that moment; she gives up her pride; she abandons her customary modesty; she fears disgrace; she fears his insincerity. Is it at all surprising, then, that even at the very last stage when she knows that she cannot stop herself, and when she no longer wishes to stop herself, she still fears the possibility of coming to bitterly repent a reckless moment of weakness? The moment after she has allowed him his way, the moment when she throws her arms about him in total submission to passion, must always be a moment of despair in a sensitive woman.

Before intimacy, even a very passionate woman can turn her feelings off at any given moment when she is not in the company of the man she loves in order to give her attention to whatever social proprieties and responsibilities have arisen. When she is with him, she has to have all her wits about her in order to act prudently and inspire maximum passion. After intimacy, she grows desperate about keeping what she has won. Besides, her pride and her ideas concerning true love lead her to throw all her energies of mind on prolonging and strengthening her lover's attachment to her.

The happiness of intimacy so far as passionate love is concerned is, bar none, the most difficult thing in the universe to express. Fortunately, I know that I have not the requisite talent, and I shall not even make the attempt. Suffice it to say that from that height all other forms of happiness seem to be beneath words.

Before quitting this subject, I would like to say a few words about what Stendhal called fiascos. He has written very admirably on the subject, and I can add nothing of consequence to his chapter.

When this unfortunate fate attends the birth of intimacy it is a much greater disaster than when habit has made lovers kind and sympathetic with regard to the follies and limitations of each other. A fiasco is embarrassing to both parties concerned (though for different reasons), but where there is tender love it should be laughed off kindly for being the trifle it is. Difficulties arise because often only physical love and petty vanity are involved.

Chapter XLIX

Of Jealousy

Jealousy produces the worst pain known to man for a very simple reason. No matter how clearly unrequited your love is, so long as the beloved is not known to be in love with someone else, you have some means to an imagined mediating position vis-à-vis her. Since the thoughts of the lover dwell constantly on one subject, he assumes that so do hers. "I love her, and yet she thinks of me without any feelings," he tells himself unhappily.

The moment he suspects her of being in love with someone else, he feels that she does not think of him at all.

Crystallization dies at the spot; or rather, every pleasure which he expected to enjoy now becomes the property of another.

La Rochefoucauld says in one of his maxims that in jealousy there is more self-love than love, and this may be one of the few instances where he is not only a little correct. Men like Montaigne, La Rochefoucauld, and Proust were ignorant of passionate love, and knew little even of vanity love; however they are on more occasions than not accurate about the actions and motives of those who are incapable of love.

The effect of jealousy is to turn the lover's attention from thoughts of the perfections of the beloved to those of his own misfortunes. Thinking of his own situation he is convinced that there is not a more undeservedly wretched soul in the world, and so he bids farewell to love.

It is thus ironic that designedly induced jealousy is such a wonderfully effective restorative for declining or uncertain love. It is a device used most effectively by intelligent women. The only time when it may seriously backfire is when her lover's faith in her moral nature was responsible for crystallization in the first place. He may take the whole thing too seriously, with some justification, and be deeply wounded. "How could she have lowered herself by acting in this manner?" It is even worse when this kind of man finds out that it was only a ploy on the part of his mistress. It speaks badly for her that she does not trust him, that she would descend to such devices, and she does not act with the noble simplicity that he thought came naturally to her. It is only excusable if he knows himself to have fallen short of her worth himself; and there is always the chance that in retrospect he will be moved by the love that inspired the ploy.

With other types of men, those moved to love slowly and dully, and in other types of love, such deliberate ploys are most wholesome in effect if carried out judiciously and in moderation.

Men sometimes use this ploy, too, but it rarely works as well. For one thing, women can easily seduce a man, and thus the lover is only too aware of how easily he may be dispensed. A woman can claim that she is just being polite to an irrepressible admirer, etc.

Conversely, jealousy produces perhaps even greater grief in women. Whatever they try to tell themselves, most women believe that it is only their physical charms that can tie their lovers to them. They employ whatever rhetorical, moral pressures they can, though they are not themselves commonly guided by moral ideas apart from fear of disgrace and ridicule, being too susceptible to the pleasures of love. But this very lack of moral honesty in themselves makes them imagine that there is no security in the words of men—I mean aside from what experience and conversation have taught them.

The number of pretty women is, as a rule, always very high, and no woman is ever absolutely certain that another woman has not singled out her lover. No matter how commonplace a man he is, since he is of some worth to her, she believes that he can be of at least equal worth to some other woman.

Since she feels that she herself only won him by her own charms and guile, she is only too sure that he may fall easy prey to a rival's, if left to himself. Worst of all, she knows, being a woman and a mistress of the art herself, that the charms may be thrown out in such a manner that they are only perceived by him, and that this very secrecy will lend them an enchantment and a sense of novelty that her own efforts cannot hope to equal.

Chapter L

Continued

Jealousy increases intensity of love because the imagination again busies itself with picturing the perfections of the beloved, only now it tells the lover what he may have lost, and what may never be his. It makes him desire to see in her the kind of response that a passionate lover always wants to see in his beloved. The most vain of lovers begin to act and speak like passionate ones when aroused to jealousy. But make no mistake about it, in these cases only so long as jealousy persists do these passionate demands continue unabated.

It is proofs of the power that he has over the beloved that jealousy makes a lover seek to discover. Love itself decreases, as its demands increase, with the onset of jealousy, since the lover no longer lives in that secure state of mind which will allow pleasures to be felt. The sole question in his mind is whether the source of those (for the moment) hypothetical pleasures will continue to be his. Thus all love, whether physical, vanity, mannered, or passionate is reduced to vanity love, or more exactly imperiled vanity love by jealousy. The lover, unless he has given up, is interested in only three things: "Is she mine any longer, or is she lost to me? How can I be certain either way? How can I ensure that she remains mine and throws over that fool?" The more tender sort of vanity lover forgets that her loving presence was only a symbol of his happiness, and comes earnestly to believe that her presence itself is happiness.

Passionate love is full of *imagined* proofs of the fact that the beloved cannot possibly be in love with one. Since he believes her to have a loving soul, it must be someone else she is in love with, or it is some other ideal man that she has in mind. Thus jealousy is a most unfailing tonic that ensures the permanence of the passionate stage. Just when you are most sure of being loved, you absurdly begin to suspect for little or no reason that you are not loved. This has a bracing effect,[1] and prevents the pleasures of happy passion from cloying the spirit. It is a necessary factor in all happy passionate affairs, as it keeps them full of the most extreme contraries of passions.

Women's responses to suspected infidelity of thought or action are usually complicated. A woman will reproach her lover; she will complain of ill-treatment, of his callousness; she can flirt outrageously with other men; she will flatter and coddle him back into line; and, if she be not possessed of too proud a character, she may gratify her wounded pride by having it out with the rival. Commonly they attempt more than one of these strategies, varying them in as unpredictable a manner as they can in order to leave their lovers uncertain of them altogether, and far from being bored.

Men rarely have the guile or the presence of mind to carry on such a war. A man of a proud and generous temperament ought to let the woman know that she is free, and that he would not think of sacrificing her happiness to his own, even if that were possible.[2] A less generous, but equally proud man will tell her clearly that he will not tolerate her seriously favoring a rival.[3] On a lower scale of pride, when only vanity and possession of the woman are at stake, the target of his wrath is his rival.

Jealousy makes you wish for the death of your rival, and often only the threat of legal punishments makes the lover resist acting upon his

---

[1]This is true only if the suspicions are groundless. To have surprised her exchanging a tender glance with another man, or even looking with special eagerness at him is another matter altogether, and calls for the most delicate and extreme maneuvers.

[2]This only after she feels sure that you do love her passionately, or she will think you false. But if Othello loved Desdemona passionately, considering his character he would have come to his senses before choosing to kill her and Cassio; and instead, with the greatest reluctance he would have bowed out of her life. In a man of different character this action that I say would have shown the existence of passion would show something different. When, sometime in the 1930's Nabokov confessed to his wife that he had a mistress, she calmly told him to choose the one who would make him happier (see Mr. Boyd's biography)—even in tender vanity love there can be generosity, although only from pride.

[3]The General in *Madame de.* If the rival is known to have received all possible favors, the lover thinks over whether he can safely kill him.

desire. Only when you are not in love do you not wish for your rival's death. And thus a voluntary sacrifice of all hopes of happiness when the object of love is seen very much inclined to someone else, a sacrifice not born of pride, is a sign of passionate love. I do not think that any but a man or woman who loves passionately can act in this manner for some reason other than pride or fear, and not feel resentment but continue to love without abatement of admiration and generosity.

Among savages, the strongest and most devious one would have had the choice of the women. A pretty savage woman was the property of whoever outlasted the others in the field of battle. This sort of attitude still exists among many men.[1]

I wonder if generous acts toward a rival exists among women at all. There is the example of Mlle de Lespinasse; however, I think (and this is only an opinion) that such generosity is rarer among women, rare enough as it is in men. I mean generosity without residual resentment. Such an inconsolably unhappy victim of love knows greater happiness than most men and women can ever even guess the existence of.

----

[1]For their information, such an attitude is reciprocally held by most commonplace women, who are, if anything, more devious, methodical, and single-minded in the pursuit of their goals; since they have fewer of them, they feel they must leave no stone unturned in securing them. Even a woman as unintelligent as Marilyn Monroe knew how to land what to her was a delectable piece of property. She would take her bicycle in a taxi to the street in Greenwich Village in New York City where a certain famous writer lived. There she would ride back and forth in front of his house expecting to be noticed. She clearly had formed some idea of what the reaction of the famous playwright would be. In a matter of months they were married. In such matters she was a genius. Having no self-respect, knowing herself to be very mediocre, unhappy at this fact, affecting ambition, and lacking confidence with regard to most people, she saw others as potentially perilous objects that must be subdued before they harmed her. She knew instinctively that she had to appear to be a helpless, beautiful doll with hopeless pretensions whom it would be a simple matter to possess. Her beauty is commonly exaggerated, but she is a perfect portrait of what a woman is when she is pretty, devoid of intelligence, but ambitious for attention. In one department at least, she will always be second to none. How many men are there who can produce such a great splash with as few talents, and do so in an equally calculated manner?

Chapter LI

Of Glances

This subject introduces an entire class of meanings.

Everything in the world anyone regards as beautiful begets its own class of meanings. Gardens, flowers, canyons, skyscrapers, oil paintings, sketches, frescoes, portraits, still lives, arias, quartets, piano concerti, faces, dance, tennis, temples, furniture, clothes, etc., each can produce shades of pleasure not duplicated by anything else, although a Haydn symphony will be in turn different from one of Beethoven's. So with glances. A hundred different nuances of interest, at least, can be expressed by glances, and even a greater number of combinations of temperaments and characters be wittingly or unwittingly reflected in them. Thus they are all important to the birth of love.

Further, they do not commit one to anything, not even acknowledgement of interest. They merely say, "If you think that you have an admirer here, you *may* not be wrong." As with everything else to do with love, the mastery that most women have of this weapon is incomparably greater than men's. They know precisely when glances will be most effective, what a glance at a particular juncture should convey and what not, and when to withhold glances entirely.

In fact, women can convey almost all of what they are capable of feeling through glances, gestures, poise, manners. All of these are commonly disguised among conventional social mannerisms. E.g., the way she pours out coffee, the way she sits, they way she looks at a supposedly interesting photograph in a magazine, the way she looks at a man, etc.,—to others who are present it seems as if for her he is the merest of acquaintances, but to him they may be invitations to a secret, shared heaven.

Only the word "love," if used with maximum effectiveness (i.e., used in the most serious and judiciously timed manner), can equal the effect of a passionate glance. All other words are trivial in effect in comparison to what a single glance can do.

After intimacy, wordless acts such as touching, kissing, and glancing, become even more important than they were earlier. Words were needed to define exactly where the lovers stood in relation with one another. But now, only feelings matter, and so considerate and tender manners, generosity, pliancy, receptivity of thoughts, and wordless acts form the foundations of a lasting love. Words are still needed, but it is only when mutual intimate happiness is disturbed or in responding to the innumerable problems of daily life that they become anything more than irreplaceable frills.

Chapter LII

Of the Differences Between the Sexes in the Arts

It is probably clear from the foregoing chapter that a woman has an advantage over a man when it comes to expressing the various nuances of love. For almost no man do as many subtleties of nuances exist as they do for a sensitive woman with regard to every aspect of love. Thus, a man can at best theorize or describe the outlines of these nuances where a woman will express them in a very much more lively and forceful manner through glances, gestures, etc.

All very lively passions come down to love in a woman; and love, even in the most liberated societies, is not a subject that a sensitive woman wants to express her deepest feelings about in public. So, with very few exceptions, only those who have felt very little and therefore have nothing above the commonplace to express set themselves up as artists or philosophers.

And for the same reason it is that almost all the great women artists are actresses, since they can hide behind the admittedly thin pretence that they are only acting, only playing roles of characters with whom they themselves have little if anything in common.

So much for why they prefer the art of acting. There remains the more important question of why they excel in it, and why they can make of it an art as expressive and intellectual as any. On this subject, no one, so far as I know, has had anything to say that is of any worth as psychological observation; Nargis is here, as usual, the exception. I find in a hack biography the following brief excerpt from an interview: "A woman can by instinct be a better artiste than a man for the simple reason that there can be much more depth and understanding in her portrayal." The psychological ideas here are *can* (i.e., possibilities), *instinct*, and more *depth and understanding* (i.e., psychological rather than moral empathy). Because instinct, the logic of sensations relatively unmediated by the logic of verbalized or abstracted ideas,[1] allows for, makes *possible*, a more *direct* psychological empathy (i.e., "there can be more depth and understanding in her portrayal"), in general, a woman by nature has (in terms of *possibilities)* a great advantage over men in acting (the opposite is true for writing).[2]

When a woman tries to find abstract ideas of beauty, she finds little: The thinness of the effects of Virginia Woolf, Gertrude Stein, Mary Cassatt.[3]

George Eliot attempted to write like a man of learning if he had the sensitivity that all women optimistically ascribe to themselves, but her masterpiece was after all only the production of an affected prude in Dorothea Brooke. All the learning and philosophy produced nothing better. I do not say that she did any worse than Milton, or Melville, or Dostoevski, or Joyce, or did as badly as James, or Lawrence, or T.S. Eliot; only that the result was only pedantry.[4]

As for Mme de Staël, she was a tolerably intelligent woman. Like George Eliot a very ugly woman, she was also forced to a manner of gratifying her vanity in other ways than women commonly do. Her desire to be thought a *moraliste* as well as a Germanic genius of sentiment is a little pitiful, were it not comic, and her vanity that made her think herself a passionate woman may seem to a dispassionate observer a trifle ridiculous.

The only contributions that such women have made to the general happiness of mankind is to awaken other women to a life less bound by

---

[1]A woman who has greatly or totally mastered the logic of sensations will attain to a great mastery of verbalized and abstracted ideas (which are but types of sensations) as well, a fact demonstrated by the above words of Nargis, someone who totally mastered the logic of sensations, just as a man can go in the other direction. It is a matter of which class of logic is used first to get to the other.

[2]There are always exceptions, even on the level of great genius: Austen and Gable; and, on a lower level, Astaire and Mme de La Fayette.

[3]See Nargis' description of the psychology of abstract pleasures known to women in *Deedar* ("Sight").

[4]A humble psychological prediction: "Who does he think he is, this would-be destroyer of pieties?" every pedant will say to him- or herself at this point. It is not in his or her power not to.

social prejudices and superstitions. So there is something to be said for them after all.[1]

Mme de La Fayette, Emily Brontë, and Kate Chopin wrote excellent works, but then they had something to express, and so did not feel the need to imitate men. They expressed themselves clearly, simply, and directly.

Everything in a spirited woman comes down to love, to what she herself feels; everything in a bold man comes down to asserting his moral superiority over everything and everyone.[2] Thus the difference between Madhubala and Shakespeare, Miss Bina Rai and Nietzsche, Grable and Fielding, Austen and Helvétius, and Hepburn and Stendhal. This difference is also the reason why these great women produced their greatest works at a much earlier age than did the men they most resembled.

Chapter LIII

Cimarosa and Meena Shorey

Cimarosa and Meena Shorey, in their lesser works, such as the former's *I Due Baroni di Rocca Azzura* and *Le Astuzie Femminili* and the latter's *Dholak* ("Drum") and *Ek Do Teen* ("One, Two, Three") expressed an equal degree, and the same class, of vanity happiness, as that of Cervantes in *Don Quixote*, the only difference being that in them the idealization is not solely that of ideal art, but that of crystallization in the abstract, i.e., of love as an ideal art passion, without any real object, as well. Crystallization brings in its train the perhaps regrettable habit of making yourself miserable over entirely imaginary matters.[3]

---

[1]The fact that most such women have had mediocre minds is telling. They have written out of a desire to prove themselves, out of petty vanity in other words. The case of Simone de Beauvoir and her desperate attempts to impress Sartre and keep him attached to her. There are some very famous contemporary names that I dare not write here.

[2]Although most such women and some such men are willing, in thought at least, to yield first place to God, society, etc. Who was prouder than Dante, and yet who placed himself so abjectly beneath his god?

[3]"This road goes on nearly straight for two miles and then curves to the right. This confirms, perhaps better than anything else, my suspicion that she will never love me."

This distinction between the art of Cervantes and that of Cimarosa and Meena Shorey is, it seems to me, perhaps not unimportant. For one thing, since crystallization has virtually vanished in our century (I speak of general occurrence, ignoring great geniuses), Cimarosa, once thought a peer of Mozart, is as unintelligible to most people today as Ophuls, Raphael, and Correggio.[1] Also, crystallization, as a motion of the soul, allows for much greater and sweeter enchantments of the imagination than the idealization of art *per se*.

The pleasures of Cervantes' masterpiece and those of Cimarosa's and Meena Shorey's secondary masterpieces are equal in degree, but very different in tone.

The difference between Cimarosa and Meena Shorey is only that of sex, their genius being identical otherwise.

For them, the idea that produced the greatest unhappiness was: "Real love cannot provide the same degree of happiness as imagined love, for no other reason than the fact that it is real. And imaginary love, love in art, etc., is better not because it is less disappointing, but only because it has not the misfortune to be real."[2] Now, how is a man or a woman who feels this pain to find happiness?

Like Cervantes, they arrived at an excellent knowledge of the mechanics of others' happiness; like him, they at some point learned to laugh at their own moral natures. And for the same reason as Cervantes, both these responses, once they had described them in a work of art, gave them sufficient happiness to delight solely in the art inspiring the pleasures of love in the abstract that they were producing, their reasons for happiness being obviously as imaginary, and comprehending as great a motion of the soul.

The fact that their moral makeup and pleasures had the element of crystallization perhaps allowed Cimarosa and Meena Shorey to do what Cervantes could not because he did not need to to be perfectly happy. Since it was the happiness of love that was involved, the pleasure solely of ideal art was bound to not be perfect happiness for them.

---

[1] I do not even speak of Meena Shorey or Jean Arthur. Surface stylistic effects and effects building on the passion of fear make *Hamlet* and *Don Giovanni* popular in spite of how little they are understood.

[2] But in Raphael and Ophuls it was: "Real love produces pleasures of the senses and vanity, but it cannot support ideas of unapproachable beauty and nobility of soul; imaginary love can, but those pleasures must then be sacrificed."

Even while producing their great secondary masterpieces, and in the course of life, the maximum degree of vanity happiness that after all is only a stable complex of motions of the soul would have left them wanting the greater happiness of the reveries of love.[1] But this, for them, was only perfect when love was unreal.

The question that must arise in such a situation, at every moment newly asked, is, "Is this then perhaps *perfect happiness?*" But this is the question when asked at each moment that is always only the prequel and concomitant of happy reveries. But nothing dispels all reveries as much as do the thoughts, "How happy am I at this moment, and how can I increase the degree of my happiness?" This is the reason why happiness, even for the great souled, is a very tricky and difficult affair.

What Cimarosa and Meena Shorey attained in their respective masterpieces *Il Matrimonio Segreto* and *Ek Thi Larki* ("A Girl There Was") was an art that asked that question at every moment and answered it with justifications for the reveries of happy *imagined* love (i.e., love in the abstract).

It is in following very closely as they operate upon the soul all the contours of what Cimarosa and Meena Shorey do that you begin to slip into the reveries that *Il Matrimonio Segreto* and *A Girl There Was* can inspire. This is an even more difficult phenomenon to explain clearly and logically than that of *Hamlet et al.*, for here we are speaking of reveries even as we speak of sustained attention to details.

I merely describe what happens; if something happens though it should not, how is one to justify his saying that it does not?

The melodic art of Shakespeare, Mozart, and Madhubala leads to the thought of possible reasons for happiness; that of Cimarosa and Meena Shorey leads to the thought of certain reasons for happiness, for vanity can only be sustained by certainty. Perhaps it is for this reason that attention to details can be concurrent with reveries. Every perceived detail adds another justification for the reveries to continue.

These are very difficult matters to describe clearly for during the experience the soul is so violently moved that it is all but impossible to think clearly, let alone remember much once the experience is past.

---

[1]The sequence of the works themselves is not important. Even after producing their masterpieces, they went back to producing ideal art works. But then, passion is known only once in a lifetime, and for only one object.

Cimarosa and Meena Shorey express the greatest reveries of happiness possible when there is no specific object that is loved. Because of this lack of object, the contours and nuances of the work of art itself become so important for the reveries to be produced, for they supply the ideas necessary. In the *Matrimonio Segreto* the accompaniments variously but consistently pose the question "Is this then perhaps *perfect happiness?*" in their every nuance, and the songs answer this question with justifications for perfect happiness. That is, the musical logic of the songs expresses ideas that produce the sensation of perfect happiness, but you must have a soul responsive to ideas of happiness to understand the songs.[1] At this stage you ignore the accompaniments, but should you lose the logical thread you begin the process again with them.

In *A Girl There Was*, Meena Shorey used glances for the same expressive purpose that Cimarosa did accompaniments in the *Matrimonio Segreto*, and all the other expressive elements of acting as Cimarosa did songs, histrionic logic replacing musical logic.

The history of the pleasure these two works give is as follows: The story situation in combination with the precisely and variously modulated asking of the implicit question puts the soul in a frame predisposed to happiness and curiosity refined of all meanness and cynical skepticism. The song or acting gives a pleasure of vanity gratified at feeling the predisposition so sweetly satisfied with a fit object. The pleasures of vanity reach the maximum possible degree as you feel in secure possession of perfection. At this point, you stop and, a little colder and more rational, congratulate yourself on your happiness and seek to define this perfection more exactly to yourself, but discover that you cannot very clearly do so. Meanwhile, the song or acting has been proceeding and to your astonishment you discover that its perfections

---

[1] For this reason, he is an extremely difficult composer to understand. Even a musical ignoramus can see the apparent musical logic of a Mozart or Beethoven, but how many musicians or composers are there who have the gift of thought? Mozart and Beethoven were themselves exceptions in being men capable of having ideas, but fortunately the expression of their ideas had the semblance of stylistic attainment. Cimarosa's ideas were of such a nature that their expression produces upon those not given to thinking much not that semblance, but only that of vivacity. Cimarosa's *I Due Baroni di Rocca Azzura* is especially instructive in this regard, for Mozart added the aria "*Alma grande, nobile core*" to its score when it came to be produced in Vienna. This aria is a work of dramatic character, and as great as the greatest arias in *Le Nozze di Figaro* and the *Zauberflöte*. It possesses the semblance of an involved, and therefore impressively emotional, style that the other songs in this opera lack, though they at least equal it in expression of ideas.

(your conviction regarding which has continued by inertia) seem to exceed the idea of them that you had formed, and this sensation is repeated every second and therefore gathers momentum of its own. Before you know it, you are convinced that you are feeling sensations too great and perfect to be known and felt by anyone, that this sensation is too perfect to be one that is actually being felt. Yet you are feeling it at the same time.

A curious fact about the pleasures of Cimarosa's and Meena Shorey's masterpieces is that they are of a nature that even as you feel the reveries you have no idea what your happiness consists of though it is perfect, for which reason these leave absolutely no memory of themselves. The other masters of reveries (Shakespeare, Raphael, Correggio, Mozart, Ophuls, Jean Arthur, Madhubala) do not express reveries that are so absolutely impervious to memory and clarity of knowledge, though to a degree so. I used to think that this is still not the happiness of passionate love, but that it is the best substitute for passion. But very lately I have come to see that in making that attainment of perfect happiness seem a certainty (through the sense of possession of perfect beauty), and not a mere promise as in Shakespeare, Mozart, Madhubala, Raphael, and Ophuls,[1] Cimarosa and Meena Shorey moved away from vanity-beauty happiness altogether toward second crystallization and passionate love. For only in passion do you feel absolute perfection as a real thing, as truly existing, but perception of it gives a sensation so violent that you do not even know what exactly you are feeling, and this sensation leaves no memory of itself.

This late discovery[2] of the nature of Cimarosa's and Meena Shorey's genius has also made clear details regarding a fact about the heart that appeared to be in no manner explainable: the exact mechanics of what happens at the birth of second crystallization. Of the three events that constitute the second crystallization, the first is the only one difficult to understand logically, for the other two follow of necessity from the first. This is how I described this event earlier:

"The beauty and perfection of the beloved seem to increase a hundred- or thousand-fold in degree beyond even the near-perfection felt during the most intense stages of the first crystallization. This illusion arises

---

[1]In Correggio and Jean Arthur there is also the feeling of perfect happiness, but not perfect beauty as well.
[2]August 1, 1994.

because an entirely different type of pleasure is being felt. The beloved is felt to be *absolutely* sublime, the *only* source of happiness the world has ever possessed. This exaggeration of her worth is accomplished at the expense of the amount of happiness that the rest of the world and its pleasures promise." The question is, "What exactly is this new type of pleasure, and whence does it arise?" There must be a series of motions of the heart that trigger this first event of the second crystallization. We owe to Cimarosa and Meena Shorey not only literally incomparable masterpieces of art but also the answer to this question.

The sequences of ideas described above regarding them are then of general truth regarding passion:

1) The greatest unhappiness arises from the idea: "Real love cannot provide the same degree of happiness as imagined love, for no other reason than the fact that it is real. And imaginary love, love in art, etc., is better not because it is less disappointing, but only because it has not the misfortune to be real."

2) Justifications are produced that overcome this idea, for without this overcoming there can be no happiness. Being artists, Meena Shorey and Cimarosa did this through practice of their arts. In the general case, justifications would also consist of acute observation of people and feelings, but manifested in crystallization of objects of love—futilely trying to match them with the qualities of unreal love, and even convincing oneself on several occasions, and sometimes for as long as days on end, that one has succeeded.

3) In spite of the intense pleasures of the previous stage, there is no happiness.

4) An object is found that allows for all the happiness that seems not to be the lot of any down here. For Cimarosa and Meena Shorey, the libretto/script of their masterpieces must have allowed them to produce such an object, though for what reason the particular libretto/script inspired this result they, in all likelihood, are the only ones who will ever know. In general, for some reason a man or woman strikes the imagination of a woman or man as possessing more promise (grading soon into certainty) of perfect happiness than he has ever imagined could exist. Even unreal love seems to pall in comparison with the certainty of happiness that seems to be contained in this object, and passionate love is born. The nature and sequence of the sensations inspired by this object I have described a page or two ago.

It seems to me now very probable that all passionate love follows this course.

For obvious reasons, neither Cimarosa nor Meena Shorey could, nor needed to, go any further. But in actual love, the soul once started on this path cannot stop here, and the second and third events described in the earlier chapter on passionate love inevitably follow.

So far as I know, only Stendhal, Nargis, and Hepburn have managed to both describe and express the reveries of passionate love. The similarity between them and Cimarosa and Meena Shorey should have been clear enough to me much earlier considering the fact that in their different ways they are the only ones who have studied the ideas of happiness itself, making them the deepest philosophers of the motions of the soul. For what is philosophy but the thorough study of motives and passions and of paths to happiness? And although the few men and women who reached the highest possible degree of vanity happiness gained in the process a thorough knowledge of motives and passions, none undertook to understand all the possible paths to happiness, which is the only way to attain to passion and the maximum intensity of happiness possible. Therefore as philosophers of the motions of the soul they fall short of the artists of passion. In consequence though perhaps little understood they are not as entirely unintelligible to the vast majority. This is true at least of the men. The women are less understood[1] because most men rarely have the imagination to understand them, and most women are too taken up with considerations of personal vanity and too little given to allowing themselves the luxury of having original ideas.

---

[1]This is very fortunate: if they had felt that they would be understood by even a few hundred from among their millions of viewers, they would (not probably, but certainly) not have dared or cared to express any of their ideas at all. See, for example, the wary evasiveness that suddenly lightens the eyes of Hepburn when, in an interview with Miss Barbara Walters, the topic suddenly turns to what she was doing in *Roman Holiday*.

Chapter LIV

Stendhal, Hepburn, and Nargis

It is my unenviable task now to describe the greatest of all masters, unenviable because they leave everyone so far behind.

Greater knowledge of happiness cannot be attained until increased knowledge of the heart is attained. You take one petty man and he will not know that much more of the secrets of the heart than another whose species of preferred pleasures arises from equally petty, but very different motives. However, there are a smaller number of those who advance to the stage where intelligence, experience, desire for more intense happiness, and application, each in large doses, have raised them to knowledge of higher pleasures.

The more clear ideas of pleasure that your happiness includes, the more you know exactly how one pleasure differs from another.

But this is hardly the end of the road. Such a stage comes relatively early in the road to the maximum happiness that can possibly be known by the human heart.

For every man and woman, a stage finally comes beyond which he or she can no longer proceed, which marks his or her greatest knowledge of happiness. As far as he or she is concerned, greater pleasures do not exist for anyone, except rhetorically.

This stage coincides exactly with that when the character of that man or woman is fully formed.

Modified though it inevitably is by circumstances and opportunities, character is nevertheless formed about the core of his or her chief passions.[1] Manners, expressions, ideas, interests, ambitions, etc. are all

---

[1]I.e., circumstances and availability of opportunities will affect how natural, how affected, how hidden, etc., his or her character will be. It is the specific response of every individual to perceived difficulties or lack of them which determines the outermost whorl of his character. This response is impossible to predict. One never knows (even about himself or herself) how he or she will react to sudden and unlooked for events. For all that, it is beyond one's power to determine what gives him or her pleasure, and what makes him happy. It is precisely this that everyone at fifteen or sixteen sets out to discover, and forms his or her character as he or she starts to get clearer ideas about what he or she wants, and how to practically go about getting it.

If, once the character is formed, a great change occurs (one loses a fortune, wins ten million dollars in a lottery, loses a limb or two in an accident), the new circumstances

completely determined by a bias in the mind that distorts all things in relation to the maximum happiness known to him or her, and its conditions and concomitants.

This bias makes awry beyond possibility of correction an individual's knowledge of the heart, and consequently, his knowledge of human motives, passions, and manners. Because a man *must* be happy or ..., he sees sensations and ideas from the point of view of his happiness or unhappiness and not as they are. Not that the errors matter much to him or her so long as he gets what he wants.

Passionate love clarifies. Because it does not partake of vanity, it leaves a man or woman free to see things clearly and as they are for the first time. Until you love passionately, you see the world through the distorting spectacles of vanity, an ironic state of affairs when you remember that passionate love itself consists of mistaking the worth of the beloved.

True passion is not born until the greatest heights of beauty and vanity have been known. It cannot be born unless you have ransacked the entire range of passions and ideas.

Knowledge of these heights is the result of the lifelong pursuit of happiness. The object of passionate love, by striking the imagination in a manner that no object has formerly done, merely sets off the last few stages that lead to the death of vanity and the birth of passion.

Passion being what it is, it made of Stendhal, Hepburn, Nargis the greatest of all masters of the heart, the ones who had the greatest knowledge of it.

About the differences between the sexes I have written enough in the course of this essay. I assume that those who can, understand the differences by this point.

The chief masterpieces of Stendhal are *De l'amour, Le rouge et le noir,* and *La Chartreuse de Parme*; of Hepburn, *Sabrina, Roman Holiday,* and *My Fair Lady;* of Nargis, *Romeo and Juliet* (a 1947 film version of Shakespeare's play), *Jogan* ("The Nun," 1950), and *Mother India* (1957).

The works of the three masters of the heart parallel each others' exactly, as was to be expected:

---

merely enable or prohibit the gratification of pleasures of the senses and vanity already known, and so the character only changes apparently. If this great change occurred earlier in life, like any other matter of circumstances, its effect is limited to the quickening or retarding of the pace of the formation of character.

De l'amour—Sabrina—Romeo and Juliet
Le rouge et le noir—Roman Holiday—Jogan
Lucien Leuwen—Breakfast at Tiffany's—The Impossible
La Chartreuse de Parme—My Fair Lady—Mother India
Lamiel—Two for the Road—Night and Day

In *Lucien Leuwen, Anhonee* ("The Impossible," 1952), and *Breakfast at Tiffany's*, Stendhal, Nargis, and Hepburn described with extreme exactness the maximum happiness actually possible in life for men and women who have never known passion. Now, the happiness of almost all men and women (excepting the greatest geniuses) are almost entirely determined in kind and degree by the society they live in. Lucien, Holly, and Mohinee[1] are just sufficiently different from the others of their society so that the worth of description is not limited by the fact that it applies to only that particular society: they are not superior beings, only a little above the common lot. The descriptions of the motions of their souls therefore can be not only exactly but also generally true, for they are allowed all that vanity may possess in actual life. The thing Stendhal, Hepburn, and Nargis describe in these works being the mechanics and limitations of vanity as these are to be seen in actual living, the ideas are bound to be very close to Helvétius' and Austen's, respectively. But even Helvétius and Austen deceived themselves about at least one thing according to the nature of their own vanity happiness (the idea of the origin of all passions exclusively from physical pleasures and pains in the former, the faith in a woman's vanity having an absolute worth as such in the latter). Even the highest and best happiness that can be known in actual domestic life by those who have never known passion (i.e., the highest happiness that can be known only by the greatest artists of vanity-beauty, those who reached the highest possible degree of vanity or beauty) is perhaps not all that enviable; in any case such highest form of happiness, as it is found in such men and women, is portrayed with great fidelity in Stendhal, Hepburn, and Nargis.

---

[1]So far as she can be considered a *character*, an inaccurate idea, but one that makes the comparison being made here more intelligible; only the fact that Nargis herself habitually used the words "chararacter" and "role" to make herself intelligible excuses this inaccurate comparison. A simple contrast with Hepburn's portrayal of Holly will show that Nargis did not conceive of and play Mohinee as a "character" (i.e., a psychologically coherent and consistent fictional personage). Her intentions were larger.

It is in these three works that the art of Hepburn, Stendhal, and Nargis seems the most labored and mannered, and there is a reason for this appearance. Their aim in these works was to describe and express the maximum vanity-beauty happiness possible in actual domestic life— i.e., in love, marriage, friendship, work, and social company. Correggio and Arthur have expressed such maximum happiness, but they only express the highest end of it, which cannot be sustained for the larger part of life, and therefore is not the expression of the maximum *habit* of happiness possible. Now, no matter how great the imaginative powers of a man or woman, the constant little thoughts that must be entertained in domestic life when the constant presence of the objects of thought prevents too much use of imagination means that those powers disappear almost entirely so far as the ideas that make for happiness in domestic life are concerned, though this does not mean that they are not felt. The ideas that made up the happiness of Mozart with his wife and family, of Gable with Carole Lombard and with his last wife and her children, of Cervantes with his friends, and wife, of Raphael with his mistress and friends, of Grable with Harry James and their children, etc. could not be the same as those that make up the expressed happiness in *Don Giovanni, Soldier of Fortune, Don Quixote, Sistine Madonna, Coney Island*, etc. In those whose maximum known vanity-beauty happiness is less than of this degree (e.g., Tasso, Nabokov, Kate Chopin, Napoleon, or to go to a lower degree still, Bach, Rembrandt, Washington, Tolstoy), the happiness of domestic life has no more ideas of pleasures than the best of ordinary men and women may know. Even of those of the highest degree, the ideas are really no greater in number, but, their habitual use of the imagination in their works of art or science being so great, the excess of energy raises the intensity of imagination in a physiological sense. The nature of the maximum vanity happiness that can be known in actual domestic life being such, Nargis, Hepburn, and Stendhal, in expressing this happiness in women and men, had to invest the rather ordinary ideas of happiness with an air of energy, and thus the overworked nuances, so that the appearance is that of overacting or overwriting (i.e., diffuseness of details).

In *Two for the Road, Raat aur Din* ("Night and Day," 1967)[1] and *Lamiel*, Hepburn, Nargis and Stendhal described the happiness of

---

[1] I refer only to the part where Nargis plays the "repressed" character of Peggy. The script of this film is that of a Freudian melodrama, which in spite of its absurdity must have

ordinary vanity, the happiness in real domestic life of all other men and women besides those who attained the highest degree of vanity or beauty. Commonplace vanity in men being a thing extremely boring to think of, Stendhal described women's, in whom its appearance is at least more lively. At this stage, he finally meets Hepburn.

Hepburn was able to give a more extended (which does not mean more complete) description of nuances of the happiness of petty vanity in *Two for the Road* than did Stendhal or Nargis in their respective equivalent works, because the backbone material was more suitable. Stendhal had to make many circuitous routes of explanation and development to give the semblance of a formal novel that was needed if the expression regarding Lamiel was to exist at all. Nargis' portrayal is limited to the perhaps half an hour to forty-five minutes when Peggy is present rather than the normal Baruna, and, further, the nature of the character within the context of the plot did not allow for varied kinds of scenes. Therefore Nargis had to express the ideas that make up petty vanity in the most general and succinct manner. For example, the love for children is not in the plot (though the reverse is), and she took the opportunity that the central song sequence gave her to express the mechanics, causes, and ideas of this love; Hepburn had a much more extensive field upon which to work, a matter of luck, since the film itself is a hackneyed piece of 1960's clichés of thoughts and film techniques—but this period being notable for its vulgarity, the film provided her with a perfect framework for the expression of the one class of ideas she had not already expressed.

De l'amour and *Romeo and Juliet* were the first works in which Stendhal and Nargis succeeded in describing the varying nuances of passion. For a man or woman to get anything out these works, he or she must fall back upon his or her knowledge of passion. What is expressed is passionate love where there is no thought of requital, for the possibility of requital does not come in.

At this point I should confess that I have not been able to find a copy of *Romeo and Juliet* anywhere.[1] It is because of what Nargis said later in

---

delighted Nargis, for the schizophrenic nature of the character gave her an excuse to express ideas she could not in a more normal role. She had retired as an actress when this role was developed for her, and came back to films only for this one final role; in my opinion, this was because there was left only one complete order of ideas of happiness she had not already expressed.

[1]This film was produced under her own banner, flopped miserably at the box office,

life that I include this work among her masterpieces. This may be taking an unpardonable liberty as an author, but considering the nature of the parallels between Hepburn and Nargis in all other areas, I am allowing myself this little speculation.

From the films I have seen that Nargis made in the years around and including 1947, *Humayun*, *Aag* ("Fire"), *Mela* ("Fair"), I think it is still possible to make out a distinction between Nargis on the one hand, and Stendhal and Hepburn on the other, in their early masterpieces.

Sabrina, the work equivalent to *De l'amour* and *Romeo and Juliet*, came after *Roman Holiday*. But I suspect that Hepburn had already done what she did again in *Sabrina* in the stage version of *Gigi*, for the title role of which Colette had selected her, thus starting her on the path to fame, for it led to her being chosen by Wyler for the role of Ann in *Roman Holiday*.

The distinction is that of temperaments; each displayed the characteristics of the melancholic temperament in love, but otherwise, Nargis was of the bilious temperament, and Stendhal and Hepburn of the sanguine. The bilious temperament makes for more sustained and intense feeding of the soul upon the chief pleasures, and may thus account for Nargis' greater ordered consistency and force of character. The sanguine temperament is by nature more given to flitting from one sensation to another, not settling into any in an involved manner.

Nargis saw facts from the point of view of the exact nature of the happiness involved, and Stendhal from the point of view of the opposition of character-beauty (the habitual manner of pursuing happiness) and the passions. Hepburn, like Stendhal, did not define in *Sabrina* states of happiness according to rules of causes and mechanics of happiness, but each individual nuance of emotion and ideas is described separately and with exact accuracy. In the latter two, passionate love is expressed as a motion of the soul, in Nargis, as a state of happiness.[1] Therefore, in her, the distinction between the motions of the soul comprehended in passionate love and those in vanity-beauty is clearly made in a manner that it is not in Stendhal and Hepburn.

---

and has not been seen by anyone I know. Considering the nature of her first great work, I imagine that its reception could only have added to her amusement at being such a popular favorite generally.

[1]The last close-up shots of her in *Fair* show this clearly, even though in this film there is not the sustained expression as there almost certainly will be in her *Romeo and Juliet*.

In *Histoire de la peinture en Italie*[1] and *De l'amour*, Stendhal's manner of describing feelings is by means of the central idea of opposition between the habitual manner of pursuing happiness, which he defines as character, and the perception of which he defines as beauty, and the strong passions, a sometimes accidental development that produce for a man a new goal in life, and in adopting this new manner of pursuing happiness, a man sacrifices more and more all others, including his own habitual one. The transports of such strong passions leave no memory behind.

Character and beauty, as Stendhal defined them, lead to the happiness of vanity, for a man forms an image and then necessarily forms an opinion of the worth of possessing as his own what this image promises him. Any strong passion (not only love) will not have this drawback. For this reason, Stendhal loved Italy, the only land then in Europe, along perhaps with Spain, where strong passions had not become largely extinct. Germany was characterized by imagination, but even such a fanciful and dreamy temper made for the pleasures of character and beauty, not of the strong passions, which take hold of the heart and prevent not only rational and prudential considerations from arising, but destroy all stable points of view (including a stably uncertain one), and which are therefore free of the pleasures of vanity so long as one is riding on their crests.

In *De l'amour*, Stendhal gave exact descriptions of the transports of love and not of the happiness of love. Now, transports of love can only be suggested by hints whereas the causes of happiness can be explicitly stated in words. For this reason, perhaps, he recorded several times in the course of the first volume (e.g., chapter XXIX) his feeling that he was

---

[1]It is not for the author of this essay to judge of the merit of this book. Whatever it is, one virtue this book has, it seems to me, is that of all the books I have read on the arts it is perhaps the only one free of pedantry and exaggerations. It would have been a greater book still had Stendhal cut the Leonardo and Michelangelo biographies to a third of their present length (i.e., had he retained only his own observations and cut most of the stolen material) and substituted one or more chapters on every important painter from Masaccio through Guercino. An example of how his book suffers in this regard may be seen by considering the following fact: He was the only man to have seen that Guercino was a dramatic artist belonging in the company of Shakespeare, yet he did not include this observation in the published version of the book. I think that he must have had hopes of commercial success at this very early stage of his career as a writer: therefore this fault arising from the wish to retain customary appearances. He was not yet the immortal Stendhal of *De l'amour*.

failing utterly to express explicitly and clearly the nature of passionate love. But even such hints can express it, as in chapter XXXIII.

In terms of happiness, in the United States today, the only form of love found is vanity love. Using Stendhal's definitions, one would have said, physical love. This is because the transports of love known here are those of physical love, but the happiness of lovers where such exists arises largely from the thought of possessing a desirable object and of not being a failure at the game of love. In India today, on the other hand, in terms of the mechanics of happiness, one finds physical love, but using Stendhal's definitions, vanity love, because what little transports of love are known there arise from the thought of possessing the sort of man or woman that custom has taught an Indian to wish for. But these give no happiness in themselves (being only part of a more general vanity of respectable appearances), and the only happiness that an Indian generally derives from love arises from its physical side, regarding which there is universally some crystallization as a result of the land's boundaries of latitudes. In the France of Stendhal's age as well as of today, love consists of vanity love, with respect both to its transports and to its happiness.

In *Sabrina*, Hepburn similarly expressed herself by describing the passion of passionate love itself, rather than the state of happiness it produces.

The final closeup shots of Soorbee in *Jogan* and of Ann in *Roman Holiday*, if compared to each other, show most succinctly the difference between the happiness of passionate love as it is felt in the bilious and sanguine temperaments.

Though passion, unlike vanity, is a single shade of happiness, the differences between the sanguine and bilious temperaments as Cabanis described these lead to a very consequential difference in the nature of happiness. Once passion is reached, the ideas are very similar in the two temperaments, but the different manner in which passion is felt will mean difference of sensations, and therefore of the precise nature of happiness.

For Hepburn and Stendhal, passion was not merely in terms of ideas that they used to express it, but in fact as well, as an experience, a motion of the soul (which is why they expressed it as such). For them passion was something felt as a *motion of the imagination* to a greater degree of intensity as a result of a greater number of ideas forming the sensation, it was not a state they could hold on to for more than a few instants at each motion. They *rose* to it and *fell* from it. Because the soul rises to and falls from passion in Stendhal and Hepburn, there are, for one thing, discrepancies between what they expressed (which was a product of sustained periods of repeated motions of the soul during passion) in their masterpieces and the idiosyncrasies of the manner in which they pursued happiness in life (where those motions of the soul were not, because they could not be, sustained repeatedly at all times). These discrepancies, which they keenly felt, are the source of that modesty and lack of confidence they often displayed, alternating with an all too clear knowledge of their complete superiority to everyone else,[1] and these two qualities come through in their self-portraits, *Henri Brulard* and *Wait Until Dark*, whereas Nargis' self-portrait (the role of Ramu as well as the very different one of the princess-*raj kumari*) in *Miss India* expresses solely the sustained knowledge (unbiased by vanity, and not inspiring its pleasures) of a sense of absolute superiority to everyone. These self-portraits are works where Stendhal, Hepburn, and Nargis wished to depict themselves detachedly, i.e., not from a point of sympathy with passion, and therefore it is revealing of the nature of their happiness that Hepburn and Stendhal wished to reveal fully both their tender and intelligent sides without self-flattery, and that Nargis instead chose to

---

[1]In spite of his natural modesty, Stendhal knew that the only men to have come close to him in depth of ideas and feelings were Cimarosa, Mozart, Shakespeare, and Correggio (Raphael not being included for reasons given in an earlier chapter), but there is never a hint that he thought his own nature resembled theirs. Hepburn, I am told by hack biographers, esteemed (among non-actors) Tolstoy, Tchaikovsky, Noël Coward, Mr. Bergman (for very utilitarian reasons, but to no practical avail), Wordsworth, among others, but in her case, since Stendhal had come earlier, she knew clearly whom she resembled so closely as to be identical save as regards her sex. See *The Children's Hour*, where, in the midst of an ordinary and non-expressive role, she found (for I doubt that she would have added this bit to the written script) among her lines the phrase "at last from the red into the black" in regard to going from financial losses to profits. There is in her acting the slightest shadow of an emphasis, but no emphasis, when she says this line, a hint which is an equivalent to staging directions or a cue to the audience (a technique that she also used to speak directly to the audience several times in *Sabrina*, and once, when forced by the script to mention the mediocrity Bernstein in the company of Nehru and Schweitzer, in *Breakfast at Tiffany's*). This hint, or a shadow of a hint, to be more precise, for it had to be one that was there but which would be noted by no one but a woman or man on her own level of mastery of the heart, who of course, could be counted upon to not point it out in her lifetime, this shadow of a hint, by virtue of its hidden nature, is the strongest, and in fact, the only kind of evidence possible (considering feminine modesty) that she understood Stendhal and her own relation to him in terms of nature of genius.

describe only the playful, prankish side of her nature. Even when she limited herself to this relatively very minor aspect of herself, she knew that the degree of *esprit* expressed by her easily surpassed the maximum degree anyone else has ever expressed (even Stendhal and Hepburn, whether or not she knew of the former), and, consequently there was the knowledge of absolute superiority to all other souls, though it was neither a product of nor led to vanity,[1] being only a soberly factual conclusion from a dispassionate consideration of evidence. In fact, if anything, far from being a source of vanity, it would have been a saddening conclusion had not the thought, "Such sadness is a product of vanity," prevented sadness.

Another consequence is that the masterpieces expressing passion of Hepburn and Stendhal do not have direct expressive power; rather, after one has seen or read one of them for several hours (once one knows them well, so that there is no effect of beauty), one easily forgets them, and it is only when one's thoughts go generally toward the subject of present or future or possible happiness that their full expressive power comes back and takes over one's soul—this is how their expression operates upon the soul. Only in *Le rouge et le noir* and *Roman Holiday* is the expression partly direct, and this because though the expression is by means of and in the nature of motions of the soul, in giving an order to the development of ideas in the souls of Julien and Ann, the states of happiness must in some manner be implied, and here they come a little closer to Nargis' *manner* of direct expression.

Contrasting *Sabrina* and *De l'amour* (and there can be no doubt that the following holds true for Nargis' *Romeo and Juliet* as well), one may make the following very important distinction between the sexes. It is obvious to any reader of Stendhal that he ransacked the entire range of experiences open to the soul; it should be equally obvious that none of his masterpieces would have been written (i.e., the Stendhal we know would never have existed) had he never met Mathilde; more precisely, a real object of passionate love was necessary before passion itself was born—whether this object actually was everything that his imagination made it out to be is irrelevant here. She is necessary for the first

---

[1]Nietzsche also emphasized the prankish side of his nature in his autobiography, but, for one thing, that side formed a very great proportion of his entire nature, and, secondly, his expression of superiority is merely that of a man who knows he has attained maximum degree of vanity, i.e., it is an expression merely of vanity.

masterpiece *De l'amour* in a sense that no object is necessary for Hepburn and Nargis—and this also leads to the difference between them and Héloïse, Mlle de Lespinasse, the Portuguese nun, for all of whom passion was born after intimacy. This was because they allowed all elements of vanity to die after an increasingly permanent doubt set in; if their souls in spite of their obvious superiority to the common run seem a little inferior to Nargis' and Hepburn's, it is because the degree of pride there was in the soul to begin with was less. It is clear from what record they have left of their ideas that they had not known the entire range of all possible ideas of happiness.

What happened in the souls of Hepburn and Nargis, and which distinguishes them from Stendhal, was the result of the fact that in women first crystallization consists of the pleasure of thinking "How much pleasure there will be to be loved by a man of such and such worth." This means that an object of love does not necessarily have to be present, since if the ideas that make up the worth may be imagined, the full pleasure of crystallization may be known (which will provide the motive for ever renewed discovery of new ideas) by a woman of supreme imaginative powers. A man, no matter how extensive and deep his knowledge of ideas nevertheless needs an object, a woman who seems absolutely sublime because she too seems to have an equally deep knowledge of all the possibilities of happiness, with regard to whom second crystallization may commence. In a woman, second crystallization is possible from merely the intense scrutiny of all ideas of happiness that the heart can know; she can study the world and her own heart so completely as to rise to passion by herself.

In this regard, it may be said that nature has apportioned her gifts equitably among the two sexes. For if one has the greater power of verbal logic and abstract pleasures, the other has an immense advantage in terms of reaching the highest degree of happiness and knowledge of the heart. For a man must imagine such a woman to really exist, otherwise he will never rise that high, but a woman may know that no man of the highest nature exists and yet rise to it herself.

Passionate love is the only stage at which the sensations of love felt in the two sexes are exactly the same. The happiness of Hepburn and Stendhal was constituted of exactly the same ideas, though what led them to it was necessarily very different, and thus the differences in what they express.

What is astonishing about Stendhal and Hepburn, what is almost impossible to understand until one understands Cimarosa and Meena Shorey, is how a man or woman of sanguine temperament could have risen to passion. The sanguine temperament does not make for dwelling upon any one passion and feeding to it all the energies of the other passions. This may therefore explain why Hepburn and Stendhal thought in a manner that allowed them to flit from one subject or passion to another with ease.[1] The resulting lack of force (not strength) of character is, in comparison to Nargis', a quality that must be admitted by the most well-disposed observer. But there was an advantage here as well, for (taking aside the effect of love) being made most unhappy by the thought, "Habitual pleasures are not a sufficiently rich food for the heart, for no other reason than merely because they are habitual," Stendhal, in overcoming this unhappiness, was able to produce a work expressive of the pleasures of vanity-beauty that ranks with *Tom Jones* and *Don Quixote* in its degree of genius, and with the *Commedia* and the works of Tacitus and Saint-Simon in its worth as a historical record of an age and people. I speak of *Rome, Naples, et Florence* where the tendency to idealize Italy reaches its zenith, and whose pleasures are sufficiently literary that I feel I may say that this book is perhaps the greatest work of literature produced by France,[2] and probably not as unintelligible to the French as Stendhal's masterpieces. Therefore I am surprised that it is relatively so little known, and those so much.[3] The pleasures that Stendhal discovered in thinking this book through from its first 1817 edition to the 1826 edition are those that are required to produce happiness in a man made unhappy for the imaginary reason just given. This completely revised edition appeared after *De l'amour* and shows the hold of the old habits of thought as well as perhaps makes more plausible the conjecture that there was a temporary rethroning of

---

[1]It may also explain why Stendhal allowed himself to slightly exaggerate the impulsive nature of the other passions beside passionate love, given much time. He put in a little more of the nature of passion into them (e.g., Mozart's *Don Giovanni*, Italy) than they really possessed.

[2]With all due respect to Mme de La Fayette (and La Rochefoucauld if he did indeed help her with her novel), and Molière. Helvétius, it is true, produced equally great books, but they are of cold philosophy not romantic imagination.

[3]More creditably, Nietzsche thought it Stendhal's best book. But he was intelligent, a quality not very uncommon, imaginative, a quality much less common, and largely free of self-deceit, a very rare quality.

the sanguine temperament in those moments when he was sufficiently cured of the pangs of passionate love.

Hepburn's equivalent work is her performance in *The Nun's Story*. She too could not be made happy by vanity; the opposite of self-love seemed to be selfless devotion to others. Here the differences between the sexes come in, for accepting received ideas, a woman would connect this idea of selfless devotion and helping of others to godly virtue, so that it takes precedence over selflessness itself. However, then she is made most unhappy by the idea, "To accept religion sincerely and without a trace of self-deception means to be unhappy because vanity is not gratified; any happiness from the thought of believing in God comes from hypocrisy, acknowledged or unacknowledged, and it is from a relatively petty idea of vanity that such happiness arises." To overcome this idea of unhappiness, Hepburn had to invent very imaginary reasons of vanity at being able to be completely selfless without any real belief in God.[1] The script of this film provided a perfect opportunity to express the highest degree of vanity happiness that may be reached by overcoming the idea that made for unhappiness. Thus, Christianity had the same importance in her film as Italy did in Stendhal's book.

Knowledge and expression of passion aside, Nargis had much the greater force of character, but produced no comparable ideal art masterpiece of the highest genius, or any ideal work, incapable as she was of lying to herself. But one cannot have everything.

What Nargis and Hepburn did, when they were offered a plot and situation that would allow them to do so, was to describe the moral makeup and passions of women who show that they, for one, have risen by themselves to knowledge of passion.

A sensitive woman never makes the slightest advances, when she knows them to be advances, because she fears nothing more than the tainting of the sense of purity that she associates with love. And besides, once serious love is born, a woman is less apt to revise her image of her lover's worth. The struggle is within her own heart only, and not with respect to his worth.

To achieve the desired expression, it sufficed for Hepburn and Nargis that the male characters their characters fell in love with were provided, at least by the end of the film, with two qualities in the plot, delicacy and

---

[1]Both Nargis and Hepburn, after they were more or less finished with filmmaking, became social workers, but their practical reasons for doing so were very different..

sensitivity born of tender respect. There could be therefore nothing sufficiently offensive to make their descriptions of ideas not true to nature.[1]

In *Le rouge et le noir, Roman Holiday,* and *Jogan,* Stendhal, Hepburn, and Nargis went a step beyond *De l'amour, Sabrina,* and *Romeo and Juliet* in pursuit of the happiness of passionate love. In Julien, Ann, and Soorbee, they drew characters who pass through various stages of vanity happiness to passion. Each stage is defined exactly, each change clearly set off.

Their chief challenge as artists had always been to find the plot and character that would allow for maximum expression.

The characters are from the beginning shown to be possessed of a rare degree of energy, the subsequent developments described being only possible in such souls. Julien had to be shown rising through all the steps to full knowledge both of the heart and of the manners, motives, and affairs of the world. Soorbee and Ann (keeping here only to some similarities they share) had to be shown increasing in self-knowledge, in self-restraint, and in the quiet pride of a desperate heart driven suddenly to disguises.

Julien had to learn of the true nature, and the true worth, of passion in the face of the many delicious temptations of vanity that the world is filled with, and chiefly the temptations of wealth, rank, and power and the freedom and certain cause for pride they bring, and those of physical vanity love. Soorbee, by force of a series of irreversible psychological conclusions, learns in attempting to think honestly that the only alternative in life is between hypocrisy and falsehood on the one hand and on the other passionate love, only the vaguest ideas of which she had in all those years at her father's palace when she used to lose herself in tender and hopeful reveries. Ann's adventures of the soul are closer to Julien's than to Soorbee's, since the sanguine temperament of Hepburn makes the general plan of the work closer to Stendhal's, but a small number of the specific ideas are naturally similar to Nargis'.

Some examples of expression in Hepburn's film: Ann looks at the pictures outside the barbershop and up until the haircut is complete: the expression of the nuance of grave fear before the impending crisis of deep crystallization; the scene at the wall of wishes: expression of the

---

[1]The plot/story is of *negligible* importance.

motion of soul involved in abandoning forever all the illusions of religion.

The plots of *Le rouge et le noir, Roman Holiday,* and *Jogan* were only frameworks, the backbones to prop up a description of characters and passions, for Stendhal, Hepburn, and Nargis; this is even more the case in Nargis' film than in the other two works.

In *La Chartreuse de Parme, Mother India,* and *My Fair Lady*, Stendhal, Nargis, and Hepburn did something odd. Exactness of description they sacrificed to the possibilities of happiness.

Le rouge et le noir, Roman Holiday, and *Jogan* express requited passionate love before intimacy. *La Chartreuse de Parme, My Fair Lady*, and *Mother India* express the happiness of intimate passionate love.

Hepburn rethought the scenario of *My Fair Lady*[1] so completely that very little of what is happening in the film has anything to do with the

---

[1]She changes the role from its apparent character and expressions as much as Nargis does in *Mother India*.

Some passages of Hepburn's own singing are presented in the videocassette accompanying the restored version of the film. If the entire original soundtrack of Hepburn's singing has been found it should be substituted for Miss Nixon's, who did a very professionally perfect job, which though is no match for expression of ideas. The brief interview of Hepburn that was included with the restored and letterboxed edition of the film shows how disappointed she was at having the songs dubbed.* The sequence of her own singing synchronized with the film as it was released that is included in this cassette shows that Hepburn was using her singing for expressive purposes, and that her disappointment arose not from injured vanity, but from the regret of knowing that her greatest masterpiece, one whose intent went far beyond vanity, and the one in which her entire soul was expressed, would not express that soul in its entirety. Even the part of the film that I used to think she had not been able to find a way of getting around the sentimentality and bad judgement of (starting at the precise moment when Eliza herself breaks into the song "Show Me" and lasting until she leaves her old cronies and begins to walk by herself, in Covent Garden) she had managed to turn to good account by the expression of harshness she gave to her voice and delivery of the song—i.e., when she was restricted so far as acting was concerned by the requirements of plot, director, producer, and adoring public, she had found in the songs a means of expression of ideas.

It is coincidental that her *My Fair Lady* should come down to posterity in an incomplete state just as the *Chartreuse* has.

*Her modesty about expressing feelings prevents a woman from telling the full truth in such circumstances. Thus, Hepburn could not say that the final parting scene in the car between Ann and Bradley in *Roman Holiday* is spoiled at its conclusion by Ann's having to cry, for she has reached too high an elevation of the soul to have any longer the kind of weakness that the end of the scene calls for. Instead, Hepburn made an amusing anecdote of the entire thing, which went thus: in spite of everything she could not make herself cry on order for that scene (the implication being that she was too young, too inexperienced as an actress then), and it was only when Wyler angrily scolded her for her failure that she

idea she is expressing at the moment, and this is even more extremely the case with Nargis in *Mother India*.

The nature of the mechanics of how these three works take hold of the soul resists description,[1] or at least that of Nargis' does.[2] This is because you can only describe the mechanics of a pleasure fully, exactly, and without exaggeration when you have risen above it to a higher one that includes it, and Nargis, and to a lesser degree, Hepburn and Stendhal in these three works expressed the greatest happiness possible down here. A natural consequence of this fact, the penalty, so to speak, is that once a man or woman has understood them, he or she falls under the illusion that, excepting the object of passionate love in his or her life, all other men and women, including even the greatest, such as for example Cimarosa, Shakespeare, Ophuls, or Jean Arthur, with all their many very worthy and admirable qualities unfortunately seem to lack or to have lacked souls. Even when he sees all the apparent proofs to the contrary that there are, he can never again fully believe that others too possess souls, or at least he can only believe that others too had or have souls if he does not allow the thought of these three masters to be present to his soul. The positive side to all of this is that anyone who is so fortunate as to not be able to understand Nargis, Stendhal, and Hepburn will not fall prey to this odd illusion inevitable in those who can, and so will never know, and therefore never regret, that he or she has missed anything of consequence, let alone the only thing in this universe that it would be a pity to have lived and never known.

---

timidly started crying, and these tears are what we see in the film. This was her way of saying that that was an unfortunate flaw in an otherwise perfectly reinterpreted portrayal.

[1] Jean Arthur and Correggio express the greatest happiness that can arise from happy love of the vanity-beauty class, and though the mechanics of such happiness is impossible to trace, this much at least can be known, that the impact upon the senses is such that the works inspire moral as well as sensuous ideas of pleasures, and this mechanics parallels happy vanity love in actual life, where the object of love is in one's arms. Correggio provides an object (the painting), whereas Jean Arthur provides responses to crystallization, which is only natural since the first crystallization in women consists of the pleasure of being loved, i.e., love arises because of the happiness of being loved by a man who seems worth being loved by.

[2] The method of Stendhal and Hepburn is to give the maximum number of shifts of imaginative focuses possible (in the case of Hepburn, these occur not in regard to the possibilities along the line of characters-story-situations axis, but in regard to the possibilities along the line of the conscious-(i.e., *psychologically* visible) act-of-acting—ostensible (i.e., physically visible but illusory)-characterization axis), so that the reader or viewer will find it impossible to reduce the total image of what is being expressed to any set of ideas. But the imaginative effort put in in the attempt to do so results, in those who have known passion in their experience, in the full expression being felt after one has finished with the work, and happens to think generally on the subject of happiness.

Chapter LIV B

Nargis

So far, I have spoken of Nargis in conjunction with Hepburn and Stendhal, in spite of the clear differences, because even more than they she reached the imaginatively very highest point of happiness. For this very reason it cannot be described completely with exactness, and the following paragraphs form an attempt whose worth I am less sure of than of anything else in this essay.

Passion being the only other possibility open to the soul besides vanity, the works of Nargis exactly parallel Stendhal's and Hepburn's, because the same stage of the happiness of passion is expressed in each equivalent work, but what exactly that happiness is is different in Nargis from what it is in the other two masters.

The distinction between Nargis on the one hand, and Hepburn and Stendhal on the other, being that Nargis stayed consistently at the level of passion whereas they rose up to and fell from it, it follows that in describing other states of happiness Nargis merely *looked down* (i.e., there was no motion of the soul involved) from her permanent perch at the uppermost peak of human possibilities. There was therefore no discrepancy between her expression in her masterpieces and her conduct in life, they were both of a piece. Also, because she had no need to move up to the state of passion, occupying it at all moments as she did, this state itself was a lasting one rather than a motion of the soul to the heights, and therefore resulted in a state where all the *outward characteristics* of the most elevated and severe pride appeared in the soul, *though there was not the slightest trace of vanity*, for vanity requires self-deceit, a quality she lacked altogether. Her happiness of passion, then, is of an entirely different quality or pitch from Stendhal's or Hepburn's, for in the latter the expression is that of maximum knowledge of the heart in combination with maximum intensity of *kind* tenderness and tender regard born of extreme unaffected modesty and maximum degree of imagination, whereas in Nargis to the expression of the same combination is added an entirely new order of ideas that transforms this combination by a severe subordination of everything to the *idea of passion pushed to a new extreme*. Instead of the most extreme tenderness stripped of all vanity, there is the most extreme strength, of which that tenderness is a part, but only a part.

The nearest thing to an exact description of her happiness I can manage I now attempt. Since passion was a habit for her, the desire solely to be loved by an absolutely sublime object, which is the motivating force of passion, itself fell under suspicion of being only a matter of vanity. In other words, she pushed, by this rejection of even holding on to that desire, the idea of passion which Stendhal and Hepburn also knew (i.e., the death of vanity) to an extreme that they did not; even that desire for love stripped of all vanity became a new source of very imaginary unhappiness born of the suspicion that it itself was possibly a form of vanity, and in overcoming this unhappiness, she reached the happiness wherein, without the slightest trace of affectation, in utter sincerity, *on account of passionate love*, life and happiness are worth nothing[1]—the highest form of happiness possible, for since there

---

[1]The seeming contradiction of terms here is not in fact a contradiction. It should be remembered that *language* is a product of imagination and memory, produced by the imagination working according to the mechanics of vanity-beauty. The idea as expressed above ("happiness wherein, *on account of passionate love*, happiness is worth nothing") is the only manner by which this product of vanity-beauty, language, can be made to express the sensation of passion of the maximum degree that Nargis created: if happiness is where happiness is worth nothing on account of passionate love, then the worthlessness of the second-mentioned happiness will make the first-mentioned (primary and actual) happiness worth nothing: what is left, in terms of the soul, is not a zero, but what in mathematics is called a null (or empty) set, i.e., an absolute absence *on account of passionate love*.* This happiness will seem to be anything but happiness to a man *governed* (literally) by vanity, for whom, since consequence is everything (being the only thing he can know of or understand, or even *perceive*), this idea of absolute absence is bound to be completely unintelligible as well as unpleasant in its tendency. It goes against his very idea of what it means for himself to exist, for *anything* to exist.

I should add here a relevant fact that my application of Cabanis' theory of temperaments in the main text obscures. This is the fact that unlike Raphael, Shakespeare, Cimarosa, Arthur, Madhubala, Hepburn, etc., who express purified and often strengthened versions of sensations that a few other people have also felt, and unlike ideal and harmonic artists who work safely within the common domain of vanity-beauty, Nargis *created* absolute absence, which, and I speak very literally here, would not exist but for *her*, and which exists now *only* because she left in her films records of her procedures of creation and their results. Although the theory of temperaments is a perhaps adequate manner of distinguishing her from Hepburn and Stendhal, it does not explain *why*, merely because passion was a habit for her, it should stop being a state of happiness, why it should not continue unimpaired as a form of happiness; it does not begin to explain why she saw the contradiction she did, and leveled *both* vanity and passion, when these are the only possibilities open to the soul, and, again I speak very literally, *created*, by clearing out their ruins, absolute absence, which is the idea of passion pushed to such an extreme that it does

is not even the *possibility* of suspicion of self-deceit and vanity left anymore (since there is literally NOTHING—no thing, no idea of worth or happiness, no desire—left anymore), there can be no more reasons for imaginary unhappiness leading to a higher state of happiness.

To know and understand the desire, the motive force, of passion fully and yet construe it as vanity requires a power of imagination that exceeds even what was needed to get to passion; *by itself* greatly exceeds in force, that is, all of the other possible imaginative powers of any and all kinds put together, which one must in any case already possess to get to passion. This is because the motion of passion contains within itself the total force, and then some, of all other possible imaginative powers of any and all kinds put together; and to be able to stop and turn this motion of passion around, as it were, once it is in motion and has gathered the supremely large momentum natural to it (amounting to the sum, and then some, of the momenta of all other motions of the imagination possible), to construe and thereby *immediately reverse* it into a form of vanity and destroy it in the process, would *necessarily* require a countering power (i.e., an effort) of the imagination that *much* exceeds all those that constitute the motion of passion.

Even the masters of the heart and of passionate love, Stendhal and Hepburn, who greatly surpass everyone else in depth and range of

---

not resemble the motions of passions as known by other people at all. For what was created was a class of happiness that she alone inhabits, which resembles that of *no one else* (literally speaking), and which must be called that of passion by default, since although she was as detached and above passion as she was above vanity, these are the only two possibilities open to the human soul *in general*, and what applies to one person *alone* in history I can see no excuse to give a general name to.

*There is no connection to the pretended selflessness (or even more affectedly, the love of nothingness) that some religions and poetry-philosophies encourage (e.g., Buddha, Schopenhauer, Mallarmé, Beckett, etc.), where, since experience as well as rhetorical ideas and conceits lead a person to esteem as worthy and true the rhetorical ideas of selflessness or nothingness, and since the consequent pursuit of this state of selflessness or consequent praise of nothingness must be *willed*, there can at best be a noble affectation—a formula which may be represented as $x=0$, where x is a natural number. Even in those cases of maximum vanity of the contradictory class (Dante, Michelangelo, Beethoven, Nietzsche, Miss Bina Rai, Ozu), the basic formula is uniformally $|0|=\infty$ (and in the case of Ozu, $0 \neq x = |0|$; and in Rumi's, $0 = x_1 = x_2 = \infty$). In the place of such inspired playacting, Nargis had the courage not to rest content with a trick of the imagination, and instead substituted a $\{\ \}$, a $\{\ \}$ which did not arise from a decision of the will, but from the impossibility of sustaining the contradiction of the state wherein the simple 0 of passion (i.e., the death of vanity) is seen to be not the nothing that it pretends to be, but a number like all others.

I apologize for these mathematical symbols, which I use solely to add *pictorial* clarity to the distinctions being made.

[285]

thought and feelings, are thus left very far behind by Nargis, who was not only one of them, but also a (and heretofore only) master OF HAPPINESS.

Chapter LV

Of Marriage

There can be two motives for marrying, and in many cases both apply. The first is security and the advancement of worldly interests. The other, love (i.e., pleasure of the senses) or weakness of character (i.e., fear of solitude and ridicule).

These two chief motives are wittily summed up by Etherege in his lively piece *The Man of Mode*. Young Bellair, who is in love with Emilia, tells the about-to-be-reformed rake Dorimant that he ought best not to think of Harriet too much, for without church security there's no taking up there. To which sage advice, Dorimant replies,

> I may fall into the snare too. But —
> The wise will find a difference in our fate;
> You wed a woman, I a good estate.

For Dorimant, a man of the world to his fingertips, a woman could not be a good match (let alone a perfect one) without a good estate, though he would marry a good estate merely on its own account only in a pinch.

There can be no doubt that for every marriage of love there have been at least several hundred thousand marriages of convenience. And that is only right, since security and survival must come first, and love is at best a super-refined luxury the absence of which merely renders life vapid.

For millennia, people married for security, to promote family ties, to increase or consolidate wealth, to keep social classes cohesive and free of admixture, etc. To talk of love in connection with such important matters would have been too ridiculous. A few imprudent souls may have flown in the face of all right thinking men and women, but they were few and far between. As the centuries passed, as symbols of *ideal* (i.e., ideal in imagination, though perilous in life) passions and actions, these reckless men and women began to be admired.[1]

But let us return to our own age, the last years of the twentieth century. A great part of the world still follows the old established traditions regarding marriage. Families decide, and young men and women do as they are told.

In such societies, meetings between the sexes are kept to a minimum. Women are taught an exaggerated respect for the worth of at least affected chastity, and the dangers of love. Men are taught not to respect women who will grant them favors, and to respect social acceptance and money only. So that, that rare poor woman who, out of weakness, gives herself imprudently to a man she loves, has little chance of being respected by him, let alone of being asked for her hand in marriage.

There is absolutely no chance of love developing out of arranged marriages, since there can be no uncertainty regarding intimacy. In the vast majority of cases, intimacy is attained on the same day that they first meet, and then it is a duty, not an exciting chance encounter that has led to breathless pleasures. Even when they have met before, or seen a photograph of each other, the pair have not the opportunity for deep crystallization, since all the foibles, follies, embarrassments, hopes, plans, strategies, wishes for luck in small things (such as weather, sitting arrangements, being able to reach her on the phone), etc., that form part of the first stages of love are ruled out.

There remains the anticipation of physical pleasures, but too much imagination, plus, in the woman's case, the need for the sudden abandonment of all customary modesty and shame, diminish the pleasures when the time comes.[2] In addition to this, there is only the hope of amicable relations, or the hope that they will be able to do what they wish to without too much interference from their future spouses— they have sacrificed so much for security already.

The best relations I have seen among those whose marriages were arranged were those of amicable business partners. This happens when both partners are of an open and easy temper. They very clearly see that they have been thrown together by chance, and their happiness lies in their putting their interests and their wits together to get the best out of

---

[1]E.g., Héloïse and Abélard. The Italian chronicles are full of such stories. The one most famous today (because of Dante) is that of Paolo and Francesca.

[2]See Montaigne's essay on the powers of the imagination.

life. They are good-natured in their manners with each other, and help each other out dutifully in the daily problems of life.[1] They may even have had a few amusing weeks or even months of pleasures when they first married, and they remain good friends ever afterwards, with a minimum of ruffled passions and resentments. Quarrels inspired by jealousy, sign of some love even in the worst of cases, are relatively uncommon among them. They are too sensible.

But few are even that fortunate. If only one or neither has the brisk, practical, and prudent temper of a merchant, the marriages are unhappy, but their societies discourage the couples from separating through very strong-armed means of persuasion. Divorce is unprofitable, for the esteem of society they enjoy will be seriously imperiled. Unless they are constantly at dagger blows, each partner persuades himself or herself that another woman or man would have as many faults as the present one, etc.

Where marriages are decided upon by inclination, the results are slightly better because they could not be worse. Men and women are free to decide for themselves how much they esteem wealth, and what they think of the social rank, the clothes, the profession, the person, and the character of a possible marriage partner. But there is also the gratification of having obtained what you wish for if things work out so that motive for some admiration does not fade away. Since passion is rare, habit, boredom, change of heart, or change of taste can make the decision seem an insipid one in retrospect, but you at least have had a brief period when you felt that you were in love.

The chief drawbacks of marriage that present themselves to those who are free to marry according to their own choice are: the possibility of finding in the future a more suitable person (more suitable in beauty, character, wealth, etc.), lack of love especially when they are very possessively loved, the curtailing of the easy pleasures of love with others, the thought of not being the masters or mistresses of their own fate, the seriousness of its duties and responsibilities, and the uncertainty as to how much marriage will suit them.

---

[1] I can give names, but they would illustrate little. So I fall back on literature. The Rostovs in *War and Peace*. Even when more superior hearts are not involved, the marriage born of love produces more amicable happiness: the Westons in *Emma*, the Gardiners in *Pride and Prejudice*, the Harvilles in *Persuasion*. I use these only as examples, and ignore the writers' intentions.

The high rate of divorce and separations only goes to show how little self-knowledge, knowledge of the heart, and love are to be found generally. If anything, it shows how little happiness besides that born of the desire for complacent security and for the respect of peers there can be in arranged marriages.

A narrator in an Ophuls film, *Le plaisir,* says that for a successful marriage, there is needed "a harmony of mood, temperaments, and of humor." Love, no matter how great it seems to the lovers, is bound to fail in the long run and be replaced by indifference or hatred unless it is based on such a spirit of compromise and amicability.[1] The man and the woman need not be similar (boring for them in the long run if they are), but they need to be willing to tolerate each other's irritating and weak points. For with few exceptions among the more sensitive, love can never remain of the degree which it first attained. But affectations lead to habits of mind, and this is the happy married love we all hear so much about.

The fact is that most of life is spent in making ends meet, in keeping up a good face to the world at large, in meeting social and financial duties, etc. The true test of the degree of love is whether all the mundane necessities and duties of life can be handled without desiccating in the least the tender and lively feelings that exist between a couple. They must continue to feel about each other as if they had just met and are not in the least certain of being even slightly loved; love dies at its own hand when you stop eagerly imagining in every spare moment of your time[2] what would most please the beloved, and attempting to act according to what you conclude.

For two good-hearted but empty-minded people, marriage is easy since it does not amount to much. It is only slightly more complicated a matter than eating at a fast-food restaurant. The education of women on rational grounds is one of the greatest advances of the twentieth century, or more exactly, the second half of the century. The difficulty that the more intelligent men used to have in finding a woman whose thoughts

---

[1]Unaffected amicability. Affected and exaggerated politeness never works, producing only unhappiness, in marriage and out of it. The case of my friend, Thomas P— and his mistress, who separated soon after I saw them together, and who had known each other for some years. Why the arranged marriages of French courtiers were generally very unhappy ones, in spite of their faultless manners.

[2]And cutting out other pleasures or duties if they infringe upon such moments of leisure.

they could respect is fast disappearing. Only a few women had the lucky combination of having a pretty head on their shoulders, a good mind in their head, and a liberal and rich father or guardian who permitted his daughter or ward to read and cultivate herself. If a woman is ignorant or silly today, it is most likely her own fault for not having the determination to escape her bondage.

Passionate love has nothing to do with marriage.

Chapter LVI

Of Relationships

By a relationship is meant the manners of a pair of lovers with respect to each other. It is, by and large, a product of the manners of the society in which they live. Ceteris paribus, its nature depends as much on the ideas and wishes of the lover less in love. Whenever conflict of interest or opinion arises, one of the two must give in a little more than the other; the one more in love fears losing the other more, and is more willing to make sacrifices. The fashionable idea today, that women have had to make all the sacrifices, describes the truth of the large majority of cases, but, taking aside the laboring class, only because women in general cannot live without some form of love in their lives.

The word *relationship* itself, as used today, is a product of the journalism of women.[1] For most men, a woman either gives herself to him, or she does not, and either way he knows where he stands. *That* is love. Depending upon his moral makeup, he is content if, in addition, he and his mistress converse about politics, gardening, shopping, money, children, neighbors, relatives, his or her job, or whatever else is of interest or importance; and he is content if his mistress takes some interest in his profession or hobbies: that is to say, he is willing to think himself loved if he has her with him, and feels no need to talk about "us."[2]

---

[1] For proof, look at the media today: the magazines, the movies, the advertisements and commercials, the *heartfelt* stories of sincere women or men, etc.

[2] The only exceptions: when a woman is unyielding, or has become so, to his wish for intimacy; and with the birth of jealousy.

But for most women, to be together is not enough. The conversation and actions should directly center around her and the man she loves. When love is seen with most women's eyes, the word relationship becomes necessary to express their sentiments, and there are no synonyms. Scarlett O'Hara described a long time ago their feelings:

> The way to get a man interested and to hold his interest
> was to talk about him, and then gradually lead the
> conversation around to yourself—and keep it there.

There, in that one sentence, are love and relationship defined from the common woman's point of view.

From the differences of the masculine and feminine point of view are born the disagreements, which, when settled and tentatively agreed upon, define the relationship between a man and a woman.

I have written in an earlier chapter that in love words have a minor consequence in comparison to glances, gestures, etc., and that only the word *love* has an effect equal to theirs. But in relationships, words are of the utmost consequence, for they determine *what* the relationship is. What you say, when you say it, how you say it, how you respond to your partner's responses to you, how you respond to your partner's words, etc., these factors determine what the relationship is.

Relationships have nothing whatsoever to do with love as a passion; only with love as a matter of prudence.

The so-called "war of the sexes" is only the predictable result of the greater honesty of women today. When only men could openly express their self-love, no such declared war existed, since women had to conform to the ideal of feminine docility in all matters save that of feminine pride and modesty before intimacy was attained.[1] But now they, too, can express their self-love without fear, and what business, besides physical pleasure and imitation of a universal fashion born of petty vanity, two self-loving people have together becomes the great question, leading to journalistic gossip about the war of the sexes. For no matter how petty his or her passions, no man or woman can abide not finding them noble, virtuous, morally justifiable. They must have their little falsehoods. Simplicity in matters of the heart they gladly leave to the sensitive, who can afford it.

---

[1]The exceptions among the aristocracy, and among the bohemians, gave birth to the war of the sexes long before the 1960's.

I know a man whose ideas and general character do not differ too markedly from mine, though oddly enough he has met with infinitely greater success in every important branch of life. He made some of these points regarding the boring subject of modern relationships to a beautiful recent acquaintance, rounding them off with a pessimistic conclusion. She began to laugh merrily at him. A little piqued, and a little curious, after the fact, whether she had taken as hints what he had poured out in a blast of philosophic over-enthusiasm—by this time her beauty had made such an impression that he would have preferred she had—he asked, "What's so amusing? Those are the facts of the matter, and how gloomy they are."

At this, she laughed more, and then suddenly became very mock-serious. "Your philosophy does not impress me a bit, Mr. L- . It is worthless, for it will never amount to anything. What does love have to do with philosophy or reason or being sensible?" She asked this question with a most charming and mischievous smile. Now, there are several very clever responses that even a not too sharp man with his wits about him could have made, but my friend, who should have known better, and not for the first time in his life, found himself at a loss for words. I cannot say that my good opinion of him did not waver for a few seconds at his having lost the battle of the sexes so ignominiously, but for some strange reason he regarded my dismay with easy humor, and left rather early an hour later, still smiling, apparently quite happy with himself.

FRAGMENTS

Some very charming women have severely taken me to task for several of the ideas concerning the sex which I have since then put down on paper. I usually ask them about Maud Gonne, the most famous woman loved by any English-speaking poet (aside from the obviously fictitious Dark Lady of Shakespeare's sonnets). This admirably strong-minded and strong-willed Irish beauty, of honest principles, a woman of political passion for justice, who, Yeats felt, perhaps found great pleasure in expressions of anger, had the sublime impudence to tell contemporaries and posterity that she had destroyed *for political reasons* most of the letters that one of the great poets of the world had written her, the woman who inspired his poetry. This was no dull mind that put forward this curious motive, she knew the world only too well. It is ridiculous to imagine that this shrewd and clever woman thought anyone would be deceived by this disingenuous excuse even had not Yeats expressed his political views clearly in his poems, essays, prefaces, letters, and speech. Was it maidenly modesty that prompted her public lie, or feminine pride and sense of secrecy and decorum? Whatever happened to the idea of proud honesty and moral integrity at all costs? And who but a politician or a woman would be so calm and assured when uttering a patently disingenuous public lie? And yet I would say that though of a cold and calculating nature, she was a rather admirable woman, but there have been countless more admirable.

*

Tolstoy tells you that he despises Shakespeare, and a critic pompously or modestly gives you fifty reasons to admire *King Lear*. Who but an idiot would not much prefer to hear Tolstoy out? Tolstoy, a great genius, may not have understood Shakespeare, but his contempt has the merit of alerting us to the very cavalier eye with which Shakespeare regarded anything to do with describing passions not raised above the commonplace degree. The critic (be he a pedant, a hack-reviewer, or a *soi-disant* sentinel at the gates of good taste and culture) would not have rest content with being what Fielding once called him[1] had he the talent to be his better.

---

[1]"My good Reptile." From Book X, Chapter I, *Tom Jones.*

*

Politeness, more so when not yet a habit, is a matter of uttering small falsehoods without conviction.

*

Autobiography as unintentional self-revelation: Augustine, Montaigne, Rousseau, Goethe, Chateaubriand, Tolstoy, Dostoevski. Autobiography as the act of self-portraiture as intended: Raphael, Stendhal, Nietzsche, Ophuls (*Lola Montes*), Nargis (*Miss India*), Hepburn (*Wait Until Dark*). As in conversation, so in books, etc., those are the most to be trusted whose sole aim is to avoid self-deceit. Then there are those who fall in the middle: Dante, Michelangelo, Titian, Rembrandt, Wordsworth, Twain, Proust, Nabokov. Mr. Robbe-Grillet in recent years. Those in politics have accustomed themselves to all forms of deceit through practice. Even Caesar and Napoleon are suspect reporters of their own characters and motives. I am more likely to believe what I read in the memoirs of a sober-minded general (Caulincourt) than in one of a man of ambition.

*

In the West,
1750: Religion or Science?
1850: Science or Religion?
1950: Science as Religion.
2000: Science and Religion.

*

Sometimes our Government is very harsh on us. Suppose you want to make a farce, a political situation today. Let somebody take an idea and make a farce on this, but our politicians have not learned to laugh at themselves. While the people abroad make just any film. I am reading a very interesting book called *Shall We Tell the President*. It's about Kennedy who might be elected President and there is a plot to assassinate him. If a book like that were published here, it would be banned. They will say, You are giving young people ideas to assassinate the head of the Government. In this country you can't laugh at the police, you can't laugh at the armed forces, you can't laugh at politicians. You can't point at them.

[294]

But were films like that made in your time?

Yes, they were made. In fact, there was not so much corruption at that time like today. So when you pointed out the corruption, then they felt guilty.

Did you feel at that time that the cultured elite did not see films because they looked down upon them.

Yes, they did. They were hypocrites at that time. They used to tell their children you must not see the film, you must not do this and that. But they had seen it themselves, because I meet them now and they tell me we have seen your films.... I met so many people who say, We have seen your films, you were our favorite, but for the last so many years, I don't see Indian films. I think that that attitude is wrong. They must see the kinds of films that are being made and then give their opinions. They can change their opinions. If politics can change, why not cinema?

Now, of the roles you played, of the portrayals you did in films. For instance, in Andaz, *the woman, the character is misunderstood, she is a victim. But which are the roles in which you projected a woman who was a positive figure, who was the central character?*

Unfortunately, in my time, the heroine had to be all good. She couldn't do anything that was wrong. She was always the victim, and I always yearned to play different types of roles. But in all of my films, which people have liked, for example *Jogan*, she has always been the victim and has been projected as the poor thing, the poor woman, the suffering woman.... But I must give credit to the films of today. They have made some films where the woman has stood up to the wrongs done to her.

... at that time, which role, for instance, did you find really fulfilling, that you really enjoyed more than any other?

Well, of course, I enjoyed *Mother India* very much. I was just twenty-five then, and it was a huge range from a young bride to an old woman. So that was a big challenge. Also, everyone told me that you shouldn't accept this role, because you are in the prime of your youth, and if you do this kind of a role where you are the mother and the grandmother, you will not be accepted as the heroine. I said, I don't care, I love this role. I can show what I can do. So I accepted the role and loved playing it. I was deeply involved in that film. *Jogan* was another film.

Who directed Jogan?

Kidar Sharma. It was a very different sort of role, of a woman who never spoke much. She was a nun; she became a nun because she was disillusioned....

A Christian nun?

No, not a Christian nun. A *sadhavi* like the Jain women you see devoted to God and devoted to religion. She was a young woman who falls in love with a man, but she can't express it to him because she is bound to her vows. That was another very difficult film, but a very beautiful one.

Who acted with you?

Dilip (Kumar). Then there was one character, one role which was immensely satisfying, and that was *Anhonee* made by Abbas. It was an excellent film with a double role of a good girl and a bad girl, bad in the sense that she was a prostitute. That was very satisfying. And of course *Raat aur Din*. That was a character of a schizophrenic girl living two lives at the same time. That was very beautiful also.

In my younger days, when I was barely fifteen-sixteen, we did Shakespeare's *Romeo and Juliet*. That was very good because I have always been fond of the character of Juliet. I had seen Norma Shearer and there was immediate identification that I must do if not better than her, then at least somewhat near it. They had kept *Romeo and Juliet* as it is, they didn't change it, even the names were the same because it was a Shakespeare play. The costumes and everything were the same except that it was in Hindi. The dialogues were superb because Kamal Amrohi had written them, a beautiful translation of Shakespeare. Sapru played Romeo. He was a very handsome man. We were very young, and it was a lovely film to do.

From an August 1979 interview with Nargis (1929-81).

*

The Germans pushed the idea of the feminine ideal beyond almost all other people. They used to talk of Woman, the Eternal Feminine, and *redemption*. In its highest form, love was a mystical experience, a divine emanation, etc.; from Gottfried through Wagner to even the vulgarized pictures of the ideal German woman in Nazi propaganda.

The Russian ideal of womanhood was established in the nineteenth century, after exposure to German ideas.

The Germanic ideas must be of very ancient origin, for they show up only a little altered to a more extreme version in traditional Hindu culture. Among Hindus as well, love was regarded as symbol or manifestation of divinity: submissiveness, docility, the bowing to duty, sense of self-sacrifice, the putting of husband and children first in every matter, these were the ideals of Indian womanhood.[1] The social esteem in which a family is held depends, aside from its wealth, upon the conduct of their women, which is why the men are so jealous of their reputation and actions, and more or less imprison them in their homes. This still happens today. But then this is only the extreme expression of feelings common to all nations.

*

The same passion shows itself in various ways among various nations. Both the Italian and the Indian are hot-blooded fellows with little politeness, and easily angered. But a fight or an act of revenge is a matter of a grim, almost quiet joy for the Indian; the Italian enjoys it with an ebullition of spirits. The Pathan acts, but it is the public display of rash pride that matters most. The Punjabi enjoys himself as some Southerners in the United States still would the delights of heavy-handed cruelty if the law allowed them. Only the Italian feels what he might call *inner or spiritual cleanliness* from the act. Naturally, I do not speak of Americans of Italian descent, whose pleasures have changed, and even those in organized crimes do not enjoy violent acts any more than do members of Chinese or Japanese gangs.

*

That self-interest was the only principle of action in all men, and that there was nothing more in nature, nothing more complicated than self-interest, no absolute good or end and no philosophic or epistemological subtleties patiently awaiting pedants' quibblings, and that to understand even the most apparently noble and heroic actions or the most abstract conceit the application of the principle of self-interest was sufficient, was the discovery of Hobbes that parallels in importance Galileo's discovery of the idea of force that acts on objects causing changes in motion. But, and here also he parallels Galileo, Hobbes could not generalize this point

---

[1]The extreme case being the practice of the sati. In some tales and poems of medieval Scandinavia there are instances of a woman being sent to her death along with the body of a rich man, though the woman was not necessarily his wife, but one who had been chosen from among his household or servants.

[297]

sufficiently, he could not demonstrate in detail its applicability to all human affairs and feelings.

In producing his philosophy, Helvétius surpassed Hobbes in a manner that Newton did not Galileo (though he did advance greatly beyond Galileo's knowledge), though both only generalized the ideas of the earlier masters, for in the middle came the stage where Helvétius was made more unhappy by this idea, "All the passions whose gratification leads to happiness depend for their existence on gross self-deception; not giving in to self-deception, not being in the power of any of the strong passions, is all very fine, but has the little drawback of making only for unhappiness," than by any other, a fact which drove him to a degree of profundity equalling that of Austen, Einstein, Hahnemann, and Kent, the spirits closest to him.

*

The greatest prudence does not arise from the greatest knowledge, for prudence is the use of knowledge in order to obtain desired results, whereas the deepest knowledge is the product of deep unhappiness at the possibility of self-deception.

Helvétius had a deeper knowledge of man than Montesquieu, but for this reason he could not give the detailed descriptions of what is needed in a republic that Montesquieu did. What made Machiavelli the greatest political thinker regarding despotism and Montesquieu the greatest political thinker regarding democratic republics arose from the very fact that their knowledge of man was limited, and their desires imaginatively of a simple kind.

Montesquieu could agree with the idealistic and entirely unscientific opinions of Locke regarding the natural state and the obligations of governments and yet think very clearly of what was required for a republic to survive intact. He could describe clearly the most important criteria regarding the practice of voting or how to sustain democracy through a balancing of power and yet think that a strong republic is moved solely through patriotism and that when love of wealth becomes as important or more so than patriotism its survival and strength are at an end.

He forgot that Solon no less than Lycurgus had to protect his city, and in that age prudence suggested that they take measures to produce a disciplined society lacking in soft luxuries and indolence in order to survive. The idea of wealth therefore was despised.

But in the eighteenth century and the nineteenth, an equally prudent and intelligent man would regard a nation's survival and power to lie in wealth since modern engineering requires education, discipline, *and* wealth. Who doubts that Hamilton had more political prudence than Jefferson?

Helvétius wisely ignored the debate regarding the natural state as being of no importance for none of the opinions was open to demonstration, and he saw all the flaws of reasoning in Montesquieu's great book that arose from a very vague and undefined understanding of man, but he saw too deeply into human nature to allow himself to propose a few detailed and effective guidelines for establishing and sustaining the best government, since the definition of best government is not, strictly speaking, possible. Therefore his influence on history has been infinitely less general and beneficial than Montesquieu's.

*

Helvétius denied the influence of climates and geography on the moral virtues and vices to be found in societies. Here again he was opposing the view of Montesquieu. But whereas Montesquieu's ideas on the influence of climate were feebly developed on the basis of too easy an acceptance of appearances as reported by perhaps all too mistaken observers, Cabanis arrived at a very specific working out of the nature of temperaments, and of the general relation between the physical and the moral. His work complements that of the homeopaths: his is more useful in philosophy, theirs in the art and science of healing.

Helvétius is no doubt right in placing the form and manner of government as by far the most important influence on the passions and manners of a people. For the climate of a land remains in comparison largely the same, but the passions and manners of its people change every century or less.

Governments determine the manner of pursuing happiness that is found in a land, and thus the passions and manners that arise there.

Climates, and to a degree, geography, determine the temperament of a people, that is, the way that they feel a given passion.

They determine the general moods and inclinations, and therefore they are bound to have an effect on people's actions, for they modify how and what an absolute ruler, say, or a greedy populace wishes for. In this manner, temperaments have an influence on laws and therefore on passions and manners of a society.

[299]

Therefore, Helvétius and Cabanis need to be used together as complements in order to understand history, politics, and manners.

*

A single, isolated, arguably innocent smile that the beloved unthinkingly bestows on some fortunate man can cause as keen a pain as her allowing him rare freedoms.

*

The ratio of cause and effect is very lopsided between suspicion and jealousy, or between jealousy and passion. The lightest suspicion may lead to the most painful pangs of jealousy; the slightest jealousy may lead to great intensification of passion. These facts ought to remind one once again that all of love is but a matter of using a very special kind of imagination, which, if at all present in a man or woman, and once employed, overrules all others, those brought into play by ambition, poetic reveries, enjoyment of the arts, of shining in society, of hobbies, other passions, etc., i.e., all the simpler forms of imagination whose function is simple idealization are marshalled to feed the imagination used in passion. The difference between their former activity and their present one is that whereas the pleasures that were their natural outcomes produced some happiness earlier, they produce none now.

*

In *happy passion* the very idea of infidelity does not exist, which is why it produces less unhappiness than any other form of happiness.

*

In ideal art, expression only comes in when the artist has something to say regarding imagination involved in love or generosity of spirit, for in all other actions and passions, the idea of happiness is less inspired. Ideal art does not express the feelings that arise in actual life. Almost all ideal artists rely purely upon emphatic use of medium. But in expressing the stronger feelings, related to ideas of love and generosity, such a method is useless. The fact that so few artists have risen to the level of expression may only mean that all the others were men of feeling who merely lacked talent, but I admit that this seems unlikely. For if you have felt something, you can always express it somehow, whether you are gifted in a particular medium or not.

Michelangelo felt the same sort of happiness that Dante did, but it was through what he saw and through images of the human body that he derived most of his ideas of pleasure, so it is in his paintings and not

[300]

his poetry where he manages to express the sensation that made up happiness for him.

One's pleasures and happiness come through in spite of everything, but perhaps in different ways: through expression in the eyes, in words, in sounds, in images, etc. And if one has a gift for certain of the arts, he or she will be made very unhappy so long as that happiness has not been satisfactorily expressed.

Héloïse's letters move me much more deeply than Petrarch's poetry, though it was the Italian poet who had the greater literary talent.

If Spenser, Picasso, or Welles had given up in despair and misery over not being able to express anything, I would have been inclined to think of them as men of feeling who unfortunately, but not out of any fault of their own, lacked talent.

For the sum of what you do expresses everything you do feel. There is never any difference between expression and knowledge or feelings.[1]

*

In a recent Wimbledon Ladies' final, the top seeded player almost lost the match, but made an astonishing comeback in the last few games to win it, thanks largely to the sudden lapse in the accuracy and assurance of play of her Czech rival. Her disappointment was so intense that when the Duchess of Kent spoke some kind words, the loser broke into tears. The curious thing about the incident is that across the face of the champion, when she saw the state of the loser whose momentary though very consequential lapse on the court she had just taken very fair advantage of, could be seen a slight though very visible tremor of sympathy and tears which she controlled in time. Self-love, extremely sensitive, and a quick sense of identification born of weakness and the vanity of being a *good, selfless, decent human being.* This fact also explains how a woman who commits mean acts without remorse

---

[1]This even in the sciences. If a physicist today who knows Newton's *Principia* well were to rewrite it entirely in his own order and words, without adding ideas that could not be known to Newton, even if he were allowed the use of the classic, the result would still be inferior to the original even if all of Newton's important ideas are included. This is because the original was the result of imaginative work driven by strong passion for truth and glory, and the result is a fine logical mesh of ideas that cannot be duplicated by a lesser man. A man who succeeds in this sort of enterprise either equals the older master (as Newton himself did Galileo or Kent did Hahnemann) or surpasses him (as Helvétius did Hobbes); in both cases the later man develops a new order of ideas that takes in most of the original one, but broadens its extent or applicability a little or much. The later man's is the genius for perfecting, as the earlier's the genius for originating.

manages to wax unaffectedly sentimental over religion: she sees no contradictions.

July 12, 1993

*

The novelist, religious moralist, and part-time misogynist Tolstoy once observed (as reported by Gorky): "With her body, woman is more sincere than man; but with her mind, she lies. And when she lies, she does not believe herself; but Rousseau lied and believed his lies."[1]

Infidelity is a ten-times worse (worse, that is, for the injured party) and more serious thing in a woman. A man does not give himself up to the woman with whom he is unfaithful. When a sensitive woman is unfaithful there is. something beyond dishonesty, insensitivity, and betrayal that the lover has to worry about: when she thus gives herself to another man, it can only mean that she regards the second much more highly, for otherwise she could not suffer herself to be touched by him when she already has a lover. So, my dear fellow, you have much more to fear from your mistress' boredom with you than she has to fear about your being bored with her.

*

If there is nothing worse than the unhappiness of passionate love, there is nothing to even compare with its happiness. This fatal piece of logic prevents the lover even when in the worst throes of desperation and misery from decamping from the field of passion.

*

The only measure of love that I accept is, How *totally* trivial are the idea and inevitability of death in comparison to your *happiness* from love? You can only call that *love* which is impudent with regard to the fact of death, which, more precisely speaking, has become absolutely *indifferent to everything* but the attaining of its special happiness. Everything else is a show or a tedious game.

*

"The whole world may be in the same state today that England and France were in 1780: with the few rich, the slightly more middling, and the majority poor. It is entirely possible that in a few centuries the greatest number of nations will be in the middle class. The good that

---

[1] See Gorky's *Reminiscences* (1946), p. 16.

[302]

will come about then is obvious, and what but good can come of such a development?"

From a recent report.

*

"I don't see the point in wasting my time seeing and hearing more than twice what men like Monet and Berlioz have to express, when I have to fit in men like Manet into my crowded schedule. We have only so many heartbeats before this magical game blows a fuse, and who knows what comes after death."

Young M. Morris to his father, the Reverend Dr. J. Morris, a great admirer of the two artists — Va., USA, 1988.

*

The nonsense spoken and written by feminists in the last two decades or so is no argument against the worth of the movement. How many idiotic ideas were expressed during the French Revolution in the heady first glow of the thought of freedom from subjection and humiliation, the thought of a more fair and more heroic future? The magnitude and importance to society in general of one are not less than those of the other. No one could or can pretend that they did not happen, and there was and is no going back to the earlier ways. What the feminist movement has done is to free women to think, feel, and do as they wish. Its great result has been not so much to give greater happiness to a greater number of women, but what is more important perhaps, to permit those women of the present and the future who happen to be born with greatness of heart and spirit to pursue happiness on an equal footing with that enjoyed by men, a problem difficult enough.

*

The man who gets up every morning and is immediately reminded by everything around him that he has a very difficult but to him very worthy task to perform and goal to obtain is never bored, unlike the fellow who feels he has everything he can ask for, and does everything for pleasure only, who in turn is less bored than he who is forced to painful tasks. Work is the great antidote to boredom. Without hard work that *he wants voluntarily to do*, a man cannot help but be bored for long stretches. It lays the foundation for happiness, but is never happiness itself.[1]

---

[1] A fact that harmonists and those who work day in and day out in order to dispel melancholic thoughts often forget.

[303]

*

Desmoulins disagrees with my ideas regarding our tastes for greatness today. He cannot see how I can say that a Baudelaire cannot arise today, and points to *Red Dwarf* as an example of a great work of art. But that show is a harmonic masterpiece, and so are the best works of Nabokov and Mr. Robbe-Grillet, the two best writers of recent decades, and harmonic excellence can arise anywhere and at any time. I do not see a great ideal artist arising today, unless he or she be on the level of a Dante or a Meena Shorey, or at least Tasso: we are at a stage today when there will only be mediocrities or very great geniuses. The middle ground of genius has been knocked out from under the feet.[1]

*

Stendhal perhaps took the name Leonora (for Mathilde) from Calderón's *No hay burlas con el amor* (*No Trifling with Love*).[2] The difference between the ideas of passionate love, and the rhetoric, fashionable especially since Petrarch endowed the idea of love with the colors of religion. Such rhetoric led in time to mannered love.

*

It appears to me that Robespierre and Lenin had exactly the same type of genius. So, why did Robespierre fail where Lenin succeeded? It is perhaps because Rousseau did not provide a sufficiently simple and straightforward substitute for religion as Marx did.

Sentiment, music, art, the vague idea of virtue, fraternity, and freedom were no doubt excellent things, but they did not provide Robespierre with a specific end, or more importantly, with a whole series of means to an end.

Marx gave a detailed romantic ideology with all the goods and evils clearly delineated, a history consisting of unenlightened past and a revolutionarily new future, and the enemies that needed to be destroyed. Therefore, where Robespierre's religion of reason failed Lenin's fanatic

---

[1]Mr. Connery, Mr. Jourdan, Mr. Adams, Miss S-, and Mr. Laurie, in my opinion the greatest living artists in the West, are on a level that always rises above its age, though not to the utterly independent degree of a Meena Shorey or Dante. Excepting Mr. Ludlum, Mr. Antonioni may be the only living ideal artist in the West not on an equally high level of genius, who nevertheless, in his two best films at least, has not fallen prey to the worst influences of his age. But considering his stated opinions on art and society, as well as the series of films very much spoiled by the affectations of their decade that he made between *L'avventura* and *The Passenger*, it seems that one must piously deem the survival of his genius a very fortunate miracle.

[2]See the first scene.

Marxism succeeded in capturing the imagination of the people, in giving them a habit of thought that was sufficiently engrossing, with both punishments and a utopian promise constantly and clearly held in front of their eyes.

The other additional advantage of Marxism was that it laid out for Lenin a *clear* set of results that had to be attained. The particular brand of fanaticism that Marxism was compelled him to make sweeping social changes with exactly defined goals inspiring them.

With Stalin, Mao, Castro, Kim Il Sung, Ho Chi Minh, and Pol Pot, the manner of Lenin became a traditional way to not only obtain but secure power. Like all imitators, none had the true sincerity of the master. Lenin himself was not imitating Robespierre; he merely had the same moral makeup. And since Russia of the late nineteenth century was in every way very different from pre-revolutionary France, his rise to power came about for a very different reason from Robespierre's.

It was Russia's misfortune that Lenin had a more practical ready-made guideline than had Robespierre, and that educated Russians were less clear-thinking and of a more enthusiastic nature than the French of the eighteenth century.

Fanaticism by its nature is a short-lived passion, and with its death the nation or empire it has created loses strength *as a society* even if the government and the military remain strong. Just as the original Arab expansion in the seventh century was soon succeeded by tyranny, so the fanaticism of the early years was bound to fall into conservative tyranny.

Stalin and Mao realized that only through the worst crimes of despotism could they keep up the appearance of the original fanaticism, and their nations were too large, and they too ambitious, to allow them to retain power in the manner of Castro or Mussolini.

There is no worse form of government than one which is uncertain of its survival, and sees only a few ideas separating it from its doom. The church in the Middle Ages and even more so after the Reformation, for example. I do not say that such a government is not very useful in the absence of alternatives.

*

It was neither Luther nor philosophers that led to the establishment of a monarchical government in Europe, as opposed to despotism.[1] It is

---

[1]See Montesquieu.

the troubadours and then Petrarch, and most importantly women, who deserve the credit for making despots wish to justify with moral reasons their power and actions. Once feudalism was crushed in France and royal power firmly established, gallantry and love of refined prettiness made it more difficult to be crudely despotic. Despotism did not disappear, but one had to invent seemingly moral and refined justifications, and this led to all the advantages and disadvantages that respect for appearances produces.

It was only after this development that the works of philosophers could have an influence on history. This development was partly a product of the climate of Europe, for though in Persia, parts of India, etc., there was also similar elevation of the idea of love in literature, the influence of this on manners was much less than in Europe, for general biliousness did not accord well with tender sentiment.

The passion of love has this degree of influence on the course of history.

*

Anyone lacking genius but ambitious for glory and success has no choice but to love the customs and conventions of his age to the degree that he may be able to convince others that he embodies the best of them excellently. For several centuries prior to the establishment of the Court of Versailles, it was through longwinded religion (and, after Petrarch, more directly Platonic poetry) that a man won glory, or at least patronage, through the arts. What the troubadours and the Italian Renaissance managed to do within such limits, when refined through the sensibility and sentiments of the ladies of that court, led to greatest honors being accorded to those who could embody everything that was felt to be called up by the words "refined" and "polite". Because of the influence of some artists maligned or ignored by their prudish contemporaries in the nineteenth century, filtered and exaggerated through the sensibility of our century, the mediocre man or woman today wishes to seem to express everything associated with impudent vulgarity and meanness of motives in order to win the highest praise. This is because those in whom lies the power to grant it belong to another class.

*

The appeal of films today is largely physical. In the name of "new wave" and "frankness," a lot of sex-appeal is projected.... That way true

[306]

naturalness has all but gone out of our films.... We have so many aids to beauty today, but do we have a *natural* beauty like Madhubala? We don't, because all those beauty aids, they are only a *means* to the end. In the end, it is what is there *in* you, the quality of your work, that counts.... It is not only sincerity that many of today's artists lack; they also lack humility. And humility, remember, is the hallmark of the true artist.

Nargis, in a 1976 interview.

*

The fact that Nargis saw the nature of Madhubala's genius very clearly as the inner expression of beauty, not the matter of a beautiful face, is at least one proof that in women as in men passionate love has this result, that all other pleasures of even the greatest souls are fully intelligible.

But for the rest, taking aside the cases where passionate love is known, even the greatest geniuses can know only the happiness of a great number of more ordinary people. To Raphael the pleasures of Titian would have been unintelligible, and vice versa. Shakespeare would no more have understood Nietzsche than Nietzsche did Shakespeare, and I doubt that Grable and Arthur knew each other's happiness.

The Sistine Chapel is the only proof that Dante was ever understood, and Mozart's objections to the manner in which Shakespeare introduced the ghost in *Hamlet* (to be expected considering the difference between music and words), which objections crystallized into the manner that Mozart treats the ghost in *Don Giovanni*, is the only proof that that play was ever even imperfectly understood. One wonders what Mozart would have felt had he read the play in the original.

*

The art of painting (as well as architecture and sculpture) is where the pedant is least free to be absurd for everything is visible at first glance, and although innumerable absurdities are found in art criticism, they yet seem to me to be less than those to be found in literary, music, and film criticism.

Therefore, general taste in paintings is not a bad index of general knowledge of pleasure in a society and age.

Generally speaking, people today, or at least those who derive real enjoyment from the arts, derive greater pleasure from Giotto than from Masaccio, from Botticelli than from Ghirlandaio, and from El Greco and Vermeer than from Guido Reni or Domenichino, and I am afraid that they are entirely sincere in their declarations of such preference.

[307]

The reason for it is that though they have lost the ability to feel deep pleasures vanity still demands that they be able to admire and enjoy the arts, and that they be able to discern beauty, originality, and nobility. But what is a person who belongs to societies governed more or less on the basis of utilitarian principles for a century or two to make of the words *beauty* and *nobility*?

Fortunately, mediocre artists like Cézanne, Picasso, Kandinsky, Pollock, de Kooning, etc., along with critics who have promoted them for want of anyone else, have made it possible for even the most frigid soul to see beauty and depth of feeling in an overworked canvas, in "tension of forms, lines, colors". The little that he does feel he finds adequately mirrored in such tensions, and his vanity is gratified at being able to feel intensely, a proof of his having a soul that can understand art. Details and form when accompanied by *technical* displays thus become the guidelines for esteem, for then you may esteem and enjoy with the least degree of hypocrisy—and once the artists who display these qualities are very generally esteemed, everything is perfect.

From this point of view, Giotto is more conducive to pleasure than Masaccio, Botticelli than Ghirlandaio, and El Greco, the excellent Caravaggio, and Vermeer than Guido Reni and Domenichino. For Masaccio, Ghirlandaio, Guido Reni, and Domenichino, in their different expressions of ideas, were forced to eliminate all details that did not help produce the impressions they sought, which tended toward different ideas of perfected beauty in Ghirlandaio, Guido Reni, and Domenichino, and of severe nobility in Masaccio. Since these are largely unintelligible to them, most people today justifiably feel less pleasure in their paintings than in Giotto's, Botticelli's, Vermeer's, or Cézanne's.

*

The woman who can see greatness of spirit in a man and loves him for it is more remarkable to me than a man who knows and loves greatness of spirit in a woman when he sees it, though both this woman and this man are rare.

*

To love truth for its own sake is a weak passion at best, for only an exceedingly mild form of vanity is gratified that way, and save in the form of rare and fortunate accidents, it never leads to the discovery of new truths.[*]

---

[*]Completed Dec. 28, 1992.

APPENDIX ONE

I have described in this essay the many ideas, all of which are subsumed by the term *happiness*. Such a description cannot be complete without a few words on the physical nature of human life. There is no happiness without health: when you are in the throes of the vicious pains that attend cancer, you cannot be entirely happy that you have a magnificent mansion, a magnificent wife, magnificent children, and a magnificent reputation.

Philosophers, so-called, and sophists have argued for millennia on the subjects of matter, energy, the body, and the soul, but it took two geniuses to show us (as far as men can see) the exact facts: Samuel Hahnemann and Albert Einstein. Hahnemann, who founded single-handedly the science of medicine, was the first to discover the exact relation between energy and matter, which is that the two are not distinguishable *in nature*. A century later, Einstein corroborated this idea in the non-biological, physical universe. For some reason, no one, to my knowledge, has seen the connection between the two greatest scientific discoveries in history.

Einstein's achievement is too well-known in this country to need my description. Hahnemann's, however, has been carefully hidden and eliminated from public knowledge by physicians here, and, to a less degree, by those abroad. Even in this age of well-paid academics, almost no one knows the fact that between the middle of the nineteenth century and the first decades of the twentieth homeopathy, the science of medicines, had grown to the degree where thirty percent of all practicing physicians in the United States took the title of homeopaths (though few were truly so), an ignorance of their own history that would have been very astonishing had it not been very deliberately and cleverly brought about by physicians.

Hahnemann's discoveries are difficult to understand, because, unlike Einstein's, they are not mathematically evident. Experimental proof is possible, but since all knowledge of man is, by virtue of the bias of vanity and pleasures, so much more likely to miscarry than are things non-human, the history of attempting such proofs has been beset with problems. Besides, Hahnemann's thought is difficult because there is no language parallel to mathematics in which he could have presented his discoveries in an easily intelligible form.[1] Most people have not the patience, the love of truth, nor the degree of imagination needed to follow him to his end.[2] I feel it to be my duty, however, as an explicator of the ideas that constitute happiness, to let Hahnemann speak in his own words:[3]

8

It is not conceivable, nor can it be proved by any experience in the world, that, after removal of all the symptoms of the disease and of the entire collection of the perceptible phenomena, there should or could remain anything else besides health, or that the morbid alteration in the interior could remain uneradicated.

9

In the healthy condition of man, the spiritual vital force, the dynamis that animates the material body (the organism), rules with unbounded sway, and retains all the parts of the organism in admirable, harmonious, vital operation, as regards both sensations and functions, so that our indwelling, reason-gifted mind can freely employ this living, healthy instrument for the higher purposes of our existence.

10

The material organism, without the vital force, is capable of no sensation, no function, no self preservation; it derives all sensation and performs all the functions of life solely by means of the immaterial being (the vital principle) which animates the material organism in health and in disease.

11

When a person falls ill, it is only this spiritual, self-acting (automatic) vital force everywhere present in his organism, that is primarily deranged by the dynamic influence upon it of a morbific agent inimical to life; it is only the vital principle, deranged to such an abnormal state, that can furnish the organism with its disagreeable sensations, and incline it to

---

[1]Or one that produces favorable impressions, as mathematical form has come to in the last three hundred fifty years.

[2]The problem faced by all geniuses who overreach the capacities of the vast majority not by an inch but by a mile. Homeopathy is more popular in France, Russia, and most of all, in the Indo-Pak subcontinent where even the general educated public has not the great faith in philosophic materialism. This popularity does not mean that Hahnemann's ideas are understood clearly, but the experimental proofs win him followers.

[3]From his *Organon of Medicine*, 6th ed. Translated by William Boericke from Hahnemann's own written revisions.

the irregular processes which we call disease; for, as the power invisible in itself, and only cognizable by its effects on the organism, its morbid derangement only makes itself known by the manifestation of disease in the sensations and functions of those parts of the organism exposed to the senses of the observer and physician, that is by *morbid symptoms*, and in no other way can it make itself known.[1]

12

It is the morbidly affected vital energy alone that produces diseases, so that the morbid phenomena perceptible to our senses express at the same time all the internal change, that is to say, the whole morbid derangement of the internal dynamis; in a word, they reveal the whole disease; also, the disappearance under treatment of all the morbid phenomena and of all the morbid alterations that differ from the healthy vital operations, certainly affects and necessarily implies the restoration of the integrity of the vital force and, therefore, the recovered health of the whole organism.

13

Therefore disease (that does not come within the province of manual surgery) considered, as it is by the allopathists, as a thing separate from the living whole, from the organism and its animating vital force, and hidden in the interior, be it of ever so subtle a character, is an absurdity, that could only be imagined by minds of a materialistic stamp, and has for thousands of years given to the prevailing system of medicine all those pernicious impulses that have made it a truly mischievous (non-healing) art.[2]

---

[1]A parallel between what Hahnemann says here and Einstein's discoveries may clarify matters. You cannot know that all matter is energy, and all energy matter until you see that when even a minute proportion of a small mass of uranium is converted to energy, in the process of its reduction by fission to simpler elements, the energy released can destroy a large city; and that a small amount of hydrogen that is allowed to fuse into helium in that superheated explosion can release an even greater amount of energy. The energy is unknown to the senses until it reveals its existence by its effect (the explosion) on the physical world.

[2]The bacterial/viral theory of disease was just being born in Hahnemann's age. Hahnemann saw that microorganisms are *concomitants* of infectious diseases, not their cause. It is because this fact is so little understood that physicians today (in 1992) are baffled that some people have AIDS, though they do not have the virus, whereas others have the virus, but do not have the symptoms. Both groups are patients, according to Hahnemann, for both have been under the effect of a non-material morbific agent of the specific disease, and both can spread the disease further, but the latter have no disease, since they have no symptoms, because their individual vital forces are not susceptible to the

[311]

14

There is, in the interior of man, nothing morbid that is curable and no morbid alteration that is curable which does not make itself known to the accurately observing physician by means of morbid signs and symptoms—an arrangement in perfect conformity with the infinite goodness of the all-wise Preserver of human life.[1]

15

The affection of the morbidly deranged, spirit-like dynamis (vital force) that animates our body in the invisible interior, and the totality of the outwardly cognizable symptoms produced by it in the organism and representing the existing malady, constitute a whole; they are one and the same. The organism is indeed the material instrument of life, but it is not conceivable without the animation imparted to it by the instinctively perceiving and regulating dynamis, just as the vital force is not conceivable without the organism, consequently the two together constitute a unity, although in thought our mind separates this unity into two distinct conceptions for the sake of easy comprehension.

16

Our vital force, as a spirit-like dynamis, cannot be attacked and affected by injurious influences on the healthy organism caused by the external inimical forces that disturb the harmonious play of life, otherwise than in a spirit-like (dynamic) way, and in like manner, all such morbid derangements (diseases) cannot be removed from it by the physician in any other way than by the spirit-like (dynamic) alternative powers of the serviceable medicines acting upon our spirit-like vital force, which perceives them through the medium of the sentient faculty of the nerves everywhere present in the organism, so that it is only by their dynamic action on the vital force that remedies are able to re-establish and do actually re-establish health and vital harmony, after the changes in the health of the patient cognizable by our senses (the totality of the symptoms) have revealed the disease to the carefully observing and investigating physician as fully as was requisite in order to enable him to cure it.

---

inimical force.

On the unscientific (or more precisely, prescientific) understanding of physical phenomena and evidence, see also the opinions of Kent and Einstein below.

[1]A fact, this, that the greatest scientific geniuses (Hahnemann, Kent, Einstein, Newton) had strong faith in the divine. Kent even said that no scientist could have been as revolutionarily great as Hahnemann had he been an atheist or agnostic.

[312]

17

Now, as in the cure effected by the removal of the whole of the perceptible signs and symptoms of the disease the internal alternation of the vital principle to which the disease is due—consequently the whole of the disease—is at the same time removed, it follows that the physician has only to remove the whole of the symptoms in order, at the same time, to abrogate and annihilate the internal change, that is to say, the morbid derangement of the vital force—consequently the totality of the disease, the *disease itself*. But, when the disease is annihilated, health is restored, and that is the highest, the sole aim of the physician who knows the true object of his mission, which consists not in learned-sounding prating, but in giving aid to the sick.

18

From this indubitable truth, that besides the totality of the symptoms, with consideration of the accompanying modalities nothing can by any means be discovered in diseases wherewith they could express their need of aid, it follows undeniably that the sum of all the symptoms and conditions in each individual case of disease must be the *sole indication*, the sole guide to direct us in the choice of remedy.

19

Now, as *diseases* are nothing more than *alterations in the state of health of the healthy individual*, which express themselves by morbid signs, and the *cure* is also only possible by a *change to the healthy condition of the state of health of the diseased individual*, it is very evident that *medicines* could never cure diseases if they did not possess the power of altering man's state of health which depends on sensations and functions; indeed, that their curative power must be owing *solely* to this power they possess of altering man's state of health.

20

This spirit-like power to alter man's state of health which lies hidden in the inner nature of medicines can in itself never be discovered by us by a mere effort of reason; it is only by experience of the phenomena it displays when acting on the state of health of man that we can become clearly cognizant of it.[1]

---

[1]Hahnemann reiterates the fact that only the effect of energy can be perceived by the senses, not the energy itself. It should be remembered that in speaking of medicines here Hahnemann means homeopathic medicines, in which the original medicinal chemical has been diluted to the degree that no atomic trace is left of it (calculating this quantity by

Hahnemann develops from this point his homeopathic theory, which is based on the Law of Similars: that diseases can only be cured (i.e., not merely suppressed as to their chief symptoms) by medicines which in a healthy man or woman would cause that disease.[1]

The degree to which he revolutionized by making logical all medical and scientific knowledge and experimentation is too great to be examined here even in summary. The reader ought to turn to the other major works of Hahnemann, and to those of other leading homeopaths, such as Hering, Allen, Lippe, and Kent (the greatest homeopath since Hahnemann, who brought the science to as nearly perfect a stage as it has attained, and who has not been equaled by any since, so far as I know).

The old-school physicians set up the American Medical Association in the nineteenth century in large part to fight the threat that homeopathy was beginning to pose to their incomes. It succeeded in nearly destroying the science by putting upon it the label of pseudo-scientific superstition, etc.[2]

When Hahnemann says, "vital force" or "life principle" he is not repeating Aristotle's notion, which was another way of saying the "soul" (in opposition to the body), for for Hahnemann, the vital force and the organism are one and the same and cannot be thought of apart, except for convenience's sake. He was not putting forward a vague poetic notion such as the Chinese *chi*, the Freudian Eros, the Christian or Islamic (or any other religion's) spirit of God and the soul, Schopenhauer's Will to Life, Bergson's *élan vital,* etc. About this part of Hahnemann's discovery, Kent wrote:

"Let us now proceed to inspect the various editions of this *Organon*, and we see what a careful man our author was. He was not a man to adopt a theory of others before having thoroughly tested it and having

---

using Avogadro's number). The great and general effect on human bodies of such a medicine in which no material presence of the original chemical is left was, in fact, the phenomenon that led Hahnemann to his discovery of the exact identity of the bodily organism and the vital force that animates it.

[1]By disease is not meant only a few painful, debilitating, or physically ugly symptoms, but the total symptom picture (physical and moral) of the patient.

[2]See, for example, the 1987 edition of *AMA's Family Guide*, which, in enumerating and briefly describing other medical systems than the fashionable one, lists them in the following order: Holistic health care, herbalism, chiropractic, acupuncture, naturopathy, spiritual healing, and homeopathy. Not stopping there, the little byte on homeopathy provides a cleverly misleading idea of the nature and practice of the theory.

observed the facts upon which the theory was based. Everywhere we see originality of thought, firmness, great power of observation, comparison, and most wonderful reasoning. Metaphysical speculation was repulsive to him, which he carefully avoided in the first edition of the *Organon*, which was published in 1810. He was eminently practical in all that he said and did. Thus, you will search in vain in all the first four editions of the *Organon* for the term and idea of the vital force. He only spoke of the interior of the organism.

"In the seventh section of the first edition: 'There must exist in the medicine a healing principle; the understanding has a presentation of it, but its essence is not recognizable by us in any way, only its utterances and actions can be known by experience.'

"Twenty-three years later, when seventy-eight years old, in the fifth edition, published in 1833, in the ninth and tenth sections, he distinctly calls a unit of action in the whole organism the vital force. From this it is evident that Hahnemann arrived at this conclusion after a long and practical experience, inasmuch as he was led up to it by his early perception of the similar vital principle contained in the medicine (see first ed., fifth section), which is only recognized by its actions upon the organism. I have shown you that it was not metaphysical speculation that led the master to the idea of the vital dynamis, but a long series of practical and experimental research."[1]

I quote from Kent's irreplaceable *Lectures on Homeopathic Philosophy*, where he makes clear the ideas of Hahnemann's books and develops them in some instances:

"[Paragraph 9 of the *Organon*][2] introduces the vital principle. It seems hardly possible that Hahnemann, in the time he lived, could say so much in a few lines.... You may get the idea from some of his expressions that the harmony itself is a force, but I do not think that Hahnemann intends to teach that way. We cannot consider the vital principle as harmony, nor harmony as principle: principle is something that is prior to harmony. Harmony is the result of principle or law.

"Hahnemann could perceive this immaterial vital principle. It was something he arrived at himself, from his own process of thinking.

---

[1]James Tyler Kent, *New Remedies, Clinical Cases, Lesser Writings, Aphorisms and Precepts*, p. 233. All quotes in this appendix are from Indian and Pakistani reprints of the original books by Hahnemann and Kent, which are no longer in print in the U.S.

[2]Paragraphs 8-20 have been quoted above.

There was paucity of individual ideas at that time. i.e., ideas outside of the accepted sciences, but Hahnemann thought much, and by thinking he arrived at the idea contained in this paragraph, which only appears in the last edition.... If he had used the words 'immaterial vital substance,' it would have been even stronger, for you will see it to be true that it is a substance.

".... Substance in simple form is just as positively substance as matter in concrete form. The question then comes up for consideration and study: What is the vital force? What is its character, quality, or *esse*? Is it true that man only has this vital force? Is it possessed by no animal, no mineral? For a number of years there has been a continuous discussion of force as force, or power to construct. The thought that force has nothing prior to it leads man's mind into insanity. If man can think of energy as something substantial he can better think of something substantial as having energy. When he thinks of something that has essence, has actual being, he must think of that *esse* as something existing, and as having something which has ultimates. He must think in a series whereby cause enters into effect and further more into a series of effects....

"Now when we consider this substance as an energy, a force, a dynamis—that is something possessing power—the subject is intelligible. Inert elements have in their nature not only their own identifying simple substance, but they have *degrees* of this identifying simple substance. The human body also has its degrees of life substance, existing in degrees suitable for all its uses. The innermost degrees of life substances are suitable to the will and understanding, the outermost degrees to the very coarsest tissue, and there is one continuous series of quality, in degrees from the innermost to the outermost. Every cell has within it the innermost and the outermost, because there is nothing in that which is coarsest but has that which is finest, too. The outermost envelopes are dominated by the coarser degrees of simple substance, and the innermost qualities are dominated by the innermost degrees.... Inert substances have their own degrees. *Silica* has its degrees of simple substance within it, which can be brought out by the process of potentization,[1] whereby it may be continuously simplified, rendered finer and finer, so that each portion which remains may, by continued potentization, be adapted to

---

[1]A method of dilution described in great detail in the *Organon*.

the higher degrees of the simple substance of man. The thirtieth potency of *Silica* will be sufficiently similar in form to reach in a curative way some of the diseases of man, viz.: such as are dominating his economy in a correspondingly superficial and coarse series of the body. But it is true that *Silica* ceases after a time to act in the thirtieth potency, and that it has to be further potentized in order that it may be similar in quality to the inner degrees, even until it reaches the very innermost or finest degrees of the simple substance....

"The morbific agents that Hahnemann refers to are simply the extremely fine forms of simple substance, or to bring them down to human thought we might call them viruses;[1] but viruses are often gross because they can sometimes be observed by the vision of man, and therefore we must remember that within the virus is the innermost and that this innermost is in itself capable of giving form to the outermost, which is the visible virus aggregated and concentrated.

"The coarser forms would be comparatively harmless were it not for their interiors. Disease products are comparatively harmless were it not for the fact that they contain an innermost, and it is the innermost itself that is causative. The bacteria are the result of conditions within, they are, as it were, evolved by a spontaneous generation —literally, that is what it is....[2]

---

[1] I.e., for the sake of convenience only.

[2] There are two sides to what Kent is saying here. First, bacteria and viruses can be detected in a body that is not suffering from the symptoms they cause by their presence in other bodies (if this were not so, the entire population of an island, such as England, should have been wiped out by a single deadly epidemic; i.e., there has to be a cause why some do not develop or die from the disease, while their brothers and sisters do). Second, after an infectious disease symptom has been suppressed by a strong medicine, there should be no bacteria left since all the symptoms have disappeared. Now, it happens that when the symptoms were but manifestations of an underlying chronic condition, they disappear entirely, but, in time, either they come back, or, some seemingly unrelated disorder, which seems to an ignorant observer to be an entirely new disease, in a different part of the body arises. When a suitable homeopathic medicine is administered, the new symptoms disappear, and the older symptoms, suppressed often *for years,** reappear *without exposure to the bacteria or virus.* That is, from no outside source the bacteria or virus is suddenly present or active again which for years could not be found through laboratory tests. The only logical conclusion is that disease is caused by something prior to the bacteria or virus. Incidentally, this phenomenon also proves the scientific invalidity of Pasteur's famous experiment that tested the theory of spontaneous generation. Since the informing immaterial vital substance had no suitably refined receptacle for its effect in the sealed or curve-necked bottles (for the vital force or simple substance can only operate on its kind, and only thus have a material—i.e. perceptible—effect), nothing could have been generated

"It is only when the vital principle is disturbed by cause of a disease character (that is the innermost of a virus in the form of a simple substance) that it gives forth any consciousness of itself...."

[Referring to the 13th paragraph of the *Organon*]: "The material notion referred to was that existing in the time of Hahnemann. Materialism is still growing. It seems impossible for the majority of men of the present day to perceive. Perception, that is, seeing with the understanding, seems to be entirely lost. The materialist refuses to believe anything that does not conform to the laws of time and space. It must be measured, it must be weighed, it must occupy space, or he has no idea of it, and will distinctly affirm that without this it is nothing and has no existence. Everything beyond this is to the material mind poetical, dreamy, mysterious. So they look in vain in the material world for cause. You will never find a material entity as in any way causing anything.[1] It has no causative power, no creative influence, no propelling influence. Causes or simple substances are, in the natural state, in motion, and

---

in them. In other words, the experiments had no scientific justification *to begin with*, and so could not have proved anything one way or the other. And, yet, Pasteur is celebrated as a great scientist. Kent noted a century ago that allopathic physicians were actively developing an air of legend around their shining stars like Pasteur to discourage the increasing popularity of homeopathy with patients.

*This discovery of Hahnemann regarding the suppression of chronic diseases, which suppressed symptoms need to be brought out and expelled to effect a cure, was stolen by the most famous pedant of this century, Freud, for his idea of repression and how to cure mental diseases; he grafted it on to the old superstitious traditions of dream interpretation and exorcism, and this combination led to other conceits too famous to need recounting.** One need only think of the fame of the resulting hodgepodge to remember that this century of collective vanity is also one of pedantry.

** Since, once he had stolen without ackowledgement (the medical profession, out of the instinct of self-preservation, had from the beginning excommunicated homeopathy from respectability) Hahnemann's idea of suppression, Freud needed a theory of repression that could be uniformly applied to all humans (being a pedant of talent, he knew that a theory that was not simple and easily comprehended could not be easily taught, and would therefore miss the mark of all successful pedantry altogether), he was forced to seek the origin of repressed ideas in the earliest possible time of life (i.e., infancy), wherein humans are most uniform in behavior, being compounded at that time of undeveloped and original animal instincts. Having arrived at this conclusion, Freud further needed some idea that would have to be repressed, all possible ideas in this domain being capable of a more or less universal application. From this realization to the so-called Oedipal complex, the unconscious, the importance of dreams, etc. was but a series of simple steps predictable in a typical pedant, as was the subsequent reliance on Sophocles and Shakespeare.

[1]All of science and philosophy begins with this one thought succinctly stated by Kent. Knowledge begins with the identification and classification of the exact nature of the motions of objects as caused by forces.

cause motion in the bodies that they occupy; the natural state for simple substance is that of power, of mobility, of activity. The natural state of matter is rest, quietude, silence; it has no power to move unless acted upon. Like the dead man, whose tissues are at rest, it has no action of its own. But the simple substance dominates matter and animates it.

"The two worlds, the world of motion, of power, and that of inertia, exist in one. There is a world of life and a world of dead matter.[1] The realm of thought and the realm of matter are the realm of cause and the realm of result. Causes are invisible, results are visible. We see the actions of material substance, but the thinking man has only to reflect to see that these actions that are visible in material form are but results of the causes that exist in the form of simple substance which is invisible to the natural eye but visible to the spiritual eye or understanding. The materialist cannot grasp this idea, he cannot think this way. We have the grandest confirmation of these things in the wonderful action of our potencies in the varying degrees in which they operate upon man, from the lowest to the highest."

Hahnemann was the first to consistently see the idea of disease with a dispassionate eye, as a thing perceived, a product of sensations, having physical and moral expressions, but in itself an abstract idea of no worth. There is no disease apart from an observer's (the patient's, the physician's, others') perception of morbid (i.e., painful) symptoms.

With a degree of logic that only a few men and women in a century ever possess, Hahnemann hit upon the simple but heretofore unknown idea that the physician's only task, his sole duty as he called it, was to cause these morbid symptoms (with attendant modalities) to disappear without bothering his head about "analysis," "pathology," and nomenclature of "diseases."[2]

And since disease is only the patient's sense of morbid sensations, his sense of his physical and moral state as having at some point distinctly *altered* for the worse from what he thinks healthy,[3] it was only logical for this great man to attempt to find a method of healing deriving from a

---

[1]By the world of life, Kent means not only biological life, but all systems of energy, such as stars.

[2]See the first paragraph of the *Organon*.

[3]There are diseased states wherein the patient on occasions seems to be content or indifferent regarding some of the moral symptoms or states, and thinks himself well, but this is almost always only a passing phase *at best*. Even euphoria becomes painful in due time if a less wearying state does not return.

comparative study of *sensations* in the healthy state in relation to those in diseased ones—disease and health being matters of relativity. Scientifically and logically looked at, every other manner of attempting cures is utterly illogical.

It was also only logical that apart from studying the effects of medicines on healthy men and women, there could be no scientific method of studying them. Since it is the alteration and its consequences that are painful, it is worthless to study effects in those already altered, in the manner of unscientific medicine practiced historically.[1] The cause of the alteration, and thus perhaps a means to reverse it, can only be studied by studying the effects of substances and potentized medicine on healthy men and women who have not suffered such alterations.

If, for example, quinine *seems* to work in cases of intermittent fever, it is only because when it is administered to *healthy* persons, a good number of them develop the morbid symptoms of intermittent fever; so that allopathic medicines either directly and violently suppress a few symptoms, or seem to work because of homeopathic relation to some symptom. But intermittent fevers have numerous modalities (patterns of intensification and amelioration of symptoms), and only a small proportion of these truly match quinine; for this reason, quinine cures only those few cases, and merely suppresses symptoms in others, leading to worse states of health later.[2]

This curative action of substances that caused symptoms in healthy men and women was a discovery of observation, not logic. Logic produces results only when you can observe accurately for yourself and not simply accept old ideas.

---

[1]The manner modern medicine still adopts.

[2]The only thing that so-called modern medicine has succeeded in has been the cure of a handful of acute diseases,* the suppression of all others. In the face of chronic diseases, this modern medicine has been utterly helpless, and the reason is that the it is basically a *palliative art*, not a science of *healing*, and the poor patient is supposed to be overjoyed that he lives in an age when so-called diseases such as arthritis, blood pressure, manic depression, etc, can be "treated" (an amusing euphemism, this, that doubtless has some placebo effect). This year ** a highly publicized public debate is taking place in the United States regarding that circus, very profitable for those in it, called the "health system" whose medical effectiveness (as opposed to its economics, fairness, administration) Americans are proud of.

*Antibiotics and other allopathic medicines need to be proved on healthy subjects; I would not be surprised if they produce many of the symptoms that they are daily employed to suppress.

** July 9, 1993.

Einstein's description (from his book *Relativity, The Special and the General Theory: A Popular Exposition*, translated by Robert Lawson) of the inadequacies of simple-minded materialism, which holds the commonly accepted ideas of space and time to be true shows that he too felt it to be a product of ignorance and lack of self-knowledge:

"In order to arrive at the idea of an objective world, an additional concept [besides those of event and time] still is necessary: the event is localized not only in time, but also in space.

"In the previous paragraphs, we have attempted to describe how the concepts of space, time, and event can be put psychologically into relation with experiences. Considered logically, they are free creations of the human intelligence, tools of thought, which are to serve the purpose of bringing experiences into relations with each other, so that in this way they can be better surveyed. The attempt to become conscious of the empirical sources of these fundamental concepts should show to what extent we are actually bound to these concepts. In this way, we become aware of our freedom, of which, in case of necessity, it is always a difficult matter to make sensible use.

"We still have something essential to add to this sketch concerning the psychological origin of the concepts space-time-event (we will call them more briefly "space-like," in contrast to concepts from the psychological sphere). We have linked up the concept of space with experiences using boxes and the arrangements of material objects in them. Thus, this formation of concepts already presupposes the concept of material objects (e.g., "boxes"). In the same way, persons, who had to be introduced for the formation of an objective concept of time, also play the role of material objects in this connection. It appears to me, therefore, that the formation of the concept of the material object must precede our concepts of time and space.

"All these space-like concepts already belonged to pre-scientific thought, along with concepts like pain, goal, purpose, etc. from the field of psychology. Now, it is characteristic of thought in physics, as of thought in natural science generally, that it endeavours in principle to make do with "space-like" concepts *alone*, and strives to express with their aid all relations having the form of laws. The physicist seeks to reduce colours and tones to vibrations, the physiologist thought and pain to nerve processes, in such a way that the psychical element as such is eliminated from the causal nexus of existence, and thus nowhere occurs as an independent link in the causal associations. It is no doubt this attitude, which considers the comprehension of all relations by the exclusive use of "space-like" concepts as being possible in principle, that is at the present time understood by the term 'materialism.'"

It was this materialism not arising logically from knowledge of human nature that Einstein attacked with his General Relativity. A century earlier Hahnemann had done the very same thing with his Law of Similars and the science of homeopathy.

Among other facts, Einstein explains in the book that the idea of "empty space" is an erroneous notion, that the concept of space arises from extension of bodies only, and that the only true idea of space is to think not of empty space, but of an infinite number of spaces in relative motion to each other.[1] The discovery of facts such as this one, or of the ones Hahnemann and Kent made, becomes possible only when the causes and effects of *sensations and ideas* are studied dispassionately. Quantum mechanics, for example, though it described well some very local phenomena, still continued to work within the absolute space-time of classical Newtonian-Galilean physics.[2] Even the wave-particle theory is subsumed under the old framework, though there was an attempt to relate it to relativity in the late 1920's—light according to this theory is a wave or particle at a certain point of absolute space and absolute time depending upon the observer and circumstances, but it cannot be both.[3] Since Einstein, theories such as the Superstring Model have produced ideas not intelligible because they do not describe anything known to the senses, and can be proved, it seems, only indirectly, by some experimental results that may correspond with a theory, perhaps by chance. And although mathematically clever, the unclear ideas when imagined as well as they can be remain within the framework of absolute

---

[1]Newton had touched upon this possibility in the *Principia* only to dismiss it in comparison to the notion of absolute space.

[2]Einstein's attempts to produce a more general theory after 1920 were unsuccessful according to the opinions of most physicists. Physics, by its nature, seems to be a science that only knows great progress after long intervals of pedantic refinements. If Einstein failed to produce a more general unified field theory, it may have been because it will take a few hundred years to obtain sufficient knowledge of as yet unknown details to make new discoveries. Considering the past, it is not improbable that at some point in the distant future, a more general (though not absolutely final) theory will be produced by some great genius.

[3]Also, to my own dismay, Mr. Hawking's theories seem to be as finely chopped a mishmash of logic as Plato's.

space-time, even though the verbal and mathematical rhetoric does not.[1]

Einstein related his ideas to those of Hume, and it is easy to see why. Hume, however, affected to see causal logic as not necessarily producing true results, which Einstein never did—and as I have said in an earlier chapter, Hume used causal logic[2] to reject the reliability of the idea of causality, making his statements worthless save as poetic principles. Einstein, like Hahnemann and Kent, used logic and observation better than most men to discover facts.

The moral relativity arising from the universal principle of interest, described by Hobbes and developed greatly a century later by Helvétius, was turned by Locke into a pedant's system of thought that allowed in time for the mild pleasures of vagueness that Berkeley and Hume sought. The uncertainty principle of quantum mechanics seems to echo Einstein's relativity in that it rests upon the element of perception, but as in the rest of quantum mechanics the priority of the material over the field has not been abandoned. So, Foucault's books about the changing ideas, among other things, of clinical madness seem to echo in a vague manner Hahnemann's establishment of an exact definition of disease as only the perception of painful moral or physical symptoms, but Foucault's theory that everything is a relative product of texts is, like Hume's, an easy, emaciated form of idealism, born of the pleasures of vagueness and of petty vanity (of a pedant[3]), far removed from the strict scientific logic of Hahnemann's ideas.

The general confusion of ideas in our own age needs no greater proof of its existence than this, that most who consider these matters will think that Hobbes and Helvétius were extreme materialists, and that Hahnemann and Kent were naive spiritualists. In fact, all four (and Einstein as well) thought of energy and matter as identical, because only errors result if they are thought of apart. I do not think that the rest of the world is about to catch up with them anytime soon. Even the discoveries of twentieth-century physics have not been understood for what they are. We must wait for the age when the mind of the average educated man will be able to unite all the relevant moral, medical, and physical sciences. As Kent himself said:

---

[1]E.g., the one-dimensional curved string that is the building block of one theory.

[2]Ineptly, one may say, as he did not take the trouble to begin with the principle of interest.

[3]This theory justifies a pedant's passing his life in a large library, for how is one to understand anything if all ideas are products of texts?

"Homeopathy will not be universally adopted for many centuries. There are many people in the world who cannot believe a great truth however much evidence is presented in its favor. We are all encumbered with tradition. Unbelief in new things is our strongest tendency. The tendency to ridicule what we do not understand is born in us. A few refined and educated minds that have been opened by circumstances are prepared to examine our principles; others have accepted the truth by force of circumstances. All who really love Homeopathy have an unlimited desire to teach it to associates and to their patients. They are often astonished that the door is closed to their willing efforts.

"Our literature has been defective, to a large extent as a teaching medium—that which has been prepared for the laity as much as that which has been prepared to teach the medical student and practitioner. Looking over our literature of the past, we observe its incongruities. Here and there we find hints. Hahnemann's ORGANON is a strong, rich source of knowledge, but it is in long sentences, and very condensed, and difficult for many to understand. When one has fully comprehended the principles, he then reads Hahnemann's ORGANON with the deepest satisfaction. The subject is so deep, so difficult to comprehend. A most scholarly, deep-thinking man said to me, 'I have read your PHILOSOPHY five times, and am still reading it, and now I begin to understand Hahnemann's ORGANON.'"

APPENDIX TWO

Alvito says that I have not gone deeply enough into the heart in my descriptions of feminine pride. For one thing, the modesty of women is only one of the many affectations of their pride.

Further, he tells me of a recent adventure (he has at least one every few months). A pretty young woman (he gave me at great length a very poetical description that I skip) slowly but surely caught his fancy. In no time at all he was convinced that she reciprocated his admiration. What should have been a smooth and straightforward undertaking was a little complicated by the fact that just as he was about to become a little serious and obvious, she abruptly rose up, made some farfetched excuse, and started to leave in earnest. He had (or at least wants me to believe he had) a choice to make, and what he did as well as its results, he tells me, can be of no interest to me.

"Why she should want to appear to be unmoved by any tender feelings at the very moment when she must have felt that her dearest wishes (and I have good reason to suppose they were just that) were about to be fulfilled—when her affected indifference could neither have the practical effect of making a slow lover act on his thoughts nor be believed by him to be true—, this, perhaps because of the exactness of the timing in this particular case, aroused my curiosity for it is neither the first, nor shall it be the last, time I encounter this manner of acting.

"I thought about this question for a few weeks, that is to say when I had some time to spare, and the only conclusion that I could make I made by comparing her thoughts to mine. At that moment, I was looking forward with delight that only the element of uncertainty kept a little in check. The only means to certainty lay in action. If rebuffed, I intended merely to redouble my efforts and pleas at that time or later, according to the manner in which she refused me. But the solution to the problem was here: I had reasons that I need not describe to you, which though they had nothing to do with her, made me think very well of myself, irrespective of the opinion of others. It must be, I said to myself at last, that she lacks such self-esteem; there can be no other reason. Keenly feeling (though reluctant to admit as much even to herself) that she has nothing solid to her mind upon which she can base her pride, she has to invent reasons, and these reasons must of course be such that her admirer and any other witness cannot help but take notice of. And there is nothing like a cold refusal to galvanize all the thoughts of a hopeful lover into respectful attention.

"I concluded that the greater the skittishness, in some women natural and in other affected, the less they feel anything in or of themselves to be justifiably proud of. You will see it in vain or proud women, and in very young ones. In the case of the latter, those same very young women act very differently after they are thirty or thirty five, or even in some cases, in their twenties, if they married early and have several children by then. Some have found justifications for pride (either worldly success, or the fact of having had many lovers), but most change because experience and disillusionment make them less open to the temptations of empty displays of pride in the face of a man they find very attractive.

"Even women in whom pride is a passion, so long as they are not content solely with the vanity of securely possessing a rich lover, though they may act in many particulars as they did when very young, for they are no less proud than in earlier years, are a little more open to the pleasures of love after some unhappy experiences. They are determined not to let any great opportunity slip by on account of a silly matter of pride. I speak of cases where a man strikes them as being especially worthy of being loved by.

"After having to think this matter through *for myself*, I must confess that I did regret, though not for more than a few moments, my most recent *petite aventure*."

I accept Alvito's criticism of my attempts to be more than a little justified. Had he read *De l'amour* or some of the sections regarding Mathilde de La Mole in *Le rouge et le noir* more carefully than he did, or, even better, for their authority on this matter is necessarily greater, had he made an attempt to understand what Nargis expresses during the second song of the flashback sequence in *Jogan*, and Hepburn expresses when, in *Roman Holiday,* upon Ann's asking Bradley to sit down, he sits down on the bed, he would perhaps have spared himself some wasted time, though not mental, or more precisely, imaginative labor.